SCULPTURE

The Great Art of the Middle Ages
from the Fifth to the Fifteenth Century

Edited by

GEORGES DUBY
and
JEAN-LUC DAVAL

© 1990 by Editions d'Art Albert Skira S.A., Geneva

Published in the United States of America in 1990 by

RIZZOLI INTERNATIONAL PUBLICATIONS, INC.
300 Park Avenue South/New York 10010

Translated from the French by Michael Heron

Library of Congress Cataloging-in-Publication Data

Duby, Georges.
  [Sculpture. English]
  Sculpture: the great art of the Middle Ages from the
fifth to the fifteenth century / by Georges Duby, Xavier
Barral i Altet, Sophie Guillot de Suduiraut.
    p.   cm.
  ISBN 0-8478-1285-5
  1. Sculpture, Medieval.   I. Barral i Altet, Xavier.   II. Guillot
de Suduiraut, Sophie.   III. Title.
  NB170.D813   1990   90-53149
  734—dc20   CIP

Printed in Switzerland

SCULPTURE

THE GREAT ART OF THE MIDDLE AGES
FROM THE FIFTH TO THE FIFTEENTH CENTURY

by

GEORGES DUBY
Xavier Barral i Altet
Sophie Guillot de Suduiraut

SKIRA
RIZZOLI
NEW YORK

CONTENTS

Christ in Majesty. Detail of the tympanum. 12th century.
Church of the Madeleine, Vézelay.

PREFACE

Georges Duby

The Middle Ages spanned more than a thousand years. Between the fifth and the sixteenth century things were constantly changing in Europe, sometimes very rapidly, indeed as abruptly as they do today. Nor should we forget that they have changed a great deal since then. Even if Joan of Arc's contemporaries spoke much the same words as we do, expressed themselves by much the same gestures and shared some of our illusions and enthusiasms, their gestures and words did not have quite the same meaning as they do today, and there are appreciable differences between their world picture and our own. We should bear those differences very much in mind when we try to imagine what the sculptures we admire meant to medieval man.

Even when they have not been wrenched from their setting to become lifeless uprooted museum pieces, even if we see them still standing exactly where the artist or his patron had chosen to place them in an ensemble from which they seem as inseparable as a particular sequence in the unfolding of a ritual, these sculptures are works of art to us. A highly cultured man of the eleventh century did not look on them in that light, and even in the fifteenth century he saw them primarily as something other than a source of aesthetic pleasure. They had a purpose and it was twofold.

The first was sacrificial. Most of these objects were liturgical adornments; they were gifts deposited before the throne of the Almighty and intended to be always in His sight. For all those statues raised up to the inaccessible heights of cathedrals were largely out of the sight of men. To make the gifts more precious and therefore more effective, so that they should please God, gladden him and induce him—in this, outdoing the donor—to bestow his blessings more generously in return, the work had to be brought to new heights of perfection by the quality of the material, the vigour of the plastic invention, the refinements of the sculptor's craft. So what we find of beauty in these forms arises primarily from the fact that they were offered to Him who reigns in the highest heaven.

Nevertheless their attraction was also directed towards men, because their function as intermediaries and intercessors between the Christian and his God did not merely imply that these works were like mirrors held up to the Almighty so that he could contemplate himself in the splendours of his creation, but also that these very mirrors should return a reflection of the divine to the faithful. In the Middle Ages sculpture took its place among the instruments of knowledge. It claimed to lead to the invisible through the visible, to lead from this world to the next, whose shape could not be grasped by the senses, but which mortals were sure they would enter one day. It claimed to reveal the secret order of the universe. By spreading God's word and the interpretations of it given by the doctors of the Church, its professed mission was to propagate the rules of good conduct. Its second role was to guide people along the path to truth and salvation. Exhibited to that end in the open air or in the enclosed spaces devoted to contemplation, medieval sculpture thus links up with the present-day advertising or propaganda poster. Like the latter, it sought to persuade, and to increase its persuasive power it did its utmost to strengthen the convincing power of the sign, especially by the use of polychromy.

The domination that religion then exercised over men's minds and actions clearly explains why great sculpture in its doubly mediatory function (at once an offering and a lesson) was so closely bound up with the sacred during these centuries. But the place it held in culture as a whole and its actual function were directly affected by fluctuations in social systems, in particular in the economy, to which statuary was more sensitive than many other cultural creations, because it is a comparatively heavy and expensive art. It had vanished at the dawn of the Middle Ages in the shipwreck of urban civilization. Its rebirth was seen in the eleventh century when trade became lively again in the course of a new expansion springing from the heart of the countryside, and the towns gradually emerged from their torpor. The leaders of the Church were the promoters of this renaissance because, enriched both by the income from their seigniories and gifts from the warlords, they raked in the lion's share of the profits from the new growth and because they discovered in monumental sculpture a means of fulfilling their office more effectively and better ensuring the salvation of the people by making liturgical ceremonies more brilliant and pointing out the strait way more clearly. They retained control of this art for a long time. But there came a moment when it partially eluded them, because continuing progress determined the steady secularization of the state, together with a reflux of the irrational and the flowering of a profane culture into which improvements in the financial system channelled ever more money. Soon there was a demand for worldly feasts to be as sumptuous as religious feasts and sculptors no longer worked solely for the monastery or the cathedral, but for princely houses as well. In the second half of the thirteenth century we already see them hastening to flatter the taste of art-lovers and striving to give them pleasure, as well as assisting their passage to paradise. A little later what we may legitimately call an art market imperceptibly came into being, so that sculpture began to reassume the role it had played in classical antiquity, to come closer to what it has become today. But it did so very slowly. The Middle Ages were over by the time sculpture had managed to throw off the ascendancy of a Christianity that had also undergone very profound changes.

FROM LATE ANTIQUITY TO THE MIDDLE AGES

by Xavier Barral i Altet

INTRODUCTION

Georges Duby

The art of the warlike tribes whose migrations precipitated the decline of the Roman Empire was an art of armourers, metal-founders, jewellers and engravers of amulets. It liked to entwine stylized animal forms in interlaces, but was loath to represent the human figure. It was the exact opposite of the art of Rome, that art of stone, of relief, which had erected effigies of the gods, heroized emperors and defunct noblemen that were true to the appearance of men in the flesh.

Rome collapsed in the tumult of the invasions and peasant rebellions, owing to epidemics, depopulation, the increase in fallow land and the decline in trade. Yet Rome survived. It fascinated the chiefs of the small tribes who had seized power and lorded it in the dying cities. The great numbers of indestructible monuments meant that it was ever present. The Christian Church, which had infiltrated the ranks of the imperial administration, remained the conservatory of its high culture, its system of education and its language. Nevertheless the fate of classical sculpture was sealed, because the bishops who strove to convert the invaders and evangelize the countryside looked on statues as the embodiment of paganism. So they set about destroying them, just as the missionaries felled the sacred trees in the forests of Germany. Moreover, was not Christianity, which extolled the superiority of the spiritual over matter, fiercely iconoclastic in its most purified form? So much so that the "barbarian" aesthetic of the abstract sign, of chasing, of sparkling gems and precious metals gradually invaded the decoration of tombs and religious ceremonies. The little that remained of the principles of antique sculpture withdrew, shutting itself up in the most secluded part of the sanctuaries, in the goldsmiths' work stored in the church treasuries, far from the gaze of the masses.

The first signs of a renaissance emerged from these residual forms at the end of the tenth century simultaneously in the southern provinces of the Christendom on which Rome had left its deepest mark and in the entourage of the sovereigns who saw themselves as the successors of the Caesars. But in both cases the aim was different. In the south, in the countries whose noblemen prided themselves on being descended from Roman senators, the leaders of the Church were forced to come to terms with the demands of secular piety. This popular devotion was firmly attached to the intercessors. It worshipped the local guardian saints, those masters of fertility and forgiveness who were able to overcome sickness and raise the dead. In order to attract the faithful and turn them away from the old agrarian cults and magic practices, it was desirable to confront them with objects in which these tutelary powers seemed to be physically present. The people were shown relics, when what they wanted to see were faces and bodies. So it was decided to reproduce enlarged examples of the anthropomorphic figures that were hidden away in the vicinity of the altar. The work of goldsmiths rather than sculptors, they took the form of glittering reliquary statues, studded with glass beads, whose enamelled eyes held in thrall the crowd of rustics prostrate in crepuscular crypts on days of pilgrimage.

The resurgence of sculpture in circles close to the imperial throne was not caused by a similar desire to please, but by a deliberate desire to link up again with Roman traditions. The Empire of the West was solemnly restored in St Peter's, Rome, in the year 800. Hailed as a new Constantine, Charlemagne felt that it was his mission to save what could again be the essence of classical culture. He had antique bronzes brought to the oratory he built near his palace at Aachen. But the pagans still went on massacring missionaries within the boundaries of his states and idols retained a formidable presence, so he did not commission statues. The return to sculpture in northern Europe was Ottonian, not Carolingian. It took place two centuries later at the culmination of a second imperial restoration, which was more decisive this time because Otto III, the emperor of the year 1000, dreamt of making Rome the capital of the world. But because the new dynasty also sank its roots in Germany, and Germany at its wildest, because the great political meetings were most frequently held there and because it was also the site of the emperor's chapel (the group of ecclesiastics, guardians of the highest culture, from whom the bishops were recruited), it was paradoxically farthest from the Mediterranean, on the borders of Christianization, on the banks of the Rhine and in the episcopal sees of Saxony, that large-scale figures inspired by Latin or Byzantine antique models reappeared. Yet, as in Aquitaine, renascent sculpture in these regions drew on the arts of the church treasury, especially in the choice of materials. Stone was excluded. The altar which Emperor Henry II offered to Basel Minster was made of gold; the crucifixes hanging in the churches of Cologne were made of wood; the imitation of Trajan's column erected by Bernward, Bishop of Hildesheim, was made of bronze. We should remember that these works were still confined to the interior of the sacred space, with the exception of the reliefs decorating the bronze doors at Hildesheim. But surely these doors, like the binding covers of Gospel Books, were both a closure forbidding access to the mysteries to the unworthy and a summons, warning and invitation to the faithful to make themselves worthy to cross the threshold?

Sarcophagus of Junius Bassus.
Scenes from the Old and New Testaments.
4th century. Vatican Museum, Rome.

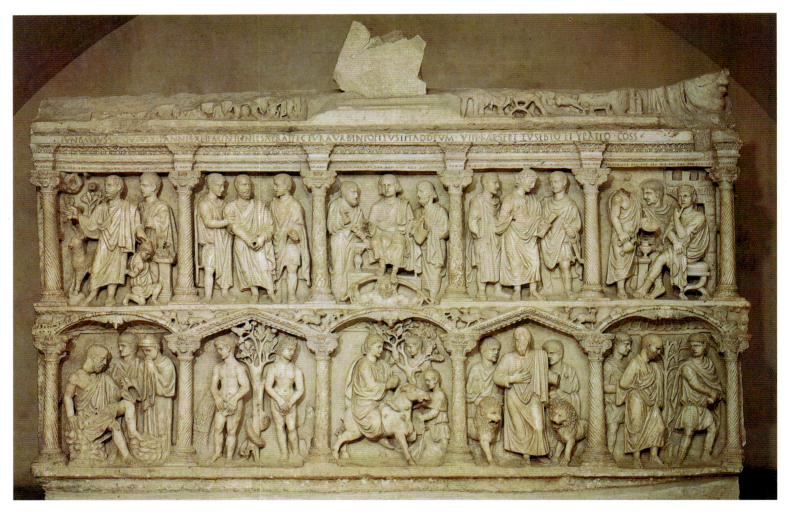

CHRISTIANS AND NON-CHRISTIANS: LATE ANTIQUITY

Forming a bridge between Christianity and the classical heritage, the civilization of Late Antiquity also occupied a novel place between the Late Roman Empire and the Middle Ages. This period began with the long reigns of Diocletian (284-305) and Constantine (307-337) and lasted for two or three centuries, its duration varying from region to region. After Diocletian had established a tetrarchic government with two "Augusti" and two "Caesares," the system became a diarchy in 313 and then, in 324, Constantine, the conqueror of Licinius, united the Empire under Christianity. This religious liberty was soon expressed in monumental form with the construction of the oldest Christian basilicas and the introduction of the first monumental decorations. In the towns, the municipal elites and the big proprietors, who often owned country residences, decorated their houses sumptuously. Public architecture strove to surpass the models of the past. The Basilica Nova in Rome was begun by Maxentius in 308 and completed by Constantine. Its three monumental aisles stood at the summit of a wide platform and were crowned by a vast western apse containing a colossal statue of the emperor.

A manifestation of the city's pomp, the triumphal arch of Constantine built by the Senate and the people of Rome in 315 stands near the Palatine Hill. The monument comprises three openings with freestanding columns outside and a group of sculptures, including reused features from earlier famous monuments, as if to confirm the imperial

Group of four Tetrarchs from Constantinople.
Early 4th century. Red porphyry.
Re-employed on the south façade
of St Mark's, Venice.

Sarcophagus with two registers.
In the centre: an illustrious couple.
From Trinquetaille. First third of the 4th century.
Musée Lapidaire, Arles.

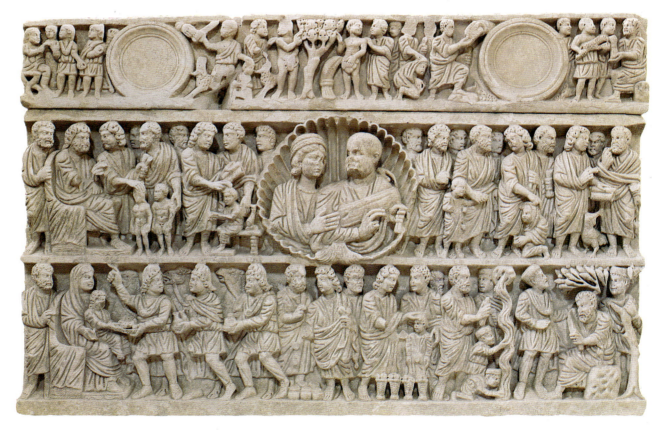

Constantine making a speech to the citizens. Detail of the north side. About 315. Arch of Constantine, Rome.

heritage. The historical frieze, in a conspicuous position halfway up, illustrates both the imperial ideology and the style of the Constantinian period. In addition to depictions of speeches to the citizens and the distribution of subsidies, a particularly noticeable feature is the setting of a hieratic court ritual in which the emperor occupies a strictly frontal position. This arrangement, emphasized by the acclaiming figures shown in profile, was adopted by consuls on ivory diptychs, by villa owners on mosaics, and even for the representation of Christ among the apostles in the semidomes of church apses.

A style common to sculpture and the arts of colour emerges during the first half of the fourth century. That is why the extremely linear and graphic rendering of the figures in the frieze on the Arch of Constantine and on contemporary sarcophagi is close to that of the figures on the mosaics of Piazza Armerina in Sicily, Santa Costanza in Rome, Aquileia in North Italy and Centcelles near Tarragona in Catalonia. The basic elements of the portrait, with wide open eyes and short hair accentuating the roundness of the head, are already observable in works produced under the Tetrarchy, the most famous of which is the porphyry group of the four sovereigns, reused in the Middle Ages on the lateral façade of the basilica of St Mark's in Venice.

During the Roman Imperial period, the Christianization of society steadily increased, but we have to wait until Late Antiquity, in particular the fourth century, to see the public expression of the new iconography. The first Christian images appeared in the Roman catacombs, those underground cemeteries with evocative names (Calixtus, Priscilla, Peter and Marcellinus), which, situated outside the city of the living, were the Roman equivalent of the surface necropolises located close to the entrances of the Empire's towns. We know those early Christian images, as well as the tastes and culture of the urban elites, from the sculptured decoration of the sarcophagi which were placed in mausoleums or private enclosures inside cemeteries.

When they were carved out of marble or porphyry, sarcophagi were ornamented with a sculptured decoration comparable in every way to the friezes of the great public monuments. These characteristic objects of Late Antiquity were sometimes "mass produced" and could be bought as standardized products by anyone who wanted to perpetuate his own memory in his lifetime or that of a close relation who had just died, as an inscription at Arles testifies: "The 17 of the Calends of April, here rests in peace Marcia Romania Celsa, a most illustrious lady, who lived 38 years, 2 months and 11 days. Flavius Januarius, a most illustrious man, former consul ordinary, placed (this epitaph) to his meritorious wife." It was also possible to have sarcophagi decorated to meet individual requirements. In the second quarter of the fourth century, Flavius Januarius ordered that his defunct wife should be portrayed as the praying figure situated in the centre of the main face of the sarcophagus between two apostles and Gospel scenes.

The sarcophagus reliefs are of different types: with spiral flutings, with a continuous frieze, on two registers, with colonnettes, etc. Pictorially, the large bucolic and pastoral scenes were soon followed by Old Testament scenes (Jonas, Daniel) in typological opposition to those from the New Testament such as the public life of Christ and the early events of his Passion. The death of Christ is

Sarcophagus with hunting scenes from Trinquetaille. Second quarter of the 4th century. Musée Lapidaire, Arles.

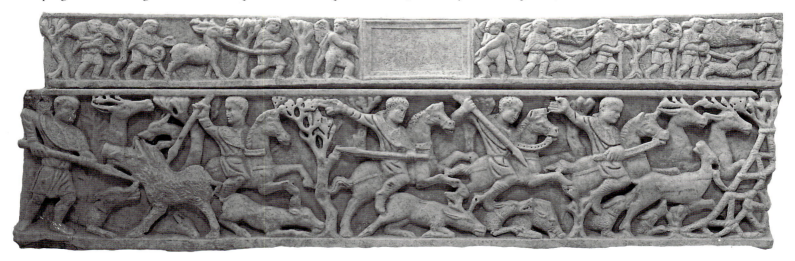

never represented; on the other hand, emphasis is laid on his resurrection, his victory over death and the promise of his return at the end of time.

Among the most significant examples, we may mention the porphyry sarcophagi of Helen and Constantine (Vatican Museum) which, between 320 and 340, display themes peculiar to the imperial iconography or the decoration of the richest villas, such as the sarcophagus decorated with hunting scenes discovered in the Trinquetaille necropolis at Arles in 1974. Of the same provenance, a sarcophagus with two registers depicting an illustrious couple is very similar to the so-called Dogmatic Sarcophagus (Vatican Museum). In addition to Old Testament episodes (Adam and Eve), it displays scenes from the New Testament, ranging from the Epiphany to Christ's miracles. These vehicles of private propaganda tell us about the very early conversion of certain elites and also about their tastes, because the Arles sarcophagus was undoubtedly bought in Rome at great expense. The sarcophagus of Junius Bassus is a particularly good illustration of the monumental quality of these works and the concentration of Christian thought they convey.

INTERLACES AND ANIMAL DECORATION

From the early fifth century, the arrival in the West of different Germanic peoples and their settlement in the territories of the ancient Roman empire brought in their train the introduction of an original culture with a Roman and a Germanic component. The first inroad took place in 401, when the Visigoths led by Alaric poured into Italy. After their arrival at the gates of Rome, this people, led by Athaulf, withdrew to southern Gaul in 412. A little earlier, at the end of 406, the Vandals, Alani and Suevi crossed the Rhine at Mainz or Worms and took the road to the Iberian peninsula. The history of these peoples' movements, their conquests and progressive sedentarization covered the whole of the fifth century. Their final settlement in specific regions constituted the first adumbration of medieval historical geography. The Franks in Gaul, the Visigoths in the Iberian peninsula and the Ostrogoths in Italy produced original works of art confined almost exclusively to goldsmithery and the arts of metal. Architecturally, they appreciated what they found in the Romanized countries. That is why, while necropolises yield funerary furnishings of clearly Germanic origin, the villas excavated by archaeologists reveal architecture and mosaics in the purest Roman tradition, some of which are even later than the seventh century. The symbiosis between these different artistic cultures laid the basis of the new medieval civilization.

The goldsmith's works of the period of the barbarian invasions were numerous. They consisted of liturgical objects, tableware, weapons and personal ornaments. Well known is the work of St Eligius, goldsmith of the Merovingian court and maker of liturgical objects, such as the Cross of Saint-Denis. But the goldsmithery of this period is mainly studied with the help of burial finds. The Sutton Hoo treasure is the most famous of the royal or princely burials of the early Anglo-Saxon period dis-

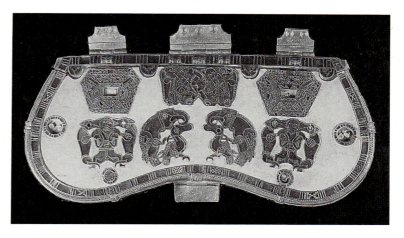

Purse cover from the Sutton Hoo Ship Burial.
7th century. Gold, garnet, enamels.
British Museum, London.

covered in England. Its contents, now in the British Museum, were exhumed from the interior of a buried ship in 1939. The objects composing this treasure included imports from the eastern Mediterranean (silver and bronze dishes), Sweden (shield), Merovingian Gaul (coins) and the Rhineland (armour). The date of interment is established by Byzantine objects made of silver on which the inspection stamps of Emperor Anastasius have been identified.

The Anglo-Saxon artifacts in the treasure from the Sutton Hoo Ship Burial consist mainly of arms, jewels and objects of everyday use. Gold is abundant and the cloisonné enamel is distributed in small differently coloured cells which articulate the surface. But while emphasizing technique, we should not neglect the decorative repertory that appears on contemporary products. Geometric forms and figurative decoration are closely fused in a tangle of curves which often describe continuous interlaces. These motifs then spread over western Europe through the circulation of artifacts and manuscripts.

In Merovingian Gaul these goldsmith's works were found in the tombs of the wealthiest individuals. Some of them still preferred burial in sarcophagi in the classical tradition. Sometimes these were local products, carved in the stone of the country, at others imports brought by way of the large rivers (Seine, Loire). Often trapezoid in shape,

Sarcophagus of the Aquitaine type from Soissons.
Merovingian period. Musée du Louvre, Paris.

Detail of a sarcophagus with boar hunt
and vine scrolls similar to mosaic decorations.
5th century. Musée des Augustins, Toulouse.

these sarcophagi, which went out of use during the eighth century, were adorned with crosses or geometric motifs. The plaster sarcophagi found in great quantities in the Paris region made up a special group and their area of diffusion extended from Rouen to the Yonne and from the Loiret to the Marne. In the south of France, the production of marble sarcophagi was prolonged until the fifth century, if not later, while in Aquitaine in particular a group of sarcophagi with saddleback covers and an all-over decoration of foliage scrolls certainly continued in production until the end of the Merovingian period. These prestigious objects travelled, but their carving was probably executed in the urban workshops of Aquitaine in connection with the exploitation of quarries. They met the demands of the great landowners of southwestern Gaul, for whom hunting was still a favourite activity, as the sarcophagus in the Musée des Augustins at Toulouse demonstrates.

Among the privileged tombs is the funerary chapel discovered to the south-east of the town of Poitiers in 1878, the sculptured decoration of which is especially important. This hypogeum, known as the Hypogée des Dunes, consisted of a "memorial chamber" provided with cult installations and it stood in a necropolis. The monument, which can be dated to the late seventh or the first third of the eighth century, was a sort of family vault containing several tombs; a lengthy inscription in the righthand door jamb states: "Here Mellebaudis, debtor and servant of Christ, I have set up for myself this little cavern in which my unworthy tomb reposes. I did this in the name of the Lord Jesus Christ whom I have loved, in whom I have believed..."

Access to the vault is by a staircase with about ten steps. The monument consists of a room enlarged by two lateral *arcosolia*. In addition to the colonnettes and capitals framing the entrance, the architectural sculpture extends over three steps of the staircase, the two door jambs and the step which raises the altar platform. This decoration in very shallow relief consists of ornamental foliage, fish and a four-stranded plait, with snakes' heads at the extremities. The monument also preserves elements of carved furniture which prove the existence of well-organized workshops. Winged figures adorn the slabs reused to close the sarcophagi standing near the altar. One of them bears the symbols of the evangelists Matthew and John, and the archangels Raphael and Rachel. Near the altar was the

sculpted base of a pillar, adorned with two figures nailed to crosses, who could be interpreted as the two thieves framing the crucifixion of Christ, now missing. Another sculptured fragment represents the lower part of a stylite identified as Simeon by an inscription.

Stylistically, these sculptures resemble seventh-century Visigothic works and monuments in northern Italy. Sociologically, the Hypogeum of the Dunes at Poitiers illustrates the phenomenon of the "aristocratization" of a section of a necropolis: a privileged ecclesiastical tomb which may have been a chapel originally and in any case was in private use. Indeed, a fragment of the lintel bears the following inscription: "The memory of Mellebaudis (*memoria*), Abbot, debtor of Christ, is here. The devout come from all sides to Him (Christ) for the offerings, and they return every year." The sculptured decoration in the Poitiers hypogeum shows, as do the lettering of the inscriptions and the vestiges of painting, that the Merovingian elites had a hybrid culture combining classical culture fostered by eastern elements and the art of interlaces which so clearly defines the plastic innovations of the early Middle Ages in the West.

Hypogeum of the Dunes. Late 7th - early 8th century.
Ornamented steps and view of the interior.
Poitiers.

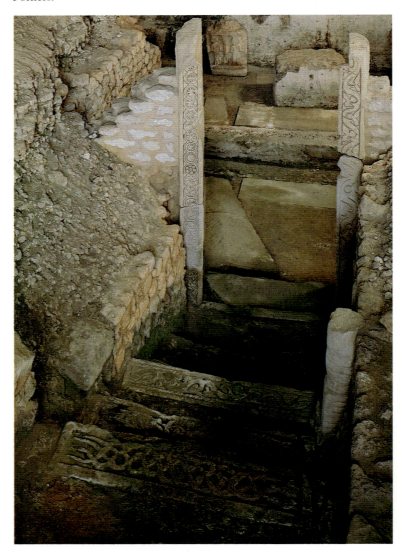

MONASTIC DECORATIONS IN MEROVINGIAN GAUL

During the second half of the sixth and the early seventh century monasticism enjoyed a new vitality in Gaul with the help of the many foundations born of the reforms introduced by St Columban (died 615) and the Irish monks. The patronage of the monarchy and the Frankish nobility encouraged this efflorescence and supplied personalities from aristocratic circles to occupy high monastic offices (St Ouen, St Philibert, St Wandrille). During the seventh century, the monasticism of Gaul was characterized by Franco-Irish influences and by the adoption of a rule combining the instructions of St Benedict and St Columban. The latter founded the monastery of Luxeuil before playing a decisive role in the foundation of a women's abbey at Jouarre in 630.

Columban represented the generation of Irish missionaries coming from an animated centre of Christian culture which had contributed since the fifth century to the preservation of many aspects of Latinity, *inter alia* by copying religious manuscripts. The development of Irish monasteries and Christian communities, often isolated from their mother churches in Gaul and Brittany, had made it necessary to reproduce bibles and psalters. The skill acquired by these workshops of scribes and illuminators is attested by the Book of Durrow and the Lindisfarne Gospels, whose geometric motifs recur in monumental sculpture, especially on certain stone crosses. These sculptures, which are also connected with the experience acquired by goldsmiths, introduced a religious iconography born of the classical heritage of early Irish monasticism.

The foundation of many monasteries in northern Gaul during the seventh century called for a great deal of building and carving. In many cases, little is known about the sculptured decoration of these monuments. So the crypt of one of the three churches of the monastery of Jouarre (Saint-Paul) comes as a fortunate exception. Agilbert, an important personality, who became bishop of Paris in 665 after having been bishop of Dorchester, though active in Northumbria, since 648, founded this crypt in which he was buried shortly after 673. Agilbert had taken refuge at Jouarre about 670 with his sister Theodechilde, abbess of the monastery.

The monument is built on a rectangular plan and separated into three aisles by columns. To the east, a funerary platform contains the tombs of four abbesses from the

Crypt of the church of Saint-Paul, Jouarre.
Sarcophagi and capitals
of the Merovingian period.
At the back, tomb of Bishop Agilbert.
To the right, cenotaph of Theodechilde.
Second half of the 7th century.
Monastery of Jouarre.

Stone cross, east side.
Mid-8th century.
Ahenny,
County Tipperary,
Ireland.

first Corinthian, the second composite. The snakes and anchors traced in shallow relief on the basket of one of the capitals with spiny acanthuses are noteworthy, especially for their links with contemporary animal art.

Most of the traces of monumental relief decoration from this period have disappeared. Moulded bricks, used in Spain and in the region of Nantes, and stucco decoration (the Carolingian ensemble of Germigny-des-Prés is a good example), were the answer when a substitute for stone or marble was sought. Inside religious buildings, the carved liturgical furnishings were intended to complete the iconographic programme of walls and vaults, at the same time that they defined the sacred space. Pilasters, closure slabs, ambo fragments, and altar panels are often to be seen in museums. One of the most coherent ensembles is that of Saint-Pierre-aux-Nonnains at Metz, which is also probably the latest sculptured monument from the Merovingian period and might date to the episcopate of Chrodegang (750-760). The panels in half-flat relief and the pilasters are carved out of local limestone. With the exception of a frontal figure of Christ, the decoration is vegetable, geometric and animal. Drawing on the Early Christian figurative tradition and the all-over geometrical adornment of the Merovingian period, the decoration of the Metz chancel opens the way to the endless series of geometrically decorated liturgical furnishings of the Carolingian period.

Detail of the carved chancel screen from Saint-Pierre-aux-Nonnains, Metz. Mid-8th century. Musée d'Art et d'Histoire, Metz.

seventh and eighth centuries surmounted by cenotaphs. Today the sarcophagus of Agilbert occupies the north recess of the crypt. At the head it is decorated with Christ and the evangelist symbols, and on its main face, with a great scene in which a number of figures in high relief acclaim Christ. It is obviously an iconographic programme organized around the theme of the Chosen for which various origins ranging from the British Isles to the classical and even Coptic Mediterranean have been suggested. The sarcophagus, which may no longer be in its original location, contributes to the creation of an all-over decoration in the monument, and to the general layout of carved sarcophagi as in the crypt of Saint-Denis, for example. The sarcophagus-shaped cenotaph of the Abbess Theodechilde is adorned with two registers of shells and shows the refinement achieved by the simple repetition of a decorative motif of classical origin.

The sculpture in the crypt of Saint-Paul at Jouarre raises some interesting problems. Where, for example, were the six marble capitals made, which are traditionally dated to the period of the crypt's construction? As with the capitals in the Poitiers baptistery, the problem here is that of identifying a localized manufacture, possibly in the Pyrenees where the marble came from. Are we dealing with carving executed near the quarry? Or with the work of itinerant workshops trained in the marble mason's craft? The dispersion of these products throughout Gaul and the differences in style and handling probably favour the latter hypothesis. The capitals at Jouarre fall into two groups: the

Examples of carved slabs:

1. Christ between two angels. Late 7th century.
   Quintanilla de las Viñas.
2. Altar frontal of Ratchis. Second quarter
   of the 8th century. Cividale.
3. End of the Agilbert sarcophagus. Late 7th century.
   Jouarre.
4. Carved lintel. Christ, apostles and angels.
   First third of the 11th century. Saint-André, Sorède.
5. Carved lintel. Christ, apostles and angels.
   Dated by the inscription to 1019-1020.
   Saint-Genis-des-Fontaines.

17

Daniel in the lions' den. Capital.
Second half of the 7th century.
San Pedro de la Nave.

VISIGOTHIC AND ASTURIAN SPAIN

Imitation of a consular diptych
on a door jamb from San Miguel de Lillo.
Mid-8th century.
Asturias.

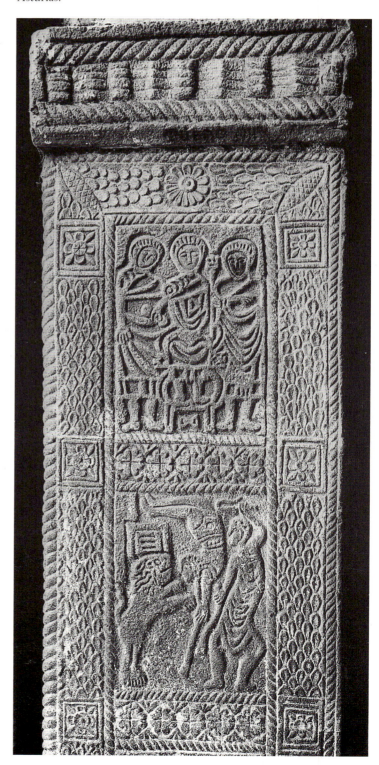

The Visigoths, driven out of Aquitaine after their defeat at Vouillé, made Toledo their capital under the reign of Leovigild (568-586). After the Third Council of Toledo (589) and the conversion of Leovigild's son, Reccared, a distinctive religious architecture appeared, mainly in the central part of the kingdom, while a rich and prestigious courtly art sprang up around Toledo.

In the field of sculptured decoration, the continuity between Late Antiquity and the Early Middle Ages is such that it is always extremely difficult to date the earlier sculptures and specify whether they actually belong to a period after the setting up of the Visigothic court at Toledo. The most reliable chronological guidemarks are found in the prestigious buildings of the seventh century. In Visigothic decoration, chancels, pillars, altar supports and other movable decorative elements vied with rich architectural elements such as friezes, cornices, imposts and capitals. Capitals enable us to establish the late antique origins of Visigothic figurative art better than any other form of decoration. Independently of regional differences, we note, among the formulas worked out at Seville, Cordova, Mérida and Toledo for adorning capitals, the Corinthian scheme with the spiny acanthus, which has sometimes been attributed to eastern models, but which undoubtedly stems from a local development of Roman capitals. At Mérida one is struck by the place which the town's Roman sculpture occupied in the output of workshops of the Visigothic period which often reused unfinished antique pieces and whose decorative choices were the reflection of an artistic culture that drew equally on local sources and the pomp and prestige of the East.

It becomes easier to define the monumental artistic features of Visigothic culture with the buildings reliably dated to the seventh century. The church of San Pedro de la Nave, with its internal partitioning, its play of proportions and the bonding used, is characteristic of the religious forms of the Visigothic period. The carved capitals with their shallow relief express an aesthetic whose classical roots merge into a new plasticity. The themes of the Sacrifice of Isaac and Daniel in the Lion's Den seem to orient an iconographic programme completed by the representations on the sculptured bases. The church of Santa María at Quintanilla de las Viñas is probably the latest building of the Visigothic period and belongs to the late seventh or early eighth century. Only a small part of the original building remains: the rectangular apse and the transept, which was formerly preceded by a nave and two side aisles. This church is well known for its sculptured decoration. Outside, the monotony of the stonework is broken by elegant sculpted bands, the decoration of which employs ornamental foliage. Animals, birds and trees are combined with geometric motifs and monograms referring to the church's benefactors. The sources of this decoration mingle late antique art with elements common in Sassanid art and Oriental fabrics. The repertory exhibits many similarities to that of contemporary Visigothic goldsmithery (crowns of Guarrazar) and is not unreminiscent of the coinage that was so characteristic of the Visigothic kings. Inside the building, the sculptured programme includes christological images which suggest a general consistency. One of the fragments represents Christ blessing, with a cruciform nimbus; another portrays two flying angels flanking Christ in the manner of antique Winged Victories accompanying the figure of the Emperor. At the entrance to the apse, personifications of the sun and moon are introduced by winged figures; two more reliefs are sculptured with figures holding a book. The dispersion of the ensemble makes it difficult to interpret a programme which has sometimes been compared with the astral and human symbolism of Christ according to Isidore of Seville. Be that as it may, these sculptures clearly belong half-way between the great decorations of Late Antiquity and those which were to culminate in Romanesque art in the centuries to come. The constricting rigidity of the frame, the flattened form of relief, the exaggerated proportions of the figures, the simultaneously frontal and profiled representation of the bodies, as well as the schematism of the eyes, hands and nose, are so many characteristic features which allow us to fit these sculptures into the framework of contemporary creations, from Irish manuscripts to north Italian reliefs. Indeed, many details are shared with the latter (Cividale), both the parallel incisions defining the drapery folds, as in wrought or repoussé metal, and the linework of the hair radiating around the head.

After the fall of the Visigoths, the Islamic retreat from the northerly regions of the Iberian peninsula helped the expansion of the Asturian monarchy from the mid-eighth century onwards. King Alfonso II (791-842) set up his court at Oviedo, maintained relations with the Carolingian world and promoted the arts. At this period the monk Beatus of Liébana had already completed an initial version of his Apocalypse commentary, destined to enjoy great success during the Middle Ages. As a continuation of the Visigothic world of Toledo, the Asturian kingdom experienced a great phase of architectural production under Ramiro I (842-850). This king initiated the construction of the palace of Naranco, San Miguel de Lillo and Santa Cristina de Lena. The most brilliant sculptured creations also date from this period. The palace of Naranco near Oviedo is a two-storey building with a rectangular plan. The size of its hewn stones recalls Visigothic architecture. The sculptured decoration of the upper storey is organized around capitals that are either Corinthian or shaped like an inverted truncated pyramid. The flat faces of the latter present decorative geometric and plant themes, as well as animals and figures, in a framework of torsades. The decoration continues in an imitation of cloth wall hangings with circular and rectangular inlaid reliefs adorned with animals and horsemen. Today the church of San Miguel de Lillo retains only a part of the original structure and the jambs of the existing entrance may be chosen to illustrate the artistic aspirations of the patrons. Actually they transpose on to stone the illustrations from ivory consular diptychs. A consul is opening games in the upper part, while a lion tamer and a tumbler perform a circus act on the lower part. This observation of Antiquity on the one hand, and the sculptured liturgical scheme preserved in the church of Santa Cristina de Lena on the other, testify to the concerns shared by the Asturian monarchy and the Carolingian empire, confirmed by the religious goldsmith's creations of the court of Oviedo.

Main hall of the palace of Naranco, dedicated in 848. Oviedo (Asturias).

Upper front of the baldachin.
Late 9th century. Stucco.
Sant'Ambrogio, Milan.

owing to their rarity, quality and the technical delicacy their execution called for. Along with consular diptychs (formed of two, usually rectangular panels with the portrayal of the magistrate and themes such as circus games), a production for private use that was increasingly prized developed between the fourth and sixth century. One of the main problems in the study of ivories concerns the whereabouts of the workshops. Depending on whether we attribute the objects to the western kingdoms or the Roman and Byzantine workshops, their basic artistic features change. Thus the diptych of St Lupicinus (Bibliothèque Nationale, Paris) and that of Saint-Andoche of Saulieu have led scholars to postulate the existence of workshops in northern Gaul during the sixth century. In Italy the same problem arises when it comes to defining the production of the workshops situated in the great capitals, Rome, Milan and Ravenna, in relation to the productions of Constantinople. The diptych of Consul Boëthius (Brescia) and that of Sts Peter and Paul (Metropolitan Museum, New York) exemplify this problem. The throne of Bishop Maximian of Ravenna, which has been reconstructed, is formed of many small ivory panels. Its iconography associates biblical themes with the traditional stock of Early Christian images adapted here to meet the patron's wishes. Stylistically, this episcopal throne divides scholars as to the existence or non-existence at Ravenna of

EARLY MEDIEVAL ITALY

During Late Antiquity, the towns of Italy maintained an architectural tradition of prestige and power. As from 353, Milan was the imperial residence on several occasions and at the end of the fourth century was indebted to St Ambrose for a spiritual influence felt throughout the western Christian world and comparable only to that of Rome. The great Milanese basilicas, San Lorenzo and Sant'Ambrogio, were given sumptuous decorations. Monumental religious art in Rome in the late fourth and during the fifth century was concentrated in venerable monuments such as San Paolo fuori le Mura, which around 385 reproduced the plan and elevation of St John Lateran and St Peter's, and Santa Maria Maggiore. The religious architecture of Milan and Rome inspired the architects of Verona, Brescia, Pavia and even Ravenna. In the last-named town, three architectural and decorative stages clearly delimited historically can be distinguished. The first half of the fifth century, with edifices such as Santa Croce or the mausoleum known as Galla Placidia, saw the town adorned with monuments which matched its role as capital of the Western Empire. The arrival of Theodoric in 493 saw the erection of a new palace, the king's mausoleum and the present-day church of Sant'Apollinare Nuovo, then dedicated to St Martin. Until then architectural sculpture had drawn on the Roman heritage of the fourth century. During the third stage, when Ravenna was conquered by the Byzantines in the sixth century, architecture and decoration looked to Constantinopolitan models, with splendid monuments such as San Vitale and Sant'Apollinare in Classe.

In connection with this last period of Ravennate art, the question of ivory carving has to be raised—luxury objects

Throne of Bishop Maximian.
546–556. Ivory.
Museo Arcivescovile, Ravenna.

Stucco decoration in the oratory
of Santa Maria in Valle.
Late 8th – early 9th century.
Cividale.

ivory carvers' workshops capable of making it and clearly differentiated from those of Constantinople.

Early medieval sculpture abounded in Italy owing to the many regional workshops which mainly produced decorations for liturgical church furnishings, while reusing antique remains as far as possible. From Aquileia to Rome, sculptors carved stone and marble in a characteristic flat relief, building up an all-over decoration of interlaces, arches and plant motifs, occasionally embellished with animals. The style changes from region to region, but the typology of chancels, ambos and baldachins, as well as the taste for this kind of decoration, remains constant. The baldachin of Sant'Apollinare in Classe, datable to about 800, belongs to the type set on bases and columns and framing the altar. Sometimes the baldachin is placed directly on the altar slab; see the example in the National Archaeological Museum in Madrid. The baldachin of the baptistery of Calixtus at Cividale symbolically protects the baptismal font. But in every case the decorative repertory is similar. Stylistically, a comparative study of the creations of the different geographical areas in the West reveals affinities such as those we observe between the reliefs of Quintanilla de las Viñas and those of the altar of Ratchis at Cividale.

Thanks to commercial routes and monastic foundations, northern Lombard Italy was in constant contact with the Frankish and Germanic world. It was to that region that the Carolingians looked when they wanted to renew the concept of empire. We have only to recall the role played by the architectural form of San Vitale at Ravenna in the erection of the palatine chapel at Aachen or, even earlier, the role of superimposed orders of columns and colonnettes backed on to the wall in the creation of monuments such as Saint-Laurent at Grenoble. Among the finest examples of monumental sculpture in Lombard Italy, the princely oratory of Santa Maria in Valle at Cividale has preserved a unique group of polychrome stucco sculptures. Six figures in salient relief stand out from the upper part of the wall on either side of a central bay. They surmount a door also embellished with geometric and plant decoration. The strictly frontal or slightly oblique presentation of the figures, the style of the drapery folds, the quality of the jewels, as well as the grandiose character of the composition have suggested a Byzantine influence that entered into the training of Lombard artists. The group's date is disputed, but comparisons with Carolingian manuscripts come down in favour of the defenders of an early date, towards the end of the eighth century, rather than those who put forward a later date at the beginning of the tenth century. Decoration in polychrome stucco or plaster is a technique common in the Middle Ages, but so fragile that little of it has survived. Among the great works executed in stucco are the monumental decorations of the baptistery of Ravenna Cathedral, of Germigny-des-Prés and Brescia, the ciborium of Sant'Ambrogio at Milan, the capitals of Saint-Remi at Reims, the Romanesque sculptures of the transept of Sant Serni of Tavèrnoles in Andorra and the tympanum of Saint-Julien at Brioude, as well as some works springing from the Germanic tradition (Hildesheim). The prestige and quality of these ensembles, illustrated here by the examples of Cividale and Milan, deservedly gives the technique of sculptured stucco a place of its own in medieval sculpture.

CAROLINGIAN ART: IVORIES AND GOLDSMITHERY

Model of the reliquary in the form of a triumphal arch given by Eginhard about 828 to the church of St Servatius at Maastricht, from an old drawing in the Bibliothèque Nationale, Paris

Binding of the Psalter of Charles the Bald, with ivory relief carving. Mid-9th century. Bibliothèque Nationale, Paris.

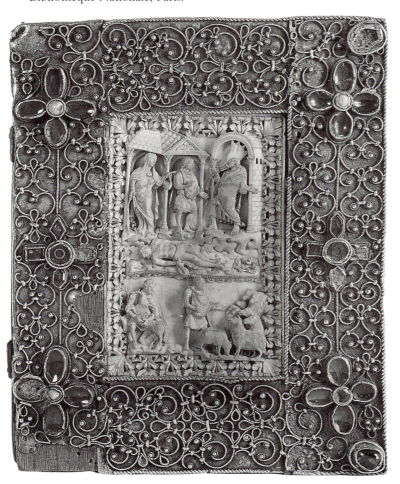

The Carolingian cultural renaissance was not produced suddenly, neither with Charlemagne's coming to power, nor with his coronation by the pope in the year 800. It had been prepared from the late seventh century in Italy, Gaul and the British Isles. Thenceforward the monastic renewal of the West was under way. Corbie, Laon, Tours, Fleury-sur-Loire and Saint-Denis were cultural centres long before the Carolingian renaissance, famous for their scriptoria and their libraries, as were the Germanic abbeys of Echternach, St Gall and Fulda. The reigns of Charlemagne and his son Louis the Pious (from 768 to 855) saw the construction of hundreds of monasteries, nearly thirty new cathedrals and close to a hundred royal residences.

The desire to vie with the prestige of Rome and Byzantium was behind Charlemagne's decision to choose a permanent residence in which to install his court, treasury and library. The palace of Charlemagne at Aachen and the palatine chapel built there on the Ravennate model at the very end of the eighth and beginning of the ninth century formed a centre for the study of letters which welcomed celebrated masters such as Alcuin. The court workshops produced illuminated books which were one of the most effective aids to the preservation of antique culture and the diffusion of contemporary artistic tastes. Among the first books illuminated at the court before the end of the eighth century was the Gospel Book of Godescalc, which reveals the growing importance of Italian and Byzantine models. The manuscripts of the Ada school, from the name of an abbess alleged to be Charlemagne's natural sister, marked a moment of diversification in the Palatine schools corresponding to Alcuin's succession by Eginhard.

Among the new artistic tendencies under Louis the Pious, the Coronation Gospels (Old Imperial Treasury, Vienna) introduced a Hellenistic or Alexandrian style. At Reims, under Archbishop Ebbo, manuscripts were illustrated in a style dominated by a movement which seems to shake the figures and their clothes. The Utrecht Psalter, written and illustrated at the abbey of Hautvilliers at the end of the first third of the ninth century, particularly characterizes this Carolingian renaissance and the school of Reims by its rapid, incisive, vibrant and nervous pen. After the death of Charlemagne and the fall of Ebbo at Reims, several artists revived the school of Saint-Martin of Tours characterized under Abbot Vivian (843-851) by the illustration of Bibles with narrative scenes arranged in superimposed registers.

The production of manuscripts created in the various specialized workshops a demand for work by the goldsmiths and craftsmen specialized in ivory carving, mainly to ornament precious bindings. This explains the close stylistic relation between illustrated manuscripts and ivory carvings. It has even been suggested that workshops were equipped to produce both genres. Thus the ivories of the Ada school are closely akin to manuscripts from the same circle. The Lorsch Gospel covers executed at the very end of the eighth century derive from Byzantine models from the period of Justinian, whereas the covers of Dagulf's Psalter find their source in Western Early Christian works. This wealth of sources also proves the role fulfilled by these

Ivory book-covers from the Psalter of Dagulf. Late 8th century, before 795. Musée du Louvre, Paris.

workshops in the transmission of models from Late Antiquity. At Metz, under the episcopate of Drogo (825–855), ivory panels (Drogo Sacramentary) reflected the movement animating the manuscripts of the same school in which contrasts with the school of Reims can be seen. Under Charles the Bald, the workshops of Corbie, Reims and Saint-Denis were particularly active and had more stylistic affinity with the Reims manuscripts. The cover of the Psalter of Charles the Bald (Bibliothèque Nationale, Paris) is especially reminiscent of the interpretation the ivory carvers made of the manuscript illustrations. In this case, the model is the Utrecht Psalter. The Munich Crucifixion, with its representation of the Resurrection beneath personifications of the sun and moon, and its antique references to Oceanus and Roma, may well be the masterpiece of this period. This ivory cover is luxuriously framed by a setting of goldwork, precious stones and enamels which invite us once again to speculate about the collaboration between ivory carvers and goldsmiths in these outstanding workshops.

The development of the cult of relics and the increasing size of the main churches were the source of the luxurious output of goldsmith's work in the Carolingian period: urns, statues, reliquaries of all kinds, book covers and other objects for liturgical use made up the essential part of a production destined to play an important role in the development of monumental sculpture. We find a good example of this in the reliquary called the Triumphal Arch of Eginhard known only from a drawing. It undoubtedly served as the foot of a cross and its rich decoration finds its inspiration in Roman and Early Christian triumphal programmes, while at the same time heralding the monumental iconographic display of the great Romanesque church portals.

The so-called Charlemagne Statuette,
representing an idealized Carolingian ruler.
Second half of the 9th century (sword and
horse remade during the Renaissance). Bronze.
Musée du Louvre, Paris.

ON THE THRESHOLD OF ROMANESQUE ART

During the tenth century, the church choirs continued to be embellished with sculptured liturgical furnishings which gave prominence to the altar. The chancel, the ambo, the ciborium and the episcopal offertory box, which had benefited by the Carolingian liturgical renewal, continued to occupy a preferential place during the tenth century with a decoration of interlaces, certain varieties of which experienced special regional developments. Thus the torsade linked with lozenges was perpetuated in the southwest of France down to the Romanesque period. The human figure is usually missing from these carved panels, but they make use of plant and animal motifs (Saint-Géraud, Aurillac). Altar slabs receive a special treatment; the most important are made of marble and assume varied shapes, mostly rectangular or semicircular. A large group in the South of France was decorated with lobes.

Along with this flowering of carved church furniture, the first attempts at decorating the façades of religious buildings began at the very end of the tenth or the beginning of the eleventh century. The marble lintels of Saint-Genis-des-Fontaines and Saint-André at Sorède in the Roussillon, together with the other sculptured motifs on the façade of the latter church, are among the first experiments in monumental sculpture and indicate contacts with the arts of ivory and goldsmithery. The Saint-Genis lintel is dated by an inscription of 1019-1020; in the centre a seated Christ in Majesty is blessing and holding the Book between Alpha and Omega, while two angels support a mandorla formed of two segments of a circle. On either side are six apostles standing under horseshoe arches. In Saint-André at Sorède, the lintel presents Christ in Majesty borne by two angels and accompanied by two seraphim and four apostles. The programme is completed by the decoration framing the upper window of the façade. It consists of the four evangelist symbols and two circles enclosing pairs of angels sounding trumpets, flanked by three seraphim. Here we see the desire to endow the entrance to the church with a genuine iconographic programme which, in its use of apocalyptic details, the concept of the Last Judgment and the vision of Ezekiel, seems to echo on the façade the decoration that usually surrounds the altar. Indeed, these reliefs have sometimes been regarded as elements of an altarpiece or an antependium reused on the outside of the building. Study of the style and technique of the vegetable elements, for example, proves that these sculptures were made in regional workshops that produced altar slabs and other items of church furnishings.

Another major work which also marks the transition to Romanesque art, in an environment much closer to the centres of power, is artistically quite different from the Roussillon reliefs. It is the altar frontal, probably executed at Fulda towards the end of the second decade of the elev-

Carolingian goldwork benefited by the progress made in the Merovingian period and combined the ancient practice of cloisonné with that of chasing and inlays. Among the most famous works are the binding of the Codex Aureus of Munich, with a decoration divided into five fields, and the ciborium of King Arnulf. Also outstanding for size, prestige and influence on sculpture is the gold and silver altar frontal of Milan, commissioned from the goldsmith Volvinius under the episcopate of Angilbert II. It has christological scenes on the front, while the back is reserved for the life of Ambrose, the Milanese saint. The differences in style observable between the two sides exactly match the situation of Carolingian art torn between a dazzling Antiquity and a new aesthetic. The bronze "Charlemagne" statuette (Louvre, Paris) clearly suggests this double dimension affirming the imperial idea. It is a reflection of the activity of the bronze-founders' workshops which have left other famous works in the Aachen chapel, such as the grilles of the galleries and the doors.

Romanesque altar slab with lobe design.
Early 11th century.
Saint-André, Sorède.

Altar frontal made by the goldsmith Volvinius under Bishop Angilbert. 824–859. Gold, silver gilt, enamel, precious stones. Sant'Ambrogio, Milan.

enth century, which stood in Basel Minster during the Middle Ages (now in the Musée de Cluny, Paris). This rectangular antependium consists essentially of chased gold panels fixed to an oak core with small nails. The field contains a series of five semicircular arches framing the following figures: Christ, at whose feet two crowned sovereigns, generally identified as the Emperor Henry II and his wife Kunigunde, are prostrating themselves; St Michael, St Benedict, and lastly the archangels Gabriel and Raphael on Christ's left. Noteworthy is the privileged place allotted to St Benedict, undoubtedly a deliberate choice of the patron, Henry II. This work, which has been the subject of a mass of specialist literature dealing variously with its technique, where it was made, its destination, patron, iconography and date, epitomizes the new Romanesque artistic context in an Ottonian milieu and the assimilation of the Carolingian past to a newly arisen, firmly monumental style.

Altar frontal from Basel Minster, probably made at Fulda about 1020. Gold and copper over oaken core. Musée de Cluny, Paris.

ROMANESQUE ART (1000-1200)

by Xavier Barral i Altet

INTRODUCTION

Georges Duby

Some hundred years elapsed before the last bastions of resistance yielded and people ventured to set up large figure compositions carved out of stone in the open air. The slow maturing that culminated in the advent of monumental sculpture had taken place throughout the eleventh century in the Benedictine monasteries of Gaul. The reform of the Church, that attempt to purify the men of prayer and, by freeing them from the defilement which kept them at a remove from holiness, to fit them to fulfil their social function better, had actually begun with the monastic institution. This enabled the latter to capture the fervour of the faithful and attract the growing flood of pious donations. The first use to which the monks put the superabundance of wealth thus acquired was to decorate the places where they silently absorbed the word of God, where they met to sing his praises at all hours of day and night. The rule of St Benedict required them to pray at such length in the name of the people so as to amass the favours of heaven for them. For it was thought that the more brilliant the liturgical office, the more generously those favours would be granted. Moreover, as liberated from the desires of the flesh as abstinence could make human beings, the monks felt that they belonged to the highest degree of terrestrial hierarchies and had come close to the realm of the angels. The church in which they chanted in unison with the choir of seraphim seemed to them the antechamber of Paradise. They wanted their house to reflect on earth the perfection of the heavenly city.

Furthermore, the Benedictine monastery was itself a city like the Roman city. Like the latter, it was enclosed in a precinct as a protection against corruption. Inside it two adjoining buildings, the basilica and the cloister, a kind of square surrounded by porticoes, formed a virtual replica of the ancient forum. The sculptors' first mission was to decorate this central space. No statues in it as yet, but at least they could decorate the tops of columns and pilasters, using what they saw on the remains of antique monuments as models. They were required to go further, to populate the profusion of plant forms stemming from the Corinthian acanthus with figures, as painters did around the initials on the parchment of lectionaries. For it was not only a question of decorating, but also of teaching, and, by means of such images that recalled scenes from the Old Testament and the Gospel, and episodes from the exemplary lives of guardian saints, of supporting the monks' meditations, of displaying before their eyes the symbols of the vices of which they had to purge themselves. The bas-reliefs decorating sarcophagi, the only elements of Roman sculpture left undestroyed, supplied models. Nevertheless it is obvious that sculptural themes were mostly borrowed from illuminated manuscripts, ivory plaques and goldsmiths' pieces, in other words they still came from the treasuries, and these forms, projected on to the wall, were still confined to the interior, to the area of withdrawal encircled by the monastic closure.

Not until the very end of the eleventh century were sculptures taken out of the sanctuaries and openly exposed to the view of the masses, because the clergy no longer feared that they would take them for the images of ancient gods. Henceforth the façade of the basilica was treated like a Roman arch of triumph. Sometimes sculptured figures covered it completely, but usually they were assembled around the portal, that key position. It was the place of transition from a depraved world to that other world of which the monastic community gave a foreshadowing by the harmony of its chants, the masterly arrangement of its processions, the heady scent of incense and the shimmering lights. The portal was the symbol of the conversion enjoined on every sinner.

The audacity that made this innovation possible grew stronger in the richest and most prestigious houses, at the nodal points of those widespread networks woven in the progress of reform, of those congregations that the monasteries assembled from one end of Christendom to the other, especially in the congregation headed by the abbey of Cluny. Closely associated with the Church of Rome from its foundation, Cluny had greatly increased the number of its daughter houses in the south of Gaul and Spain, in the highly Romanized provinces. Then, at the height of its renown, it laid claim to the cultural heritage of the Empire and took over the role once held by the imperial chapel. This return to great outdoor sculpture was firstly an affirmation of power. By half-opening the door, allowing a glimpse of the pomp of the liturgical feast and giving a foretaste of the joys promised purified souls, monasticism displayed its power to intercede. So decorative sculpture primarily fulfilled what we might call a political function, such as it had assumed in Antiquity, when it demonstrated on church portals the authority emanating from the city. But once it became public, sculpture also sought to be a demonstration of orthodoxy. In opposition to the threatening sects whose leaders, denounced as heretics, were pursued and burnt when they persisted in rejecting the incarnation, destroying crucifixes and claiming that man could communicate directly with God, and that ecclesiastical intermediaries were unnecessary, the tympana, the lintels and the column statues proclaimed first and foremost that God blessed those who erected magnificent monuments to his glory. Showing the apostles, prophets and Christ too in the body, they proclaimed that the Word was made flesh, that he had lived among men. Thus in the adornment of the monastic church, that impregnable fortress raising the trophies of daily victories won over the forces of evil, the aim of drawing the faithful on to the paths of truth was already evident. Showing at Moissac the risen Christ surrounded by the twenty-four Elders as the author of the Apocalypse had seen him at Patmos, giving on Autun Cathedral a glimpse of the Last Judgment, meant lifting a corner of the veil, inaugurating the apostolate by which the good news was spread to the far corners of the world, as the great scene exposed for the instruction of pilgrims on the tympanum at Vézelay has demonstrated in masterly fashion for nine centuries.

The dream of the Three Magi.
Capital. About 1125-1130.
Saint-Lazare, Autun.

◁ The prophet Isaiah.
Mid-12th century.
Souillac.

▷ Leaf of the bronze door
with Old Testament scenes.
Early 11th century.
Hildesheim Cathedral.

FORMATION OF THE STYLE

OTTONIAN SCULPTURE

At the beginning of Romanesque art, the medieval West was divided into two large geographical zones, a southern and a northern one. The former was characterized, during the second quarter of the eleventh century, by the spread of a sombre vaulted type of religious building. It had no sculptured decoration, but the small regular stonework used in its construction made its own contribution to the architectural decoration by means of small blind arcades and mural bands. This early southern Romanesque art spread rapidly from northern Italy, southern France and Catalonia. An early northern Romanesque art (also known as proto-Romanesque) was characterized in the Ottonian and Salian imperial regions by a return to the architectural formulas of the first Christian basilicas (timber-roofed, well-lit buildings) expressing the political desire of the Carolingian and Holy Roman Empires for a renewal of the old Roman Empire. Essentially, Ottonian art comprised two great phases, the first covering the second half of the tenth century and the first quarter of the eleventh until the death of Henry II in 1024 and the extinction of the Saxon dynasty, and the second continuing under the Salians until approximately the end of the third quarter of the eleventh century.

The great masterpieces of Ottonian sculpture were church fittings with monumental aspirations, made of bronze. The technique of casting an alloy of copper, tin and zinc in a mould, known since Antiquity, was particularly developed in the Ottonian centres in the Rhineland and northern Germany (Hildesheim, Augsburg, Mainz, Magdeburg). In addition to the very rapid diffusion of small objects such as crucifixes, Ottonian bronze-founding became famous at Hildesheim under Bishop Bernward (993–1022), the tutor of Otto III, and two imposing monuments have been preserved, the doors and the triumphal column. These works stand out forcibly in buildings characterized by the purity of their forms and architectural bareness. They provide brilliant testimony to the antique and Carolingian vision that presided over Ottonian artistic creation close to the centres of power. They are the jewels of the Hildesheim bronze workshops which also produced and exported a number of small-scale works (candlesticks, chandeliers, crucifixes).

The technical skill represented by the founding of each of the leaves of the Hildesheim door in one piece is only

Bronze column commissioned by Bishop Bernward for the church of the Holy Cross. About 1015-1020. Hildesheim Cathedral. Above: detail with scene from the life of Christ.

equalled by the plastic effort employed to animate a flat surface with figures in high relief. The scenes from the Old and New Testaments, depicted in cycles on separate registers, show a combination of the static force of antique models and the movement inherited from Carolingian illuminations. This pictorial summary of the Christian doctrine standing at the very entrance to the church had its counterpart in the interior in other fittings of bronze and gold, as well as in the painted decorations. The bronze column, luckily still there today, is a major monument of Western art because it reflects the political and religious aspirations of the circles of power. This triumphal monument, 12½ feet high with a diameter of 23 inches, erected to the glory of Christ, is modelled on the Roman triumphal columns of Trajan and Marcus Aurelius. Trajan's exploits are matched here by events from the public life of Christ; his victories over death and evil correspond to the emperor's victories over the barbarians. The underlying imperial ideology is reflected in one of the most beautiful illustrations of art in the service of a power which the quality of the style only enhances.

Beside these prodigious works of art, architectural sculpture played a minor role in the Ottonian realm. The Carolingian column capital derived from the classical Corinthian model (Essen, Paderborn) was almost entirely abandoned, and capitals ornamented with figures or masks are very rare (Gernrode, Zyfflich). The Ottonian capital *par excellence* is cubic in shape; the basket is a cube whose lower corners are rounded. This structure, very simple to rough-hew, which provides four smooth bare faces, was probably intended to receive the addition of painted decoration in certain cases.

Crypt with cubic capitals. About 1030-1035. Speier Cathedral.

THE ELABORATION OF
THE ROMANESQUE CAPITAL

The architectural decoration of religious buildings in the second half of the tenth century was usually very simple. It consisted of decorated panels, moulded imposts and a few reused capitals from immediately preceding periods. The large-size capital was very rare insofar as the large buildings used rectangular pillars as an element of separation between nave and side aisles. Only small churches or crypts used columns needing a carved capital. Among the examples of this period which extend and continue the last capitals of Late Antiquity we find the pre-Romanesque capitals of Brescia and Capua in Italy, and the Mozarabic formulas of San Cebrián de Mazote (Valladolid) in the Iberian peninsula.

The first regional experiments in carving capitals represent one of the essential aspects of the rise of monumental Romanesque sculpture during the first half of the eleventh century. They are part of the working out of the different features of early Romanesque architecture. These regional experiments are apparently unconnected, but they testify to a common concern destined to culminate in Romanesque art proper. In northern Italy, early Romanesque, with little ornamentation, welcomed capitals in crypts and ambulatories, as in San Stefano at Verona. During the first half of the eleventh century (around 1038 at Caorle), a group of capitals characterized by faithful and direct imitation of the antique Corinthian model appeared in basilicas at the head of the Adriatic, between Venice (San Nicolò di

Capital with interlace pattern. About 1020. Sant Pere de Roda.

Capital inspired by antique Corinthian. About 1020-1030. The abacus is Gothic. Basilica of Aquileia.

Lido) and Trieste (San Giusto). The acanthus leaves are handled slackly and the volutes curve back under the corners and under the dado of each face of the basket. At Aquileia, around 1020-1030, under the patriarchate of Poppo, the workshop was inspired by an antique capital in carving all the capitals in the basilica and its members were so proud of the result that they had no hesitation about placing and exhibiting the original in a privileged location, at the crossing of the transept. The two Corinthian capitals re-employed at Romainmôtier (Switzerland) in the second quarter of the eleventh century testify to a similar dependence on antique sculpture. At Aquileia the fidelity of the copy does not conceal what constitutes the essential aesthetic transformation of the new Romanesque capital as compared with the antique model: the evolution of the acanthus leaf to the palmette.

At about the same time, in the south of France and Catalonia, there was a search for the technical means to solve the problem of adapting the surface motif used on panels (interlacings, palmettes and rosettes) to the rough-hewn surfaces of the capital. From the end of the first third of the eleventh century at Le Puy, Tournus and Sant Pere de Roda there appeared a series of capitals based on the Corinthian scheme which show the pre-Romanesque shallow relief giving way to chamfering and deep grooving. This tendency continues in the ambulatory of Tournus, at Issoudun, and then before the end of the century in the cathedral and Saint-Allyre at Clermont-Ferrand. A second group of capitals with squaring and proportions closer to cubic forms has baskets completely covered with interlacings blossoming into palmettes and foliage: Sant Pere de Roda, Sainte-Foy at Conques and Aurillac. Links with pre-Romanesque relief work appear more clearly in the sculptured capitals with animal and plant themes in shallow relief in the church of Saint-Martin-du-Canigou in Conflent, reliably dated to the early eleventh century.

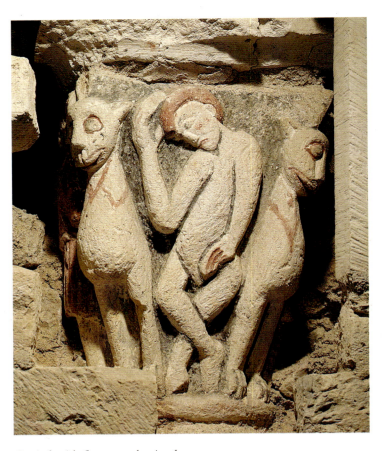

The transition from ornamental to figurative in the decoration of the capital researched by Henri Focillon and the role of the figure intended to emphasize and lighten its function are only two aspects of the amazing wealth of experiments which helped to form the style peculiar to Romanesque plastic art and give it its architectural character during the eleventh century. In northern France, where the forms of cubic capitals can be compared with those of the Ottonian world, the capitals of Vignory, ornamented with geometric, plant and animal motifs in a half-flat technique, testify to concerns similar to those observed in the south of France. At Saint-Remi of Reims some stucco capitals with a varied repertory of foliage, animals and figures are preserved. In Normandy, the two series of capitals at Bernay, the older of which may go back to 1020-1040, relate both to Burgundy and the Loire region; these contacts have been partly explained by the activities of a celebrated prelate, William of Volpiano, summoned to Burgundy by the Duke of Normandy at the very beginning of the eleventh century. Shortly after the mid-century, the duchy looked towards England, notably after the conquests of William the Bastard (later the Conqueror) in 1066. The best evidence of this is at Jumièges, Bayeux, Thaon, Rouen and, in the third quarter of the century, the geometrized decoration of the basilica of the Trinity and the chapel of Sainte-Croix at Caen. Sub-

Capital with figures and animals.
Before 1029.
Crypt of Saint-Aignan, Orléans.

View of the crypt. 1059-1080.
Church of La Trinité (Abbaye aux Dames), Caen.

sequently Normandy adopted highly geometrized and schematic abstract motifs, making them one of the characteristics of a Romanesque style whose contribution to Western art was essentially architectural. Interregional connections were also established between Burgundy and the region of the Loire and the Rhone valley. From the early eleventh century, Burgundy possessed monuments of the first importance: Cluny, Romainmôtier, Saint-Philibert of Tournus, Saint-Bénigne of Dijon. The last-named abbey church, which played such a large part in the flowering of the Romanesque apse during the first two decades of the century, under William of Volpiano, has in the present-day crypt some magnificent capitals decorated with complicated monsters accompanying corner masks and figures; their innovative nature makes them one of the most striking experimens as regards style. In Paris, the capitals from Saint-Germain-des-Prés in the Musée de Cluny contrast with these series by the monumentality of the Christ in Majesty represented on them and add fresh fuel to the controversy over the chronology of these works. At the centre of Capetian power, the capitals of the cathedral of Sainte-Croix at Orléans and those in the crypt of Saint-Aignan pose both the problem of dating the birth of Romanesque sculpture in the valley of the Loire and that of tracing the sources of inspiration of these varied experiments.

Capital in the rotunda.
Early experiment in Romanesque sculpture.
Before 1018.
Saint-Bénigne, Dijon.

Christ blessing.
Capital from Saint-Germain-des-Prés, Paris.
Mid-11th century.
Musée de Cluny, Paris.

THE TOWER-PORCH OF SAINT-BENOÎT-SUR-LOIRE

Corinthian capital signed Unbertus.
Ground level of the tower-porch.
Mid-11th century.
Saint-Benoît-sur-Loire.

At the beginning of Romanesque art, the Loire basin was a geographical zone of intense artistic activity. Helgaud, the monk of Fleury, has left handsome witness to the wealth of foundations by Robert the Pious at Orléans, which include for example the construction at Saint-Aignan of Orléans before 1029 of a chevet modelled on that of Clermont Cathedral perhaps with an ambulatory and radiating chapels. An ambulatory may also have existed in the basilica (dedicated in 1014) of Saint-Martin of Tours (unless it belonged entirely to the apse built after the fire of 1096). The dating of this church at Tours has been the subject of scholarly polemics for more than a hundred years, like those which surround the chronology of the best preserved monument in the region: the tower-porch of Saint-Benoît-sur-Loire.

This abbey (Saint-Benoît-de-Fleury), standing on the banks of the Loire, has a very old history, since its foundation goes back to 651. Reformed between 930 and 943 by Odo of Cluny, the abbey of Fleury became one of the main intellectual centres in the West under the abbacies of Abbo (988-1004) and Gauzlin (1004-1030). A centre of studies, with a large library and a highly reputed scriptorium, the abbey, during the eleventh century, was one of the repositories of the antique culture in which the medieval monastic culture was forged. Archaeological excavations have partially disclosed the flat chevet and the transept of the monastery church built during the last quarter of the ninth century, after the Norman invasions. This edifice probably already possessed a western tower. A fierce fire devastated the abbey in 1026 under the abbacy of Gauzlin, who decided on the construction of a tower at the west end. The chevet of the present church was only built by Abbot William (1067-1080); it was consecrated in 1107. The nave in its turn was not rebuilt until the twelfth century. As for the tower-porch with its exceptional wealth of sculpture, when does it date from? From the years following the fire and thus from the abbacy of Gauzlin? Was there a direct relation between the fire and the reconstruction of the tower? How many years after the actual fire was this reconstruction? Was it one of the works of Abbot William?

The tower-porch of Saint-Benoît-sur-Loire, built on an almost square plan, has a ground floor and one upper storey in its existing state. Each of its external façades is pierced by three openings on both levels. To the east, the central door, framed by two niches, is flanked by the doors to spiral staircases which allow access to the upper part. Each level is subdivided into nine bays with an almost square plan by large piers confined by semi-columns, although the shapes vary according to their position and

Ground level of the tower-porch.
Mid-11th century.
Saint-Benoît-sur-Loire.

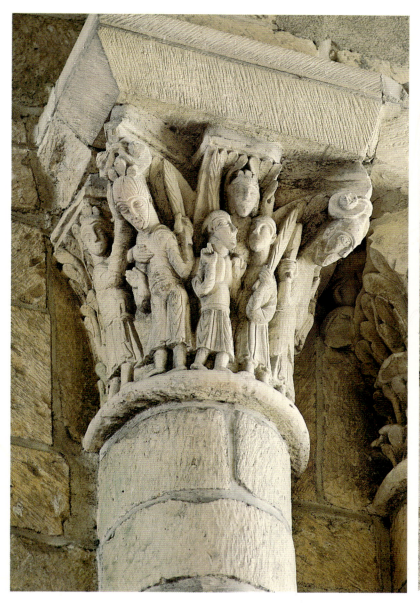

Historiated capital representing martyrs.
Upper level of the tower-porch.
Third quarter of the 11th century.
Saint-Benoît-sur-Loire.

Historiated capital representing the Visitation.
Ground level of the tower-porch.
Mid-11th century.
Saint-Benoît-sur-Loire.

storey. They support groined vaults, except in the three bays which precede the three minor apses hollowed out of the thickness of the east wall of the upper storey.

This monument, whose architecture already marks it out as Romanesque, is exceptional for the series of capitals decorating it. On the ground floor, the acanthus reigns on large capitals reflecting the antique culture of the master who engraved his name (*Unbertus me fecit*) on one of the most conspicuous capitals. The Romanesque synthesis he effected was nurtured by certain drawings, a few sheets of which have been discovered in Rome and Paris, by observation of the antique and the desire to create new schemata with the help of the palmette, for example. In a second group of capitals, the acanthus disappears and the style is dryer and more linear. The human figure, which invades the capitals on the upper floor, already appears on the ground floor, in the representations of the Annunciation, the Visitation and the Flight into Egypt.

The relations between the ground-floor capitals of the porch of Saint-Benoît-sur-Loire and those of Méobecq, and comparisons with the capitals of disputed date in Saint-Hilaire of Poitiers, Saint-Martin of Tours and Maillezais pose interesting methodological problems concerning the chronology of early Romanesque sculpture in France. How should we situate the model and its copies? Can mentions of the construction work be used to date the completion of the sculptures? As regards style, the hand of one member of Unbertus's workshop has been detected at Méobecq (Indre), a monument dedicated in 1048; but to which of the successive buildings at Méobecq does the dedication refer? Supporters of an early date think that the Saint-Benoît capitals belong to the worksite opened around 1026; hence their importance for the origins of Romanesque sculpture. But is it conceivable that Unbertus's experiments with the Corinthian scheme and the appearance of the historiated capitals at Saint-Benoît are more than half a century earlier than the first Corinthian capitals of Saint-Sernin at Toulouse or those of about 1100 at Vézelay? That is unacceptable to defenders of an evolutionist theory of Romanesque sculpture, for whom the Romanesque style, once formed, followed a regular course.

Bernard Gilduin. Marble altar slab consecrated in 1096. Saint-Sernin, Toulouse.

FROM TOULOUSE TO COMPOSTELA:
THE EFFLORESCENCE OF SCULPTURE

After the nineteenth-century discussions emphasizing the national origins of the medieval art of each country within the framework of romantic resurgences, Emile Mâle initiated in 1922 a polemic putting the origins of French Romanesque art on an essentially nationalist basis. Mâle held that monumental sculpture reappeared in the south of France at the end of the eleventh century under the influence of the miniature. The home of this renaissance was Toulouse. "Spain or Toulouse?": that was the question raised in reply by the American art historian Arthur Kingsley Porter (1924) who believed that Hispanic creations preceded those of France–a point of view taken up and expanded by Manuel Gomez Moreno (1925). An early addition to this controversy, which has been steadily supplied with ammunition during our century, was the theory of the pilgrimage roads, a means of penetration into Spain for French sculptors according to Emile Bertaux (1906), or of artistic exchanges according to Paul Deschamps (1923). In 1923 A. Kingsley Porter improperly entitled his monumental compilation in ten volumes *Romanesque Sculpture of the Pilgrimage Roads*. In 1938 Georges Gaillard made an intensive and direct study of the oldest Hispanic works and established that early Romanesque sculpture was characterized on both sides of the Pyrenees by a large variety of forms owing to the diversity of sources and talents.

The origins of Romanesque sculpture during the second half of the eleventh century are evidenced on both the north and the south side of the Pyrenees. Among the oldest buildings is the abbey church of San Salvador de Leyre in Navarre, consecrated in 1057, with its two groups of capitals situated in the crypt and the church above. As yet they do not exhibit the decoration of fleurons and palmettes which was destined to become one of the favourite themes of Romanesque sculpture in south-western France and northern Spain; that ornamentation asserted itself progressively during the last quarter of the century at Santa María de Ujué, before 1089, and at Santa María de Iguácel at about the same time. Nevertheless, the history of major Romanesque sculpture is directly dependent on the views we may hold about the opening and progress of the great worksites of Toulouse, Moissac, Jaca, León and Compostela.

The cathedral of Santiago de Compostela and the collegiate church of Saint-Sernin at Toulouse are two edifices of comparable importance. Their plans are similar and the construction of both began about the same time, shortly after 1070. Both contain a sculpture programme of amazing scope. About 260 Romanesque capitals are preserved at Saint-Sernin, placed at the springing of the semicircular arches in the interior of the building. Showing great stylistic continuity and a progression from the apse towards the nave, the following groups can be distinguished: densely decorated capitals in the lower parts of the chevet and the transept, capitals derived from the Corinthian column in the ambulatory, historiated capitals in the interior of the apse whose style can be followed into the galleries of the choir, and lastly capitals in the side aisles outside the nave ornamented almost exclusively with leafwork. In order to arrange these works chronologically, we should assess the full importance of the years 1075-1083, a period when reform was introduced at Saint-Sernin and an aggressive canonic policy was pursued. In another connection, we know that a man named Raymond Gayrard, who founded a hospital near Saint-Sernin around 1075-1078, took part in the work in the nave of the Romanesque church until his death in 1118. Lastly, the altar slab signed by an artist named Bernard Gilduin was consecrated by

Lid of the Alfonso Ansúrez sarcophagus from Sahagún. About 1093. Museo Arqueológico Nacional, Madrid.

Commemorative relief
of Abbot Durand.
About 1100.
Cloister, Moissac.

Relief with an apostle
re-employed in the ambulatory
of Saint-Sernin, Toulouse.
About 1100.

the ciborium which sheltered the altar of Santiago de Compostela at approximately the same time. At Toulouse itself, seven re-employed marble panels, possibly cut from antique columns, are now disposed in the ambulatory of Saint-Sernin. They come from a choir decoration that has disappeared and can be attributed to the school of Bernard Gilduin. They show a Christ in Majesty enclosed by the evangelist symbols, a cherub, a seraph, two angels and two apostles. The first three panels are very close to the period of the altar slab; the other four could be approximately dated to 1100 if we compare them with the apostles or the abbot on the pillars in the cloister at Moissac, another great artistic creation from the very end of the eleventh century.

In addition to borrowings from goldsmithery and ivory work, references to Antiquity are one of the great contributions of the production of Bernard Gilduin and his workshop, which also carved a certain number of capitals in the transept galleries of Saint-Sernin (figures carrying a funerary altar in the tradition of antique sarcophagi) and others beyond Toulouse as far as Saint-Caprais at Agen. Antiquizing plastic art also characterizes the sculpture of a worksite that was formerly dated as far back as 1065, but which recent scholarship places towards the end of the century: that of Jaca Cathedral. Besides capitals as well known as that of the sacrifice of a naked Isaac almost in the round, whose details are directly copied from antique

Pope Urban II in 1096. These facts help to establish a chronology around which our understanding of the Romanesque sculpture in this region pivots.

The basilica of Saint-Sernin at Toulouse, whose oldest parts are in the chevet, is also important for defining a type of Romanesque "pilgrimage architecture," which also includes the basilicas of Sainte-Foy at Conques, Saint-Martin of Tours, Saint-Martial of Limoges and Santiago de Compostela. Saint-Sernin has a nave with double side aisles, characterized in elevation by galleries, a vast, strongly projecting transept with single side aisles and a chevet with ambulatory and radiating chapels. At Santiago de Compostela we find the same plan, only magnified, in a monument begun in 1078 or perhaps a little earlier. Construction, interrupted around 1088 at the ground-floor level of the ambulatory, was vigorously resumed before the turn of the century. The oldest capitals in Santiago de Compostela make much use of animal decoration which does not fully merge with the plant motifs. As an exact parallel, in the tower known as the Pantheon of the Kings in San Isidoro of León, we find carved capitals from the time, it is now thought, of Urraca, daughter of Ferdinand and Sancha, who died in 1101. Today León, Toulouse and Compostela are seen as contemporary worksites opened shortly after the 1070s.

Let us return to Toulouse to follow the style of Master Bernard Gilduin which characterizes the early 1100s. With him liturgical furniture holds the place of honour. He signed a marble altar slab ornamented with lobes on its upper part and christological scenes on the side. It is connected with earlier monuments of the same type listed in Gallia Narbonensis, but is distinguished from them by the layout of the decoration: the beardless Christ is carried by angels and flanked by the Virgin, St John and several apostles. Close to goldsmithery, the decoration of the Saint-Sernin altar slab evokes vanished monuments such as

View of the nave with carved capitals.
About 1100. San Martín, Frómista.

sarcophagi and are re-echoed at San Martín de Frómista, Bernard Gilduin's style appears in a modillion today reused in the apse of Jaca Cathedral. Exchanges or at least stylistic contacts between these different worksites are now confirmed. Thus, while capitals close to those at Jaca recur later at Loarre, a capital of the Jaca-Frómista type appears in the south arm of the transept of Saint-Sernin at Toulouse contemporaneously with the works by Bernard Gilduin's atelier. The demonstration could be extended to the formidable influence of these different workshops by the study, for example, of the different phases of the sculptured decoration of the church of Saint-Sever-sur-l'Adour, begun around 1070 at the earliest; work on it continued during the first quarter of the twelfth century. Here the Toulouse worksite left its mark on several capitals in the church's west gallery, and we could add the cathedral of Lescar, Saint-Sever-de-Rustan and Saint-Jean of Mazères. Artistic exchanges, migratory movements towards the reconquered Spanish towns, the renewed prestige of architectural sculpture, emulation and rivalry between the worksites: the last decades of the eleventh century are marked on both sides of the Pyrenees by massive collective investments in the field of construction on a scale unheard of until then. Such enterprises confirmed the profitability of pilgrimages, the importance of gifts and the material power of the abbeys, chapters and their

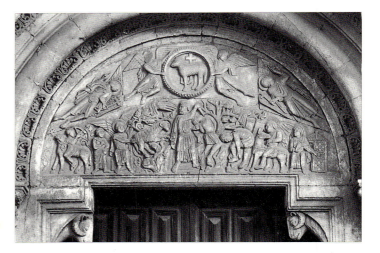

Sacrifice of Isaac. Tympanum of the Portal of the Lamb.
About 1110-1115.
San Isidoro, León.

Two women with lion and ram from Saint-Sernin, Toulouse.
Shortly before 1118.
Musée des Augustins, Toulouse.

patrons. If buildings appear henceforth with a sculptured decoration enriching the architecture and deploying an iconographic programme inside the church, the patrons were at the same time preparing to display all this wealth and the profundity of Christian thought on the sculptured portal outside the church.

Preceding the work of Bernard Gilduin, the Door of the Counts at Saint-Sernin of Toulouse, possibly executed even before the last decade of the eleventh century, opens into the south arm of the transept by two twin bays. The structure is visually inspired by the monumental doors of Antiquity and its architectural role only leaves room for the decoration of the capitals (for which an integration with the general iconography of the interior of the apse has been proposed) and the presence of bas-reliefs in the spandrels. A similar arrangement would probably have been used for the south portal of Jaca Cathedral, a church which already had its west portal decorated with a sculptured tympanum. The chrism, a traditional Pyrenean feature, but here suggesting a Trinitarian significance, is flanked by two lions, the one on the right trampling a basilisk and a bear underfoot, the one on the left protecting a man holding a snake in his hand. The meaning is explained by the inscriptions: the lions represent Christ in two roles, on the right as conqueror of the empire of death, and on the left showing mercy to the repentant sinner, with an exhortation to penitence. The meaning is completed by the capitals of the portal, one of which represents Daniel in the lions' den visited by Habakkuk. The Portal of the Lamb at San Isidoro of León, which fits into the Jaca sequence around 1110-1115, presents an iconography already fully worked out, with the incorporation of typological images such as the Sacrifice of Abraham into the framework of a programme tailored to meet political wishes after the reconquest of Spain. It is crowned by a zodiac in which the illustration of a Christian intellectual renaissance has been recognized. Thus, iconographical ambition and stylistic research go hand in hand, as evidenced by the powerful relief in which Sts Isidore and Vincent, who flank the tympanum, have been executed. This programme, however, is not much earlier than the great tympana of mature Romanesque art.

On the road to Compostela, the search for a façade decoration was in full swing from the early twelfth century, as proved by the Door of France and the Door of the

Miègeville Door.
About 1105-1115.
Saint-Sernin, Toulouse.

David.
Relief re-employed in the
Door of the Goldsmiths.
About 1110.
Santiago de Compostela.

Goldsmiths at Santiago de Compostela executed before 1112. The latter, which today presents a sculptural jigsaw puzzle that art historians are trying to solve, preserves two tympana and many fragments from a programme that emphasized the dual nature of Christ. The whole was crowned by an apostolic frieze, a prelude to those which were to triumph on Spanish façades. In Saint-Sernin of Toulouse, the Miègeville Door, finished shortly before the death of Raymond Gayrard (1118), evinces a similar evolution and the combination of stylistic links already mentioned. Begun shortly after 1100 in the entourage of Bernard Gilduin, it was later completed by sculptors who were familiar with Compostela. Certain capitals framing the portal are historiated and represent the Annunciation, the Visitation, the Massacre of the Innocents and the Expulsion from Paradise. On the lintel, which rests on two consoles representing King David and two figures sitting astride lions, are the twelve apostles and two angels who are watching the Ascension of Christ depicted on the tympanum. On either side of Christ, the apostles Peter and James are accompanied by Simon Magus and other personages. The great historiated Romanesque portal, which should have added lustre to the west façade of the basilica of Saint-Sernin, would undoubtedly have gathered the fruits of these decades when the style was being worked out. Judging by the extant capitals, it was under construction when work on the site was interrupted in 1118. Martial and Saturninus would have occupied a privileged position on it. Perhaps the masterpiece preserved in the Musée des Augustins representing two women with legs crossed, with one foot shod and the other bare, and carrying a lion and a ram respectively, came from it? Comparison with the attitude of the David on the Door of the Goldsmiths at Santiago de Compostela (which may have come from the Door of France) illustrates to what point the progression of the style seems to be formed in this environment of rivalry and emulation between sculptors whose names and artistic motivations we should like to know better.

THE PRESTIGE OF CLUNY

One of the major events in the history of the Middle Ages was the foundation of Cluny by William III of Aquitaine in 910. A great centre of reform in the observance of the Old Benedictine Rule, Cluny, under the direction of men of exceptional ability such as Mayeul and Odilo, rapidly created an unparalleled network of monastic daughter houses. Among the most prestigious buildings of the late tenth century figures the abbey church of Cluny II (960-981), which had a chevet with staggered apses, a comparatively narrow transept, a nave with side aisles and a galilee–a plan used by many eleventh-century churches. As it soon proved too small, and ill-adapted to the economic expansion of the mother house of the Cluniac order, a new church was founded in 1088; although partially consecrated by Pope Urban II in 1095, construction continued until the solemn consecration of 1130. It was an enormous building, whose design is reflected in many smaller churches, primarily in Burgundy (Paray-le-Monial, La Charité-sur-Loire, Autun). It had five aisles preceded by a galilee and two façade towers, a double transept and an apse with ambulatory and radiating chapels. The vaults rose to a very great height above three storeys. The unfortunate demolition of this building between 1798 and 1823 has deprived us of a unique monument known only by archaeological researches and a few surviving elements.

This abbey church which all Christianity envied was decorated with sculptures, paintings and mosaics; an echo of them is found in the great Burgundian complexes such as Vézelay for sculpture and Berzé-la-Ville for painting.

The west front, from which numerous remains of richly polychromed sculpture have been rediscovered, has been restored on a hypothetical basis by the American archaeologist K. J. Conant; its tympanum was decorated with a theophany in the spirit of the one formerly on the tympanum of the Monte Cassino basilica, and still to be seen on several Burgundian churches (Charlieu, Perrecy-les-Forges). The unrivalled quality of the Cluny sculpture, its beauty and its role in the subsequent development of medieval sculpture, can be grasped from rediscovered fragments of the choir screen and eight surviving capitals from columns in the ambulatory of the great basilica. The importance of the foliage sculpture is well known, not only on the capital entirely decorated with leafwork derived very closely from the antique Corinthian, but also on the other capitals. They are surprising for the absence of an architectural frame and for the way in which the figures fit into the foliage of the Corinthian squaring. Figures instead of palmettes appear at the corners of the baskets, whereas elsewhere they occupy the centre of a single face, magnified by mandorlas. A coherent iconographic programme centred on a moral and cosmological symbolism incorporates the Virtues, the tones of the Gregorian music scale, the Seasons and the Rivers of Paradise. It must have fitted into the larger ensemble of paintings and sculptures, to judge by two extant engaged capitals representing the Sacrifice of Abraham and Adam and Eve. The mastery of the nude, the forceful modelling, the movement of the drapery folds, and the restless linework reminiscent of illuminations, as well as the majestic handling of the Corinthian scheme, are noteworthy features of these masterworks which the monks of Cluny raised to the summit of Western art, shortly before 1120 (possibly even about 1110).

The rivers of Paradise. Capital from the ambulatory of Cluny. About 1115. Musée Lapidaire, Cluny.

The tones of music. Capital from the ambulatory of Cluny. About 1115. Musée Lapidaire, Cluny.

Eve. Part of the lintel from the north transept door of Saint-Lazare, Autun. About 1130. Musée Rolin, Autun.

THE MEANING OF THE IMAGERY

THE TYMPANUM AND THE SOCIAL ORDER

The Romanesque church contained sculptured picture cycles on capitals either facing and answering each other or arranged in series in particular parts of the building, such as the crypt (cycle of St Benedict in Saint-Denis) and especially the choir enclosure and ambulatory, as in the churches of Auvergne: Issoire (Passion of Christ), Mozat (Resurrection) and Saint-Nectaire. This iconography hidden at the back of the sacred space invites us to consider each capital in relation to the nearby wall paintings and to its position in the building. Essentially it consists of images of the Passion, the Salvation, the Resurrection, the Last Judgment, lives of the Saints, struggles between the Virtues and Vices, and typological correspondences between the Old and New Testaments. Beside these decorations reserved in principle for those at prayer, the church displayed outside, especially at the entrance, on the façade, portal and tympanum, large sculpted frescoes intended to offer the passerby both a synthesis of Christian doctrine and the Church's conception of the world order: this was the great iconographic triumph of the Romanesque period.

The façade design is centred on the tympanum which rests on a lintel and concentrates the spectator's attention by its semicircular form. Its iconography always fits in directly with that of the portal and in a broader sense with the façade as a whole. The latter is made up of different architectural elements, each of which has a place and plays a specific role in the structure of the whole. With its portals, round windows, rose window, high windows, gable and towers, the façade is a screen which lends itself admirably to the display of a carved or painted decoration which the ecclesiastical and civil powers utilized with dexterity. The meaning of the images is nearly always spelled out by inscriptions which sometimes identify specific elements, but more usually provide the interpretative key to the whole work, like the formula surrounding the mandorla containing Christ in Majesty accompanied by the Tetramorph on the north tympanum of the twelfth-century church of San Miguel d'Estella in Navarre: "This present image that you see is neither God nor man, but he is God and man whom this sacred image figures."

The great Romanesque tympana bear witness to a remarkable architectonic calculation, to careful iconographic planning and uncommon technical skill; and they show that large sums of money were available to buy the materials and pay the artists. The latter, sculptors or masters of works, were a force to be reckoned with from the moment when they dared to sign their work, as at Autun beneath the feet of Christ in Majesty, in the midst of religious inscriptions, using the somewhat presumptuous formula *Gislebertus hoc fecit*. The close tie between iconographic conception and artistic execution is clearly emphasized in the phrase inscribed on the twelfth-century tympanum of the church of Autry-Issards (Bourbonnais) accompanying the divine glory carried by angels: "God made everything. Man makes, has remade everything. Natalis made me." It should, of course, be added that the execution of the great Romanesque tympana was a team undertaking. At Conques, as at Autun and elsewhere, the tympanum is made up of juxtaposed blocks of stone carved before they were put in place. Technical observa-

Portal and tympanum with the Last Judgment. About 1140–1145. Saint-Lazare, Autun.

tion of the bonding shows how complicated the sculptors' researches were before completion of the definitive formula for putting the stones in place. The main problem was to ensure the coincidence, which was not always sought for (Autun), of the stone-cutting with the cutting up of the iconography (Conques, Vézelay).

By its monumentality, the sculpture of the Romanesque tympanum completed by that on the archivolts sometimes forms the only decoration of the whole façade (Conques). At other times, the tympanum is integrated with the façade, as in the little chapel of Saint-Michel-d'Aiguilhe at Le Puy where the lobes surrounding the tympanum are ornamented with an Adoration of the Lamb by the Elders of the Apocalypse, while on the upper part of the façade there is a frieze of figures, situated on either side of the Divine Majesty, which cannot be left out of a global interpretation. But the tympanum is first of all an integral part of the portal and its meaning has to be

Portal and tympanum with the Mission of the Apostles. About 1135–1140. La Madeleine, Vézelay.

clarified by that of the sculptures on the trumeau and the embrasures, as well as those on other portals of the façade, as at Vézelay, for example. The images are integrated into a liturgical context that we forget only too often when interpreting them, sometimes for lack of adequate documentation. Thus the lintel fragment from the portal of the north transept of Saint-Lazare at Autun which represents the enigmatic figure of a reclining Eve picking the apple with her left hand, resting her head on her right hand, and with foliage placed in the centre of the relief modestly hiding her sex, has been explained in different ways. Her posture had suggested that the artist was obeying a formal imperative, imposed by the dimensions of the lintel or by the iconographic intention to show Eve leaning towards Adam and whispering in his ear the idea of the sin. In reality, Adam, like Eve, was originally also depicted reclining on the lintel, because, condemned by God, they had been punished for the Original Sin and were likened

The weighing of souls and Hell.
Detail of the Last Judgment tympanum.
About 1140-1145.
Saint-Lazare, Autun.

Signature of Gislebertus
and separation of the Chosen and the Damned.
Detail of the tympanum.
About 1140-1145.
Saint-Lazare, Autun.

to the demoniacal serpent. A risen Lazarus was represented standing upright on the tympanum, emphasizing the iconographic intent by a strong formal contrast. But Eve's reclining position must also be connected with the liturgy for Ash Wednesday, when sinners entered the basilica of Autun through this portal prostrate, and did not stand erect until they had been pardoned by the sacrament of penance. (The faithful also passed beneath the coffin of St Lazarus in his mausoleum at Autun on their knees or stooping.) If the sacramental liturgy was particularly suited to a sculptural interpretation at the entrance to the church, it found numerous iconographical allusions on Romanesque tympana. The exhortation to public repentance took place between Ash Wednesday and Maundy Thursday, and often throughout Lent, in front of the church door, in the porch or the atrium, places occupied by the penitents until the Easter remission of sins. The tympanum of the west portal of Jaca Cathedral, which has already been mentioned, may also be interpreted in this way. Thus we are entitled to extend this approach to Romanesque tympana in a more general way to the whole iconographic environment of the Original Sin, to the scenes of healing and resurrection which often constitute the essential part of the iconography of the capitals flanking the portal. Penitence leading to the Eucharist summarizes the meaning of the portal giving access to the church when it is passed through by the penitent who prays, in Daniel's words: "I have sinned, I have committed iniquity, I have done wickedly, have pity on me, Lord."

The illustration of Good and Evil, the sculptured presentation of the social order, of the models which had to be followed to be a good Christian, of the prizes reserved for the just and the punishment awaiting those who strayed from the right path, were clearly and inexorably displayed on the tympana of the Last Judgment. At Conques and Autun, the Divine Majesty sits in Paradise welcoming the chosen with one hand and rejecting the damned without appeal with the other. At Autun, the inscription engraved on the mandorla of Christ clearly stresses his role as judge. At Conques, another inscription warns: "O sinners, if you do not change your lives, know that a harsh Judgment awaits you." When the angels announce the Resurrection and the Last Judgment, the dead leave their graves to stand before the supreme Judge. Michael weighs the souls and presides over the general

Tympanum with the Last Judgment. About 1125-1135. Sainte-Foy, Conques.

organization of the tympanum into two zones: the chosen on the right, the damned on the left. The contrast is striking. On the side of the chosen, calm, happiness, order and rhythm are opposed to the disorder, agitation, ugliness and horror prevailing on the side of the damned. At Conques, the symmetry between Abraham welcoming the chosen to his bosom and Satan sitting in Hell accentuates the contrasts. A procession presided over by the Virgin and St Peter includes those whose task it is, in twelfth-century society, to preserve the faith and the feudal order, the kings, bishops, abbots and monks, while, following the model of St Foy, pilgrims and Christians in general are awaited in paradise in glory and perpetual peace. Among the damned, languishing in despair, torments and the horror of deformity and monstrosity, the sins of Christian society, lust, lying, adultery, avarice and pride, are punished with tortures, but so are the sins which harm the smooth running of the feudal society represented here by the counterfeiter and the bad soldier. Stylistically, the Autun sculptor has found the best way to accentuate the contrasts in the plastic rendering. The scene of souls being weighed is exemplary in this respect. The angel gently bears the dish of the chosen from which the innocent souls already rise in the beatitude of contemplation and have no difficulty in making the scales weigh down on their side, in spite of the desperate efforts of the infernal monster, in whose skeleton-like rendering the artist has given of his best. The inclusion of the group in the general iconography of the Salvation is emphasized at Conques by the appearance, below Christ, of the Cross and the instruments of the Passion, a reminder of the Redemption and Christ's victory over death and sin, a victory which is expressed here, as in antique imperial iconography, by the

exhibition of the trophies and the instruments of this victory.

The iconography of the Last Judgment as the last stage in the work of Redemption can be connected with the iconographies more directly associated with the work of Salvation, and so once again with the images which accentuate the penitential role of the tympana. A fine example is the tympanum of the Descent from the Cross on the Portal of Forgiveness of San Isidoro at León. Between the last stages of this work of Redemption and the coming of Christ for the Last Judgment come other theophanic visions illustrated on tympana, such as the Ascension and the Transfiguration. At La Charité-sur-Loire, an important

Descent from the Cross.
Tympanum of the south transept door (Portal of Forgiveness).
First quarter of the 12th century. San Isidoro, León.

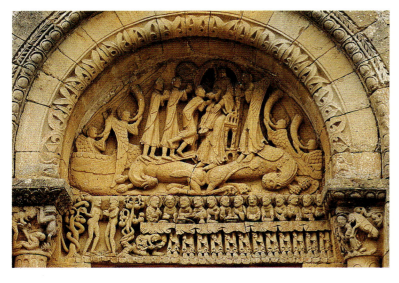

Tympanum and lintel with the Epiphany and the meal in Simon's house. Second quarter of the 12th century. La Madeleine, Neuilly-en-Donjon.

Tympanum with the Ascension of Christ. About 1140-1150. Cathedral of Saint-Etienne, Cahors.

Cluniac priory, two tympana are decorated (about 1135), one with the Epiphany, the Presentation in the Temple and the Transfiguration, while the other represents, for the first time in Romanesque art, the welcome of the Virgin Mary by her son in the heavenly Jerusalem (Assumption). While the illustration of the Transfiguration can be related to the introduction of the feast of the Transfiguration to the Order of Cluny by Peter the Venerable, it is particu-

Detail of the tympanum, lintel and arch moulding. About 1135-1140. La Madeleine, Vézelay.

larly close to the Ascension of Christ on the formal level. The Assumption of the Virgin, which is attributable to the Venerable's belief in the corporal assumption of Mary, should also be related to the fact that the patronal feast was celebrated at La Charité on the day of the Assumption. Henceforth the presence of the Virgin forms one of the essential concepts of Romanesque visionary iconography. We have found her presiding over the procession of the chosen on the tympana of the Last Judgment, and she also appears about 1140-1150 on the tympanum of the cathedral of Saint-Etienne at Cahors where, surrounded by the apostles, she watches the Ascension of Christ standing in a mandorla (a theme more frequently portrayed afterwards: Lucca Cathedral). The originality of the Cahors tympanum lies in the representation of episodes from the martyrdom of Stephen, the church's patron saint, insofar as he had been present at the vision of the Trinitary God.

At Vézelay, after 1135, the great central tympanum evokes the Ascension, the Second Coming, the Sending of the Holy Spirit, and the Mission of the Apostles in the setting of a large triumphal theophany. Synthesized images and cyclical representations are sometimes associated in the iconography of the great Romanesque tympana. At Neuilly-en-Donjon, for example, juxtaposition of images and coherence of interpretation are particularly explicit. The Virgin, who never won access to the tympanum on her own until the Gothic period, here finds herself in a privileged position thanks to the episode of the Epiphany, which, however, is a direct reference to the homage of the nations to Christ (as on many Romanesque tympana: the Door of the Goldsmiths at Compostela, Notre-Dame-du-Port at Clermont, Pompierre, Fontfroide, Beaucaire, Saint-Gilles-du-Gard). At Neuilly, the figures walk on the backs of two impressive beasts occupying the lower zone of the tympanum. The angels sounding the trumpet recall the resurrection of the dead. The lintel is occupied by the representation of the Original Sin which emphasizes another basic idea of this complicated iconography, the opposition Mary/Eve, and by the depiction of the meal in Simon's house, through which pierces another penitential image, that of Mary Magdalene, whose penitence is generally considered as having made amends for Eve's fault. She appears here above the entrance door of a church which is dedicated to her, as at Vézelay.

THE APOCALYPSE AND THE VISION OF MATTHEW

The visionary iconography of the great Romanesque tympana took its inspiration from the textual sources, the Old and New Testaments, with a preference for the apocalyptic text of St John and the vision of St Matthew (XXIV–XXV). The west portal of Anzy-le-Duc (Saône-et-Loire), executed by two sculptors' workshops, including one from Charlieu (but not at the early date sometimes attributed to it), shows the simple handling of the various sources, since it presents on the tympanum a Christ in the act of blessing in a mandorla borne by two angels appear-

ing on the firmament, on the lintel, the twelve apostles of the Ascension standing, presided over by the Virgin, and on the archivolt, the Elders of the Apocalypse. More simply still, a number of Romanesque tympana represent only the *Majestas Domini* between the evangelist symbols or in a mandorla carried by angels, as we have seen at Cluny. At Moradillo de Sedano (Burgos), an image of the Majesty in the mandorla is surrounded by the evangelist symbols, carried by angels. The twenty-four Elders occupy the first arch moulding while the apostles Peter and

Portal with the Vision of the Apocalypse.
About 1130-1135.
Former Abbey Church, Moissac.

Tympanum with the
apocalyptic vision of St John.
Mid-12th century.
La Lande-de-Fronsac.

Paul, who usually stand on either side of the door, are here incorporated into the tympanum. So there is a wide variety of formulas for showing the faithful the great synthetic visions in which the theophany sometimes merges with the image of the Last Judgment.

Among the great theophanies, the vision of the Apocalypse is one of the most valued by Romanesque patrons. The most spectacular example is provided, about 1130-1135, by the Moissac tympanum which stands at the back of a porch whose lateral registers, backed against two buttresses, are also sculptured and, since the early nineteenth century, exposed to superficial weathering which is the object of technical investigations today. On it Christ is sitting on a throne surrounded by the four Living (turned into evangelist symbols by the presence of books) and two angels. The twenty-four Elders, seated and crowned, appear on three registers, their heads turned towards the Apparition. The synthesis corresponds closely to the textual model, because even such a detail as the sea of glass is represented. Many interpretations have been put forward to explain the deeper meaning behind this apparently simple vision. Emile Mâle, for example, saw it as the transcription into stone of an illumination of the type of that on folios 121v-122 of the Saint-Sever Apocalypse. But the Moissac tympanum is a distinctly Romanesque work, a

synthetic and triumphant vision in which the seraphim, strangers to the Apocalyptic vision, establish a noteworthy bond with the non-apocalyptic theophanic visions. If we take into consideration the sculptures carved on the side walls of the porch, the meaning of the Christ on the tympanum is slightly modified because they include a summary of the story of the Salvation, from the Incarnation to the promise of the Last Judgment.

In a less thorough way, certain Romanesque tympana reproduce concrete passages from St John's visionary text. The one at La Lande-de-Fronsac represents the moment when John in his preparatory vision, ready to transmit his message to the seven churches of Asia, turns round and sees the Son of Man with the sword, the seven candlesticks and the seven stars. But here again the presence of the Majesty standing in the centre of the tympanum refers more broadly to the Romanesque Majesties already mentioned.

Too often considered as directly dependent on the art of the Moissac tympanum, the portal of Beaulieu (Corrèze) illustrates with especial brilliance the vision of the apparition of Christ at the end of time according to St Matthew (xxiv-xxv). The triumphal sense of this image, which has even been compared to representations of the victorious emperor and at which the prophet Daniel is present among a multitude of witnesses, is enhanced by the representation of the cross adorned with carved precious stones and carried by angels. It is the trophy we referred to when describing the tympanum of Conques. Here Christ also appears victorious over all the animals displayed on the double lintel. The three temptations are represented on one of the engaged piers of the porch, the story of Daniel on the other. Note the importance of the association of the vision of Matthew with Daniel and of the appearance of the cross-trophy which also refers to the cross-sign which will shine in the sky to announce the resurrection of the dead and so by implication the Last Judgment; the theme at Beaulieu is not however the Last Judgment, but the revelation of Christ's second coming. How should we situate this triumphal image in relation to the art of the Master of Moissac? It is a question much discussed among art historians, especially since Emile Mâle saw in the Beaulieu tympanum a model for the one at Saint-Denis. This question being set aside, as well as the chronological anomalies that such an assertion implied, a date shortly before the mid-twelfth century seems more probable. It is also suitable for the sculptured façade of Souillac which must have had a similar porch: an illustration of the miracle of Theophilus occupied the inner face of one of the side walls of the porch.

Tympanum with Christ appearing
at the end of time.
Mid-12th century.
Saint-Pierre, Beaulieu.

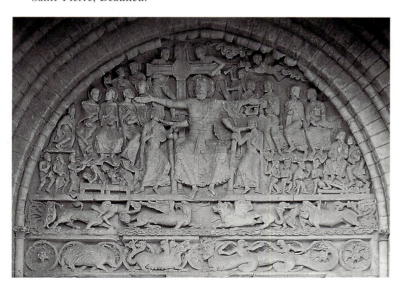

Sculptured portal and façade.
About 1190.
Saint-Trophime, Arles.

THE TRIUMPHAL FAÇADE

Shortly after 1100, stimulated by the rediscovery of Antiquity, Romanesque sculpture arose in north-western Spain, at Toulouse and in northern Italy. At Santiago de Compostela and San Salvador de Leyre in Navarre, the search for monumentality is expressed by the proliferation of decoration over the whole surface of the church façade. The vertical series of prophets under arches which appear at Modena in the worksite of Wiligelmo are another response to this quest. Throughout the twelfth century, Romanesque sculptors pursue this conquest of the façade destined to become a great display of monumental sculpture in different forms. A particularly striking example, in spite of the many restorations it has undergone since the Middle Ages, is the façade of Angoulême Cathedral which reproduces an eschatological vision distributed over the whole front. The decoration is no longer concentrated solely on the tympanum; it spreads out and develops into a complex composition made of particular images subject to the overall meaning. The idea of translating a monumental decoration on to a façade is not strictly speaking a Romanesque innovation, because monuments such as Old St Peter's, Rome, and the basilica of Poreç (Parenzo) had already shown the way by means of pictorial techniques. Romanesque artists looked back to Antiquity, to the formulas of triumphal arches and town gates, to find monumental models and solemnify the entrance to the heavenly Jerusalem, the holy town that is the church.

Protecting the entrance symbolically, the porch may adopt the form of a triumphal arch as at Civita Castellana or that of a ciborium resting on columns (*protiro*, in Italian)

Triumphal porch. Early 13th century.
Civita Castellana.

Protiro resting on two lions.
About 1135-1140.
San Zeno, Verona.

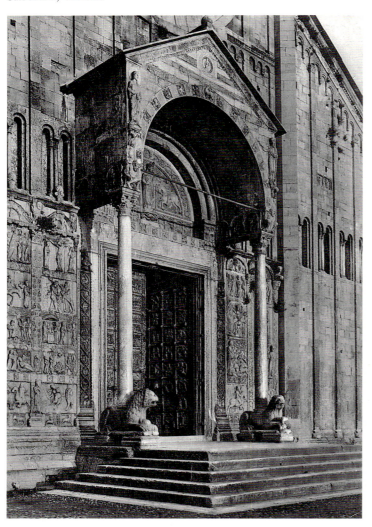

as at Modena, Cremona, Piacenza and San Zeno in Verona. In this case, we often find a pair of lions couchant bearing the columns which support the edifice. These wild beasts, as impressive as those which appear to Charlemagne in a dream in the *Chanson de Roland*, are generally represented holding a quarry between their paws, a human form, a ram, deer or some other animal. Bearers of the monument since they are sometimes replaced by genuine atlantes (Piacenza), the lions pinned to the ground by the columns, guard the entrance to the building according to a very old tradition (Salerno Cathedral) which medieval symbolism modifies through the text of the Bestiaries. From the early twelfth century, the porches of northern Italy may have answered to a political desire to imitate the Christian monuments of papal Rome; at the same time they served as the focal point of religious, judicial or simply civic ceremonies.

Like the lions, each element of the porch, portal and façade may be studied individually, not forgetting for all that the general impact of an iconography with which the scenes on the church doors were also integrated in the Middle Ages. The antiquizing trend, which may also be underscored by the arrangement of decorations in superposed reliefs, is always more or less present on the formal level. The Romanesque sculptor made progress in his craft through the study of antique sculpture. Antiquity sometimes supplied pieces to be reused directly, for example the Gallo-Roman lintel ornamented with a *suevetaurilia* from Beaujeu (Musée de Lyon) which also seems to have inspired the Romanesque lintel of Charlieu. There are a great many examples of this inspiration, such as the frieze on the façade of Nîmes Cathedral, for which the sculptors sought models in antique sarcophagi. Observation of Antiquity and Romanesque visionary iconography coalesce on the west portal of Saint-Trophime of Arles, which, set against the façade of the church, combines the theme of the apocalyptic vision with that of the Last Judgment; its architectural structure gives great prominence to the architraves and frieze, as also to the main colonnade which serves as a frame for the large statues. The portal of Saint-Trophime of Arles comes at the end of Romanesque development around 1190. On it we can observe the course followed by the sculptors in their search for a monumental rendering of the triumphal façade.

Essentially, the flowering of the sculptured triumphal façade occurred rather late in Romanesque art, after the middle of the twelfth century, when the iconographical and formal novelties of Gothic art had already proved themselves on cathedral façades in northern France. As we shall see later, one of the main contributions of the Gothic façade was the emergence of the column statue. The degree to which Romanesque art of the second half of the twelfth century was susceptible to infiltration by Gothic innovations is the subject of constant research. The column statues on the portal of Santa María la Real de Sangüesa, for example, have been thought to be inspired by the sculpture of Chartres, either directly, or through the intermediary of Burgundy, because of their elongated proportions and the verticality of the narrow, pleated drapery folds. The reality is more complex and the differences outweigh the similarities. The large statues which adorn the splays of the portal at Ripoll in Catalonia had also been linked with Saint-Denis and Chartres, within the framework of the general theory of the radiation of French art.

It is true that at Ripoll we are already far from the Moissac reliefs or again from those on the pillars of Sts Peter and Paul at Saint-Michel-de-Cuxa. The Ripoll statues are no longer bas-reliefs, but genuine works in the round, which replace the column up to the height of the figures' shoulders. The latter, although tending to replace the column, are not load-bearing elements; they have the essentially iconographic role of a disengaged statue. The Ripoll apostles seem as if they were frozen in the splays of the portal. This domination of representation over function is even more prominent at Saint-Gilles-du-Gard in a diversity which testifies to the thematic and stylistic issues with which Romanesque sculptors were confronted in the elaboration of the great façades.

A richly sculptured triumphal entrance, set against the façade of the eleventh-century church, was conceived shortly after the middle of the twelfth century at the celebrated abbey of Santa María de Ripoll in Catalonia. The façade is formed of juxtaposed blocks, without mortar. The very sandy material used contains calcareous cement, absorbs water and is very sensitive to the corrosive action of the air, the reason for the serious conservation problems from which the reliefs suffer. The portal, without tympanum, which has the figures of Peter and Paul and episodes from their lives in its splays, also houses the stories of Cain and Abel, Jonah, and Daniel, as well as personifications of the months of the year depicted on the jambs of the entrance proper. A vast composition arranged in storeyed friezes is presented on the great rectangular façade. At the summit God in Majesty sits on a throne, blessing the faithful and presenting the book, surrounded by four angels and two of the evangelist symbols, the other two being located on the lower storey. The twenty-four Elders of the Apocalypse are arranged standing upright in the upper frieze, carrying cups and cithers. They dominate the next register which is decorated with twenty-four of the blessed, among them apostles and prophets, praising the Lord. The fourth and fifth friezes present scenes taken from the cycle of *Exodus* and the *Book of Kings*. The lower levels are occupied on the left by David and his musicians and on the right by Christ accompanied by four personages, including an ecclesiastic, surmounting representations of animals, a centaur, a horseman and, in very high

Façade crowned with an *apostolado* and portal with column statues. Third quarter of the 12th century. Santa María la Real, Sangüesa.

Façade with pilasters, columns and porticoes. Second half of the 12th century. Saint-Gilles-du-Gard.

Façade ordered in the antique manner.
Second half of the 12th century.
Saint-Gilles-du-Gard.

relief on either side of the portal, a lion grasping an animal in its claws. The base is also embellished with other historiated and animal scenes, while the lateral returns of the façade complete the iconography of the whole.

The triumphal meaning of the Ripoll portal is directly emphasized by the form and composition of the architecture of the sculptured façade. In their deliberate imitation of an antique triumphal arch, the builders have shown a profound knowledge of this type of monument, enabling them to organize the complex on two superposed levels underscored by the tiered arrangement of the corner columns and crowned by a continuous frieze. Comparison with the decoration of the Carolingian reliquary in the form of a triumphal arch offered by Eginhard to the abbey of St Servatius at Maastricht points up the triumphal symbolism, for in both cases the upper register is occupied by an image of the triumph of Christ surmounting the figurations of historical persons who have announced, prepared or contributed to the fulfilment on earth of the kingdom

of Christ. What we have is a Christian version of Roman programmes for the glorification of the emperor.

The general symbolism of the Romanesque façade is also expressed on the formal level by a progression towards the summit of the axis of the door. The image of Christ overhangs the composition, while the eyes of the figures on the upper register converge on him and the whole façade is composed as a sort of monumental triangle, with the Almighty at the top. Some scholars have even seen in it the complete reproduction of what must have been the painted decor of many Romanesque buildings, the upper part corresponding to the decor of the flattened apsidal dome and the middle registers to that of the walls in the nave. Indeed, in Italian apses, historical personages do accompany the image of the theophany. The Ripoll façade, whose prodigious iconography is open to every possible exegesis, also stresses a verticality which in some ways recalls another of the great themes of Romanesque art, the Trinitary concept. Beneath the feet of the enthroned Christ on the upper register, in the centre of the outside arch moulding of the portal, the Lamb is shown carrying the cross in a disc, adored by two angels; lower down, in the intrados of the arch of the door, still in the axis, the image of Christ in a medallion is accompanied by incense-bearing angels. This correspondence in verticality, which has already been noted in the choir mosaic of San Vitale at Ravenna, recurs in the majority of Romanesque façades.

Let us pause now to examine one of the reliefs on the lower register of the façade which represents a horseman armed with lance and shield, for it recalls the large number of Romanesque horsemen from the west of France, Italy, Spain and elsewhere, even from the north (Ham-en-Artois), which generally occupy a prominent position on the church façade, sometimes trampling a beaten enemy beneath the horse's feet and accompanied by a female figure. In some cases, these horsemen have been identified, often wrongly, with St James or, more plausibly, with Constantine and Helen, but a seigniorial interpretation, possibly even connected with the donors, is more fitting in many cases. The local historical and political circumstances in which it was decided to erect such façades often elude us. We have already mentioned the links between the tympanum of León and the peninsular Reconquest. The monastery of Ripoll became the pantheon of the Catalan dynasty from the time the façade was put in place. The style of its sculptures, moreover, has much in common with that of the sarcophagus reliefs of the Count of Barcelona, Raymond Berenguer III (died 1131), preserved in the church. Neither façade nor sarcophagus were executed until some years after the count's death, when his son Raymond Berenguer IV had completed the reconquest of Tarragona and southern Catalonia from Islam.

The iconographic conception of a façade may adopt the formula of a sculptured crowning in the form of a frieze of standing figures (apostolado) as at Sangüesa in Navarre and other Spanish churches, accompanying the Divine Majesty and the Tetramorph (Carrión de los Condes, Moarbes) or again quite simply, as at Saint-Gabriel in Provence, taking advantage solely of the architectural motif of the round window to associate with it the four evangelist symbols.

The overflowing of images on to the façade implies the integration of the portal iconography with the façade, as at Saint-Gilles-du-Gard. In an architectural design modelled on the Roman triumphal arch, the façade of Saint-Gilles is articulated into three portals which incorporate tympana, archivolts, lintels and splays in an interplay of columns and sculptures. Two antique structures are superposed: the façade ornamented by pilasters with figures and the columned portico surmounted by an entablature. Can we even imagine the impact that such an ensemble and its iconography, framed by the tympana of the Epiphany and the Crucifixion, must have had before the end of the twelfth century? It implies the adoption of everything that Provence could offer by way of antique monuments in the service of the triumph of Christianity.

Façade designed as an "arch of triumph."
Second half of the 12th century.
Santa María, Ripoll.

THE PORTALS
WITH ARCH MOULDINGS
OF WESTERN FRANCE
AND THE CYCLE OF TIME

Carved arch mouldings. Second half of the 12th century. Collegiate Church, Toro.

Among the different regional groups of Romanesque portal, the group in the west of France is very characteristic during the twelfth century by its architectural, iconographical and stylistic coherence. The façade generally exhibits a vertical division into three zones separated by buttress columns and is closed at the extremities by clusters of columns surmounted by a lantern topped by a pyramid. In the centre, the façade proper is crowned by a gable and pierced by bays on the ground floor and the upper storey. The articulation of the wall by columns and niches is common to the majority of façades in Poitou and Saintonge: Parthenay-le-Vieux, Aulnay-de-Saintonge, Saint-Hilaire at Melle, Notre-Dame-la-Grande at Poitiers and the Abbaye des Dames at Saintes, to name only a few. The tympanum is still absent from the portals which are characterized by the multiplication of arch mouldings sculptured with figural elements finely carved in a soft limestone which permits exceptional ornamental subtleties. Sculpture extends to the façade as a whole, to the niches, capitals and archivolts, but, in the form of work in the round or simple sculptured slabs, it also stands within niches, on the wall and the gable. Generally the portal is set in the thickness of the wall, while the latter is given an elegant rhythm and softened by niches and sometimes even by a thinning down of the upper part. At Saint-Jouin-de-Marnes (Deux-Sèvres), the façade has an enormous central window and the portal pierced in a fore-part is unusually deep. In all these monuments, the sculptured capitals and arch mouldings set off the portal and the other architectural elements of the façade, making them seem like chiselwork carved in stone.

There are close connections between the formal structure, iconography and style of the façades of all these churches, which form a homogeneous regional group, with some differences of course, mainly reflected in the stylistic handling. Even if an outside hand appears here and there, the local and regional tradition is attested by monuments of secondary importance which vouch for the existence of sculptors' workshops specializing in the large-scale production of these repetitive arch mouldings, pre-carved in series depending on the size of the portal for which they were intended. The skill of this regional school brought it considerable success during the Romanesque Middle Ages, as proved by the diffusion of some of its basic plastic concepts (Sicily). Small Romanesque portals with decorated gables are found as far as the Gironde, following the model of prestigious buildings such as those of Poitiers, Angoulême and Périgueux. The actual form of the portal with arch mouldings extended over a wide area, towards Brittany for example (Dinan) and especially southwards (Morlaàs) and even to Spain where it appears from the early second half of the twelfth century at Santa María de Uncastillo (Aragon). Then it recurs in other edifices; witness the magnificent north portal of the collegiate church of Santa María de Toro (Zamora). The latter shows the twenty-four Elders of the Apocalypse arranged radially on either side of Christ flanked by St John and the Virgin on the outer arch moulding; the intermediate one is adorned

Ground level of the façade. Second half of the 12th century. Saint-Pierre, Aulnay-de-Saintonge.

with plant motifs, the lower one with censer-bearing angels on either side of Christ, and these angels reappear inside the lobes of the portal.

The iconographic programme of façades often includes at the top a representation of the Cross or Christ, as at Saint-Jouin-de-Marnes, and statues distributed freely over the façade or set in niches which represent saints and other figures standing or on horseback, including the famous horseman mentioned earlier, and episodes from the Old and New Testaments. A wealth of imagery appears on the modillions (minstrels, musicians, sculptors at work) and on the archivolts of portals whose arch mouldings are invaded by familiar and picturesque scenes. Among the latter, personifications of the months are very popular, decorating the entrance of both modest and imposing churches. They picture men and women carrying out the work appropriate to each month of the year. This theme is common in the Romanesque period, whether as a linear arrangement with the personifications of the months juxtaposed on either side of the portal or, as in the buildings of the west, set out on the arch mouldings around the portal. Accompanied by the signs of the zodiac, these images fit into the cosmic figurations of the world, the cycle of time, the rhythm of the seasons and everyday activities.

The development of the calendar on the portals with arch mouldings of the west of France is quite remarkable and systematic. Sometimes the battle of the Virtues and Vices is associated with the calendar; so are the Wise and Foolish Virgins (Aulnay, Civray) or other themes like the Elders of the Apocalypse (Saint-Jouin). In January, the peasant is resting (Civray) or Janus may illustrate the beginning of the year (Saint-Jouin). In February, the peasant warms himself by the fire. Then the year continues, with various agricultural labours and images illustrating the start of a season, as at Civray where the month of April is personified by a young man standing between two trees; in July we find the harvest, in August threshing, in September picking or treading the grapes. Finally, the year ends with the month of December when the peasant is usually sitting at table, in the shelter of home. The limestone used by the sculptors has suffered from weathering and many façade carvings are almost illegible today. But the general sequence of themes is easy to discern; whereas at Aulnay each month is carved on an arch-stone flanked by the corresponding sign of the zodiac, more frequently each of these elements occupies one arch-stone or even two, as at Cognac, Argenton, Fenioux and Civray. Sometimes inscriptions throw light on the theme.

In the Middle Ages, the representations of the months referring to the activities peculiar to each region are often accompanied by the seasons, the Rivers of Paradise and other features which have to do with the interpretation of time and the cycle of annual life. These images are presided over by the figuration of the year. The months surround the year just as the apostles or the Elders of the Apocalypse surround Christ in Majesty. On the sculpted façades of religious buildings, the representations of the months are often placed around the portal; the personification of the year does not occur here because it is implicitly replaced by the image of Christ enthroned in Majesty portrayed elsewhere. Thus the geographical and cosmological order of the world is displayed at the church entrance by way of the cycle of the seasons and the months, and refers directly or indirectly to Him who governs the order of things, the world and the creation.

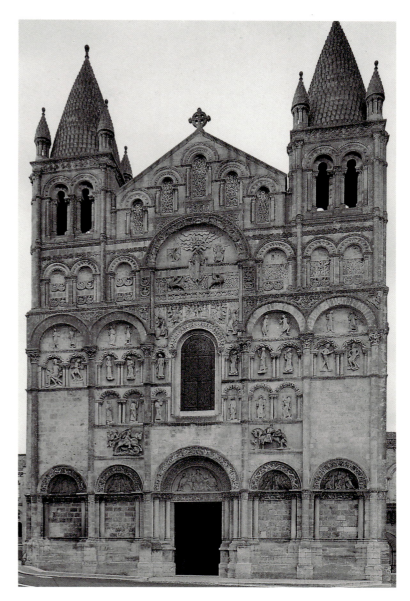

Romanesque façade heavily restored in the 19th century by Paul Abadie. Cathedral of Saint-Pierre, Angoulême.

Façade with clustered corner columns. Before 1174. Notre-Dame-la-Grande, Poitiers.

THE HISTORIATED CLOISTER

The cloister is a porticoed court on a square or trapezoidal plan situated at the heart of the clerical community; around it stand the buildings of everyday monastic life (chapter, cathedral, collegiate church or monastery proper). The cloister acts as a service gallery, a covered walk, a place of passage and meditation. Typologically, the Romanesque cloister derives from the atrium of the Roman house and the late antique basilica by its form and its organizing purpose. The atrium of the basilica of San Lorenzo at Milan is of quite special interest for the origin of the medieval cloister, for it possessed a series of small side rooms to which access was had by means of two staircases located in two lateral *avant-corps*. The atrium of the medieval cathedral at Salerno has a series of small loges behind which are the rooms where the canons lived. In a wider sense, the word cloister was often applied to the monastery as a whole in the Middle Ages.

The cloister stood at the heart of monastic life from a very early period. During the eleventh century, it generally had no sculptures. Of irregular plan or having four equal galleries often with semicircular barrel vaulting, its cloister walks in the eleventh century opened on to the

Christ with doubting Thomas and apostles. Relief on a cloister pillar. First half of the 12th century. San Domingo, Silos.

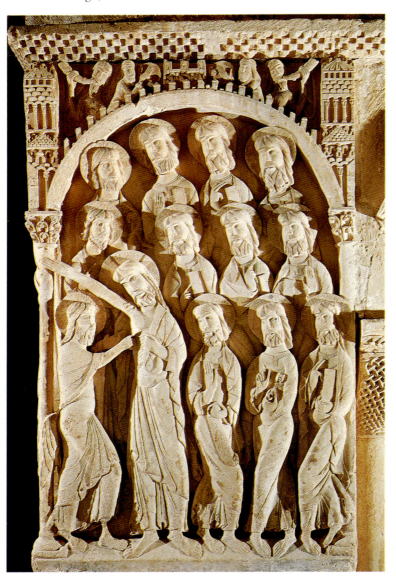

court by arcades supported by massive masonry pillars following the Carolingian model. It was not until the twelfth century that the cloister was invaded by a wealth of sculpture covering columns and pillars. Since the nineteenth century the quality of these works and the ease with which they could be dismantled have attracted the covetousness of collectors and antique dealers. One of the most astonishing products of this collecting zeal is The Cloisters in New York. It originated with the collection formed by the sculptor George Grey Barnard who lived in France before 1914 and bought many pieces from the cloisters of Saint-Guilhem-le-Désert, Bonnefont and Saint-Michel-de-Cuxa, among others, which he wished to use as models for his American students at the Beaux-Arts. Purchased by the Metropolitan Museum of Art in 1925, the Barnard Collection has become a museum of medieval art whose architectural conception is that of a monastery with several cloisters. The history of medieval cloisters is indeed eventful, especially in France after the Revolution, or even before it, as was the case with the cloister of Notre-Dame-en-Vaux at Châlons-sur-Marne which has now been restored by archaeologists. The history of the cloisters of Saint-Etienne and La Daurade at Toulouse is exemplary in this connection. Their dispersion was soon followed by regret and the desire to restore them. Hence the decision to create a historical and didactic museum headed by an erudite scholar who, along with others, had much to do with the image we now have of the Middle Ages: Alexandre du Mège. As early as 1817 du Mège began setting up the sculptures on a continuous plinth so that they should serve as "objects of study for those who cherish the knowledge of Antiquity." He reconstructed the door of the chapter house of La Daurade, the precursor of further reconstructions of celebrated cloisters, closer to us and based on other criteria, such as that undertaken by the Historical Monuments Service at Saint-Michel-de-Cuxa.

The oldest historiated Romanesque cloister was built shortly before 1100 in the abbey of Moissac. Its model may have been the cloister commissioned by Odilo at Cluny before 1048. A daughter house of the abbey of Cluny from 1047-1048, Moissac flourished to an extraordinary degree, its prosperity leading to the construction of a new abbey church consecrated in 1063. This was a building with nave and narrow side aisles, and an ambulatory revealed by excavations, although it has not been possible to determine whether it already had sculptured capitals. The cloister was built nearer the end of the century, as indicated by an inscription engraved on the central pillar of the west gallery: "In the year of the incarnation of the Prince Eternal 1100, this cloister was finished in the days of the Lord Abbot Ansquitil. Amen." The porticoed cloister walks had alternating single and twin marble colonnettes adorned with rich capitals carved with geometric and plant motifs, historiated scenes and animals. The style of these works also betrays their date, because certain abaci decorated with busts of figures are very close to the Toulouse works of Bernard Gilduin. The essential contribution of the Moissac cloister was to give the sculptured pillars a privileged place in the overall disposition. Eight apostles occupy the corner pillars, which tallies with their symbolism as pillars of the universal Church. A ninth, Simon, stands today on the central pillar of the west cloister walk. Abbot Ansquitil took the decision to have the image of his predecessor, Durand, sculpted on the central pillar of the east cloister walk, which has something to tell us about

East walk of the cloister. Late 12th century. Saint-Trophime, Arles.

the high place the monastic order sought to occupy in the contemporary Church. Stylistically, these figures, like those of the Saint-Sernin reliefs at Toulouse, seem to be particularly inspired by ivories and goldsmith's works. Iconographically, the sculpture of the forty-one historiated capitals centres on the Gospel story, the Old Testament, apocalyptic and eschatological scenes, the martyrdoms of Peter and Paul, Stephen, Saturninus, Fructuosus, Augurius and Eulogius, as well as the miracles of St Benedict and St Martin.

Whereas at Moissac the scenes are isolated on each capital, a step forward was taken at La Daurade in Toulouse where we find a continuous story arranged on a group of capitals, just as illuminated Bibles continued an illustrated narration over several pages. This is the formula adopted during the twelfth century in a certain number of cloister walks: Gerona, Sant Cugat del Vallés, Tarragona. The oldest series of reliefs in the Silos cloister forms an Easter cycle continuing down to Whitsuntide; the pillar with doubting St Thomas naturally finds a place there. The north walk of the Saint-Trophime cloister at Arles, dating to about 1180, is a model of iconographic cohesion; it incorporates both the statue figures and the scenes on bas-reliefs and capitals, the latter so arranged as to be seen solely from the covered walk. The programme, strictly focused on the glory of Christ, with allusions to the Old Testament, also includes the saints venerated at Arles, Trophimus and Stephen.

During the Middle Ages, the decoration of the Romanesque cloister with figure carvings gave rise to lively religious discussions which in part sum up the notion we have formed of monastic ideals. While the Moissac cloister seems to have been completed at the very end of the eleventh century, it was certainly the outcome of earlier experiments and tensions that we know little about. Hence the eloquent anecdote about the abbey of Saint-Florent near Saumur, whose cloister Abbot Roger of Blois (985-1011) had already undertaken to decorate with polychrome stone sculptures accompanied by inscriptions: *claustralis fabrica mira lapidum sculptura cum versuum indiciis ac picturarum splendoribus est polita*. But under Frederick, an abbot of the first half of the eleventh century (1022-1056), discussion turned into action when he ordered the limbs and heads of these cloister carvings to be smashed with a hammer. True, it is difficult to equate this source with what we know of the date of the sculpture's appearance in the cloisters, and the phrase *claustralis fabrica* is ambiguous; but it at least allows us to evoke the important role that painting must have played in the decoration of the early cloisters. Moreover, this incident seems to be a premonitory sign of the vigour with which St Bernard (c. 1124), and with him the Cistercian Order in general, expressed his opposition to the richly ornamented Cluniac cloister: "What are these ridiculous monsters, this deformed beauty and this beautiful deformity doing in the cloisters beneath the eyes of the brothers intent on their reading?

ceilings of the walk; and lastly they sometimes adorn the upper walk (Saint-Guilhem-le-Désert). Apart from the presence of an inscription or the effigy of the founding abbot (Cuxa, Ripoll), a reference to the rule (column-statue of St Benedict in Saint-Père of Chartres, wall painting of St Augustine in Saint-Sernin of Toulouse, capital of St Ursus at Aosta) and some illustrations alluding to the communal life or its models (Entry into Jerusalem, Washing of the Feet, Last Supper), we have to admit that the cloister imagery is extremely varied, open and receptive to the outside world. The incoherence of some cloisters is due to the fact that the walks were often built successively or subject to interruptions that might last more than a century (Elne, Ripoll). The type of homogeneous cloister like Monreale in Sicily, with its colonnette shafts carved or adorned with mosaics, is the exception rather than the rule. The monotony of some cloisters has been explained by the "mass production" practised by specialized marble masons (Subiaco, Cuxa); the richness and fantasy of others by the many different functions of the cloister and by the possibility that the walks were open to the faithful on certain days and at certain hours, especially in urban settings. But this explanation is inadequate, for the richly decorated upper cloister walk of Saint-Guilhem-le-Désert was only accessible to the monks from the gallery of the abbey church or their own dormitory and had no direct communication with the lower walk.

The iconography of the cloister is not limited to carved capitals or wall paintings. The doors giving access to the church or the monastic buildings are often adorned with archivolts, capitals and even a sculpted tympanum. The tombs of benefactors or members of the community helped to embellish the cloister walks, often on a monumental scale. Of all the monastic halls surrounding the cloister (refectory, dormitory, etc.), the chapter house is the most decorated (wall paintings at Brauweiler and Sigena). The splay statues of the chapter house of Saint-Etienne at Toulouse brilliantly illustrate an intermediate formula between the bas-relief (Saint-Caprais at Agen) and the column figure (Saint-Georges-de-Boscherville);

What are these disgusting monkeys doing? These ferocious lions? These monstrous centaurs?"

In accordance with the rule, the Cistercian cloisters, especially the older ones (Le Thoronet), had no decoration at all, and this was of course the case with the Carthusians, the Premonstratensians and the Grandmontians. But the moment has come to ask if there is an iconography peculiar to the Romanesque cloister. We should note that the images and their locations are extremely varied. They may be purely ornamental or fantastic or taken from Bestiaries or from everyday life, like a gaze turned on the outside world. They may be connected with the façade decoration or objects in the treasury. They may be concentrated in one part of the cloister or on a single capital, or unfold through a whole cloister walk in a complete cycle. Sometimes they assume the form of pillar reliefs or column statues, or extend as paintings along the walls or

△ Ascension of Alexander the Great. Cloister capital. Shortly before 1100. Saint-Pierre, Moissac.

◁ View of the cloister and washing fountain. About 1175-1185. Cathedral of Monreale.

▷△ Capital with secular subject in the east walk of the cloister. First half of the 13th century. Santa María del Estany.

▷ Entrance of the chapter house. About 1175. Saint-Georges-de-Boscherville.

they portray the apostles, models of the communal life. The chapter house entrance at Saint-Georges-de-Boscherville in Normandy (about 1175), decorated with column statues and capitals, illustrates the passage from the Rule of St Benedict devoted to the abbot's duties with depictions of life, death and monastic discipline; this, together with other examples, proves that sometimes an iconography peculiar to the cloister actually did exist during the twelfth century. The chapter house is not always in the same location. In England it is often large and spacious, and to give it height it is not designed to open directly into the cloister, but into an access-giving corridor behind it. Worcester is the oldest known example. In the Gothic period, it assumes an octagonal shape (York) or is organized in relation to a central column (Westminster). In Lower Normandy, chapter houses are built along an axis parallel to that of the church and project from the wall of the dormitory. Three are built directly against the church, fourteen are separated from it by the sacristy, three by the sacristy and a staircase, and one (Longues) is built over the refectory. The Cistercian chapter house was a rectangle divided into aisles by pillars.

The cloister basin or fountain, which bore a striking resemblance to baptismal fonts, stood in the middle of the cloister garth. Sometimes it was housed in a small building and placed in the middle of the cloister walk opposite the church or at the corner of two walks. It served for the monks' ablutions and took the form of an outer basin fed with water from a raised central dispenser (Conques, Monreale, Poblet). These fountains are decorated with masks (Lagrasse) or heads of a more learned iconography (Saint-Denis), with colonnettes and capitals (Cuxa), and may be surmounted by a prestigious crowning feature such as the later horseman on the bronze fountain of Saint-Bertin at Saint-Omer. The Gothic cloister, with its delicate colonnettes and foliage capitals, puts the emphasis on a new aesthetic. Nevertheless, the twelfth-century Gothic cloisters in the north, contemporary with Romanesque cloisters in the south of France, are still richly sculptured. Column-statues smaller than those of the portal splays

adorned the cloister of Saint-Denis around the middle of the twelfth century; they are known from the drawings of Montfaucon. The cloister of the collegiate church of Notre-Dame-en-Vaux at Châlons-sur-Marne, to be discussed later, possessed some fifty column statues and an equal number of historiated capitals justifying the admiration in which twelfth-century monastic commentators held this cloister, sometimes interpreted as an *imago mundi* and compared to Paradise and the Heavenly Jerusalem by Honorius of Autun and Hugh of Fouilloy. The recent reconstruction of an apocalyptic programme with the Four Horsemen and the Elders comprising a zodiacal group in the dispersed cloister of Saint-Avit-Sénier in Périgord reinforces the links between the iconography of cloisters and façades (possibly about the second quarter of the twelfth century) and confirms the idea of the cloister as prefiguring the advent of the heavenly city.

Romanesque tympanum from a secular building.
Musée Curtius, Liège.

THE EMBELLISHMENT OF TOWNS

In the medieval town of southern Europe, the urban structure was still fundamentally antique and many monuments from Antiquity still formed the essential part of the townscape. Ibrâhîm b. Ya'qûb, travelling in Europe about 965, observed in his description of Bordeaux that "the town has very high buildings supported by enormous columns." But the most impressive ancient city in the twelfth century was Rome–an urban myth for the whole of Western Christianity. The ancient topography had not changed much and the Roman wall surrounded the whole city. New churches and bell-towers, as well as new districts, arose on the other side of the Tiber between St Peter's and the Castel Sant'Angelo. The Capitol became a place of dwellings, as did the Roman amphitheatre at Nîmes. From the eleventh century on, new towns sprang up everywhere. Linear development from a landscape feature (the river at Lübeck, the road at Castrojeriz) and concentric development (around the palace at Aachen and the hill at Cordes) were the most common. The growth of monasteries on the edge of Roman cities created towns, sometimes with their own surrounding walls (Tours, Paris). In other cases, an isolated monastery was the origin of the town (Saint-Denis, Cluny, Conques). Other towns grew up around a castle. From the late eleventh century, newly founded towns sometimes adopted a strict grid pattern along two axes at the intersection of which was a central public square (Sangüesa). But other forms were also adopted, linear plans, envelopment plans or radial plans centred on a market, as in Great Britain. Venice is an entirely original case.

In Venice we can admire the outer and inner aspect of the medieval decorated urban palace. A broad arcaded façade usually on two levels developed the heritage of Late Antiquity (Fondaco dei Turchi). Designed to house the prince and his retinue, the palace consisted of living quarters and common rooms; a meeting hall or *aula* was the public centre. The other pole was the chapel, generally on two floors. As the Middle Ages progressed, the urban newly rich vied with the feudal lords and ecclesiastical dignitaries in their desire to construct dwellings with particularly elegant façades. A large portal occupied the ground floor; the windows of the upper floor were generally divided into two lights and their ornamentation was rich: bases, capitals, reliefs, and tympana.

In the town of the Romanesque period, cathedral or church was the jewel of an urban embellishment which also included private and public monuments, adorned with rich sculptured capitals: episcopal palace of Auxerre, Casa de la Paeria at Lleida (Lérida), public baths as at Gerona. Public decoration was not necessarily Christian; the Jewish quarter, for example, had its synagogues adorned with sculpture (Besalú, Rouen). The discovery in 1976 of a synagogue within the precincts of the Palais de Justice at Rouen shows an architectural structure akin to the palaces and a sculptured decoration similar to that of other Norman monuments from the late eleventh or the first quarter of the twelfth century, such as Saint-Georges-de-Boscherville. This confirms that artists and craftsmen from the same circle conceived and decorated Jewish and Christian buildings in the same town.

Except for the Romanesque reliefs carved on circular or lancette-shaped marble plaques (*patere* and *formelle*) which decorate Venetian façades with fighting animals and monsters, private houses are generally adorned very simply

Sculptured decoration of the public baths.
Late 12th century.
"Arab Baths," Gerona.

with decorative capitals on the ground floor and even more on the first floor (Rome, Tournai) or more exceptionally with historiated capitals (Roland's exploit on the beautiful façade of the Estella palace in Navarre). Often, the house fronts of well-to-do townsmen assume the aspect of palace façades (Cluny, Burlats). The handsome Jewish homes built from the mid-twelfth century in Norwich, Lincoln and Bury St Edmunds differ in no way from the homes of Christian burghers. In some cases, the town house is given an outer decoration as exceptional as that of the church (Saint-Gilles-du-Gard, Céreste). The Saint-Antonin house (Tarn-et-Garonne) is a three-storeyed private building whose owners belonged to the new bourgeoisie that grew rich about the middle of the twelfth century. Two monuments adjoin each other, a main building and a tower. The openwork of the first floor is punctuated by three groups of three colonnettes whose capitals have a handsome iconography. They are separated by pillars. The latter are embellished with sculptures in high relief representing Adam and Eve and the Judgment of Solomon. This sculptured gallery on the façade, which corresponds to the position of the large reception hall

Granolhet House. Mid-12th century.
Saint-Antonin.

Adam and Eve. Pillar on the first floor of the Granolhet House.

inside, was far from unique in Romanesque towns. The sculptors who carved these decorations also worked on religious monuments, and the same is true of wall painters. Incidentally, carved tympana were peculiar to abbey churches and cathedrals. Houses possessed them, too, as demonstrated by the very fine twelfth-century example at Reims from the so-called Maison de la Chrétienté, now displayed in the new rooms of the Musée Saint-Remi at Reims: it illustrates the allegories of Knowledge, Strength and Love. The Victoria and Albert Museum in London preserves a magnificent triple window, adorned with six small tympana carved with fantastic animals, sirens and a centaur attacking a basilisk; it comes from a late twelfth-century house front at Trie-Château (Oise). It is astonishingly like a Chartres triple window. Another major work of secular Romanesque architecture is the Bourdon House at Liège, now in the local Archaeological Museum. Each of three medallions contains a figure accompanied by inscriptions: Work, kneeling, offers a bowl of honey to Honour, who accepts it, turning away from Solicitude and the absinthe she is proferring. This is a scene of offering, of homage, a true act of justice which proves that the great lords and certain institutions commissioned secular sculptured programmes which are quite the equal of the decorated church tympana. Showing the other side of the coin, the tympanum of Saint-Ursin at Bourges illustrates secular themes on a church door. The lower register displays the iconography of the months of the year, the unusual centre register has a great stag and wild-boar hunt inspired by a Roman sarcophagus, and the upper register shows episodes from fables (the donkey schoolmaster, the wolf and the stork, the burial of Renard). In addition to a sport practised by the ruling class, the patron had requested the sculptor who signed the tympanum, Girauldus, to represent the cycle of the fields and life, and the fables, as an explanation of the world and nature.

THE VARIETIES OF CREATION

ROMANESQUE STYLE AND GEOGRAPHY IN FRANCE

During the nineteenth and at least the first third of the twentieth century, most students of Romanesque art in France viewed it in terms of "regional schools" begetting a stylistic geography and raising problems of influences and the diffusion of forms. Even before 1840, the Norman archaeologist Arcisse de Caumont defended the idea of the existence of "monumental regions" and attempted to classify Romanesque art into schools based on the old provincial geography on the one hand and the external aspect of churches and their decorations on the other. He distinguished seven: the school of northern France with Champagne and the Orléanais, the school of Normandy and Brittany, that of Poitou and the Angoumois, those of Aquitaine and Auvergne, the school of Burgundy and Provence, and lastly that of the Rhenish provinces. Another nineteenth-century French archaeologist, Jules Quicherat, the first professor of archaeology at the Ecole des Chartes, worked out a theory based primarily on the way churches were vaulted. In his turn, Viollet-le-Duc formulated a system incorporating both Romanesque and Gothic churches. This meant that, in spite of improved methods of study as the decades passed, the majority of art historians dealing with the Middle Ages (Anthyme Saint-Paul, Choisy, Enlart, Brutails, Lefèvre-Pontalis) attempted to define regional artistic schools by attacking the problem, in both architecture and sculpture, of the anteriority of some schools in relation to others and in relation to those of neighbouring countries. Today these problematics seem to be out of date on the theoretical level, although this does not preclude agreement about the local and regional peculiarities of Romanesque art, especially of its sculpture. What is in question is the validity of using modern political and administrative frontiers to establish a Romanesque geography which does not always coincide with the medieval historical divisions.

Auvergne should be given a place apart for the coherence of its medieval art and the character given to its sculpture by the coarse-grained stone used there. The term school has often been applied to a group of Romanesque churches with nave and two side aisles, a projecting transept with a small apse attached to each of its arms, an ambulatory and radiating chapels, and whose elevation comprises galleries and a dome on squinches at the transept crossing. Localized around Clermont-Ferrand, its cathedral and Notre-Dame-du-Port, the group includes Orcival, Issoire, Saint-Nectaire and Saint-Saturnin. The regional reality is much wider because it extends to the Velay (Le Puy) and Gévaudan. Auvergnat sculpture is fairly well localized geographically and drew on outside sources (Burgundy, Languedoc), while having very little influence beyond its own frontiers. Auvergne does not offer the monumental façade decorated with tympana like that at Conques, but does preserve important tympana such as those of Notre-Dame-du-Port and Saint-Michel-

View of the choir and ambulatory.
Third quarter of the 12th century.
Notre-Dame-du-Port, Clermont-Ferrand.

d'Aiguilhe at Le Puy. Among the decorated tympana are those of Mauriac (Ascension) and Saint-Julien of Brioude. An original feature of the portals is the pentagonal shape of the saddleback lintel; sometimes it is the only sculptured part of the façade (Thuret, Mozat).

Inside the Auvergnat Romanesque church, one grasps better than elsewhere the general programme governing the decoration of the sculptured capitals. Even though foliage capitals greatly outnumber historiated capitals, the latter are often grouped in very specific parts of the building, the ambulatory in particular. The ambulatory of Issoire contains a cycle of Christ's Passion and we find the Resurrection at Mozat. The ambulatory of Notre-Dame-du-Port associates the Virgin with the theme of the contest of the Vices and Virtues. At Saint-Nectaire, the life of Christ, the Passion and the Resurrection are accompanied by the vision of the Apocalypse and the Last Judgment, while the life of Nectarius, the patron saint, is shown as a counterpart of that of Christ. This iconography is not peculiar to Auvergne, for it focuses on images of the Salvation, the lives of the saints and typological correspondences between the Old and New Testaments. Nor is it confined to the ambulatory; the reliefs in the transept at Issoire, for example, portray Abraham, Isaac and the Multiplication of the Loaves.

The first Romanesque sculpture workshops show their hands, as we have already seen, on the apse and transept capitals of Le Puy Cathedral. At the same time a monumental decoration akin to it appears at Aurillac and Conques. The cathedral sculpture at Le Puy evolves towards the façade, but to understand the sculpture of the late eleventh century two fundamental links are missing in Auvergne: the cathedral of Clermont-Ferrand and the abbey church of La Chaise-Dieu. Although the origins of Romanesque sculpture in Auvergne have been clarified thanks to study of the capitals in the cathedral of Le Puy and the abbey church of Aurillac, the chronology of Romanesque sculpture in this region, which has divided scholars for more than a century, remains problematic. The lack of archives makes dating a subjective matter of stylistic analysis, with dates varying from the late eleventh century to the late twelfth. To this is added the difficulty entailed by the apparent homogeneity of the Auvergnat churches which makes it hard to distribute them in successive groups.

The sculpture of the former abbey of Mozat (Mozac, Riom), conceived under the influence of Clermont Cathedral and presumably reflecting to some extent the vanished sculpture of Clermont, might stand at the origin of the known Auvergnat series, at the beginning of the second quarter of the eleventh century, at least as regards the ambulatory capitals adorned with stocky static figures which reveal traces of an antique heritage. The more freely composed side-aisle capitals, with personages and other figurative elements set among abundant plant motifs, imply some knowledge of the Burgundian flowering in the first decades of the twelfth century. If the role attributed to the capitals in the Mozat ambulatory may appear excessive compared with monuments like Conques and Brioude, it has the advantage of making the dates of the great Auvergnat figure sculpture agree with those of Languedoc. Comparisons drawn with certain capitals at Brioude, Conques and Chanteuges have been used to strengthen the attribution of an early date to the Mozat sculpture. Issoire, with its capitals adorned with figures distributed by groups on each of the faces of the basket, is a little isolated within the development of Auvergnat sculpture. The flaring of the drapery in three folds is

St Nectarius bringing Bradulus back to life.
Capital in the ambulatory.
Third quarter of the 12th century.
Saint-Nectaire.

St Foy before the Proconsul Dacian. Capital in the nave.
First third of the 12th century.
Sainte-Foy, Conques.

comparable to the sculptures of the Rhone valley and Provence in the second quarter of the twelfth century. The two major ensembles, Notre-Dame-du-Port at Clermont-Ferrand and Saint-Nectaire, exhibit a very massive, majestic, graphic and decorative sculpture, for which we know the name of at least one artist, Robert, who signed the capital of the life of the Virgin in Notre-Dame-du-Port. The main problem is that of relations with the style of the Conques tympanum, for art historians have found it hard to agree on which came first. Nevertheless, notable differences exist and there is no doubt that the scales are balanced in favour of Conques. The chronology of Saint-Nectaire depends on the trust we place in two bulls issued by La Chaise-Dieu. One bull in 1178 mentions Saint-Nectaire as one of the possessions of La Chaise; the other, in 1145, does not yet mention it, which encourages us to date its construction to the third quarter of the twelfth century. In 1185, the worksite of Notre-Dame-du-Port had not yet been closed, which would seem to indicate that the sculptures of the south portal were not very far chronologically from those of Saint-Nectaire. The question of the place we should allot to the other Auvergnat churches in relation to these two type worksites remains open.

We have already mentioned the great Romanesque regions with a well-defined style in the west of France and in Languedoc around Toulouse, with Moissac, Souillac and Beaulieu on the one hand, and their extensions to the southwest on the other (Saint-Sever). Some churches, like Saint-Eutrope at Saintes, show the interplay of exchanges: the capitals in the crypt (1081-1096) look towards Anjou, Poitou and Maine, while in the choir the influence of

Poitou steadily grows; by the early twelfth century Languedoc had prevailed, marking a change of orientation in the sculpture of Saintonge and Aquitaine. Romanesque sculpture in this southern region subsequently developed on lines of its own, not unconnected with Languedoc and western France on the one hand and with the south side of the Pyrenees on the other (Morlaàs, Oloron-Sainte-Marie). The river Garonne played a key part in diffusing southern forms and materials towards northwestern France.

Something has already been said about Burgundian sculpture, which for sheer quantity is the foremost group in France (together with the sculpture of Toulouse). It is time now to sketch out the main stages of its chronological and stylistic evolution, at the centre of which stand the ambulatory capitals of Cluny, together with the chancel screen and west front of the great abbey. The dating of these exceptionally fine sculptures was long a matter of sharp controversy, but today it is generally agreed that work on the choir and consequently the carving of the capitals was completed about 1118-1120 under the abbacy of Pons de Melgueil (1109-1122).

One of the Cluny masters probably went to Vézelay after the closing of the Cluniac worksite around 1120, for the sculpture in the nave of La Madeleine at Vézelay bears the mark of his easily recognizable hand. Indeed these stylistic observations agree with what we know of the history of Vézelay when the nave was built after a fire which ravaged the abbey church in 1120 (the consecration of 1132 is now attributed to the nave). Work on the tympanum of the west front therefore only began with the end of work on the nave.

Whatever stylistic conclusions one draws from the presence of the Cluny master at Vézelay, the chronological

St Andrew.
Statue from the tomb
of St Lazarus.
Mid-12th century.
Musée Rolin, Autun.

Visitation, Annunciation to the Shepherds, and Nativity.
Detail of the tympanum, south portal of the façade.
About 1135-1140.
La Madeleine, Vézelay.

Capital with the Flight into Egypt. Mid-12th century. Saint-Andoche, Saulieu.

relation between the two buildings seems to be pretty well established. Moreover, the dating of other Burgundian carvings (at Perrecy-les-Forges, Montceaux-l'Etoile, even Charlieu and Anzy-le-Duc) depends on this chronology. In another great monument of this region, Saint-Lazare of Autun, the work, which began with the apse, seems to be almost contemporary, since an initial consecration took place in 1130; but the tympanum would be more than a decade later than this date. Gislebertus seems to have directed a large part of the work, to judge by the style of the sculpture which, unlike that of the Vézelay basilica, is very unified here. Its handling is one of the most easily recognizable in the whole of Romanesque art owing to the excessive elongation of the bodies and the swirling drapery folds indicated by parallel lines. The realistic attitudes of the figures are accentuated by the extreme linearity and delicacy of the execution. But not all the Autun sculpture was done by a single carver. Among the capitals in the church, we can easily distinguish works by the same hand (Pilgrims of Emmaus, Mary Magdalene, Martyrdom of St Stephen), whereas others are workshop products (Nativity, Daniel). These stylistic observations give us a better grasp of the collective output of the sculpture workshop, the movements of artists and the influences exerted by one worksite on another. At Vézelay, each sculptor seems to have specialized in a specific set of themes. In the work of Gislebertus as in the Vézelay sculpture, we perceive the influence of a common source emanating from the workshops of Toulouse and Languedoc sculptors. In Burgundy these great works were exceptionally influential, both in iconography and style. One has only to compare the capitals which reproduce the same theme from one church to another (Flight into Egypt at Saulieu). From the mid-twelfth century, Burgundy occupies an original place between Romanesque and Gothic art, as testified at the time by the porch of Saint-Bénigne at Dijon, which, while recalling Burgundian models, reveals the penetration of the new style from the Ile-de-France. An equally original work, in which Romanesque traditions strongly resist the new Gothic canons, is the sculptured tomb of St Lazarus

at Autun. In plan, it reproduced a church in miniature, with transept and apse. Inside it, Lazarus lay in a sarcophagus whose cover was carried by four men. At his feet were the statues of Christ, Peter and Andrew; at his head, Mary Magdalene and Martha. The work was probably executed around the known date of the transfer of the relics in 1146-1147.

The Rhone valley between Burgundy and Provence is famous for the construction of a great monument of the Burgundian type which took the church of Cluny III as its model: the cathedral of Vienne. The influence of Burgundian types, also observable in Saint-Martin-d'Ainay at Lyons, is equally reflected in the field of sculpture and confirms the original position of this geographical transit zone between Burgundy and Provence. During the eleventh century and the early twelfth, beside researches peculiar to early Romanesque (Cruas), certain groups (Chabrillan, La Clastre) provide evidence of an artistic trend uninfluenced by the antique capital. At Saint-André-le-Bas in Vienne, in the very middle of the twelfth century, the full power of the Rhone style is displayed in an original art which in part derives from the sculptured models of the St Maurice Cathedral in Vienne, and subsequently influenced the workshops of Lyons. Vienne Cathedral also contributes something to the style of the carved capitals in the nave of Saint-Barnard at Romans which, about 1140, reflects the attraction of Burgundy as well. The regional turning point comes with the introduction of the style of the antiquizing workshops of Provence, which can be seen in the apostle figures on the jambs of the west portal of Saint-Barnard during the third quarter of the twelfth century. But relations between Vienne and Burgundy continued. The chief originality of the central Rhone valley with its two great centres, Lyons and Vienne, not forgetting Valence and even Avignon, lies in this multilateral relation, which did not preclude a large measure of independence. The cloister of Avignon Cathedral shows a closer connection with Italy, although we must not forget the relations which existed with Languedoc and Catalonia, and which in the twelfth century were based on the political links of Provence with the Counts of Toulouse and the Counts of Barcelona. A white marble capital discovered at Valence in 1974, representing the Resurrection and the Women at the Tomb, exhibits all the richness but also the complexity of Rhone valley sculpture in the late twelfth century under the influence of Byzantinizing painting and contacts with Italy, facilitated because the region on the left bank of the Rhone belonged to the Empire.

The architectural and sculptural influence of Burgundy even reached Provence, as evidenced by the plan of Saint-Gilles-du-Gard and, among others, by the capital decorated with scenes from the childhood of Christ in Nîmes

Museum, which is not intelligible without the sculpture of Saulieu and Burgundy. As we shall see later, the Saint-Gilles worksite was active during the last three quarters of the twelfth century. But Provence has other buildings that are characteristic on the regional level with a single wide nave backed by thick buttresses and crowned with a semi-circular apse. The interior of the apse is patterned with blind arcades resting on columns adorned with capitals. Considered in a broad historical sense, Provence offers a type of nave capital in its religious monuments. It is found at Notre-Dame-des-Doms at Avignon, Saint-Trophime at Arles, Saint-Sauveur at Aix, Cavaillon, Saint-Restitut and Carpentras, as well as Pernes, Saint-André at Rosans and Saint-Paul-Trois-Châteaux, over a period covering much of the twelfth century, especially its later phases. Among them, we can clearly distinguish the capitals which reject the classical style in favour of decoration in two zones (Aix, Avignon) from those which are marked by the antique renewal of the cloister and portal of Arles, for example (Saint-Paul-Trois-Châteaux). If discussion still continues about certain early datings in relation to the chronology of Burgundian sculpture (Avignon, Aix), there is now agreement about the late chronologies of the great flowering of Provençal Romanesque sculpture fostered by contacts with Italy and the observation of Antiquity. This will be discussed later.

Now it is time to turn to the northern regions often left to one side in the geographical presentation of French Romanesque sculpture because of the precocious and brilliant success of Gothic forms from the middle of the twelfth century. Normandy, for example, whose sculpture has been rehabilitated during the last few decades, is not rich solely for its eleventh-century monuments (Bernay, Mont-Saint-Michel, Coutances, Rouen, Caen, Bayeux, Jumièges). Even though its architecture has left so deep a mark on the progress of medieval art, the history of Norman Romanesque sculpture is primarily shaped by exchanges with England. Even before 1066, the insular art appeared at Jumièges. Subsequent comparisons are eloquent: the Abbaye aux Dames at Caen and the crypt of Canterbury Cathedral, capitals of Fécamp and Steyning, influence of the Caen abbeys at Stogursey, York Minster and Blyth, and of Cerisy-la-Forêt at Norwich, Alton and Christchurch. At Saint-Georges-de-Boscherville, about 1115–1125, we can assess the receptivity of Norman art to that of the Ile-de-France, the Soissonnais and the Beauvaisis districts, but their influence was small in comparison to the insular impact. The commemorative tomb of the first two Dukes of Normandy, Richard I and Richard II

(1162), vouches for the quality of another type of Norman figure sculpture on the threshold of Gothic art.

In the Ile-de-France and Champagne, Romanesque sculpture has a very short life, beyond the traditions of the eleventh-century capitals, owing to the precocious emergence of Gothic art. Works of quality exist, however, as demonstrated by the north portal of Saint-Etienne of Beauvais, with a flower-filled decoration, or that of the Sainte-Madeleine at Trie-Château (Oise). The west front of Saint-Denis, built by Abbot Suger shortly before 1140, illustrates everything it owes to Romanesque art by certain details of its decoration (calendar). A relief discovered in 1947, with the twelve apostles standing under arches, was immediately pitched into the centre of the debate about the transition from Romanesque to Gothic on the strength of its decorative and compositional heritage, its connection with Burgundy which might date it around the middle of the century, and the presence of stylistic details that are already Gothic.

From a homogeneous group of Romanesque sculptures originates an abundant production which extends over the first two decades of the twelfth century, starting with the series at Cambrai, Arras and the now vanished abbey church of Saint-Bertin at Saint-Omer. Although contacts with Norman sculpture of the early twelfth century have been detected, it is primarily towards the astonishing artistic output of Tournai that we should look. The ensemble at Tournai Cathedral formed of more than 1500 capitals and the remains of several portals, made of that blue-grey stone which was so widely diffused during the Middle Ages, is one of the most exceptional examples in the West and is equally referable to northern France and England or to northern Italy, between 1120–1140 and the consecration of 1171. During the Middle Ages the Tournai workshops produced many pieces of church furniture, funerary sculptures and above all baptismal fonts which were exported from the regions of the Meuse and the Scheldt not only to nearby territories like northern France and the Rhineland, but also to more distant parts like England and Scandinavia. The baptismal basins resting on a base are usually circular or square. Frequently adorned with small blind arcades, plant motifs and masks, they sometimes portray the baptism and life of Christ, Old Testament episodes and hagiographic stories on the outer surround of the basin. The Last Supper at Notre-Dame of Termonde is a fine example of this iconography. The style of these works, which vary greatly in quality, reveals the hand of sculptors used to carving capitals and other elements of monumental decoration, but trained as metalworkers.

Relief with the apostles. Mid-12th century. Basilica of Saint-Denis.

Master of Cabestany. Martyrdom of St Saturninus of Toulouse. White marble sarcophagus. Last quarter of the 12th century. Saint-Hilaire-d'Aude.

THE PYRENEAN MARBLE-CUTTERS

During the twelfth century, both sides of the eastern extremity of the Pyrenean chain are marked by the massive exploitation of marble quarries and by the recarving of antique marbles. Several generations of craftsmen specialized in producing works much imitated in limestone sculpture. The recent discovery of a red marble slab depicting Abbot Gregory, originally from the cloister of

Master of Cabestany. Jesus walking on the water towards his disciples. Façade of Sant Pere de Roda. Last quarter of the 12th century. White marble. Museo Federico Marés, Barcelona.

Saint-Michel-de-Cuxa, has definitely confirmed that the latter is accurately dated to around 1146-1150. It is one of the earliest pieces of the red marble carving of the eastern Pyrenees, reflecting the whimsies of sculptors whose hand is clearly recognizable. Variations on lions, sometimes alone, sometimes in groups, with two bodies and a single head, fighting or rigid, eagles and plant life, make up the only repertory used by these artists to decorate the capitals and arcades of the Cuxa cloister. The gallery of Serrabone, dating from the consecration of the church in 1151, depends stylistically on that of Cuxa. In it we find the same Corinthian heritage with varied monsters and animals whose bodies are bent around the corners of the capital. Much more original is the decoration of the galleries which stood opposite the faithful in the middle of the church. That of Cuxa is dispersed, but several elements have been preserved, in particular two pillars portraying Peter and Paul, which, as in many Romanesque portals, may have stood on either side of the gallery. At Serrabone, the original arrangement is essentially preserved, following models known both in the south of France (Cruas) and Italy (Vezzolano). The gallery, roofed with groined vaults resting on columns with capitals, displays a façade on which the evangelist symbols are represented.

The art of Cuxa and Serrabone was highly influential at the regional level. Echoes of it are even found on the other side of the Pyrenees, as the source of the rich and abundant output of the workshops of Ripoll and Vic, which were also nurtured by Italian and Toulouse trends. The monastery of Santa María de Ripoll was the scene of intensive artistic activity during the second half of the twelfth century with the construction of the monumental façade, a very fine altar baldachin, whose bases have been preserved, an extensive series of tombs and architectural sculptures, and above all the north and earliest walk of the Romanesque cloister. Still preserved there on a corner pillar, although very worn, is a large slab of the Cuxa type representing Abbot Berga (1172-1206) standing in a strictly frontal position under an arch. This relief affords a valuable chronological clue for the latest stages of the Ripoll sculpture which is contemporary with that of Vic Cathedral and many other important Catalan ensembles (Besalú, Sant Joan de les Abadesses).

This marble masons' art flourished very late and was even prolonged beyond the turn of the century. Exceptional personalities were deeply involved in it, testifying on this side of the Mediterranean to a development parallel to what we observe in Italy. Incidentally, the Italian training of the best of these masters, or rather the new vigour that Italian apprenticeship gave the Pyrenean marble-cutters, is the source of the finest productions of late Romanesque towards 1200. An anonymous sculptor known as the Master of Cabestany took his name–at a time when scholars looked to Romanesque sculpture for evidence of the itineraries of the principal artists–from the village of Cabestany near Perpignan where his best known work is found. It is a tympanum, already exceptional for the iconography of the Virgin (episode of the miraculous girdle), and even more so for the style the sculptor displays: dry, hard faces carved on two planes, with slanting eyes and huge hands. The artist worked with the best re-used white marble and employed a drill like the artists of Late Antiquity by whom he was inspired (Sant Pere de Roda, Saint-Hilaire-d'Aude). His influence has been detected in Tuscany and his work is found in the Aude district and through Roussillon and Catalonia as far as Navarre, and also the Bordelais. The façade of the church of Sant Pere de Roda was probably his major work. Only a few elements of it survive, but it is known to have represented Passion scenes. The relief in the Marès Museum, Barcelona, with Christ appearing to his disciples on the water, well conveys the quality of his work during the last quarter of the twelfth century.

Gallery. Mid-12th century. Red marble. Church, Serrabone.

Master Wiligelmo. Detail of the façade. About 1105-1115. Modena Cathedral.

CENTRAL AND NORTHERN ITALY: BETWEEN MEDITERRANEAN AND ADRIATIC

During the first half of the eleventh century, northern Italy was characterized by the precocious flowering of an early Romanesque art which spread rapidly to the south of France and the northern regions. This architecture of masons using small, neatly hewn ashlar, reflecting the care devoted to the vaulting, nevertheless left room in parts of northern Italy for the timber-roofed church of the Early Christian tradition. It welcomed, with more originality than was shown by regions further west, a sculptured decoration mainly concentrated on the crypt capitals, from Aosta Cathedral to the crypts of basilicas nearer to the Adriatic, from Pavia and Parma to the antiquizing trends that we have noted in Aquileia Cathedral, for example.

Around 1100 or shortly afterwards, there came a sudden flowering which still remains partly unexplained. It looks as if the attainment of certain economic and social conditions, plus a higher degree of technical skill, had created a climate in which new religious constructions were looked on as stark and bare unless adorned with handsome carvings. Our geographical survey tends to show the contemporaneity of these different trends: it cannot be explained solely by the movement of artists from place to place, nor by technical exchanges, nor by the development of pilgrimages and commercial routes, but rather by a deeper transformation of social and cultural attitudes, by the place which the Church and its wealth now assumed in society, and by early twelfth-century man's new conception of himself and his past, of nature and God. Monumental art illustrating different aspects of both religious and secular culture was not only a necessity for all those whom the new wealth had helped to raise to the peak of society, but also a duty to God and men. It was in well-defined social contexts, evolving on parallel lines, that we see the emergence in Toulouse and northern Spain, in Burgundy and northern Italy, of sculptors with strong personalities whose task was to translate into stone, perhaps as had hitherto been done in the field of the precious arts, a monumental illustration fitted to preach and educate, a reflection of the rules of feudal society, enriched with vivid polychromy, and nurtured by the observation of Antiquity and the study of its artistic canons. As already noted for the sculpture of the first half of the eleventh century, what we find after 1100 is not the diffusion of a style from one source or the brilliant work of one master, but the proliferation of regional trends around creative, well-trained masters–phenomena accordant with the history and the religious and political geography of the period. Without claiming that it coincides exactly with the latter, we have to recognize that this art, especially in the form of public monuments which are nearly always monumental sculptures, constitutes a remarkable testimony to the new forces at work and to the formidable rise of men who observe themselves with interest and observe their contemporaries as well.

Pausing briefly in an attempt to understand the deeper reality behind the emergence of major Romanesque sculpture in the West between 1080 and 1120 (taking here a broad time-span on which all art historians agree) helps to give us a better insight into the work of the first of the Italian sculptors, but does not enable us to explain all the sources. The dating of the façade of Modena Cathedral on

St Matthew. Portal of the Princes, detail. About 1110. Modena Cathedral.

which Wiligelmo signed his name depends on the interpretation one gives to the date when work on the building began (1099) and on one's assessment of the point construction had reached when it was consecrated in 1106. Wiligelmo's work is later than the latter date. In an antiquizing spirit, he sets out a vertical alignment of figures under arches. The style is sober and the emphasis dramatic. He probably worked on them for a good fifteen years, at the same time carving various items of church furniture. This is oddly reminiscent of Bernard Gilduin's artistic activity at Toulouse, but not of course his style. There can be no doubt about Wiligelmo's influence. It appears equally on the portal of Nonantola and in the prophet statues of the Duomo at Cremona. Features of his workshop style also appear on the Porta della Pescheria of Modena Cathedral, so popular for the episodes from the Arthurian legend that the artists carved on it. Wiligelmo's essential work, however, is the series of reliefs on the façade of Modena Cathedral arranged in juxtaposed scenes on separate panels. They represent episodes from Genesis, beginning with Christ in Majesty in a mandorla, supported by two angels, the creation of Adam and Eve, and the Temptation. Executed in a narrative style similar to that of Carolingian and Romanesque Bibles, these reliefs prove by certain details, such as the initial image comprising a synthesis of the six days of Creation, that the artist was familiar with models common to the famous Cotton Genesis and the Carolingian Bibles of the School of Tours. They belonged to a general façade programme inspired by the earliest known examples of the semiliturgical drama, such as the *Adam* mystery play.

The first quarter of the twelfth century saw the introduction in northern Italy of a type of screen-façade which had a great success and which left a large wall space suitable for sculptured reliefs. It formed a great parapet-wall wrought with niches and arcades over the doors, deriving from the Early Christian tripartite structure with a central raised gable (Modena, Verona), or adopting the more characteristic form of a screen-wall rising to the summit of the central nave and crowned by a saddleback cornice surmounting a system of arcades (Parma, Pavia, Piacenza). The façade of the church of San Michele at Pavia illustrates the application to the screen-façade of the so-called Como formula using ornamental friezes, here without an architectural framework, in association with portals whose splays are covered with sculptured decoration.

At the beginning of the second third of the twelfth century, the master mason Niccolò, thought to be a disciple of Wiligelmo, engraved his name on the façades of Ferrara Cathedral and San Zeno at Verona about 1135-1140, both carved with a delicacy of line and a monumentality which have prompted art historians to seek stylistic analogies in southwestern France and northern Spain, or again in Byzantine art. The splay statues which fit with the utmost elegance into the pattern of set-offs and colonnettes on the Verona façade, are somewhat reminiscent of the almost contemporaneous work of Gilabertus at Toulouse. Essentially, a large part of Romanesque sculpture in northern Italy arises in relation to the work of these two masters. The second half of the century is firmly set on a path which in some ways recalls the parallel evolution of the Provençal region. It is exemplified at Lodi and Piacenza by the work of sculptors who employ expressive naturalism in their search for a refined style that lays emphasis on form and

Scenes from the Breton Cycle. Porta della Pescheria.
About 1120-1130.
Modena Cathedral.

Stylistic evolution of Romanesque.
Right: Isaiah, jamb shaft of the portal.
About 1120. Cremona Cathedral.
Left: Eve, jamb shaft of the portal.
Last quarter of the 12th century.
Lodi Cathedral.

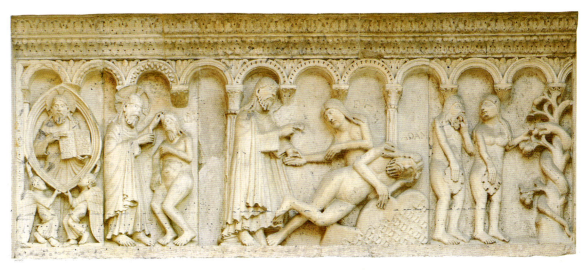

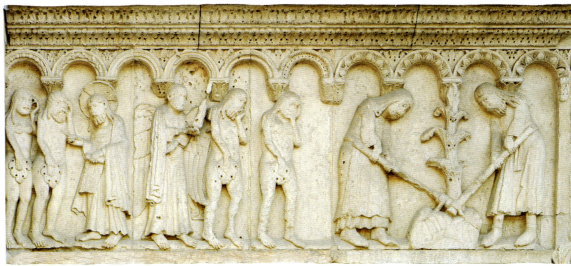

Master Wiligelmo.
Relief with scenes
from Genesis.
West front.
About 1110.
Modena Cathedral.

aims at creating plastic concepts which are original in relation to antique art. More will be said about this production when we come to deal with Antelami.

North and central Italy lies between the Mediterranean and the Adriatic; that is, between West and East. At Venice, for example, we find markedly eastern creations in the field of mosaics, whereas monumental sculpture is very receptive to the trends of Lombardy and Emilia which, combining with the influence of Byzantine models, culminate around 1200 in the last great Romanesque achievement: the portals of the west front of St Mark's, Venice. Romanesque art of the eastern Adriatic is even more receptive to Byzantine trends (Zadar, Split), while maintaining special relations with Apulia (Dubrovnik) and northern Italy. The reliefs of the Parma baptistery, perhaps those of St Mark's at Venice and certainly the Labours of the Months at Ferrara, are reflected in a monument on the Dalmatian coast: the portal of Trogir Cathedral. Its inscription records a very late date for this piece of Romanesque sculpture: "This portal was built in the year 1240 after the travail of the Glorious Virgin by Radovan, the best in this art, as appears from the statues and reliefs, under Bishop Treguan the Tuscan, of the Town of Flowers."

The monumental Romanesque art of Tuscany is illustrated by the cathedral, baptistery and bell-tower of Pisa, buildings of prodigious prestige thanks to the wealth of their marble carving, which medieval sources repeatedly

refer to and extol. Such architectural decoration is already impressively majestic in San Michele in Foro and San Martino at Lucca. The highly decorative treatment of façades continues into the Gothic period, as shown by the work of Nicola Pisano on the Pisa baptistery about the middle of the thirteenth century. Architectural polychromy was especially popular in Florence. The churches of Spoleto, in Umbria, have façades with a rose window surrounded by carvings. It is standard practice for the sculptors of this region to employ an antiquizing style more or less inspired by northern art. Among the great artists, Roberto signed the baptismal font of San Frediano at Lucca in 1151, and Guglielmo the ambo at Cagliari in Sardinia. But the style is tantamount to a signature if one knows how to follow it with an expert eye; the distinctive style of the Master of Cabestany has been found at San Giovanni in Sugana and at Sant'Antimo. Biduino is perhaps the sculptor who best sums up the culmination of Tuscan Romanesque thanks to three signed lintels, including that of the church of San Cassiano at Settimo near Pisa, dated to 1180. It is directly inspired by fourth-century Christian sarcophagi. This distinguishes his art from Guglielmo's no less antiquizing but much more varied experiments, especially in the handling of space. This milieu, in which the proximity of the Carrara and Luni quarries turned sculptors into marble-cutters equally skilled in recarving antique marbles, was the cradle of great Gothic artists such as Nicola Pisano.

Master Niccolò. Façade.
About 1135-1140.
San Zeno, Verona.

THE ROMAN MARBLE-CUTTERS

Master Vassalletto.
Candalabrum.
Late 12th century.
San Paolo fuori le Mura,
Rome.

Much more than in Tuscany, Roman and Early Christian Antiquity is ubiquitous in the city of Rome, which during the Romanesque period made a spectacular return to the monumental and iconographic sources of early Christianity, in conjunction with a Church policy aimed at prestige. This return to Late Antiquity was deliberately initiated by Desiderius, abbot of Monte Cassino, and the reform-minded pope, Gregory VII (1073-1085), who were intent on reviving the political and cultural symbolism of the early Christian period. In the architectural domain, the basilica of Monte Cassino, rebuilt by Desiderius from 1066, reverts to the Early Christian plan, as does Salerno Cathedral as rebuilt by Alfanus. This pre-Renaissance, which precedes that of Frederick II in the thirteenth century, appears equally in Rome, Campania and Sicily. For example, antique capitals were reused in many monuments, notably in the cathedrals of Salerno, Amalfi and Monreale, while the antique materials of the city of Rome were eagerly sought after. We know from Leo of Ostia that columns, bases and other elements used at Monte Cassino were shipped from Rome down to the mouth of the Tiber, then along the coast and up the river Garigliano. The porphyry for the tombs of the Norman kings of Sicily also came from Rome. This says much for the ideological value attaching to ancient Roman materials during the Romanesque period. After the advent of Pope Paschal II (1099-1118) a specifically Roman Romanesque art spread to the whole of Latium. The Roman churches reconstructed in the twelfth century, such as Santi Quattro Coronati and San Clemente, illustrate the return to Early Christian art, both in the plan and the decorative programme of paintings, mosaics and sculpture.

Another characteristic example is the church of Santa Maria in Cosmedin refurbished under Calixtus II (1119-1124), which preserves a very complete liturgical arrangement. This revival of sculpture is demonstrated in the decision to carve Ionic capitals to decorate the porches of San Lorenzo in Lucina, SS. Giovanni e Paolo, San Giorgio in Velabro and San Lorenzo fuori le Mura.

Roman sculpture during the Middle Ages was produced by specialized marble-cutting workshops active in Rome and Latium and employing both sculptors and mosaic workers. They were equally at home making cloisters and campaniles, liturgical furniture and sepulchral monuments, pavements and wall mosaics. They are known as Cosmati workers from the name of a prominent family of carvers, called Cosmas. We can easily follow the genealogy of these family groups, as well as the majority of their works, because, to our great good fortune, they signed and dated their creations. Apart from the Cosmas family, the Mellini and Vassalletto families are among the best known. Their work is characterized by an extensive use of the marbles then to be found in Rome and its environs in the form of antique columns, capitals and inscriptions, ready to be sawn and recut. Besides church furniture (chancels, ambos, altars, etc.), their art is impressively displayed in cloisters. That of St John Lateran, built between 1225 and 1236 by the Vassalletto brothers, provides the richest model by the varied forms of its colonnettes and the interplay of carved and mosaic decoration. Still larger, the cloister of San Paolo fuori le Mura, begun in 1205 and finished in 1241, testifies by its dates to the very late character of this construction. In these Roman workshops, the masons also carved wholly prefabricated cloisters ready

Roman marble carvers.
Liturgical fittings and mosaics
restored in 1883 by Giovenale.
12th century (baldachin of the
late 13th or early 14th century,
signed by the Cosmati
marble carver Deodatus).
Santa Maria in Cosmedin, Rome.

for export. Thus in 1232 Pietro de Maria, a Roman marble-cutter, carved with his disciples, in his workshop at Rome, various elements of the Sassovivo cloister at Foligno, in Umbria, and undertook to supervise the transport of the marbles, when ready, and to assemble them *in situ*. At Subiaco, the cloister of Santa Scolastica, in which an inscription records that it was executed at Rome, has preserved in the south walk the mason's marks intended to guide the assembly of the arcades after delivery.

In addition to sculptures in the round such as lions, monumental candelabra were among the finest products of these workshops. The one in San Paolo fuori le Mura was carved in the late twelfth century by Vassalletto, harking back to antique triumphal columns, with a series of superimposed registers portraying scenes of the Passion, the Resurrection and the Ascension. Very close to it in form, that of Gaeta unfolds a cycle from the childhood of Christ to the Passion and also focuses on the local saint, Erasmus. The Paschal candlestick of Anagni illustrates the commonest model: a twisted column ornamented with mosaic work on a sculpted base, crowned by a telamon supporting the dish holding the candle.

This Roman art, stemming from both the city and its surrounding territory, had a far-reaching influence owing to the movements of workshops from place to place and the export of their works, and extended southwards to Campania.

SOUTHERN ITALY AND SICILY

For many long decades, students of medieval sculpture argued over the question whether Sicily or Campania came first in a production which broadly connects these two regions within the much larger framework of the whole southern kingdom. After the arrival of Robert Guiscard in 1072, Sicily became an independent Norman state, which also annexed Apulia and Capua under Roger II (1105-1154). This was an outstanding period, continuing under William I (1154-1166) and William II (1166-1189). Then were built such sumptuous monuments as the Cappella Palatina and La Martorana at Palermo, and the cathedrals of Cefalù and Monreale. In a land successively Roman, Byzantine, Islamic and Norman, outside contributions constantly stimulated an artistic production in which art historians have looked for links with Provence, western France, the Rhineland, Rome and Byzantium, on historical but mainly on stylistic evidence.

The sculpture of Sicily and Campania shows very close mutual relations, corroborated by those which the Norman kings maintained with Salerno and Rome. Yet it would seem that the main sources are to be sought in a Roman past still very much present and an antique sculpture which Romanesque artists studied with care.

Cloister. 1205-1241. San Paolo fuori le Mura, Rome.

The revival of monumental sculpture in these two regions is essentially in the field of church furniture, with the exception of some monumental projects such as the archivolt of the cathedral of Sessa Aurunca, executed about 1190 by Sicilian sculptors, and the cloisters of Monreale, Santa Sofia at Benevento and La Cava dei Tirreni. The ambo of Ravello Cathedral, of rectangular plan, supplies one example of this furniture; another is that of Salerno Cathedral, which stands on four columns. Fidelity to Antiquity appears not only in the carving of capitals, but also in the iconographic choice of the story of Jonah, which figures on a number of ambos. Other themes, such as the cycle of the Months at Lentini in Sicily and Sessa Aurunca in Campania, the bearded heads on certain ambos, but above all the ornamental foliage containing figures, confirm a tendency which, having been observed in Provence, has sometimes tempted scholars to make a direct connection between these three regions. The cloister of the abbey of Monreale, built like the basilica by William II between 1172 and 1190, houses 228 twin colonnettes with shafts either carved or adorned with mosaics, surmounted by capitals with a rich ornamental or historiated decor on which several artists worked. Here we find subjects taken from contemporary events, episodes from the Testaments and animals. Stylistically, in spite of the similarities which have been established between one of the artists and Provence, and which in the case of the cloister of Cefalù have been extended to the southern Rhone valley and

Vienne, fidelity to local classical art prevails, as it does in Campania. One of the Monreale artists at least was a Roman: his name was Constantine the marble mason and he called himself a son of Rome.

In the twelfth century, Apulia produced another cultural synthesis between East and West with its great religious constructions. The architecture of Bari, Barletta, Bitonto, Trani and Troia forms a regional group. The monumental sculpture of Apulia is particularly rich. The façade of the Duomo at Troia, which recalls Tuscan forms, provides a majestic framework for the famous bronze doors dated to 1119. But the originality of Apulian sculpture is very early reflected in a series of decidedly Romanesque sculptured thrones (Monte Sant'Angelo, Canosa, Siponte, Taranto).

The throne of Abbot Elia (died 1105) in San Nicola at Bari has often been considered as illustrating the renewal of monumental sculpture in southern Italy around 1100 (the throne of Canosa is reliably dated between 1078 and 1089). Three atlantes support the richly carved chair and the whole is cut out of a single block of marble. The forcefulness of the artist's style is such, the quality of the sculpture in the round so fine, his monumental inspiration so direct, that one is tempted to regard this throne as a commemorative work, executed during the third quarter of the twelfth century by a master fully aware of the trends in Sicily, northern Italy and France, and heralding the art to come under Frederick II.

Romanesque throne of Abbot Elia.
About 1100. Marble.
San Nicola, Bari.

Apostles. Façade relief from
the Romanesque cathedral of Vic.
About 1170-1180.
Victoria and Albert Museum, London.

THE CHRISTIAN IBERIAN PENINSULA FACE TO FACE WITH ISLAM

The Romanesque art of the Iberian peninsula corresponds to the geographic parcelling out of the Christian kingdoms which took form confronting Islam. Catalonia, to the east, was a conglomerate of countships among which Barcelona won the hegemony, before uniting with Aragon to form the prosperous kingdom of the Crown of Aragon. To the west, Navarre remained staunchly Pyrenean, while León and Castile, which very soon crossed the Duero, also united. At the western extremity, Galicia and then Portugal constitued another solid political power on Christian territory. During the twelfth century, monumental sculpture flourished in all these regions. In Catalonia, wealth and political stability led the towns to reconstruct all the cathedrals and many urban monasteries. Arising under the stimulus of the first Romanesque art, what has been called the second Romanesque art spread beyond the Pyrenean regions to reach the recently conquered territories of Tarragona and Lleida (Lérida) where, as we shall see, the finest works are all very late and mark the transition to Gothic. To characterize twelfth-century sculpture in this region, one may choose the art of Ripoll and Vic, of Sant Joan de les Abadesses and Besalú, the handiwork of Pyrenean marble masons, or, further south, the cloisters of Sant Cugat del Vallés and Tarragona. In

neighbouring Aragon, the lower parts of the apse of Saragossa Cathedral, begun around 1180, characterize Romanesque art, together with the cloisters of San Pedro el Viejo at Huesca and San Juan de la Peña. The astonishing quality of the apostle statues in the apse of Saragossa Cathedral points up the novelty of the scheme. Navarre, which was traversed by important roads in the Romanesque period in spite of its Pyrenean location, preserves major monuments such as Tudela Cathedral and funerary chapels such as those of Torres del Río and Eunate. As far as sculpture is concerned, along with the churches of Tudela, especially the tympanum of San Nicolás, and the cloister of the collegiate cathedral, we should mention the major ensembles of Estella and Sangüesa. The façade of San Miguel d'Estella, also a late work begun during the last quarter of the twelfth century, is characteristic of northern Spain, where reliefs tend to invade the façade in an apparent disorder which has led art historians to regard them as unfinished. Rich iconography, strong relief, a treatment of drapery folds which testifies to a style that was long in the making, are some of the features inseparable from this varied and profuse decoration. The capitals of the former cloister of Pamplona Cathedral, with episodes from the Old and New Testaments, are among the most important works in Navarre. The fully developed Romanesque sculpture of Castile is no older than that of the other kingdoms, for the apse sculptures in the cathedral of Santo Domingo de la Calzada (Logroño) were not carved until about 1160. Avila, Carrión de los Condes and Silos are the three main centres of activity, belonging for the most part to the very end of the century; they will be discussed later. In the former kingdom of León, Zamora

Statues at the springing of the vaults.
Third quarter of the 12th century.
Salamanca Cathedral.

Cathedral, between 1150 and 1175, was given a decorative dome over the transept crossing, imitated by Salamanca Cathedral at the same time. The Zamora dome is one of the most superlative examples since Roman times of monumental sculpture integrated with the architecture. The ribs starting from the keystone rest on two storeys of a drum pierced with richly decorated windows. The model is taken up again at Toro. The capitals of Salamanca Cathedral and the statues under the dome are late elegant creations, whose Romanesque maturity reflects the considered assimilation of the productions of Burgundy, Aquitaine, and Italy, and the whole tradition of regional sculpture. The tomb in the Iglesia de la Madalena at Zamora is a fine example of Romanesque scenography,

together with that of the martyrs in San Vicente at Avila. In Galicia, architectural and sculptural activity is dominated by the work of Master Mateo, towards the end of the third quarter of the twelfth century, seen at his best in the last decades of the century in the Porch of the Glory of the cathedral of Santiago de Compostela. This prodigious creation eclipses that of other Galician cathedrals (Orense). In present-day Portugal, the imprint of the art of Compostela finds only a pale reflection in rural monuments. The triumphal façade of Coimbra Cathedral, in which King Sanchez I was crowned in 1185, shows, like the architecture of the church, the influence of Compostela and the originality and exoticism of the two known masters who directed the works, Bernard and Robert of Lisbon.

Façade with sculptured portal.
Last quarter of the 12th century.
San Miguel, Estella.

Virgin and Child from the church of Saint-Laurent, Liège.
Mid-12th century. Carboniferous sandstone.
Musée Curtius, Liège.

THE GERMANIC WORLD
AND CENTRAL EUROPE

The Ottonian heritage marks twelfth-century Romanesque religious architecture in Germanic countries. There, too, the quality of the metal work of the Carolingian and Ottonian periods influenced the Romanesque sculptors. Monumental sculpture in the northern lands does not have

the same architectural dimensions as in the Mediterranean countries. Goldsmith's work holds the place of honour. Between the Rhine and the Meuse, apart from the exceptional ensemble of Tournai Cathedral which is related to different geographic and artistic realities, Romanesque sculpture can be regrouped into regional series of varying degrees of importance. While the architecture of Cologne is notable for the rarity of carvings, in St Servatius at Maastricht we observe the impact of different geographic zones and a style of sculpture which has been described as goldsmithery in stone. At Liège, the so-called Dom Rupert Virgin is characteristic of this type of work by its style, as are the St Cecilia tympanum and the Siegburg Madonna in Cologne. The Cologne goldsmiths' workshops were so important in the twelfth century that stone carving depended on them. So it is by no means surprising that carved church furniture plays an essential role in this context. Between the holy sepulchre reliefs in St Cyriacus at Gernrode and the choir screen of St Michael's at Hildesheim, separated by nearly a century, a whole tradition of stucco work and funerary relief carving is reflected. At Gernrode we also find two essential features of Germanic sculpture: the Ottonian tradition in the figures and the influx of North Italian trends in the decoration of architectural frameworks. The former is responsible for the archaic style revealed in the stiffness of certain Germanic works throughout the twelfth century and already around 1115 in the rock relief of the Descent from the Cross at Externsteine. With the second we may associate, among others (Remagen), the St Jakob portal at Regensburg which vouches for the importance of this North Italian trend in the twelfth century; it also affected the splaying with decorated colonnettes and the reliefs which extend along the wall of the façade. The tympanum with busts of Christ, the Virgin and St John shows that we must not look solely in the direction of Italy to explain this South German sculpture. The Andlau portal in Alsace is more directly connected with this Lombardic trend. But the basic questions concerning these relations may be raised about the north portal of the Grossmünster in Zurich which, about 1180, adopts a form of triumphal arch and a sculptured decoration with plant motifs and figures, whose smooth drapery folds recall those of the Vic reliefs in Catalonia. In parallel with these international trends, a local production is particularly well illustrated in Switzerland at Chur, Castro and Müstair. The apse relief of naive design in the

West choir screen. Late 12th century. Stucco. Church of St Michael, Hildesheim.

church at Schöngrabern in Austria has been explained by the intervention of sculptors from the west of France; but we need a better assessment of the emergence of a late local production coming at the end of an evolution shaped by southern, western and Germanic exchanges. We can thus better understand the Hungarian sculptures of the cathedral of Pécs. In these regions of central Europe, which were also in contact with Byzantine art, sculpture deserves to be studied on its own, outside strictly western trends. Major works, like the bronze doors of Gniezno Cathedral, were created on the territory of present-day Poland. For all that, the sculptured columns and the tympanum of the abbey church at Strzelno are somewhat isolated and could effectively be explained by artistic exchanges. The same exchanges influenced much more distant countries and produced the portal of Lund Cathedral about the middle of the twelfth century. In addition to carved portals and a few tympana, sculpture in Scandinavia figures mainly on baptismal fonts; more than a thousand of them have been recorded in Jutland alone. Nevertheless, woodcarving clearly prevails in those regions, notably in the Norwegian churches with portals richly framed by an all-enveloping decorative sculpture consisting of ornamental foliage peopled by figures and animals, the study of which constitutes a separate chapter in the history of sculpture.

Mary Magdalene.
Holy Sepulchre relief.
Early 12th century. Stucco.
Church of St Cyriacus, Gernrode.

Statue of a king
(Charlemagne?).
12th century.
Church of St John, Müstair.

Descent from the Cross.
Rock relief.
First quarter of
the 12th century.
Externsteine, Horn.

THE INSULAR PHENOMENON

English Romanesque sculpture shows great originality that the discoveries yielded by archaeological excavations are continually enriching. At times akin to illumination and the precious arts, at others stemming from local traditions of stone-working, these carvings present an amazing synthesis in which both continental contributions and Scandinavian features play a part. The Norman conquest of England in 1066 has often been seen as the political event marking the advent of Romanesque with the arrival of Norman sculptors. That is to underrate the role of Edward the Confessor (1043-1066) in the reconstruction of Westminster Abbey and the importance of Anglo-Saxon sculp-

South side door known as the Prior's Doorway.
1130-1139.
Ely Cathedral.

ture. It is true, however, that with the Conquest a purely Norman style appears in the capitals of York Minster and those in the crypt of Rochester Cathedral. It is also noteworthy that the carved tympanum occurs very early, if we accept the date of 1071 for the one (completely geometric, to be sure) at Chepstow Castle. The preponderance of Norman sculpture in England immediately after the Conquest has been explained by the massive importation of limestone from Caen and sculptures partially carved in the local quarries before embarkation; but here again the Anglo-Saxon tradition of stone-working should not be minimized. Today we also know that some of the stone used in England came from Flanders, which gives a more diversified view of the early work. Major architectural sculpture appears after 1100. The capitals of the crypt of Canterbury Cathedral, with a dense plant and animal decoration, illustrate an innovating style datable to before 1120. This date is important, because a series of monuments depend on it, such as Romsey Abbey, Reading, the south transept of Worcester Cathedral, etc. During the first half of the twelfth century, regional styles begin to emerge: Herefordshire, Yorkshire, Ely, etc. The choir and transept of Ely Cathedral were given capitals with cubic squaring at a very early date, between 1093 and 1106. The portals, belonging to the third decade of the twelfth century, are situated on the side aisle and south arm of the transept. The one most richly carved exhibits an extremely dense plant decoration on the splayings and arch mouldings surrounding a tympanum adorned with a theophany. Even if the iconography brings to mind contemporary continental work, the style, similar to that of illuminated manuscripts, recurs in Norwich Cathedral. The influence of illumination on Romanesque sculpture in England is considerable, which is explained by the importance of royal and episcopal patronage. Among the most compelling works for their dramatic intensity are the fragments of a choir screen at Chichester Cathedral, with scenes from the life of Lazarus; they can hardly antedate the 1140s. During the second half of the twelfth century, English Romanesque art benefited by Gothic innovations. The portal of Rochester Cathedral certainly refers back to the Ile-de-France as regards its tympanum and splay statues. The arrival of William of Sens for the reconstruction of Canterbury Cathedral after the fire of 1174 is a famous example of continental influence. Contacts with Mosan art have been recognized; they led to numerous imports of sculptures made of Tournai stone. The definitive introduction of Gothic and the weight of the Romanesque tradition go hand in hand at York in the fine series of splay statues possibly coming from the chapter house of the former abbey of St Mary. Parallel to this great production, English monumental sculpture workshops also executed tombs, choir screens and baptismal fonts.

Romanesque sculpture in Ireland skilfully mixes the local tradition of interlacings with borrowings from England and the continent before and after the conquest of 1171. The tympana of Cormac's Chapel at Cashel vie with those having human and animal heads at the corners of the set-offs. The most original creations are the sculptured stone crosses which stand in isolation near a church, in a cemetery or at the boundaries of a monastery. The Old and New Testaments, lives of the saints, representations of animals and abundant plant motifs contribute to the highly decorative and calligraphic character of Romanesque sculpture in Ireland.

One of the two facing tympana under the south porch. About 1155-1170. St Mary and St Aldhelm, Malmesbury.

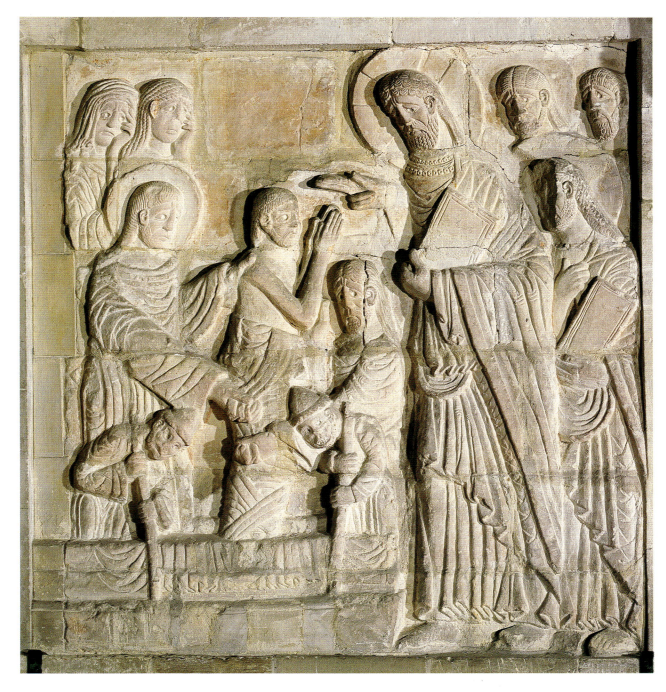

Raising of Lazarus.
Choir screen.
About 1140.
Chichester Cathedral.

THE WEALTH
OF TECHNIQUES

"Here is the portrait of the sculptor Arnau Catell,
who has built this cloister for eternity."
Later 12th century. Cloister, Sant Cugat del Vallés.

SIGNATURE AND WORK
OF THE ROMANESQUE
SCULPTOR

For a long time art historians believed in the anonymity
of the Romanesque artist and built up a legend asserting
that medieval artists never signed their work, preferring
to die in nameless glory. Even Viollet-le-Duc helped to
propagate this point of view when he wrote that "in the
twelfth century, when lay craftsmen began to work, the
chroniclers of the abbeys... organized a conspiracy of
silence against those outside the congregation. And it
worked quite well, because few of the names of the
twelfth- and thirteenth-century masters have come down
to us." Nothing could be further from the truth, for the
signatures of Romanesque artists are numbered in their
thousands and sculptors signed their works without false
modesty and quite unambiguously, on the strength of the
social recognition they enjoyed and the high esteem in
which they held their own creations.

Let us take a few examples: "Thy sculpture, Wiligel-
mus, shows today how worthy thou art of honour
amongst sculptors" (façade of Modena Cathedral); "The
monk Martin, admirable worker in stone, carved this
work under the episcopate of the great Stephen" (tomb of
St Lazarus, Autun); "Here is the portrait of the sculptor
Arnau Catell, who has built this cloister for eternity"
(Sant Cugat del Vallés); "Gilabert, who is not an unknown, sculptured me" (statues, Saint-Etienne of
Toulouse); "Petrus Janitor made this capital, the first"
(Châtillon-sur-Indre); "Carved by Simeon of Ragusa, in-
habitant of Trani (portal, Barletta Cathedral); "Look on
this, Master Sighraf" (baptismal fonts at Aakirkeby, island
of Bornholm, Denmark); "Raymond de Bianya (or R. de
Via) made me and I shall be statue" (tombstone, Elne); "In
1178, the sculptor executed this work in the second month,
this sculptor was Benedetto Antelami" (Deposition from
the Cross, Parma Cathedral); "Twice two being taken
from 1200 [i.e. 1196] the sculptor called Benedetto began
this work (baptistery, Parma); "This work is worthy of
great praise, John had it made; by this divine gift, honour
and praise to Pellegrino who carved such a work. His
work is resplendent everywhere" (candelabrum, Sessa
Aurunca).

Some specialized craftsmen described themselves as
magister marmolarius, a common designation among
Roman marble masons. One example is Guidetto, who
signed himself in this way on a scroll held by a youth on
one of the columns on the upper façade of the cathedral
of San Martino at Lucca. So the names of sculptors are very
numerous, as indeed are those of architects and masters of
works who are described as *architectus, artifex* or *magister
operis*. Some inscriptions are as explicit as this one on the
Pórtico de la Gloria at Santiago de Compostela: "In the
year of the incarnation of the Lord 1188... the lintels of
the main doors of the Santiago church were put in place by
Master Mateo, who was in charge from the foundations of
these portals." Problems arise when the artist's specialization is not mentioned. For example, we may think that the
inscription "Girauldus made these doors" at Saint-Ursin,
Bourges, probably refers to the sculptor, but what are we
to make of Gislebertus of Autun who signed beneath the
feet of Christ in the middle of the tympanum, *Gislebertus
hoc fecit*, of Leodegarius who signed the column-statue
of the Virgin on the portal of Santa María la Real at

Stages in the carving of a capital and the finished work. Cloister relief. Second half of the 12th century. Gerona Cathedral.

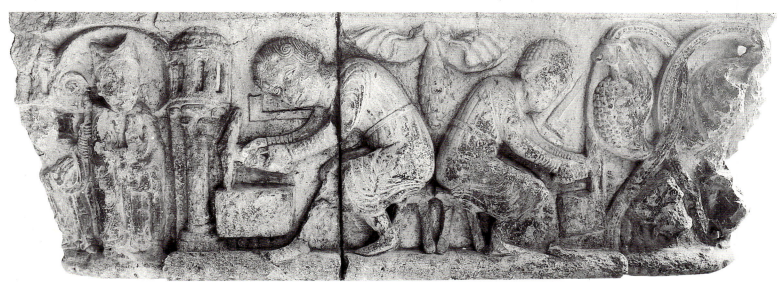

Sangüesa, *Leodegarius me fecit*, or the signature of the portal statues of Saint-Gilles-du-Gard, *Brunus me fecit*, and many laconic statements of the same nature engraved on a capital at Saint-Benoît-sur-Loire, Chauvigny and elsewhere? For it is not impossible that the place chosen by the architect or master of works to sign his name was precisely that of a really outstanding sculpture. The sculptors themselves are sometimes portrayed while at work (Sant Cugat del Vallés), with their tools (modillions of Saintonge and Poitou) or with the features of a personage we find it hard to recognize because he forms part of a scene or because he is not identified by an inscription as at Tournai. The work of a sculptor is teamwork involving a master and stone-cutters. Several teams worked simultaneously, especially on the great worksites. The materials, particularly when they were of high quality, might come from afar, as shown by a letter of Pope Adrian IV addressed to the archpriest and canons of Pisa on 20 April 1156, in which he announced the arrival of brothers sent to Italy to carve the stones and colonnettes for the cloister of Saint-Ruf-lès-Valence (or that of Avignon). The blocks could be rough-hewn in the quarries, as the fate of Hugues, master of works at the church at Conques, tells us. His legs were crushed by a cart drawn by twenty-six pairs of oxen which was carrying capitals and column bases from the quarry to the church. A relief in the cloister of Gerona Cathedral shows the phases of squaring a block for the carving of a capital, the

mass production of which has been proved in many cases, especially in the case of capitals with bare leaves, whose chiselling remained unfinished (Saint-Michel-d'Aiguilhe at Le Puy). We have already seen how the blocks of the great tympana were prepared before being put in position. The work of Roman marble masons shows that cloisters were prepared in workshops before installation and testifies to the existence of a master sculptor whose name later figures on the finished cloister (Vassalletto, in the cloister of St John Lateran, is described as "noble and skilful in the art"), and who directs the work as a whole and its putting in place. The mass production of all the elements, bases, colonnettes, capitals, arch-stones, fell to stone-cutters and their assistants, whose craft was handed down from father to son. The engraving of inscriptions, as in Antiquity and as on a Romanesque capital at Maastricht, was probably entrusted to specialists.

The interdependence of artistic techniques is fundamental, notably between painting, goldsmith's work, ivory work and sculpture using stone or wood. Although specialization was the general rule, one artist at Bury St Edmunds was master of several techniques. In the second quarter of the twelfth century, Master Hugo is mentioned as having executed a Bible, the bronze doors of the abbey, a bell and a wooden Crucifixion with the Virgin and St John. Major Romanesque sculpture implies a close relationship between the work of sculptors and painters. All the great tympana were painted, as the vestiges of colouring at Vézelay and Cluny demonstrate. The capitals with bare leaves were intended to be painted. The capitals at Berzé-la-Ville, for example, once carved, were passed to the hands of painters so that they could add the leafwork. This completely changes our view of capitals which are often thought of today as unfinished. It has been shown that on the Vézelay tympanum the sculptor left even the most elegant details at the painter's disposal so that he could put the finishing touches to them. This final intervention was foreseen from the beginning. This allows us to return to the question of inscriptions, because in the same way that the sculpture of capitals formed an integral part of the iconography of the painted decoration, and that sculptured scenes whose meaning today remains obscure were explained by painted inscriptions (Vézelay), many works that remain anonymous to us are sculptures whose painted signature has disappeared.

△ Weight-bearing figure
leaning out towards the spectator.
The master mason?
Second half of the 12th century.
Cathedral of Tournai.

"Gofridus made me."
Capital of the Epiphany.
Second half of the 12th century.
Saint-Pierre, Chauvigny.

Altar frontal from Santa María, Taüll. 12th century. Polychrome wood. Museu d'Art de Catalunya, Barcelona.

WOODCARVING

Wood was an essential material for the construction of private houses, religious and municipal buildings, bridges and town walls. Boats and floating were generally used to transport it by river. Several groups of craftsmen specialized in working wood in the Romanesque period and, to judge by the treatise of Theophilus, they should not be confused with those working with other materials. In the thirteenth century Etienne Boileau's *Livre des métiers* (Book of Crafts) illustrates the growing specialization which separates joiners from carpenters, but associates the crucifix carvers with the men who whittled knife handles and all the other forms of carving, whether in bone or ivory. The furniture-making workshops were probably the most numerous, for the illustrations and the few examples preserved show the wide variety of cupboards, chests, church pews, armchairs, chairs and altars then being made. Furniture and statuary, together with architectural decoration, were the main products carved out of wood. In all cases, the wood was local, importation from distant parts being very rare. The first stage of the work was trimming, followed by cutting, but a very important place was given to assemblage. The size of the material, the tree-trunk, governed the work. Romanesque Virgins were often carved out of a single block, to which the separately carved child was added. At other times, some twenty pieces of wood might be assembled to form the statues. Wooden Christs were generally made out of two or three pieces; either two trunks were assembled to form the cross, or one piece was used for the body and two more for the arms. According to the *Book of Crafts*, skilful assemblage was the main quality of the craftsman in wood. Once the work was carved and assembled, it was smeared with a preparation before the polychrome painting was added, which clearly shows the relations between image-makers and painters, unless the two crafts were concentrated in the hands of the same people. We know that many Romanesque abbeys had woodcarving workshops, in addition to painting and illumination workshops. Although statues were always intended to be covered with polychromy, they were also given a metallic facing if resources permitted. Thus the bust of St Baudime at Saint-Nectaire was made of a wooden core covered with gilded repoussé sheets of copper, with the head and hands in cast copper and the hands chased (late twelfth century). In contrast, the bust of St Caesarius of Arles, preserved in the church of Maurs (Cantal), was given an application of silver and gilded copper on the body only, while the head and hands were painted straight onto the wood. A restoration of the bust of St Chaffre at Le Monastier (Haute-Loire) throws light on the different stages of the commission and the work. The wooden torso was prepared, from its conception, to receive a facing of silver embossed *in situ*, whereas the head was first conceived simply to be painted. The decision to cover it with metal only came later when the necessary funds were available. The Virgin and Child at Orcival, today faced with silver-gilt and copper except for the heads and hands, was originally carved independently of this precious coating, as shown by the quality and detail of the drapery folds, which do not correspond with the handling of the metal.

Among the monumental wooden works that are preserved, we have, in addition to the decoration of Norwegian churches, church doors with relief carving of the kind found at St Maria im Kapitol in Cologne and Santa Maria in Cellis at Carsoli in Italy, or with carving close to champlevé, whose decorations stand out in very shallow relief against hollowed out grounds. Of the latter, some are concentrated in the Velay in France. Among them, the doors of Le Puy Cathedral, signed by Gauzfredus, are dated by an inscription which mentions the patron, Bishop Peter III (1143-1155). In addition to the life of Christ (Cologne, Gurk in Carinthia) and Old Testament scenes, we find personifications of the Months at the entrance to the church (Blesle in the Velay).

Around the altar, the baldachin, like the altar itself with its antependium or altar frontal, and certain exceptional works such as the lectern from Alpirsbach, are often made of wood; in Italy the altarpiece appears very early. But the best known work of Roman woodcarving workshops is statuary: Virgins and Child and crucifixes. The Virgin seated facing the viewer with the Child on her knees is perhaps the most characteristic type image of Romanesque art. The representation of Mary, the Throne of Wisdom, a concise expression of the dogma of the Incarnation, developed slowly until about 1200, when the rigidity of the composition gradually disappeared in favour of the depiction of feelings of tenderness between mother and child. These statues, objects of great veneration and worship, links between heaven and earth to which the piety of the faithful ascribed miracles, were nearly always reliquaries and were used in the Middle Ages for the staging of liturgical dramas such as that of the Epiphany. The statue might be placed on an altar, but became portable for processions. In France, Auvergne is the region which has preserved the greatest number and the regional style is characterized by the very calligraphic design of the drapery (Orcival, Saint-Flour). The stone Virgin on the south portal of Notre-Dame-du-Port at Clermont-Ferrand supplies a chronological reference point (1160-1180) for the always difficult classification of this abundant production. In the Pyrénées-Orientales, the Virgins of Corneilla-de-Conflent and Cuxa appear as extensions of many Catalan Virgins, two large groups of which can be singled out around Gerona and La Seu d'Urgell. The black wooden Virgin of Montserrat, coloured well after its original execution like all its fellows, is, together with the stone Virgin and Child with Toulouse accents in Solsona Cathedral, one of the major works of Romanesque Catalonia. Regional creations can be studied in northern Spain, Burgundy, Italy, Switzerland and Germany, especially the Ottonian Virgins of Cologne, Hildesheim, Paderborn and Frankfurt, and in the Scandinavian countries. Many of these works pose the more general problem of relations between wooden statuary and monumental sculpture in stone.

Scene from the life of Christ: Presentation in the Temple.
Detail of the wooden doors.
Between 1143 and 1155.
Cathedral of Le Puy.

Wooden doors.
Second half of the 11th century.
St Maria im Capitol, Cologne.

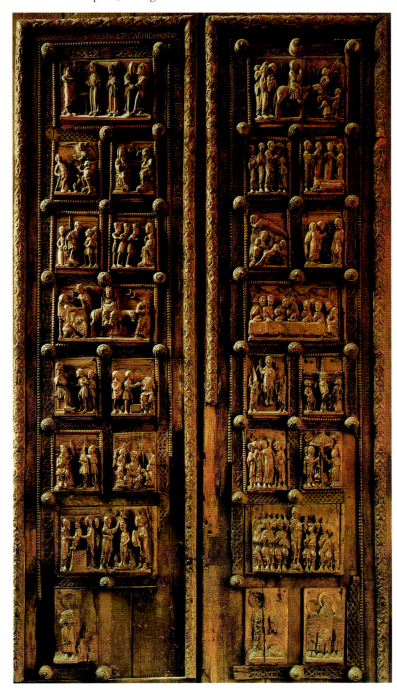

Virgin known as Notre-Dame-de-Bon-Espoir.
About 1180. Painted wood.
Notre-Dame, Dijon.

to Burgundian stone sculptures from the entourage of Gislebertus. Notre-Dame-de-Bon-Espoir of Dijon, which was not black originally, reflects the rise of Gothic about 1180. The Virgins of the Fogg Art Museum and Jouy-en-Josas are not far stylistically from the façade sculptures at Senlis. Two large heads in the monastery of Sahagún in Spain have also been compared with works in stone. In the abbey of St Hubert in Belgium, an artist named Fulco is reputed to have been equally skilful in working wood and stone, and in illuminating manuscripts, which does not seem to have been exceptional in monastic circles (Hugo at Bury St Edmunds). One of the more explicit comparisons is that which scholars have been tempted to make

Virgin and Child.
12th century. Painted wood.
Museu d'Art de Catalunya, Barcelona.

In the absence of records, stylistic comparisons provide chronological and geographical arguments and enable us to reflect on the relations in working methods between the stonecarving and the woodcarving workshops. The Virgin of Autun, preserved in The Cloisters in New York, shows a handling of the drapery which has been compared between the Romanesque Christ on the Cross at Moissac and the Majesty on the tympanum. Nailed to the plant-like cross, the wooden Christ's only covering is a cloth from the waist to the knees. The treatment of the broken folds and borders, as well as that of the hair and face, is very close, almost identical, to that of several elements of the Moissac portal sculpture, in particular to the head and clothing of the Christ in Majesty on the tympanum. Although the iconographical type may be a little isolated during the first half of the twelfth century (which has sometimes suggested a later dating), stylistic comparisons with the sculpture on the portal allow us to assign this work to the team of the tympanum sculptors.

Virgin and Child.
12th century. Painted wood.
Saint-Nectaire.

Virgin and Child known as "La Diège."
Late 12th century. Painted wood.
Jouy-en-Josas.

The Romanesque wooden Christ is depicted alive on the cross wearing a long tunic or simply a loincloth. The *Volto Santo* at Lucca, executed in the twelfth or early thirteenth century, enjoys great fame for its long tunic falling in large folds, its majestic air and the legend surrounding its making and its arrival in Lucca. Nevertheless, a similar work existed previously from which many twelfth-century Christs derive, in spite of regional variations: the crucifixes of Bocca di Magra, Milan, Barcelona (Batlló Majesty), Saint-Michel-d'Aiguilhe, and Brunswick (signed by its carver Imervard on the two straps of the girdle). In the Mosan and Rhineland regions, the Christs on the Cross of Notre-Dame at Tongres and of St George at Cologne illustrate the development of the Ottonian tradition and the relations with goldsmith's work.

The groups of the Descent from the Cross constitute the most spectacular dramatic setting of wooden church furniture. Christ crucified is welcomed by Joseph of Arimathea, accompanied by Nicodemus, the Virgin, St John and the two thieves. Depending on the region, Christ is presented in a position corresponding to different moments in the story. He may be shown still nailed to the cross, with his right hand or both hands already unnailed, or with his body detached from the cross. Many crucifixes exhibited in museums come from scattered groups; about fifteen late elements of them are preserved in Italy, the oldest remnant being the Christ of Badia di Sant'Antimo in Tuscany carved about 1170. The only two groups still intact in Italy are those of Volterra and Tivoli Cathedral, dating to the first quarter of the thirteenth century.

Virgin and Child. Late 12th – early 13th century. Chased silver over wooden core. Beaulieu.

Descent from the Cross.
First quarter of the 13th century.
Painted wood.
Volterra.

◁◁ Christ on the Cross known as the "Batlló Majesty."
Mid-12th century. Painted wood.
Museu d'Art de Catalunya, Barcelona.

◁ Christ on the Cross known as the "Volto Santo."
Late 12th or early 13th century.
Painted wood.
Cathedral of San Martino, Lucca.

Descent from the Cross.
Mid-13th century.
Painted wood.
Cathedral of Tivoli.

Wooden statues of the Virgin and St John
from the Descent from the Cross
of Erill-la-Vall.
Second half of the 12th century.
Museu d'Art de Catalunya, Barcelona.

They are a little earlier than the group in the Louvre executed in central Italy in the mid-thirteenth century. A
workshop specializing in groups of the Descent from the
Cross has been located in the Pyrenees near Erill-la-Vall;
another worked with La Seu d'Urgell as its base. The most
prestigious of the Catalan groups is preserved at Sant Joan
de les Abadesses. Seven statues in a very sober style recalling the Ripoll sculpture are arranged around Christ and
the host or relics which were lodged in cavities made in his
forehead and back. The group is exceptionally well documented. A layman of the town called Dulcet commissioned Canon Ripoll Tarascó to have a group executed
at his expense; he intended it for the abbey, specifically for
the altar of the Virgin. He arranged for the delivery of

Central group of the Descent from the Cross
from Erill-la-Vall.
Second half of the 12th century.
Museu Episcopal, Vic.

Lectern with the four evangelists
bearing the reading desk.
From the monastery of Alpirsbach.
Third quarter of the 12th century.
Painted wood.
Stadtkirche, Freudenstadt.

walnut and pine wood and specified the composition he
wanted. This is an example of a form of patronage common in the Romanesque period when a donor financed a
work of art for a religious institution and entrusted the
supervision of the work to one of its members. Consecrated on 16 June 1251, the group was placed on the high
altar of the church or close to it. These groups, which are
associated with the sacred representations of the Easter
period, may occupy different points in the nave or a lofty
position at the apse entrance or on the screen separating the
clergy from the congregation, as in the monastery of Las
Huelgas Reales at Burgos and in Italy. Several Germanic
Crucifixion groups (Halberstadt, Ratzeburg) preserve this
theatrical arrangement.

Christ on the Cross.
From the church of
St George, Cologne.
Last third of the 11th century.
Wood.
Schnütgen-Museum, Cologne.

BRONZE

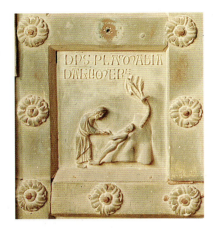

Bonanno of Pisa.
Detail of the
bronze doors.
Before 1186.
Cathedral of Monreale.

Bronze and brass are alloys of copper, the metal most frequently used in artistic metallurgy for its hardness, malleability and resistance to atmospheric agents. The average alloy is seventy per cent copper and thirty per cent of other metals, as in Antiquity. Among the bronzes, alloys containing high percentages of tin or zinc possess the quality of being very fluid in the state of fusion and of circulating easily inside moulds, while reproducing the least details of the inside wall; but they are very difficult to complete or correct when cold. So the Romanesque bronze doors were cast in an alloy rich in lead and tin which faithfully reproduced the modelling impressed on the wax and then on the terracotta mould. To cite one example, the doors of Trani Cathedral are composed of seventy-three per cent copper, eleven to twenty per cent tin, and four to fourteen per cent lead; the percentage of copper is very low, as it often was in the Middle Ages. It is obvious that stylistic characteristics depend equally on the choice of materials and the technical qualities; in the case of bronze, the relations between style and technique are extremely close. The colour of bronze varies according to the percentage of the metals composing it. Brass is particularly appreciated for its yellow colour obtained by re-heating and the addition of calamine. The founding of large objects such as doors, thrones and baptismal fonts was often the work of masters specializing in bell-founding, because they were experts in the preparation of large-scale moulds for direct casting and in handling enormous quantities of metal.

We know the names of many of the medieval master bronze-founders, among them Renier of Huy who executed the baptismal fonts preserved in Saint-Barthélemy at Liège in the early twelfth century. There were also Oderisius of Benevento, maker of the bronze doors of Troia Cathedral (1127) donated by Bishop William II, as well as the vanished doors of San Giovanni at Capua and San Bartolomeo at Benevento; Barisanus of Trani, who executed the doors of the cathedrals of Ravello, Trani (central portal), and Monreale (north portal) during the last quarter of the twelfth century; not to mention the celebrated Bonanno of Pisa, founder of the bronze doors of the Duomo at Pisa and those of the main entrance of Monreale Cathedral (before 1186). There is still the problem of how the tasks were distributed between sculptor and founder, unless they were one and the same person. When the decision was taken at Florence to provide the baptistery with bronze doors, a master was sent to Pisa to copy Bonanno's doors and another to look for founders in

Renier de Huy. Baptismal font. Early 12th century. Bronze. Saint-Barthélemy, Liège.

Bronze doors from Plock. About 1150-1155.
St Sophia, Novgorod.

Bronze doors. Second quarter of the 12th century.
San Zeno, Verona.

Venice skilled in the Byzantine technique to execute the moulds for the work of Andrea Pisano.

Bronze doors form one of the major monuments of the Romanesque Middle Ages. Coveted by all the great religious centres, they are preserved both in Italy, from Venice to Sicily, and in the northern countries. The Byzantine doors of Venice, Salerno, San Paolo fuori le Mura at Rome and Monte Sant'Angelo are engraved and inlaid with silver, a technique marked by the influence of illumination which was also adopted by Oderisius for Troia Cathedral. The work of Barisanus at Trani, Ravello and Monreale is characterized by the presence of reliefs obtained by stamping, but Byzantine influence dominates the style. In northern Italy, the door leaves of San Zeno at Verona are composed of panels assembled on a wooden core executed by different masters in a firmly Romanesque style; they present an iconography mainly centred on the Old and New Testaments, but also including apocalyptic themes and the story of Zeno. Different dates, which should fall in the second quarter of the twelfth century, have been assigned to the various styles. The doors of Plock Cathedral on the Vistula, today at Novgorod, show portraits of master-founders and donor bishops, and a general iconography also centred on the Old and New Testaments, crowned by two rectangular panels depicting the Ascension and the theophany. Executed about the middle of the twelfth century at Magdeburg by

bronze-founders, whose tomb of Archbishop Friedrich von Wettin is also preserved, these doors testify to a tradition of founding which goes back to the prestigious Ottonian works of Bernward of Hildesheim and is famous in Germanic regions for the production of candlesticks (Erfurt), the feet of crosses (Luneburg), aquamaniles (Hamburg, Boston), crucifixes (Amrichshausen, Cologne) and censers (Trier). The Mosan region, with Stavelot and Liège, is one of the main centres of production and the bronze doors of Gniezno Cathedral in Poland (c. 1175), devoted to the life of St Adalbert, apostle of Bohemia and Poland, should be attributed to its influence. The brass baptismal fonts by Renier of Huy which the abbot of Notre-Dame of Liège, Hellin (1107-1118), had executed for his church, reveal all the possibilities of the material. Various baptismal scenes are illustrated by figures standing out in strong relief from the ground of a basin cast in one piece and carried by protomes of oxen. By its monumentality, the quality of the work, and the delicacy of execution, this remarkable work of Mosan art proves the priority given by ecclesiastical dignitaries to certain pieces of liturgical furniture (such as the Trier censer and the candlesticks of Gloucester, Winchester, Canterbury and Durham) which become, by the nature of the material and the dazzling power of the art employed, prestigious symbols of the economic and spiritual power of the Church.

Altar cross
from Bury St Edmunds.
Second quarter of
the 12th century.
Ivory.
The Cloisters
Collection,
The Metropolitan
Museum of Art,
New York.

GOLDWORK

The treasury was perhaps the essential feature of the medieval church. An accumulation of precious metal, it was the tangible expression of the wealth of an abbey or a church, and could be melted down at any moment to become saleable metal again. It was also a spiritual symbol because it housed the venerated relics which attracted the pilgrims who ensured the fame of the holy place and its material prosperity. The treasury was formed by numerous gifts as is proved about the year 1000, by Helgaud, the biographer of Robert the Pious, referring to Aignan, patron saint of Orléans: "Burning to honour such a great bishop . . . the king had the front of the shrine of St Aignan ornamented with the best fine gold, precious stones and pure silver, and he had the *mensa* of the altar of St Peter, to whom the sanctuary is dedicated, covered with fine gold." The king "placed his contentment in the relics of the saints which he caused to be faced with gold and silver, in white vestments, sacerdotal ornaments, precious crosses, gold chalices, censers in which rare incense burns and silver vessels for the priest's ablutions."

In the artistic realm, Romanesque goldsmithery played a considerable part not only in the birth and development of monumental sculpture, but also in the training of artists. The reputation of the goldsmiths crossed frontiers and their works were often cited as models. It was said of Godefroid of Huy that he "had no equal in the field of goldsmithery; in various regions, he had made many reliquaries and objects for the kings." Repoussé work was one of the most fashionable techniques with goldsmiths because it rendered the relief better on the foil which, laid over a wooden core for reliquaries and altarpieces, translated on a smaller scale the aspirations of monumental

sculpture. The work of reliquary busts certainly made the greatest impact on the efflorescence of Romanesque sculpture. In the *Book of the Miracles of St Foy*, written about 1014 by Bernard, master of the episcopal school at Angers, we find a remarkable testimony: "A venerable and antique custom exists both in the lands of Auvergne, Rodez and Toulouse, and in the neighbouring regions. Each district erects a statue to its saint, of gold, silver or another metal, depending on its means, inside which either the saint's head or some other venerable part of his body is enclosed . . . I contemplated for the first time the statue of St Géraud standing on an altar. A statue remarkable for its very fine gold, its stones of great price and reproducing with such art the features of a human face that the peasants who looked on it felt themselves pierced by a penetrating gaze and sometimes thought that they glimpsed in the rays from his eyes the indication of a favour more indulgent to their wishes . . . Finally, on the third day, we came near to Sainte-Foy [of Conques]. It happened, by good fortune and by chance, that when we entered the monastery the secluded place was open where the venerable image is kept. When we arrived before it, we were so cramped because of the great number of the prostrate faithful that we ourselves could not bow down. This annoyed me and I remained standing to look at the image."

The reliquary statue of St Foy at Conques has been preserved. It is a ninth-century statue faced with gold, reusing a head from Late Antiquity, modified in the late tenth century and then during later periods with the addition of many items of goldsmithery, thanks to the gifts of pilgrims anxious to enrich its majesty. The wide diffusion of reliquary busts during the Middle Ages has already been mentioned in connection with woodcarving. In the

Reliquary bust of St Baudime.
Second half of the 12th century. Copper-gilt over wooden core.
Saint-Nectaire.

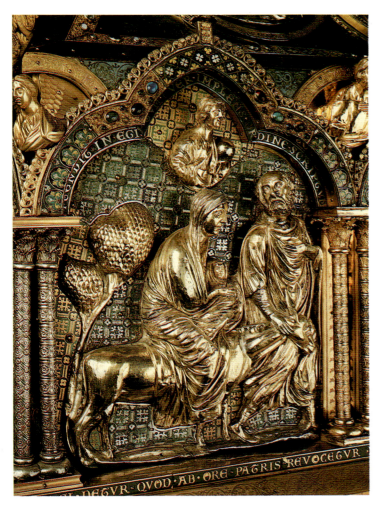

Nicolas de Verdun. The Flight into Egypt.
Detail of the Shrine of the Virgin.
1205. Silver-gilt, copper-gilt, enamel, over wooden core.
Treasury of Tournai Cathedral.

great cross from the altar of Bury St Edmunds, now in The Cloisters, New York, carved during the second quarter of the twelfth century, offers a quite exceptional iconographic programme, but now lacks the Christ that was attached to it. Its style, which shows singular affinities in the treatment of the drapery folds with the Bury Bible illuminated by Master Hugo about 1135, illustrates once again the interdependence of artistic techniques.

Reliquary statue of St Foy.
9th–10th centuries and later periods.
Gold and silver-gilt over wooden core.
Church Treasury, Conques.

Mosan region, the head of Pope Alexander was ordered by Abbot Wibald (1130-1158) for his monastery of Stavelot in order to welcome the relics of the Pope in 1145; figuring among the most prestigious objects in church treasuries, it is a securely dated landmark of twelfth-century Romanesque wooden sculpture in the round. At the time, under the patronage of Wibald, Godefroid of Huy executed the great altarpiece disposed around the reliquary of St Remacle, surmounted by a large tympanum devoted, like the great façade tympana, to the theophany. Stavelot is also the source of the portable altar, now in the Royal Museums in Brussels, supported by statuettes of the four evangelists cast in gilt bronze and which has been compared to the beautiful altarpiece of the Pentecost in the Musée de Cluny. Towards the end of the century, Nicolas of Verdun, the most celebrated goldsmith between Romanesque and Gothic art, appeared, again in the very fertile Mosan area. The date of two of his works is known: the celebrated altarpiece, originally the precious facing of the ambo of the rood loft of St Augustine at Klosterneuburg near Vienna, which, with its fifty-one scenes, represents the most important enamelled piece of the twelfth century (1181); and the Shrine of the Virgin in Tournai Cathedral (1205). The reliquary of the Three Kings in Cologne Cathedral belongs between the two. Noteworthy as being akin to monumental sculpture are ivory carvings, made by specialized workshops and preserved in church treasuries: pyxides, reliquaries, and above all inlaid and facing panels for subsequent assembling. To cite only one example, the

THE LAST BURST OF VITALITY

St Michael. Detail of the façade. Third quarter of the 12th century. Saint-Gilles-du-Gard.

PROVENCE AND ANTIQUITY

An exceptional monument dominates Provençal sculpture of the second half of the twelfth century: the façade of Saint-Gilles-du-Gard. Three portals with statues and reliefs spilling over on to the façade adorned with pilasters, columns and porticoes, form a coherent group within a carefully planned architectural and iconographic programme, whose style influenced the whole of late Mediterranean Romanesque art. Its unique character makes it one of the most studied monuments in the period as a whole, and the absence of inscriptions and specific documentary sources also makes it one of the most controversial. Some twenty chronologies have been put forward, ranging from the late eleventh century to the late twelfth century. In a region in which a great number of antique monuments, both urban and rural, were still standing during the Romanesque period, the men who conceived the façade of Saint-Gilles would have had no difficulty in finding models of architectural arrangements in triumphal arches or the stage walls of theatres. This impression of imitating Antiquity is further accentuated by the reliefs forming friezes and the arrangement and allure of the majestic statues which embellish the whole. Saint-Gilles was an important monastery and the decision to embark on such an undertaking is inconceivable unless weighty political and economic events had occurred within the abbey. Its Mediterranean situation facilitated stylistic exchanges and made it a much frequented place and a beacon for Christianity fighting in the East. We do not know any

more about it, except the determination to provide a programme which emphasizes the work of salvation through episodes from the life of Christ, which establishes its thought on the statues of the apostles, and which is based on the organization of the three tympana adorned with the Epiphany and the Crucifixion on either side of a theophany.

Here style and chronology are at the centre of a very subjective debate concerning the place to be assigned to the sculpture of Saint-Gilles-du-Gard in the art of the second half and end of the twelfth century. Only two apostle statues are signed by one Brunus about whom we know nothing. At the very most we can attribute the statues of Matthew and Bartholomew in a heavy, austere antiquizing style to this master. Those of Thomas, James the Less and Peter, with a more frankly Romanesque look and the linear animated treatment of sculptures of the west of France, come from the hands of another artist who may also be responsible for the bas-reliefs on the central portal. Much closer to Brunus, a third sculptor handles the supple drapery softly and enjoys modelling the folds around arms and legs as we see on the first two statues of the righthand between-portal, on the north tympanum and the relief with the Denial of St Peter in the left splaying of the central portal. The south portal with its tympanum of the Crucifixion and the last two apostle statues to the right of the façade were executed by an artist who gives a hard volume to the drapery folds by accentuating the contrasts of light and shade; and one of his stylistic characteristics is the spiral treatment of certain folds. The personality of a fifth master is revealed by the St Michael which is attributed to him for an agitated style of great expressiveness recalling Burgundian art. It is obvious that such a stylistic grouping is primarily based on the desire of art historians to put a gigantic ensemble in order. We should imagine not only a long period of execution, as witness the alterations made during the execution (frieze of the Passion), but also the work of a large number of sculptors who must have succeeded each other on the site with their teams. It was once thought that such a creation could only be the final outcome of the whole elaboration of Romanesque art. It is more probable to suppose that, as with the façade of Ripoll, the work begins at the moment of the plenitude of the style about the mid-twelfth century, but that the execution extends, with interruptions, to at least the end of the century. We know nothing about the time of experimentation doubtless required by the masters capable of taking over the work after the departure or death of a preceding master, nor about the circumstances in which different teams may have coexisted on the same site. We can only measure what such a large complex required in months or years of sculpture, especially if we compare it with achievements nearer to us carried out in a wholly medieval spirit, such as the sculptured programmes of Washington Cathedral and the Sagrada Familia at Barcelona.

Thus the influence of the sculpture of Saint-Gilles was exercised over a very long period during which visitors, sightseers, specialists and pilgrims, flocked from all parts to admire the miracle in the course of construction. Many were inspired by it. The artists and teams that had worked there were soon in request elsewhere. We find echoes of the fame of this work at first in Provence, Mediterranean Languedoc, and the lower valley of the Rhone (Arles, Saint-Guilhem-le-Désert, Maguelone, Beaucaire, Saint-Barnard of Romans, Valence), then in Italy (*pontile* of Modena, Antelami), in Sicily, in the Iberian peninsula and even in the Rhineland. So we see that the chronology of Saint-Gilles depends largely on the view we hold of European sculpture in the late twelfth century.

In the neighbouring town of Arles, a second great worksite was in operation. The west portal of Saint-Trophime, set against the façade, exhibits a structure close to that of Saint-Gilles, but reduced to a single door. Again we find a composition with architraves and frieze, and the principle of a colonnade embellished with statues. Several styles can be detected here, but the whole gives the impression of having been executed in a short time. The artist who carved the statue of St Paul seems to have received inspiration from the central portal of Saint-Gilles, with a treatment of tight, narrow pleats which fall stiffly in a very realistic rendering. We find his hand again in certain figures on the tympanum. At the time when the portal was completed (about 1190), the Romanesque cloister walk had been in place for less than a decade; there again one detects, through the general antiquizing tendency, the presence of sculptors from Saint-Gilles, although other hands enrich the work with a new expressiveness. The St Paul holding a phylactery on the northeast pillar of the cloister sums up the styles by the fine, deeply incised treatment of folds which hang down far below the elbows; it has been compared with the St John and St Paul of the central portal at Saint-Gilles. The influence of Arles is impressive in its turn (Montmajour, Avignon) and, in many cases, we can no longer individualize it in relation to that of Saint-Gilles, especially as far as more distant works (Catalonia, southern Italy, the Holy Land) are concerned.

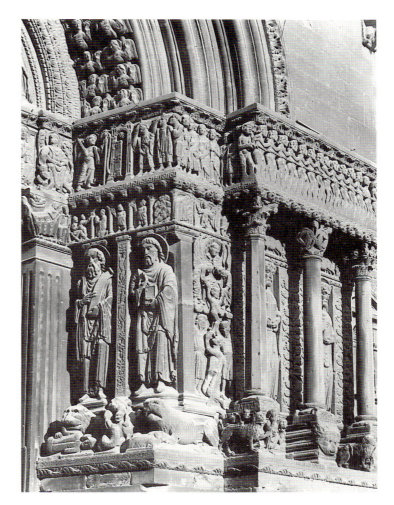

Detail of the west portal.
1180-1190.
Saint-Trophime, Arles.

Tympanum and lintel,
right-hand portal
of the façade.
Second half of
the 12th century.
Saint-Gilles-du-Gard.

ANTELAMI OR THE NEW MANNERS

Antelamian relief: personification of the month of November and zodiac sign of Sagittarius.
About 1200.
Baptistery, Parma.

Romanesque sculpture was at the height of its vitality during the last third of the twelfth and even at the beginning of the thirteenth century, with a sophisticated, varied, studied style which welcomed the first breakthroughs of Gothic art in places, but did not systematically try to take up the challenge of the early sculpture of the new art. The quest for new paths began about 1180 by the adoption of a position vis-à-vis the antique, a detailed observation of the precious arts and illumination, and by the appearance of strong personalities. Among them, Benedetto Antelami is perhaps the sculptor whose fame has lasted longest or at least the one who has caused the keenest controversies among art historians when it comes to attributing works to him. Apart from him, the *pontile* or rood screen of Modena Cathedral shows, with the statues of Adam and Eve on the portal of Lodi Cathedral, the state of the elaboration of the style, the appearance of an expressive naturalism which seeks to master the contours of the form. These works reflect some knowledge of the first Gothic sculpture, combined with a firm rejection of its acquired experience, and point to contacts with the Provençal sculpture of Arles. For a better understanding of the state of sculptured production at the time when Antelami's powerful personality emerged, we must remember that many of the works we have already mentioned in Tuscany and southern Italy were contemporary with the master's activity, whereas the creations of the Roman marble masons mostly come after it. Nevertheless, the quality of Antelami's style makes him an artist without compare between Romanesque and Gothic art. In 1178 he signed the Descent from the Cross in Parma Cathedral with the long inscription already mentioned, which occupies a whole line immediately above the scene depicted, on either side of the upright of the cross. Meticulous care presided over the wording of the inscription, in the fashion of Leonine verse, and its engraving; the letters are large and clear enough to be still legible from a certain distance, and the beauty of the lettering contributes to the decorative effect of the whole. The majestic composition of the scene with figures arranged in a frieze and the rendering of the drapery in tight narrow pleats define the master's style in the first of his documented works. A second inscription engraved on the north portal of the Parma baptistery, also elegant and well set off, gives the date 1196 for the beginning of the work, and the already mentioned signature of the sculptor: Benedictus. In this case, he would have directed the decoration work on the monument, the word *opus* referring not only to the nearby sculptures, but to the building itself. We know that the building was already used for baptising on 9 April 1216 (Easter Saturday), which leaves barely twenty years for the considerable works of architecture and sculpture of the lower parts of the monument (after an interruption, work was resumed in 1281). It has been observed that all the inscriptions accompanying the sculptured parts of the exterior of the baptistery were the work of a single hand at the beginning of the thirteenth century: three tympana (Epiphany, Last Judgment, Sun-Moon), lintels of the north portal (John the Baptist) and the south portal (Agnus Dei and John the Baptist), archivolts of the north (prophets) and west (apostles Andrew and Peter) portals, engaged piers of the south portal, etc. The sculptured ensemble is a large one. The architectural design of the building is that of an octagonal tower with an interior elevation on three levels, covered with a ribbed dome; the thickness of the basement is lightened in the interior by niches and pierced by three portals. Study of the architecture reveals a section in the antique tradition and borrowings from northern Gothic, which partly corresponds to Benedetto Antelami's way of approaching sculpture. There remains the polemical problem of unsigned works attributed to the master or his entourage, especially the façade sculpture of Fidenza Cathedral, a mixed group including statues of the prophets which have been particularly subject to scrutiny by the critics. The influence of Antelami's latest style is observed at Mantua and Vercelli, in the reliefs of the Months in Ferrara Cathedral and even the central portal of St Mark's, Venice, at the end of the first quarter of the thirteenth century. Inevitably it has been suggested that the baptistery inscription might refer to another sculptor with the same name of *Benedictus*, but in reply it could be objected that as the inscription was engraved long after the beginning of the works, the master was then celebrated enough to abbreviate his name. Moreover, stylistic analysis clearly proves that Antelami worked there with his assistants. The greatest care is mandatory with regard to the multitude of works all round the Mediterranean attributed to Antelami's influence, for they merely testify to the advance of stylistic formulas which made themselves felt during the last decade of the twelfth century, in which Antelami also took part, though undoubtedly with more genius than the others.

Statue and reliefs whose attribution to Antelami remains controversial.
Detail of the façade. Early 13th century.
Cathedral of Fidenza.

Benedetto Antelami.
Descent from the Cross. Signed and dated 1178.
Parma Cathedral.

Capitals in the Seu Vella.
First quarter of the 13th century.
Old cathedral of Lleida.

The Musée Calvet at Avignon houses a relief in white veined marble representing two half-naked figures facing each other, treated in a singular style and portraying the Twins. It can be compared with the illustration of Aquarius preserved in the Museum of Lyons. For a long time specialists wrongly attributed these slabs to Antiquity. They come from a group at Nîmes dating from the first quarter of the thirteenth century and have much to tell us about the evolution of Romanesque sculpture after Saint-Gilles, Arles and the work of Antelami. We observe the variety of replies given to the same problematics in the upper walk of the cloister of Saint-Guilhem-le-Désert, on the Roussillon tombs signed by Raymond de Bianya, one of which is dated to shortly after 1200, as well as in the south walk of the Elne cloister and in the extant sculptures from the portal of the collegiate church of Saint-Jean-Baptiste at Perpignan. Incidentally, Raymond de Bianya's style testifies to researches parallel to those

SOUTHERN ECLECTICISM IN THE 1200s

Annunciation from the church of the Cordeliers, Toulouse.
About 1200.
Musée des Augustins, Toulouse.

Confronted with the appeal of Gothic and the peak reached by Provençal and Sicilian works, and those by such masters as Cabestany and Antelami, renewal seemed difficult to those who refused to adhere to the new style. Nevertheless, a very late Romanesque sculpture, contemporary with Gothic creations and which we have already met on several occasions in our survey, did exist from Italy to Galicia. It proposes eclectic solutions, but among other permanent characteristics possesses a renewed penchant for certain aspects of the art of Late Antiquity and the resumption of artistic exchanges with distant parts. As early as the 1180s, the northern fashion of a portal with column statues was introduced in the cloister of the Benedictine priory of La Daurade at Toulouse, although the local tradition exemplified by the portal of the chapter house of the cathedral of Saint-Etienne seems to prevail over the novelties represented by the Gothic column figures. Cloister art also experienced a new burst of vitality in certain corner capitals from La Daurade now in the Musée des Augustins at Toulouse, but especially in the series of historiated Catalan cloisters at Sant Cugat del Vallés and Tarragona. In Languedoc, the group of the Annunciation which probably came from Les Cordeliers at Toulouse crowns this development. On the one hand, the idea of placing these statues on a portal shows that much attention was paid to the northern novelties, but the style still depends on the local tradition of Gilabertus, while fitting into the antiquizing trend and into an interplay of what were once again very close exchanges with northern Spain (San Vicente at Avila, La Guardia). Among the examples which crown this last creative impulse in southwestern France, we find Saint-Bertrand-de-Comminges and Valcabrère, Saint-Caprais at Agen, Mimizan, as well as the beautiful series of capitals with heads in the Bordelais. But they are only minor isolated examples compared with what was developing in Mediterranean Languedoc and on the other side of the Pyrenees.

demonstrated by Antelami's works at Parma. The beautifully fashioned early sculptures of the "old" cathedral of Lleida (Lérida) are not anterior to the second decade of the thirteenth century. The new canons which are proposed, with full volumes, firm modelling and monumental proportions, prompt us once again to refer to the chronological and stylistic landmark of Antelami's sculpture. The altar frontal of about 1220 in Tarragona Cathedral illustrates the connection with the masters of Lleida (Virgin Annunciate); its style is further reflected in the sculpture on the south side of the Tarragona cloister, where one also detects echoes of Antiquity, contemporary Italy and Languedoc.

In the more western regions of the Iberian peninsula sculptors tried to overcome the exhaustion of the style by a similar research. Sangüesa, Carrión de los Condes and Avila put forward formulas receptive to Gothic novelties in varying degrees. At Santiago de Compostela, Master

Annunciation on a cloister pillar.
About 1200.
San Domingo, Silos.

Annunciation on the south portal.
Shortly after 1200.
San Vicente, Avila.

Mateo directs the worksite of the Porch of the Glory during the last decade of the century, but we assign a quite special importance to this work which will have its due place when we come to deal with the early Gothic experiments. The transition to the new formulas appears in the more or less contemporary apostle statues of the Cámara Santa at Oviedo and the tomb of St Vincent at Avila. These works mark a turning point. In the cloister of the monastery of Silos, the most recent sculptures executed around 1200, as well as the rediscovered elements of the north porch of the church, show, if we compare them with the relief of Doubting Thomas from the first half of the twelfth century, how difficult it is to describe them as still Romanesque. The Annunciation relief occupying one side of the pillars depicts a Virgin in Majesty crowned by two soaring angels; she receives, by way of annunciation, the homage of an angel kneeling at her feet. Like the relief of the Tree of Jesse, it presents an elegance in the supple handling of the drapery and an aesthetic which can already be considered as Gothic, in spite of the lingering influence of the Romanesque tradition.

103

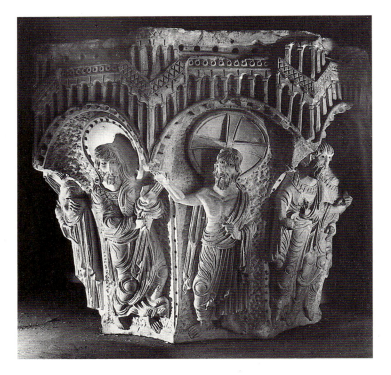

Christ and doubting Thomas
from the cathedral of Nazareth.
Third quarter of the 12th century.
Museum of the Greek Orthodox Patriarchate, Jerusalem.

Capital with the temptations of Christ
from the cathedral of Nazareth.
Third quarter of the 12th century.
Museum of the Greek Orthodox Patriarchate, Jerusalem.

THE SCULPTURE OF THE CRUSADES

The Latin kingdom of Jerusalem born of the First Crusade in 1099 lived through two eventful centuries until 1291. Four Christian states then shared the East: the countship of Edessa, the principality of Antioch, the countship of Tripoli and the kingdom of Jerusalem proper. A vast amount of construction is known to have gone on there, with the large-scale use of sculptured decoration which, with the scholarly research of recent years, has become one of the most exciting and innovative subjects of Romanesque and Gothic art. Building on Western techniques and styles, Crusader sculpture produced an individual artistic culture of such quality and power that it was exported in its turn. In the course of two centuries, several generations contributed to endowing the Holy Land with a Western culture. One of its essential qualities arose from the rich local substratum and the strong tradition of Syro-Byzantine sculpture which supplied models for sculptors and earlier remains suitable for re-use. In 1125 Foucher of Chartres refers to the new colonists who, leaving Reims and Chartres, became citizens of Tyre and Antioch, married Syrian or Saracen women, and were then joined by other members of their family, avid for the new wealth which this land of the East offered so generously. Both architecture and sculpture were then imported from France. With the restoration of the Holy Sepulchre at Jerusalem, which was consecrated in 1149, we have a chronological reference point to help us to date the marble lintels adorned respectively with scenes from the life of Christ and a very fine foliated scroll containing figures.

But the richest sculpture comes later. Discoveries in the esplanade of the temple and in the quarter of the Holy Sepulchre now help to give us a better grasp of the style of the years 1170-1180 by way of the fragments which decorated the tomb of Baldwin V (1185-1186), the church of St John the Hospitaller, the church of St Anne, etc. A Provençal stylistic trend combines with certain basic Burgundian traits, for example in the plant elements which frame the figures and in the treatment of bodies. The rediscovered sculptures from the church of the Annunciation at Nazareth have made possible a trial reconstruction of the trumeau-tympanum group. Essentially we know of five capitals carved in white limestone on the theme of the Mission of the Apostles. Their date probably falls in the third quarter of the twelfth century. A large fragment of the tympanum is close to the style of certain Burgundian tympana (Saint-Julien-de-Jonzy). Thus, even if our conclusions remain tentative, the circulation of artists and their output must first be seen as going from France to the Holy Land thanks to the movements of artists mainly coming from Provence, but among whom sculptors from the Rhone valley, Burgundy, Nivernais, Berry, the Poitou-Charentes region and possibly even Toulouse are found in the twelfth century. Their contributions are successive and are superposed on the local substratum and on an autonomous development which in its turn becomes sufficiently esteemed to export its output and its artists to southern Italy, regardless of the religious and political motives (fall of Jerusalem?).

▷ Figures from the Old Testament.
West front, central portal.
1145-1155.
Chartres Cathedral.

THE EXPANSION OF GOTHIC

(1150-1280)

by Xavier Barral i Altet

INTRODUCTION

The twelfth-century sculptures that can be accurately dated are few in number. It is likely, however, that the sculptors finished their work in the narthex of the abbey church of Vézelay and on the Royal Portal at Chartres at approximately the same time. Art historians classify Vézelay as Romanesque and Chartres as Gothic, the reason being that they relate them to their formal characteristics, not to the chronology. Now the evolution of these characteristics took place less abruptly in sculpture than in architecture. The faces on the tympanum at Autun, several years earlier than that at Vézelay and also classified as Romanesque, already adumbrate the features which the faces at Chartres were to have. It was the emplacement and functions assigned to sculpture, much more clearly than its forms, which changed between 1120 and 1150.

This change was the result of several combined modifications, firstly the restoration of order to the ecclesiastical institution. From the monasteries, moral reform had reached the senior clergy. When the process of purging the morals of the episcopal personnel, begun in the mid-eleventh century under the direction of the Bishop of Rome, achieved its goal seventy years later (it was at the very moment when large-scale monastic sculpture was flourishing), the Pope, who was not a former monk like his predecessors, but an archbishop, was able to re-establish the primitive hierarchies, reduce the pretensions of the monastic communities and again place them under the control of the diocesan bishops. This transfer of authority was decisive, because the leaders of the Church again had all the resources of artistic creation in their hands. The secular clergy took the lead from the regular clergy in this and other fields.

Other transformations affecting the material bases of culture came into play. Since late Roman times, the bishops had had their sees in a city. The extension of their power was inseparable from the revival of the towns, from that profound movement which caused a virtual return to antique structures during the twelfth century. Drawing new forces from the continuous development of rural production, the cities gradually spread beyond the lowlands, their populations increased and they grew rich because their markets were the scene of trading in the increasing surpluses from agriculture, viticulture and stock breeding. By the end of the twelfth century they dominated the low-lying countrysides where they had nearly foundered during the early Middle Ages. Thenceforth the town was a power. The princes reckoned with it; through it they controlled the surrounding country; from it they collected the money they needed more and more. For that was where money abounded, in other words the means to rebuild, to decorate, to engage sculptors. From the twelfth century onwards in Europe, the great building sites, the avant-garde workshops, the centres of research and innovation, never left the towns.

I have said that monumental sculpture was re-established in places whose role corresponded to that played by the forum in the past. In the monastery, that ideal city, it was the basilica and the cloister. In the real and reinvigorated city, it was not the main square where the merchants met, for the main urban function was political, not economic. It was the cathedral and its annexes, because the word was uttered from the heights of the pulpit, as it was from the heights of the tribune in antiquity, the word that judged, corrected, exhorted. The cathedral was the mother church of the city, but also of the bishop and chapter, of the attendant community of canons, and it was their mission to guide the people by the word. A mission which then seemed vital.

The general progress which awoke the towns from their lethargy strengthened the idea that the Christian could not delegate the task of his salvation to others, that he must save himself by making his actions conform to the precepts of the Gospel. As he became conscious of this necessity, he questioned the semi-magical mission of intercession the monks had allotted themselves; and the education of the faithful was seen to be necessary if they were to be responsible for themselves and not to be caught passively, like nocturnal insects, by the shimmering flame of a paradise glimpsed on the threshold of miraculous sanctuaries. In the Cluniac order, the monks, to tell the truth, cared little about teaching the people. They muttered the text of the Scriptures among themselves. They contemplated. The teaching task was the responsibility of the clerks, men who did not turn their backs on the world, but on the contrary plunged into it to save it from sin. The bishop's duty was to train the men who assisted his pastoral function in this ministry, to develop the school attached to the cathedral where the art of discourse was perfected by exercises in grammar, rhetoric and dialectic. Nevertheless, before the bishop adapted himself to becoming fully accessible to the common people, the image seemed to be the most effective instrument of education. The monks had used sculpture as a bait. Under the control of the chapter and its wisest members, it became the mainstay of a systematic method of teaching. To that end it became more legible. It abandoned the walls of the abbeys to cover the walls of the cathedral.

The monasteries were still felt to be indispensable in the twelfth century, but they were supposed to be at the service of the priests, helping preachers to flesh out their sermons with the fruits of a meditation pursued in renunciation, solitude and silence. The new monastic congregations which then spread throughout Europe, founded, like Cîteaux, on a strict interpretation of the rule of St Benedict, or, like La Chartreuse, on the example of the eastern anchorites, fulfilled this function submissively. Islands of perfection, springs welling up with spiritual values, their houses increasingly withdrew, establishing themselves in the wilderness, in forests and precipitous places. Denouncing the pomp which was still displayed at Saint-Denis in 1140, they were stripped of all ornamentation. It was logical for sculptures to disappear from the façades of their churches, since the latter, in total isolation, no longer had portals in the true sense of the word. They were entered through narrow doors by the monks and lay brothers returning from work in the fields. Sculptures were also banished from cloister and sanctuary where the images seemed not only superfluous but above all troubling, seducing the soul from the bare path which gradually leads to the encounter with God.

The bishop and his canons personally professed abstinence, forbidding themselves to yield to the seductions of the flesh. So the interior of the cathedral adopted the austerity of Cistercian buildings. No sculpted figures on the inside walls, not even on the pier capitals, whose decoration, when not abstract, was limited to a few variations on plant themes. Nevertheless, the great churches welcomed in the people of the diocese whom they had to instruct through wide portals. So some sculpture was allowed in the churches, but sparingly, confined around the central point from which the exhortation was launched and towards which the public was supposed to turn its attention, namely the pulpit. It was also allowed on the walls of the closure surrounding the choir where the chapter shut themselves in for the office and on that sort of iconostasis, the rood screen. It was outside that sculptured work flourished freely, so that by its attraction, profusion and complexity of signs, it succeeded, standing permanently in full view of the passers-by, in striking and intriguing the stolidest and most indifferent people and thus propagating the message from the centre of the city to the depths of the popular masses.

The pedagogic purpose justified the sumptuousness of this decoration. It was not pride which, to enhance its brilliance, led to such expenditure, to the frustration of the poor, replied the Bishop of Paris in 1180 to his detractors, the rigid moralists, but the aim of strengthening pastoral action. An excessive amplification of the portal of the Romanesque basilica, cathedral porches spread out in the thirteenth century, displaying to the West, North and South, as if on vast platforms, the combined elements of a visual demonstration of what the Christian ought to believe. In the background, on columns, arch mouldings and uprights, they offered the viewer a compendium of the knowledge which was steadily being widened in the schools, an encyclopedia, a whole explanation of the world. In this decoration, actors were distributed in a series of tableaux. They had to be persuasive so that their presence was felt and everyone could identify them by their costumes and emblems. The statues stood out from the wall; they came to life. Their bodies were inflected beneath their draperies and the scholars who directed the sculptors' work insisted that they impart the pulsation of life to the eyelids, the lips, and those faces which were mute, but still eager to bring the Word.

In this preoccupation with achieving truth to life, the progress of monumental sculpture fitted in with that of scholarly thought. Sustained by the tales of the Crusades which brought back from the Holy Land the memory of the places where Jesus had lived, supported by the ever firmer belief that religious experience is that of one person advancing towards another, and by the conviction, reinforced by the briskness of economic growth, that what is related to things material is not wholly bad, that man was urged by the Creator to make the most of the Garden of Eden, to associate himself with Him in the continuous act which is creation, the reflection of theologians was concentrated on God's humanity. Thus sculptors were encouraged to remove the image of Christ from the nimbus with which Romanesque sculptors had surrounded him to express his transcendency, to represent him among men, in the same attitudes, in the same proportions, as part of the long line of men of which he was the descendant, among that group of men, his friends, who had accompanied him on earth. They were also encouraged to depict him in the guise of a master or a doctor, book in hand, in this aspect confirming that he was brother to the bishop and canons, but also brother to all men, and sufficiently close to the faithful for them to feel capable of following him as his disciples had followed him. And yet distant, living, but not of this world, separated from everyday life, as indeed were the minor actors in the scenes, by an invisible partition, by that indefinite distance from which emanates the fascination sometimes exercised by the theatre through the wealth of means at its disposal.

The close union between sculpture and school emerged with absolute clarity at precisely this point, the union between the sculptor's workshop and that other workshop, close by, where the clerks pored over the sacred texts and scrutinized nature in search of its rhythms and laws. These investigators sought lucidity, taking great pains to eliminate chimeras, hewing a way through obscurity and clearing away the undergrowth. With the help of the light of reason, with their eyes about them, they explored the universe, intent on discovering beneath the accidental, the disordered, the perishable, beyond the deceptiveness of appearances, the original thread, the master plan, the simple framework of beings and things as the divine spirit had conceived them for eternity in their purity and harmony. The churchmen imposed the same approach on the sculptors of Chartres, Reims, Amiens, Paris and Bourges. That is why statuary achieved for a brief moment in the early decades of the thirteenth century such an admirable and fragile equilibrium between realism and abstraction, between nature and the supernatural.

▷ The Gothic Cathedral of Chartres in the heart of the town.

SCULPTURE AND ARCHITECTURE

THE CATHEDRAL IN THE TOWN

In the Gothic period, the cathedral dominated the town not only by its lofty silhouette, but also through its religious, economic and political influence. The cathedral is the monument which in itself goes to define what we call Gothic art. This term, given prominence by the Romantics, was applied to the new style that originated in the Ile-de-France and flourished first in northern France, spreading to the neighbouring lands during the second half of the twelfth century and the two following centuries. Monumentally speaking, the sculpture of the period of Gothic expansion was primarily conceived for the embellishment of cathedrals.

The interest that nineteenth-century Frenchmen showed in the study of Gothic cathedrals had dual roots in ideology and architectural technology. They saw in the cathedral and its decoration the symbol of a communal organization, of a secular spirit which had taken precedence over monasticism and feudalism. But, while neo-Gothic tendencies in architecture became very popular throughout Europe from the end of the eighteenth century, Viollet-le-Duc embarked on the study of the architectural structure, without which, as far as he was concerned, there could be no form in Gothic art: for him it was a dynamic system based on the interplay of thrusts

and the study of the ribbed vault. Since then, many other approaches to the interpretation of the Gothic cathedral have been suggested–formal, symbolic and technical. Illustration of the Heavenly Jerusalem, image of Paradise, echo of scholastic philosophy, monumental embodiment of the postulate that God is light, the cathedral has been the subject of many attempts at a global interpretation.

The cathedral was an urban monument whose rise went hand in hand with the revival of the episcopate and the expansion of the town. Benefiting to some extent by the increasingly obvious decline of the monastic orders during the thirteenth century, the bishops played an important part in a spiritual reform in which the mendicant orders also shared. The Fourth Lateran Council, which in 1215 codified the new religious obligations of the faithful, while raising their minimal requirements, contributed to the increase in secular piety. Around the bishop, the canons lived in a quarter near the cathedral in individual houses which reduced community life to a strict minimum. These chapters, which offered openings to the upper classes of the population, provided work for many town-dwellers. The cathedral, in its capacity of episcopal see, was also a centre of culture for it housed within its perimeter the episcopal school, which sometimes became a university, as in Paris.

So to understand the amazing rise of the Gothic cathedral whose heyday falls in the half-century known in France as the age of Philip Augustus, from about 1175 to 1225, we must grasp the setting in which it arose and the phenomenon of urban expansion in which it shared. There

Leodegarius. Chartres-type column statue of the portal. Third quarter of the 12th century. Santa María la Real, Sangüesa.

Column statue probably from a cloister. Third quarter of the 12th century. Musée de la Société Archéologique, Saint-Maur-des-Fossés.

THE COLUMN STATUE: AN EXPRESSION OF THE NEW STYLE

Major Gothic sculpture was born and evolved to the rhythm of the cathedrals of which it was the external embellishment, in the same way as the precious decorations of the great Gothic shrines made by goldsmiths. Sculpture invaded the cathedral façades, being intimately wedded to their severe architecture and helping to pattern their division into storeys. The towers which stood over the side aisles enclosed the central part of the façade and rose heavenwards solidly supported by the powerful buttresses. The latter were masked at ground level by the fullness and depth given to the splayed jambs of portals, which monumental sculpture helped to lighten. The ensemble of the tympanum, the arch mouldings, the trumeau, the statues and plinths of the splaying, makes up the historiated Gothic portal. Its iconography considerably enlarged the religious content of Romanesque façades by closely associating the arch mouldings and splays with the tympanum. Among the themes carved on them, besides the Apocalypse and the Last Judgment, we find Old Testament scenes corresponding typologically with those of the New Testament. Each event from the time of the Old Covenant refers to an episode of the New Covenant. Thus Jonah's sojourn inside the whale prefigures Christ in the tomb, and Abraham sacrificing Isaac evokes the sacrifice of the Cross. Matthew, the Fathers of the Church and certain medieval theologians have set forth these typological comparisons very clearly. A large number of portals offered the faithful the example of saints' lives. The Virgin occupied a privileged place, to which we shall return later. According to the classification put forward by Emile Mâle, the ensemble corresponds to the different mirrors of Gothic Christianity: nature, and moral and historical science.

Monumental sculpture also invaded the upper parts of the Gothic façade: gables, galleries, rose windows, etc. Outside the building, flying buttresses and spurs formed aerial emplacements, almost like tabernacles, where statues were housed. In the interior, architectural sculpture may cover the mural surfaces, as on the inner façade of Reims Cathedral, but that is unusual, as are sculptured pillars like the one in Strasbourg Cathedral. On the other hand, statues very soon appeared on the pillars of choir and nave as in the Sainte-Chapelle at Paris and Cologne Cathedral. In contrast, carved capitals no longer play the iconographic role they had in the Romanesque period. The rood screen closing off the liturgical choir afforded a new sculptured wall. But the cathedral was also adorned with carved furniture, cult statues, altarpieces and tombs, whose careful arrangement made them essential elements in the general iconography. The place occupied by sculpture in the early Gothic cloisters has already been mentioned in the section on Romanesque art.

In the historiated portal of early Gothic, the most original and innovative creation is the statue carved out of the same block as the column, whose form and function it espoused. It is known as the column statue. It confers a vertical dimension on the porch and appears on the jamb, an integral part of the general programme of the portal.

was indeed a widespread increase in building, as demonstrated by town walls, like those of Paris, Reims, Troyes, Provins and Bourges, the multiplication of parishes and the construction or reconstruction of many churches, and the renewal of public and civil architecture (collective buildings, bridges, markets), as well as private architecture (houses). This growth had repercussions in the neighbouring countryside and reflected the city's new industrial and commercial roles. The cathedral worksite occupied an essential place among all this new wealth. Immense resources were needed which came from the fertile surrounding country, from gifts and alms, as well as from the increased pressure of feudal taxation on urban populations. But the worksite, too, contributed to the general economy by giving direct or indirect employment to a very large number of people.

Besides these social and economic factors, the cathedral was the centre where the essential inventions of Gothic architecture were worked out: the pointed arch, the cross-ribbed vault, the flying buttress. Treatment of the walls and openings led to a progressive enlargement of the latter which led in turn to the installation of stained glass windows that captured the light and transformed it into a transcendental expression of religious thought. But what made the monumental progress of the new style possible was primarily the new organization of the worksite, of its provision with stone and wood, and especially the standardized cutting and mounting of blocks of stone. Rational working methods affected both the project and its realization, and extended to sculpture which was put in place to keep time with work on the masonry. In this way a new bond was created between architecture and sculpture.

The earliest examples were those on the west front of the abbey church of Saint-Denis, dispersed or destroyed before the end of the eighteenth century, but fortunately known to us from the drawings reproduced by Montfaucon in his *Monuments de la monarchie française* (1729). The façade of Saint-Denis, as we shall see, had a decisive influence on the origins of Gothic art. The slender, elongated column statues, with a frozen elegance, decorated with fine, severe pleating, became the favourite theme of the sculptors of the second half of the twelfth century and grew progressively more animated. Portals, and also cloisters, were thronged with them.

Standing at the church door like the portico columns of King Solomon's temple, column statues have been the subject of different iconographic interpretations. They have variously been seen as the kings of France and biblical heroes; they have even been identified with legendary figures. Today we know that they fit into the typological iconography already mentioned. So we find column figures of prophets, patriarchs and kings: Abraham, Moses, Aaron, David, Solomon, Josiah, Elijah, Isaiah, Jeremiah, Daniel, John the Baptist, and the Queen of Sheba among the women. The importance assigned to the Old Testament kings in these iconographic programmes of northern France should be related to the progress of the monarchic institution, whose ideal portrait is the representation of Solomon. His judgment was interpreted in the Middle Ages as the image of the divine judgment between Church and Synagogue. The wisdom of Solomon attracted the Queen of Sheba, who stands for the Church. There are many iconographic variations between portals which portray Old Testament figures exclusively and those where the presence of Peter and Paul, who traditionally flank the door, confirms the connections between the two Testaments. The portals in which column statues fit into the framework of the iconography of the Virgin belong to a separate category. But when studying the disposition of column statues in cathedrals we should not forget that they have sometimes been moved from their original position; even in the Middle Ages the master masons had a tendency to move and reuse sculptured works at will (as in the St Anne portal at Notre-Dame in Paris, in the transepts at Bourges, in the north transept of Saint-Denis).

Splaying of the central and north portals of the west front (the present state shows some reordering). 1145-1155. Chartres Cathedral.

111

SAINT-DENIS, CHARTRES, PARIS: ORIGINS OF GOTHIC SCULPTURE

The Gothic style did not make its appearance in a cathedral, but in the abbey church of Saint-Denis, a showplace of French history for it had housed the tombs of French kings since the early Middle Ages. Its reconstruction was the work of Abbot Suger (1122-1151), whose religious and political role measured up to the ambitions he cherished for his abbey. Suger has left us several writings which testify to the planning of his undertaking and the constant attention he devoted to the architectural and decorative work. His *De consecratione* and *De administratione* are full of spiritual, financial and artistic information. The first deals with the abbey church's two consecrations; the west section was consecrated on 9 June 1140 and the apse with radiating chapels and crypt on 11 June 1144. In 1145, the monks of Saint-Denis assembled in chapter asked the abbot to write the second document, which is a report on his administration. According to Suger's own words, his great artistic enterprises were the consequence of his policy aimed at financial recovery "both by the acquisition of new domains, the recuperation of rights fallen into disuse, all the progress made in exploiting land, and by reconstruction campaigns and the addition to the treasury of goldsmith's works set off with precious stones and sumptuous fabrics."

Work on the new abbey church destined to replace the Carolingian monument began with the construction of a massive west vault connected to the Carolingian nave by two bays; then work continued eastwards between 1140 and 1144. The two blocks were to have been connected by a nave which Suger did not begin until shortly before his death. These two extremities of an unfinished building proved decisive for the advent of a new style which is

Central portal
of the west front
as restored in
the 19th century.
Before 1140.
Basilica of Saint-Denis.

Detail of the jamb shaft, right portal of the west front.
The Labours of the Months. Before 1140.
Basilica of Saint-Denis.

apparent in the architecture, sculpture and stained glass windows. For our purposes, it is the façade erected by Suger and already completed in 1140 (on which he had himself depicted kneeling at the feet of the Christ on the central tympanum) which represents an essential milestone in early Gothic sculpture. Three portals, with splays adorned with eight column statues on the central portal and six on each of the side portals representing Old Testament figures, comprised sculptured tympana, arch mouldings and jamb shafts. The column statues of Saint-Denis symbolized the *imperium* (the three French dynasties) in the guise of the *sacerdotium* (kings, high priests and prophets of Israel), an interpretation confirmed by Suger when, as Regent of France during the Second Crusade, he convoked the peers, archbishops and bishops at Soissons in 1149 in the name of "the indissoluble unity of the *regnum* and the *sacerdotium*." The central portal was organized around the Last Judgment on the tympanum and the arch mouldings, and also comprised the Elders of the Apocalypse and the Wise and Foolish Virgins. The leaves of the door presented Passion scenes and a statue of St Denis occupied the trumeau. The righthand portal was devoted to the legend of St Denis and his companions, and thus inaugurated the series of Gothic tympana devoted to the history of the church's patron saint. The engaged piers displayed a calendar, whose counterpart is on the engaged piers of the lefthand portal representing the signs of the zodiac. The tympanum of this portal was adorned with a mosaic (an unusual technique in France at this period) portraying a theme of the Virgin, to which the archivolts and column statues were also devoted (royal ancestors of the Virgin).

Today the façade sculptures of Saint-Denis are not preserved in their entirety. We have already mentioned the dispersal of the column statues, although we are fortunate enough to know them quite well from the drawings published in Montfaucon's book of 1729. What remained of the sculptured façade was heavily restored by the team of the sculptor Brun under the direction of François Debret (1839-1840). This restoration has never really been understood and since its completion has been the subject of criticisms as violent as that of A.-N. Didron who, in 1846, condemned "the disfigured façade, deprived for ever of historical interest and very ugly into the bargain." Emile Mâle made no mistake when, looking beyond the restorations, he detected many surviving original features. Since then, air pollution has helped to give the whole a misleading appearance of unity. Current scholarship has made it possible to discern what is old and what is modern in the central portal, and Sumner McKnight Crosby has proved that many more authentic stones remain than was formerly believed. Moreover, heads from the column statues continue to be identified thanks to the preparatory drawings made for Montfaucon's engravings. Until recently, four heads were known: two in the Walters Art Gallery, Baltimore, one in the Fogg Art Museum, Cambridge, Massachusetts, and the fourth is the head of a queen in the Musée de Cluny in Paris. A fifth, representing Moses, has recently increased the number and has fortunately been acquired by the last-named museum.

The problem of the style of the sculptures on the west front of Saint-Denis is a highly controversial one. Certain features, such as the months of the year and the signs of the zodiac on the jamb shafts and the whole ornamental repertory surrounding them, are still firmly bound up with Romanesque art. Moreover, Suger seems to have been aware of this influence from the past when he described the tympanum mosaic as "out of date." The essential novelty lies in the column statues, the decoration of the arch mouldings and certain basic stylistic features (calmer style,

Column statues of the west front
of the basilica of Saint-Denis (before 1140),
after Bernard de Montfaucon, 1729.

113

relief composed of independent volumes) of the older parts of the central tympanum. Henceforth the problem of the style of the column statues can be better understood with the help of the heads still preserved. After Wilhelm Vöge's study at the end of the nineteenth century, the view persisted that the sculptors of Saint-Denis had been schooled at Toulouse and Moissac. Today scholars look exclusively northwards, because the best elements for comparison are in northern France, in the capitals of Saint-Etienne at Dreux, for example, or in the more international milieu of goldsmiths and metal craftsmen.

The second essential monument for the rise of the Gothic style in sculpture is the much better preserved set of three west portals (Royal Portal) at Chartres. The twenty-four column statues originally existing there are probably the most famous works in the whole of Gothic sculpture. They have undergone various attempts at restoration from the plaster casts made by Lassus in 1840 and the removal of two statues in 1961 to the treatment of the stone *in situ* carried out from 1979 to 1983. A fire in 1134

was the point of departure for the idea of the cathedral's reconstruction. At first the works were focused on the north tower; then they spread to the whole west front, the portals being executed between 1145 and 1155. The façade as a whole should be understood in relation to the existence of the preceding building; it was largely responsible for the high narrow proportions that prevail. The design with three portals included statues on the splaying (nineteen of them are extant) representing Old Testament kings, queens and patriarchs, and historiated capitals forming a cycle devoted to the childhood and life of Christ, which begins, to the left of the central portal, with the story of the birth and childhood of Mary according to the Proto-Gospel of James. The enigmatic signature of the sculptor Rogerus appears on one of the pilasters adorned with figures in high relief beneath the frieze of the Last Supper. The three tympana are decorated as follows: south side, the Virgin in Majesty flanked by angels surmounting a double lintel with the boyhood of Christ, with the Liberal Arts on the arch mouldings; north side, the Ascension in

Tympanum with Christ in Majesty, on the lintel the standing apostles, on the arch moulding the Elders of the Apocalypse and angels. Central portal of the west front. 1145-1155. Chartres Cathedral.

Virgin in Majesty, double lintel with Childhood of Christ,
Liberal Arts on the arch mouldings.
Right portal, west front. 1145-1155.
Chartres Cathedral.

Tympanum dedicated to the Virgin and the Childhood of Christ,
with later additions.
Portal of St Anne. 1140/45-1150.
Notre-Dame, Paris.

a three-tiered composition, including the seated apostles in
its lower part; in the centre, Christ in Majesty surrounded
by the four Beasts and the twenty-four Elders of the Apocalypse on the arch mouldings, and the standing apostles
on the lintel. It is a programme of great breadth and
coherence, but its style betrays the hand of several artists.
Art historians have picked out the sculptor of the central
tympanum to define the predominant style. However, the
different types of drapery folds, the treatment of faces and
the proportions of the figures enable us to distinguish
several different artists. To the monumentality of the principal master are opposed the dry linear folds of the maker
of the exterior column statues, while a third artist is characterized by proportions that are perhaps more archaic,
broad and thickset. The problem of the origins of all these
works and the schooling of the sculptors is still very much
under discussion. Great emphasis has been laid on the role
of Burgundy, Autun, Vézelay and La Charité-sur-Loire,
while the creative ferment of the arts in the Ile-de-France
may have been underestimated, since that area alone could
have provided a synthesis of the best outside currents in the
creation of the style. Today it is no longer thought that
Provence could have played any sort of role in this elaboration; in contrast, the masters of Saint-Denis, the royal
statues of Saint-Remi at Reims and above all the Parisian
creations proper (Saint-Martin-des-Champs, Sainte-
Geneviève, Saint-Germain-des-Prés) restake their claim.

This reassessment was initiated by the cleaning of the
portal of St Anne at Notre-Dame in Paris which, until
about twenty years ago, had been dated too late and was
misunderstood in consequence. This south portal of the
present-day west front, which should really be called the
Portal of the Virgin, is a work from the years 1140/45-1150
designed for the church preceding Maurice de Sully's
cathedral (c. 1160), then put back in place with numerous

Façade restored from 1853.
About 1195-1205 for the portals.
Cathedral of Laon.

115

Tympanum from Saint-Bénigne of Dijon. About 1150.
Musée Archéologique, Dijon.

additions on the new façade begun in 1210. For this operation, the builders proceeded not only to add some necessary elements, but also to recarve others, such as the St Paul discovered in 1977 with numerous fragments which added their testimony to the observations made when the façade was cleaned in 1969. Then what scholars had begun to divine became factual evidence on the occasion of the "de-restoration" of the only trumeau preserved from the first great Gothic portals, the St Marcellus in the Musée de Cluny which was removed from the centre of the portal of St Anne in 1857 by Geoffroy Dechaume. The tight pleats with their supple movement and the high plastic quality of the St Marcellus (headless today) entitle this portal to a place of the highest order in early Gothic sculpture between Romanesque (lintel) and contacts with Chartres (Virgin). Here a new problem is posed, that of the existence of a project for the reconstruction of a cathedral anterior to the present one and in which Suger himself was interested enough to donate to it a stained glass window devoted to the Virgin before his death.

Give or take a few years, the portals of Saint-Denis (the oldest), Paris and Chartres are contemporary. Around them gravitate some ensembles with column statues, notably the south portal of the collegiate church of Etampes; the style of its sculptures, with their recently recovered polychromy, is close to the two outside statues of the left splaying of the left portal of Chartres, to those of Saint-Bénigne at Dijon for which a redating to before 1150 has been suggested, to the south portal of Le Mans Cathedral (a portal possibly antedating Chartres, some now think), and to the column statues in the cloister of Saint-Denis which mark the art of the first two decades of the second half of the twelfth century. During these years 1150-1170 Gothic sculpture followed multiple paths naturally marked by the rapid diffusion of portals with column statues; their variety vouches for the existence of many different workshops. In certain cases, the style is shaped in relation to Chartres, as in Notre-Dame at Corbeil; in others, as in La Madeleine at Châteaudun a little earlier, the style of the Paris Basin merges with the diffusion of late Romanesque from western France. Among the many new creations, special mention should be made of the west portal of Saint-Germain-des-Prés in Paris, the west portal of Angers Cathedral, that of Saint-Loup-de-Naud, the side portals of Bourges Cathedral, then the door of the north transept of Saint-Denis (c. 1170–1175) and the façades of Senlis and Mantes (1170-1180). Reciprocal influences between the greater and lesser ensembles cannot be singled out here; the list would be wearisome, for comparisons such as those linking Corbeil to the rediscovered fragments of Nesle-la-Reposte belong to the very specialized field of the diffusion of the style in a region which saw profound changes during the second half of the twelfth century. The example most brilliantly restored to prominence recently is that of the cloister of Notre-Dame-en-Vaux at Châlons-sur-Marne whose fifty odd rediscovered column statues testify to the stylistic diversity of the years 1170-1180, the complexity of relations between artists from one monument to another (the relations between Senlis and Mantes, for example) and of joint work on a single site by several masters (five principals have been identified at Châlons) who, while sharing the concerns of their age, interpreted artistic tendencies in terms of the technical practices and stylistic features born of their different schooling.

Column statues from the cloister (demolished in 1759).
Apostle and Bishop. About 1170-1180.
Notre-Dame-en-Vaux, Châlons-sur-Marne.

THE TYMPANUM OF SENLIS AND THE NEW MARIAN CULT

During the twelfth century the Virgin Mary progressively acquired a privileged place in Western iconography, both in monumental sculpture and church furniture. Not that she had been ignored before, but for various reasons connected with the veneration in which eminent prelates held her on the one hand and the new inclusion of feminine values in society on the other, the Virgin Mary became more present in Western piety. We have already seen the place her figure held in Romanesque iconography and how, often through the intermediary of the Epiphany, she won access to apses and portals, the sites traditionally reserved for theophanies of Christ. As the Mother of God, or through her Son, she began to take a monumental place and play an intercessory role. Her cult, which was spread far wider in the East than the West, grew rapidly and the Virgin was present in everyday piety and the collective imagination, supported by the sermons of a Fulbert of Chartres, by the hymns and writings of Peter the Venerable and Bernard of Clairvaux, by the poems of Gautier of Coincy.

In the monumental iconography of the Virgin, western sculptured façades retained different themes, among which dominated the representation of Mary, seat of wisdom, shown frontally, holding the Child, associated with the Three Kings, or depicted in the centre of the apse or the tympanum surrounded by a few favoured personages. Apse decorations in Rome already show this Marian figure during the early Middle Ages, then it became common in the Romanesque period on the sculptured tympana of Corneilla-de-Conflent, Neuilly-en-Donjon, Anzy-le-Duc, and in the early Gothic period on the portal of St Anne at Notre-Dame in Paris, the south tympanum of the Royal Portal of Chartres, the north transept of Reims and at Laon Cathedral–to mention a few examples. Moreover, each of these images fitted into a context peculiar to it, into the framework of an iconography which acquired its full dimensions in terms of the scenes surrounding it. The Virgin also figures in the Ascension of Christ, presiding over the apostolic college, at Cahors and Anzy-le-Duc; she becomes even more autonomous in the representation of her own Assumption at La Charité-sur-Loire where she is welcomed by her Son in the Heavenly Jerusalem. The novelty of this image lies in the special emphasis put on the concept of bodily assumption, belief in which spread from the beginning of the twelfth century. It was around 1135 that Peter the Venerable defended it in a letter addressed to one of his monks. The special veneration in which the Virgin was held at Chartres was of long standing, while in England Marian devotion and more especially the cult of the Immaculate Conception was celebrated even before the Conquest. So it is not the growth of the cult of the Virgin as such which is in question at the beginning of Gothic art (we should remember that late southern Romanesque had represented the miracle of Theophilus at Souillac and the episode of the Virgin's girdle at Cabestany), but rather the transition from the theme of the triumph of the Virgin to that of her coronation and more especially the creation of a type of portal entirely built up around this iconographic theme.

Virgin and Child: central part of an Epiphany
with Joseph on the right, from the abbey of Fontfroide.
Romanesque art, second half of the 12th century.
Musée de la Société Archéologique, Montpellier.

The tympanum of La Charité-sur-Loire, the mosaic of Santa Maria in Trastevere at Rome, the tympanum of the south portal of Quenington church in England, present three variants of the triumphant Virgin welcomed by her Son in celestial glory. At Notre-Dame in Chartres, the tympanum devoted to the glory of the Virgin and Child, and surmounting episodes from the boyhood of Christ in which the Virgin Mother intervenes, is accompanied (elsewhere on the façade, to be sure) by a cycle, entirely new

Christ and the Virgin.
Central theme of the tympanum. Shortly before 1216.
Saint-Yved, Braine.

in the West, of the birth and childhood of the Virgin. A similar context (glory of the Virgin and Child, childhood of Christ) is presented on the tympanum of the portal of St Anne coming from the earlier portal dedicated to the Virgin at Notre-Dame in Paris. The iconography here is complicated, because the ensemble was re-assembled; what is known of the original arch mouldings tells us that they were apparently destined for a decorated portal of the Majesty of Christ, other fragments of which were found

Virgin and Child from
Saint-Martin-des-Champs, Paris.
Third quarter of the 12th century.
Polychrome wood.
Basilica of Saint-Denis.

by Viollet-le-Duc. The two historical personages, a bishop and a king, who accompany the censing angels on either side of the Virgin and Child, were formerly identified as Maurice de Sully and Louis VII. More recently, it has been suggested that they are St Germain and Childebert, two historical figures who had a decisive say in the construction of the cathedral. Looking a little further, we might be dealing here with an allusion, already mentioned in connection with Saint-Denis, to the symbolic representation of the secular and ecclesiastical powers brought together by the Virgin: the bishop standing to the right of Mary asserts his pre-eminence over the king kneeling on her left. This is an interpretation which fits in with twelfth-century ecclesiological thinking and which acquires a new significance today in a Parisian context because of the much earlier dating of this ensemble.

It used to be assumed that Abbot Suger played a leading part in the creation and diffusion of Marian iconography, but this theory, which Emile Mâle found so seductive, has since been regularly contradicted. Yet, according to the latest research, the west front of the basilica of Saint-Denis does seem to have included a portal dedicated to the Virgin, whose triumph was depicted on the tympanum mosaic. Before his death, Abbot Suger is said to have offered Notre-Dame in Paris a stained glass window representing a Marian theme–possibly the earliest example of the coronation of the Virgin. It is a difficult point to prove, although we do know from an eighteenth-century description that this window portrayed a Marian triumph.

According to our present state of knowledge, the iconography of the Virgin broke new ground on the west portal of the cathedral of Notre-Dame at Senlis, where we find the fully worked out theme of the crowned Virgin for the first time. The two known dates (1150-1155 under Bishop Theobald for the decision to rebuild and 1191 for the consecration) are too far apart to fix the chronology of the façade accurately. Stylistic comparisons, on the other hand, favour a dating of about 1170, although the style, formed of supple curves full of nuances in contrast to Chartres verticality, is original enough to make it a somewhat isolated phenomenon and one that had little following.

The west portal of Senlis Cathedral consists of a sculptured tympanum set on a wide lintel, protected by four archivolts decorated with figures which rest on splays with column statues, the plinth being adorned with a calendar. On the lintel, to the left, are the death of the Virgin and the placing of her body in a sarcophagus by the apostles (Dormition). In the upper part of this scene, angels soar up with the Virgin's soul represented as a small figure over which they hold a crown. To the right, a group of angels attend the resurrection of the Virgin, supporting her on her emergence from the tomb, while one of them also holds a crown over her head. On the tympanum, the Virgin and Christ, both crowned, are depicted seated and conversing, in Majesty and symmetrically arranged on either side of the central axis. The two figures are placed on an equal footing, which establishes a marked difference from, for example, the apse mosaic of Santa Maria in Trastevere at Rome (c. 1145), in which Christ occupies the centre. At Senlis this dialogue between the two crowned sovereigns is magnified by a pattern of arches, whose central double curve brings to mind the outline of the uncial M. All around, angels censing or holding candles appear under the small lateral arches and in the *oculi*. It should be pointed

Holy Conversation
between Christ
and the Crowned Virgin.
Portal of the west front.
About 1170.
Senlis Cathedral.

out that the Senlis Christ does not actually crown the Virgin; instead the emphasis is more on the links which unite the two divine figures, the Virgin being already crowned.

Introducing the ensemble, the eight column statues, heavily restored and completed by the sculptor Robinet in 1845-1846, represent, from outside to inside, John the Baptist, Aaron, Moses and Abraham on the left, and David, Isaiah, Jeremiah and Simeon on the right. They all bear the attributes indicating their role as prophets of the Incarnation (right) or foreshadowers of Christ the Redeemer (left) and, in this capacity, refer more to Christ than the Virgin. Doubt still exists about the identity of the figure that might have occupied a putative trumeau which has disappeared today. Christ or the Virgin? A very similar arrangement of column statues is found on the portals of Saint-Nicolas of Amiens (destroyed during the Revolution) and of the north transept of Chartres (central portal), there with Peter and Melchizedek. It will be noted that the statues on the splaying pose a general problem it would be interesting to study, namely the nature of the changes these series originally conceived for portals with the iconography of the Redemption might have undergone when

they had to accompany the new iconography of the coronation of the Virgin in its early stages.

The west portal of Senlis is completed by the arch mouldings carved with figures representing the genealogy of Christ and the Virgin (Abraham, Jesse, David, Solomon) amid the branches of a Tree of Jesse. This lineage culminates symbolically in the Virgin and the Christ on the tympanum. Thus the general programme of the Senlis portal becomes clear through the different stages of the history of Humanity redeemed by the blood of Christ, stages in which the Church played an essential part. By comparing the Virgin of the tympanum sitting beside Christ to the betrothed of the *Song of Songs*, the virtual equation of the Virgin with the Church becomes stronger. The essential novelty is that the place the Virgin occupies on the tympanum puts her on the same footing as Christ. The corporal resurrection of Mary, which is based on belief in the Assumption of the Virgin, is accompanied here by the celestial glorification of the Mother of God.

Even if the term Coronation of the Virgin does not exactly fit the scene on the tympanum of the main portal of Senlis, this figuration subsequently becomes the major

Portal with the Coronation of the Virgin.
North transept.
Shortly before 1210.
Chartres Cathedral.

theme of Marian tympana. The central portal of the west front of the collegiate church of Notre-Dame at Mantes, whose dating must be very close to that of Senlis, if slightly later, presents a monumental version of the Senlis images, although with certain differences (a richer cycle of the Virgin, a slightly different Assumption). In contrast, the theme of the tympanum and arch mouldings is revived on it with a complement which serves to reinforce the meaning of the Senlis portal: a cross appears above the central couple. The west front of Laon Cathedral has two portals devoted to the Virgin executed at the very end of the twelfth or during the first few years of the thirteenth cen-

Coronation of the Virgin.
West portal.
Second half of the 13th century.
Santa María la Mayor, Toro.

tury; they complete the righthand portal dominated by the Last Judgment. The central portal takes up the Senlis scheme again, whereas the lefthand portal breaks new ground in Marian iconography, heralding the north transept of Chartres and Amiens. The tympanum represents an Epiphany with the familiar formula of a lintel adorned with the Annunciation, the Nativity and the Annunciation to the Shepherds. The arch mouldings deserve attention insofar as they contain prefigurations of the virginity of Mary. Figures and symbols of the chosen people are assembled on the third arch moulding: the new Eve, Daniel in the lion's den, Habbakuk, Gideon, Moses before the burning bush, the Ark of the Covenant, the Temple, Isaiah. The fourth exhibits figures and themes from pagan Antiquity associated or not with the history of Israel: the unicorn, Virgil, Isaac blessing Jacob, Balaam, Simeon, the statue in Nebuchadnezzar's dream, Nebuchadnezzar asleep, the coronation of David, the Sibyl, the three Hebrews in the fiery furnace. Typologically speaking, we find here a summation of the testimonies of Jews and Gentiles about the virgin birth of Christ and the coming of his kingdom on earth, which is portrayed at Laon in the scenes on the lintel and tympanum. At Saint-Yved at Braine, shortly before the dedication of the church in 1216, the Virgin turning towards Christ is shown in profile in the attitude of prayer. The subsequent evolution of Marian iconography assigns an essential place to the coronation proper and repeats this scene *ad infinitum* as we see it even before the end of the first decade of the thirteenth century on the central portal of the north transept of Chartres. Then the Annunciation and the Visitation take their place among the column statues on the splaying of the lefthand portal of the same transept.

During the thirteenth century statues of the Virgin holding the Child and standing became common in the Ile-de-France and elsewhere. In monumental sculpture, the tradition of the seated Romanesque Virgin holding the Child continues and culminates about 1180 on the trumeau of the central portal of Noyon Cathedral. The appearance of the standing Virgin and Child on the trumeau poses a problem. It is recorded at Moutiers-Saint-Jean in Burgundy at a date close to that of the Virgin and Child on the righthand splaying of the west portal of Notre-Dame of Vermenton (c. 1170). The role of Paris in the diffusion of the trumeau Virgin must have been decisive, judging by the crowned Virgin trampling the snake underfoot, accompanied by saints on the splays, who figured about 1210 on the lefthand portal, below the Coronation of the Virgin, of the west front of Notre-Dame in Paris. This model (destroyed during the Revolution) was taken up again at Amiens and then in many monuments. The figure of St Anne holding Mary in her arms (portal of the Coronation of the Virgin, north transept of Chartres) stands out as an important stage in the Marian iconography of the façade shortly before 1210, insofar as it refers to the story of Mary's childhood, quite apart from the presence of relics of St Anne at Chartres. Formerly the Annunciation to Joachim could be seen on the plinth. The introduction of the monumental iconography of the Virgin testifies by its great popularity to the theological elaboration which, during the second half of the twelfth century, governed the cult of this Lady, mother of Our Lord, fiancée of Christ and embodiment of the Mystery of the Church. It is one of the major innovations in the new Gothic cathedral sculpture.

SCULPTURE IN NORTHERN FRANCE AROUND 1200

To define the changing art of the age of Philip Augustus, increasing use has been made for some decades of the term "1200 style" applied to the notion of a transitional style and covering the years on either side of 1200. Its field extends to the artistic production represented in book illumination by the Ingeborg Psalter, but also to goldsmith's work which, beginning with outstanding monuments like the shrine of the Three Kings in Cologne Cathedral and the work of Nicolas of Verdun, played a decisive role in the definition of the styles adopted in monumental sculpture. Other forms of the "1200 style" also appear in distant geographical areas such as southern France and Italy under Frederick II.

The major sculpture of northern France just before the turn of the century is marked by a new monumentality and by antiquizing tendencies. The sculpture of Laon Cathedral denotes the first turning point in relation to the style of Senlis and Mantes. The two characteristics just mentioned are expressed here on the arch mouldings of the portal of the Virgin, for example, in a completely assured manner for the first time. These major stylistic upheavals recur and mature on the worksite of Sens Cathedral. This monument, which was destined to be one of the first of early Gothic art, for it was begun under Bishop Henri Sanglier (1122-1142), belongs to the years 1185-1205, as far as the west front is concerned, except for the tympanum of the central portal and the righthand portal which were rebuilt in the mid-thirteenth century. The figures appear in groups on the arch mouldings of the lefthand portal adorned with a cycle of John the Baptist. Medallions invade the mural surface in the lower parts. On the arch mouldings of the central portal, a new antiquizing style appears in the fluid and delicate treatment of the drapery thanks to a play of lines slightly curved and in any case less severe than in the past, defining the style which finds

Figure from the Old Testament.
Right portal of the north transept. About 1220.
Chartres Cathedral.

Judgment of Solomon.
Lintel, right portal of the north transept.
About 1220.
Chartres Cathedral.

its highest expression in the St Stephen on the trumeau of the central portal around the turn of the century and in a few heads which escaped mutilation in 1793. This style had a certain influence even beyond monumental sculpture, as the tomb of an abbot preserved at Nesle-la-Reposte testifies.

The stylistic experiments at Laon and Sens lead to the north transept of Chartres, especially the statues on the splaying of the central portal. The monumental formula which consisted in treating the extremities of transept arms as genuine west fronts was perfected on the worksite of Chartres Cathedral. To help fix the chronology, we know that the head of St Anne was given to the cathedral in 1204-1205 and that the trumeau of the north portal must be dated very similarly. The cathedral of Chartres was rebuilt after the fire of 1196 and the canons were already installed in the new choir in 1221. The comparative chronology of the building and stylistic study of the portals and porches show that the central portal is the oldest, the others dating only to the second decade of the thirteenth century. During these early decades, Chartres was a centre producing quite exceptional sculpture which reached a peak about 1230 and even a little later with a monumental rood screen illustrating the childhood and Passion of Christ, many fragments of which have been preserved. It was one of the finest monuments of all Gothic sculpture in the thirteenth century.

When dealing with the stylistic mutation of the first decades of the thirteenth century, one of whose major currents led to the marvellous antiquizing statues of the central portal of Reims Cathedral, we should take into account the vast worksite which the reconstruction of the west front of Notre-Dame represented in Paris, from about 1210. There we find the result of antiquizing research (angel's head in the Musée de Cluny) and of the forms perfected at Laon and Sens. The Last Judgment on the central portal and the Coronation of the Virgin on the north portal embody a formula of wide superimposed registers that are more clearly integrated with the rhythm of the arch mouldings. A greater verticality characterizes the style of the sculptures, which have already abandoned the antiquizing mode and announce the expressiveness of the Amiens statues. The extraordinary discovery of 1977 has improved our knowledge of certain stylistic aspects of the Notre-Dame façade, in particular the heads of the arcade of kings which date to the latest stage, around 1230.

Moses. Head of a statue from the splaying.
Central portal.
About 1180.
Notre-Dame, Mantes-la-Jolie.

Head of an Old Testament King discovered in 1977.
From the Arcade of Kings on the west front, Notre-Dame, Paris.
1225-1230.
Musée de Cluny, Paris.

AMIENS CATHEDRAL

Amiens Cathedral is one of the greatest French buildings of the thirteenth century. A labyrinth which was situated in the middle of the nave gave the date of the works begun in 1220 by Bishop Evrard de Fouilloy (1211-1222) and the names of the architects Robert de Luzarches, Thomas de Cormont and his son Renaud de Cormont. 1288, the date when the labyrinth was made, indicates that by then construction was completed. It began with the nave and continued after the terrain was cleared (destruction of Saint-Firmin to the east and displacement of the Hôtel-Dieu to the west), the façade being erected shortly after 1236 and the apse begun about 1241. The plan of Amiens Cathedral is formed of a nave with ten bays flanked by single side aisles, a wide transept also with side aisles, and three straight bays with double side aisles preceding the apse with radiating chapels, including the deep axial one, and an ambulatory. The building is also characteristic for its elevation on three levels. The external sculpture extends widely over the west front and the south arm of the transept.

The chronology of the west front of Amiens Cathedral remains in question. Work was thought to have proceeded, more or less, according to a linear evolution, which would have brought the workmen to the façade only ten years or so after the beginning of the nave. After a colloquy organized in 1974 by the Société Française d'Archéologie, the façade was judged to be not particularly coherent and later in date, with successive additions marking the progress of its attachment to the main body of the cathedral. This point of view is opposed to a chronology in three building campaigns, from 1220-1235 to 1248-1263. Apart from the fact that it takes into consideration the numerous technical observations made in the nineteenth century during the radical restoration undertaken by Viollet-le-Duc (1844-1847), it brings the sculpture of the west front into line with that of the portal of the *Vierge Dorée* of the south transept. Thus the role of the Amiens workshops is essentially concentrated on some ten years around 1240. Certain sculptures might belong to an initial façade design; for example, the statue of St Ulphia on the lefthand splay of the St Firmin portal, with its antiquizing air due to the employment of damp-fold drapery. With that remark, we return to the general prob-

West front. About 1230-1240. Amiens Cathedral.

The "Golden Virgin."
Trumeau statue,
portal of the
south transept.
About 1240-1245.
Amiens Cathedral.

lem of the differences of style between the sculptures on the great façades. Are they evidence of different moments in the execution of the works or do they simply point to the presence of sculptors with varied origins and training? Because, when looking at the façade of Amiens Cathedral, we observe, in addition to the innovating hand of the Master of the *Beau Dieu*, whose style is comparable to the Christ on the trumeau of Notre-Dame in Paris, the hand of several masters at work on each of the portals.

The west front of Notre-Dame of Amiens, with two towers and rose window, has an elevation on several levels. The monumental sculptures are concentrated on the arcade of kings and the three portals. Each portal is designed with trumeau and tympanum, and flanked by deep splayings. The unity of the whole is due to the fact that the statues and the reliefs in quatrefoils on the substructure continue without interruption onto the splays and buttresses. As a result the ground floor of the façade offers a close symbiosis between architecture and sculpture. As in Paris, the tympanum of the central portal is devoted to the Last Judgment; its programme is set out on three large registers. The separation of the Chosen from the Damned continues on the lower part of the first arch moulding. The programme unfolds on the arch mouldings with angels, martyrs, priests, women, the Elders of the Apocalypse and the Tree of Jesse. As in Paris, the trumeau depicts Christ blessing (known as the *Beau Dieu*), one of the major works of sculpture at Amiens, while the apostles, much restored, occupy the splays. The righthand portal is devoted to the Virgin, who is standing on the trumeau and crowned on the tympanum. The statues on the splays represent the Three Kings, Herod, Solomon and the Queen of Sheba on the left, and the Annunciation, the Visitation and the Presentation in the Temple on the right. The lefthand portal is devoted (henceforth the established norm for the great programmes) to local hagiography: on the trumeau, St Firmin, first Bishop of Amiens, whose story unfolds on the registers of the tympanum; the statues on the splays represent twelve saints. On the buttresses are arranged prophet statues, forming an original composition in conjunction with the reliefs of the substructure.

Together with the bronze plaque from the tomb of Bishop Evrard de Fouilloy (died 1222), in a style without direct relation with that of the façade and an important example of the bronze-founders' art, Amiens Cathedral possesses another major work of thirteenth-century sculpture: the St Honoratus portal of the south transept. Today the evolution of the worksite and the style of the sculptures enable us to date it to the years 1235-1240 (possibly even 1245), with the additional help of an architectural study of the actual installation of the portal. The latter is famous for the so-called *Vierge Dorée* on the trumeau. As an innovation, the apostles, grouped in conversing pairs, stand out in the round on the lintel. The originality of the programme of the arch mouldings is enhanced by that of the tympanum which recounts the life of St Honoratus, former Bishop of Amiens, on four registers. The style of the sculptures on the portal of the Golden Virgin offers many points of comparison with that of the sculptures on the west front. It had been wrongly assigned a later date than the west portals of Reims and the transept of Notre-Dame in Paris. However, the present chronology has the advantage of placing the originality of the lintel and the style of the Virgin more accurately in the framework of the evolution of thirteenth-century sculpture.

Gothic foliage capital. Scene of rural life. 13th century.
Reims Cathedral.

REIMS CATHEDRAL

Reims Cathedral is a masterpiece of French medieval art which had made a profound impression on people's minds, sometimes less for its role as a coronation cathedral than for the damage inflicted on it during the First World War and the discussions which ensued about the deterioration of the sculptures, their removal and restoration. In 1210, after a fire, Archbishop Aubry de Humbert (died 1218) decided to rebuild the church and the axial chapel was in use by 1221. The subsequent history of the cathedral's construction was full of incident and interruptions on the worksite. The west front was begun in 1255 and finished in 1275 (except for the upper parts), but from the outset statuary had invaded the exterior of the building. A labyrinth supplied the names of four architects, Jean d'Orbais, Jean Le Loup, Gaucher of Reims and Bernard of Soissons, but not the details of their intervention. The plan of the building comprises a nave with nine bays flanked by single side aisles, a slightly projecting transept with a supplementary side aisle which is prolonged by two straight bays preceding a choir with radiating chapels and ambulatory. On the exterior, the present-day building lacks the transept towers, but has a façade firmly anchored on the two lateral towers, which endow it with a characteristic vertical upthrust. The great profusion of sculptures testifies to an immense project, successive additions and a rare decorative ambition.

The west front of Reims is a wonderful illustration of this flood of sculpture, covering portals, buttresses and gables, as well as the tabernacles placed in the buttresses and the upper parts. The Coronation of the Virgin on the central portal reaches up into the gable, the tympana being pierced. The Virgin and Child occupy the trumeau, while the statues on the splays are devoted to the boyhood of Christ and the life of the Virgin. The lefthand portal is dominated by a monumental Crucifixion and the arch mouldings contain a christological cycle. Saul's conversion is represented on the lintel, while the splay statues represent saints, angels and apostles. The Christ as Judge on the gable of the righthand portal is accompanied by an Apocalypse cycle on the arch mouldings; prophets and saints stand on the splays.

The decision to replace the mid-twelfth-century façade was probably taken some thirty years before work actually began. So the design of the west front would date to the 1220s or shortly afterwards, which would explain why the great splay statues with their antiquizing air (Mary and Elizabeth representing the Visitation, for example) had already been executed before 1240-1245, at the same time that the statues on the upper parts of the choir and transept were being made. It has recently been suggested that the delay in setting up the façade workshop could be attributed to serious financial difficulties in the diocese of Reims. From 1255, work on the portals, which demonstrate a knowledge of the west front of Amiens, got under way. The first group of reliefs was executed by sculptors coming from Amiens or Paris. Shortly after 1260, the model of the north transept of Notre-Dame in Paris led to

St Firmin.
Trumeau, left portal
of the west front.
About 1230-1235.
Amiens Cathedral.

St Calixtus.
Trumeau, central portal
of the north transept.
About 1225-1230.
Reims Cathedral.

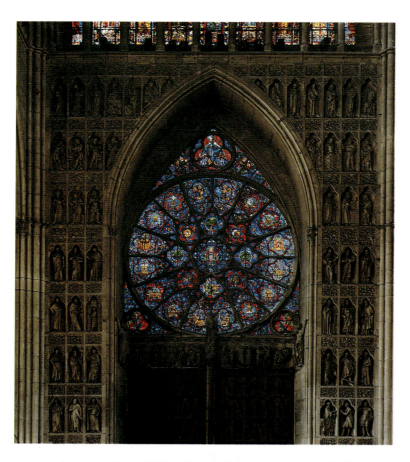

an enlargement of the side buttresses and is reflected in the upper parts and the style of the inner wall of the façade. Indeed, the programme of the upper parts of the portals continues in the interior by means of a succession of niches containing figures referring to St John the Baptist on the north half of the wall of the main nave and to the Virgin on the south half, while prophets appear in the side aisles, with scenes from the New Testament and the Apocalypse. The lintels are also embellished on their inner face. On the principal trumeau is St Nicasius facing the main nave; on the lintels of the side portals is the martyrdom of St Stephen. Its location made this programme quite exceptional, although it was probably not unique in the Middle Ages. On the exterior, contributions from Amiens (reliefs of the legend of St John, the preaching of St Paul, and the lintels) precede those from Paris (relief of the Apocalypse). The large statues reveal some Parisian features (smiling angel, Helen), but essentially they show great diversity and are mostly later than 1261, as an important recent book has proved.

Inner west wall of the nave.
About 1255-1275 (lower parts), 1275-1299 (level of the rose window).
Reims Cathedral.

Annunciation and Visitation. Splaying, central portal of the west front.
Mary and Elizabeth (right) are in an antiquizing style; the Virgin of the Annunciation (second from left) derives from Amiens.
They were carved before the façade was erected in 1260-1274. Reims Cathedral.

FRESH INSPIRATION IN PARIS

So the history of Gothic sculpture in the middle and early second half of the thirteenth century starts in the 1240s with the fundamental changes in monumental sculpture we have seen emerging at Paris and Amiens. Some Parisian works should also be mentioned, beside the more recent sculptures carved for the late installation (c. 1240) of the central portal of Notre-Dame (Christ, angel with nails, left section of the lintel, trumeau Christ, six archstones in the first arch moulding), breaking with the style of the 1220s, as does the King Childebert from the refectory trumeau of Saint-Germain-des-Prés in the Louvre, reliably dated to the abbacy of Simon (1239-1244), whose restoration has revealed its polychromy and forceful style. Although space only allows a brief mention, we should not forget the importance of the apostles of the Sainte-Chapelle (some originals in the chapel, others in the Musée de Cluny, c. 1241-1248), the elegant portal of the north transept of Notre-Dame, and above all the fine quality of the statue of a naked Adam in the Musée de Cluny, from the inner south transept of Notre-Dame; it is contemporary with the magnificent inner and outer decoration of that façade, whose first stone was laid by Jean de Chelles in 1258. The treatment of the nude is akin to that of the bodies of Adam and Eve on a rood screen fragment from Notre-Dame preserved in the Louvre.

In comparison with the works executed in Paris shortly before the middle of the thirteenth century, Bourges stands out for the rood screen sculptures, a remarkable composition with heavy drapery folds and full decorative forms, and for the central portal of the west front, possibly slightly later than the rood screen and so from the middle of the thirteenth century, with its classical air and a remarkable freedom in the treatment of the nudes. These stylistic tendencies recur on the portal of La Calende at Rouen, at Rampillon, and in the south transept of Saint-Denis. The reconstruction of Saint-Denis in the thirteenth century is important for the history of Gothic architecture. The retables of the choir chapels, showing obvious affinities with the Bourges sculptures and the Sainte-Chapelle apostles, attest the Parisian production of the years 1250-1260 and the role that carved church furniture played in the evolution of Gothic art. The large relief with St Denis, St Rusticus and St Eleutherius (Louvre), probably from the rood screen of Saint-Denis, already belongs to the end of the century. The new dating (before 1265-1279) of the major ivory statuette of the Virgin and Child (Louvre), known as the Sainte-Chapelle or Soltykoff Virgin, confirms the importance of Paris as an artistic nursery. Many other works do not deserve to be left in the shade: the portals of the west front of Auxerre Cathedral and especially the abundant output of funerary sculpture which, in the context of relations maintained with monumental sculpture, leads from the *gisants* of Fontevrault to those of Amiens, then to the funerary statue of Constance of Arles (Saint-Denis) and the head of the *gisant* of Jeanne of Toulouse (1271-1285), on the threshold of the new artistic tendencies of the late thirteenth century.

Adam. Statue from the inner south transept of Notre-Dame, Paris. About 1260. Musée de Cluny, Paris.

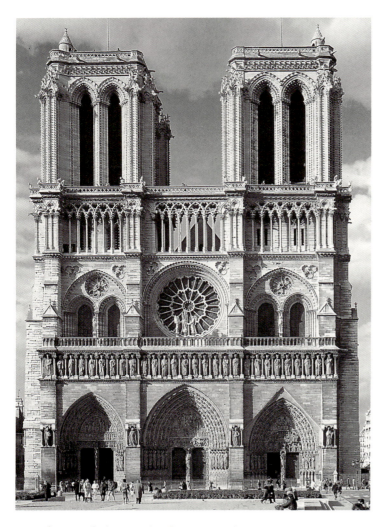

West front with the Arcade of Kings (modern statues).
From about 1210 (arcades, about 1225-1230).
Notre-Dame, Paris.

HISTORY, RELIGION, POLITICS: THE ARCADES OF KINGS

During the first decades of the thirteenth century, Gothic sculpture made innovations in many fields. Statues, for example, owing to a twisting movement which made the legs face in an opposite direction to the torso, or a slouching from the hips with the weight on one leg (the Gothic sway), tend to stand out visually from the architectural setting. Again, statues began to smile and there was a growing taste for the anatomical study of the nude. We have already dwelt on the novelties in the iconography of the Virgin. Parallel to them, from the beginning of the thirteenth century, monumental Gothic sculpture shows a predilection for the representation of crowned kings, for a royal iconography. The west portals of Saint-Denis and Chartres had already established the type of the royal biblical statue on the splay, with the book or *rotulus* as attribute. Generally, the figures wear an open cloak, held in on the right shoulder, which falls in straight tight folds. During the first half of the thirteenth century, the robe falls to the feet and is drawn in at the waist; an open cloak is held in over the chest. But the main novelty is the appearance of royal figures aligned on the upper part of the façade: the famous arcades of kings.

In April 1977, 364 sculptured fragments from the cathedral of Paris were discovered during restoration work on the Hôtel Moreau, Rue de la Chaussée-d'Antin. In 1793, in the desire to suppress emblems of royalty after smashing the crowns on statues, the revolutionaries decided to pull them down and destroy them. Out of religious and undoubtedly monarchic respect, many fragments were buried and so faint was the memory of them that Viollet-le-Duc had to use his imagination when restoring them. Among the pieces found in 1977 were twenty-one heads from the arcade of kings at Notre-Dame, which establish the Parisian style of the years 1225-1230, that is to say an intermediary period little known before, and supply valuable information about the polychromy of medieval statues. Their formal aspect is fairly coherent: a crown with fleurons that have disappeared, hair divided into long strands often hiding the ears, beard and moustache nearly always abundant. In contrast, only a very few fragments were found of the bodies, from which the heads had been carefully removed.

Much has been written about the identification of the statues in the arcades of kings. The Notre-Dame arcade represents the kings of Judah and so constitutes a sort of horizontal Tree of Jesse, better explained today by the authentification of the central group which surmounted the arcade. It represented the Virgin and Child flanked by two angels restored in the nineteenth century on the initiative of Viollet-le-Duc. In contrast, the restored statues of Adam and Eve on either side, in front of the towers, have turned out to be a product of the restorers' imagination. So the role of Notre-Dame in Paris in the monumental glorification of the Virgin is even better known than it was when the only artistic creation of that genre attributed to it was the standing Virgin on the trumeau.

When looking for the origins of the arcade of kings, a distinction should be made between the architectural motif and the iconography, because the row of figures under arches developed very early in medieval art, in painting and mosaics, at the back of apses or sculptured on façades in western France and northern Spain. Many

Interior of the Sainte-Chapelle, Paris,
as restored in the 19th century
with statues of the apostles (about 1241-1248).
Some of the originals are in
the Musée de Cluny, Paris.

The *apostolado* arcade.
Upper part of the façade.
First third of the 13th century.
Cathedral of Ciudad Rodrigo.

Façade of the south transept.
About 1210-1235.
Chartres Cathedral.

Spanish façades display *apostolados* or registers of apostles, as at Santiago de Compostela, Moarves, Carrión de los Condes, Sangüesa and later at Ciudad Rodrigo, a monumental transposition of a theme frequently found on altar frontals. Incidentally, the Epiphany is incorporated into the frieze at Carrión de los Condes. The arcade of kings of Notre-Dame, Paris, as well as those of Chartres (south arm of the transept and west front), Amiens (west front) and Reims (buttresses and transept towers) signify the emergence and diffusion of a new theme in which the royal ancestors of the Old Testament were very soon confused with the "ancestors" of the kingdom of France. The fact is that the emerging theme of the arcade of kings cannot be dissociated from the growing prestige of the Capetian dynasty beginning with the reign of Louis VI, from the shaping of the notion of royal legitimacy, from the reflection on the image of the king which was a central concern in the aulic circles of the France of Philip Augustus. The royal statues in the upper parts of the transept of Reims show, by the artistic and iconographic scope of the cycle, the close connection deliberately sought between religious iconography and the idea of royalty through its symbols. The important ecclesiastical and political personalities who intervened in commissioning works were directly involved in the emergence of an architectural motif which illustrates the culmination of thinking about medieval genealogies. As a façade theme, the arcade of kings also enjoyed an obvious and rapid success outside France (Burgos, Wells, Lichfield, Exeter, Lincoln).

ENGLISH GOTHIC

Fragment of a head
from Wolvesey Palace, episcopal
residence of Henry de Blois.
The style recalls that of Saint-Denis.
About 1145-1150.
City Museum, Winchester.

REJECTION OF THE GREAT SCULPTURED PORTAL

The great English religious buildings before the Conquest belonged to three types of communities: the secular cathedrals such as Wells, Salisbury and Lincoln (composed of non-resident canons and administered by a dean and chapter), the monasteries (essentially Benedictine, Cluniac, Cistercian and Augustinian) and the episcopal priories which are unique to Britain (episcopal sees with a monastic community led by a prior). Durham is a typical example of the last-named and has groups of separate buildings for the bishop, to the north of the cathedral, and the prior, to the south. The first fully achieved example of Gothic architecture in England is traditionally regarded as the reconstruction work on Canterbury Cathedral after the fire which destroyed the Romanesque choir in 1174. Gervais, a monk and chronicler, has left a particularly detailed account of this undertaking for which the French architect William of Sens was called in. His replacement by an English architect after a fatal fall from a scaffold in 1178 marked a new orientation of English Gothic, combining the new tendencies from northern France and a national evolution with its own regional idiosyncrasies; a Gothic art dominated by the important role of the episcopate and royal patronage. English art historians have adopted their own terminology for Gothic architecture, one which essentially goes back to the nineteenth century. The first Gothic architecture is called Early English, for which Episcopal style has been suggested as a substitute (Canterbury, Wells, Lincoln, Peterborough, Salisbury, Westminster). For more recent periods, we find the terms Decorated style (Exeter, York, Ely) and Perpendicular style (Cambridge) corresponding to the Rayonnant and Flamboyant styles of French terminology respectively. The period that concerns us here begins about 1150, ex-

tends over the second half of the twelfth century and is illustrated by a gradual transition at the regional level from Romanesque to Gothic architecture. We find a variety of experiments that gradually become standardized during the first half of the thirteenth century until the opening of the worksite at Westminster, which marks a new aesthetic and cultural interpretation in the middle of the thirteenth century.

The first Gothic sculpture in England, and for that matter in Scotland, Wales and Ireland, does not play the same innovatory role in the development of medieval art as architecture and indicates a clear rejection of the model represented by the great façades of northern France. During the second half of the twelfth century, sculpture is chiefly architectural and decorative (Worcester, Winchester). Apart from the portal of Rochester which includes and interprets, shortly after the mid-twelfth century, the type of column statues on the west front of Chartres, no great ensemble develops a cycle of façade sculptures similar to French creations. The novelties mostly come from the realm of architectural sculpture. Thus sculptures of exceptional quality appear in Wolvesey Palace in Winchester and at Glastonbury towards the middle of the century, under the patronage of Henry of Blois. And it is the study of capitals that enables us to follow the progress and tendencies of early Gothic art in England. The different types testify to the various influences on the buildings of each region during the second half of the twelfth century. It has been rightly assumed that sculptors from France accompanied William of Sens to the Canterbury worksite, where we see the appearance in the Trinity Chapel of the crocket capitals destined to have an ephemeral success in England, but soon to be replaced by the stiff-leaf capital. For a better understanding of this development, we may concentrate on the single worksite of Wells, to which we shall return, and follow the elaboration of the type from the narrow separate leaves of the choir capitals executed about 1180-1185 to the full, deeply carved foliage with an

West front. First quarter of the 13th century.
Peterborough Cathedral.

effusive baroque air, endowed with an intense movement, of the west capitals of the nave dating to the early thirteenth century. Nevertheless, one should guard against generalizing insofar as regional developments retained a large measure of autonomy. In the north, for example, the capital with smooth leaves had a greater vogue and consequently the stiff-leaf capital did not appear there until later.

Much of the originality of the architectural decoration of Early English Gothic is based on the polychromy born of the use of a black marble, from the Isle of Purbeck in Dorset. As early as the Romanesque period, English patrons had shown a predilection for dark stone exemplified in the importations of fonts and funerary slabs carved out of Tournai stone. The exploitation of Purbeck marble was already known in the Romanesque period, but the opulence of the material really shines forth in the new construction at Canterbury, on the plinth of the shrine, the piers of the Trinity Chapel and especially the shafts in which the lie of the stone in the quarry was placed vertically when dressed. The last-named became characteristic of the Early English style.

If the Rochester portal remains an isolated phenomenon, the same is true of the column statues of St Mary's Abbey at York, now in the Yorkshire Museum, which stylistic analysis of the treatment of faces and drapery folds allows us to date to 1200-1210, based on comparison with the French worksites of Senlis, Mantes and Sens. The best known and best preserved are the figures of John the Baptist and Moses with the rounded movement of the drapery folds that has become famous. The thirteen statues extant, including seven in a very good state, were discovered in January 1829 in the ruins of the conventual church. The stocky proportions of these statues are more easily understood today if we accept the theory that they may not have come from a portal, but from piers supporting the springing of the ribs of the chapter house, which was also sumptuously adorned with fo-

Moses.
Statue from St Mary's Abbey, York.
About 1200-1210.
Yorkshire Museum, York.

West front. Second third of the 13th century.
Salisbury Cathedral.

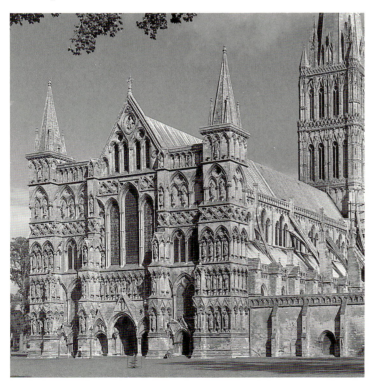

liage capitals. Moreover, each pier must have included the typological figuration of an apostle surmounting a prophet. It is a portal arrangement (Bamberg) unprecedented for a chapter house, but it has the advantage of explaining the general aspect of the statues and it would confirm the pre-eminent role of chapter houses in the development of English Gothic.

THE SCREEN FAÇADE

During the first half of the thirteenth century, the principal English cathedrals under construction or reconstruction were given façades like immense screens which received vast cycles of sculpture. In marked contrast to French cathedral fronts, the emphasis was on their horizontal extension rather than the vertical soaring effect.

131

West front.
About 1240.
Wells Cathedral.

Although the Anglo-Norman tradition of façades with two towers persists, certain features also derive from the Romanesque façades of the west of France with their rich lode of sculpture. Contrary to the French tendency which favoured the splays of portals, England developed a flat conception of monumental sculpture in which each element or statue was incorporated until it seemed to merge into the immense decorative scheme of the façade.

The main cycle of sculpture from the first half of the thirteenth century is that of Wells Cathedral, a building begun shortly after 1180 and so almost contemporary with the reconstruction of the Canterbury apse. Progress made on the works led the builders to the west front in the 1240s. Of gigantic proportions, with a double transept, the architecture of Wells Cathedral is distinguished from that of Canterbury by its linear conception. The building has an elevation on three levels patterned by the horizontal continuity of the triforium. The richest west front of all English cathedrals, Wells is impressive for the amplitude of its horizontal levels, for the increased breadth acquired by the towers projecting laterally over the side aisles, and for the quantity of sculptures displayed on it. The bare substructure is pierced by three doors which disappear between the buttresses. The tiers of arches on the central level display stylistic changes as they move upwards until they terminate in the Perpendicular style. The skeletal appearance of the building was accentuated originally when the lancets of the lower parts of the towers were pierced. The portals play only a secondary role in the façade's iconographic programme. The central portal, devoted to the Virgin, is surmounted by the scene of her coronation. The quatrefoils of the lower storey contain angels and episodes from the Old and New Testaments. The intermediate level is covered with statues of prophets, patriarchs, martyrs, confessors and various local saints. In the centre of the upper part, superimposed friezes display the resurrection of the dead, the orders of angels, the twelve apostles and Christ in Majesty dominating the whole at the summit: a supreme celestial vision, whose expressiveness was further enhanced in the Middle Ages by the

statues' brilliant polychromy, many traces of which have been discovered. The execution of an ensemble like this undoubtedly lasted for one or two decades around 1240 (1230-1250), as the stylistic progress of the sculptures from below to above shows. The style testifies to an autochthonous development which was also aware of the great creations of the period, the west front of Notre-Dame in Paris and Amiens, and the south transept of Chartres.

Roughly contemporary or slightly earlier, the façade of Lincoln Cathedral is of considerable breadth, but with a different pattern from that of Wells. The high towers stand in the background, enclosing the nave and its façade gable, while the latter broadens out on either side, beyond the side aisles. This section of the building, which reveals a high opening in the centre, made it possible to incorporate the old Romanesque façade in this new, essentially decorative conception. The skilful assemblage of blind arcades and bays which create the originality of this type of façade is also noteworthy, with proportions made taller and slimmer by the height of the porches, in the façade of Peterborough Cathedral. At Salisbury we again find the general equilibrium of the Wells façade, with which it is almost contemporary, with its translation on to the façade of the internal proportions, the towers that project sideways and the profusion of sculpture.

SCULPTURE AS INTERIOR DECORATION: WESTMINSTER

The variety of styles that flourished in England towards the middle of the thirteenth century can best be seen in the sculptured decoration adorning church interiors: rood screens and architectural sculpture, but also funerary sculpture in which England was outstanding. The use of Purbeck marble produced a polish close to that of bronze (tomb effigy of King John Lackland, Worcester, 1225-

Tomb effigy of John Lackland.
About 1225-1235. Purbeck marble.
Worcester Cathedral.

1235). The drapery style with small tight parallel pleats of the first half of the century gave way about 1270 to a more voluminous design with full supple folds (tomb of Bishop Giles de Bridport, Salisbury). Iconographically, the chief novelty lies in the presenting of the tomb effigy, no longer immobile, but slightly turned on to one side with hand on hip. This tendency to movement culminated in the effigy with crossed legs characteristic of the following period, to which we shall return.

The evolution of monumental sculpture is the result of a constant dialectic between native apprenticeship to the craft on long-lived worksites and receptivity to the forms worked out on their great continental counterparts. The headless statue of a woman from Winchester, variously identified as the Church, the Synagogue or one of the Cardinal Virtues, is a good illustration of this play of exchanges, because its antiquizing character, which reveals the influence of Reims (Queen of Sheba) or Chartres (north porch), allows us to date it to about 1230-1235, on the strength of these French analogies. Many other examples could be cited, but they are all eclipsed by the opening shortly after 1240 of the worksite of Westminster, which, on the initiative of King Henry III, brought sculptors of various origins together to adorn an edifice conceived as a monumental reliquary and which was to be richly adorned in the interior, like a shrine treated with goldsmith's work. A large number of later works derive from this great worksite in which Roman mosaicists worked side by side with artists from the most reputable circles. Important elements of the sculptured decoration have been preserved, including the Annunciation group from the niches flanking the inner portal of the chapter house, which still poses many problems because of the differences in style between the two statues on the one hand and the iconographic differences in comparison with French groups on the other. The treatment of the bodies and the rendering of the draperies in large hanging folds recall the queens on the west front of Wells Cathedral, and are comparable to the style of certain English manuscripts, notably the Douce Apocalypse illuminated shortly afterwards in the circle of the palace and Westminster Abbey. The influence of these sculptures, which have been associated with a payment made in 1253, reached as far as Scandinavia, as shown by the St Michael slaying the Dragon in the museum of Trondheim, Norway.

Westminster also saw the fruition of a plastic conception which became characteristic of English sculpture and which consisted in fitting great sculptured figures into the spandrels of arches inside buildings. Beginning with this period, angels invade the upper parts of the Gothic church and embody the idea of the basilica as the image of paradise. Those adorning the triforium of the Westminster transept (c. 1250-1259) have affinities with the Annunciation group by the treatment of the bodies and draperies, but their timid smile and facial structure betray knowledge of innovations from Reims or answer to parallel international tendencies. The artist who carved these masterpieces was probably involved in the execution of the three keystones of the hall of the archives, the sculptures on the west spandrel of the arcature of the Chapel of St Paul, on the spandrel in the middle of the arcature of the Chapel of St Edmund, and of the keystone of the Annunciation. The base of the apse triforium which shows a man laughing, sometimes identified as a portrait of the first architect mentioned, Henry of Reyns (1244-1256), might also be attributed to him. It is an output of astonishing richness, characterized by the vigorous handling, the way bodies stand out from the background, and the dexterity of the style, although the sculptor's task was not made any easier in the case of the spandrels by the position of the sculptures. The fragments from the wall arcade of the Chapel of St John Baptist illustrate once again around the middle of the century the artistic ambition underlying the introduction of an iconographic programme which already appears in the Lady Chapel shortly after 1220.

These artistic tendencies, which arose in a royal setting, show that the importance of thirteenth-century English sculpture has too often been underestimated in favour of illumination. The fragments discovered prove the quality of an output attested by the corbel heads from the nave of Gloucester Cathedral and the head from Clarendon Palace preserved at Salisbury. During the twenty years following the middle of the century, the influence of Westminster reached the Last Judgment portal at Lincoln Cathedral, whose sculpture, especially the statues on the engaged piers, illustrates by the modelling and the elegant treatment of the draperies a handling common to the art of the illuminators working at Crowland Abbey. A second ensemble, the famous Angel Choir at Lincoln, begun in 1256 and consecrated in 1280, gathers the fruits of all this heritage and announces the new paths of the last third of the century, already observable in the Virtues and Vices in the vestibule of the chapter house at Salisbury and especially in the Christ in Majesty at Rievaulx Abbey, or again in the censing angels from Sawley (Derbyshire) today in the Victoria and Albert Museum.

Interior of the church.
About 1240-1270.
Westminster Abbey, London.

DIFFUSION OF GOTHIC IN THE EMPIRE

Adam from
the splaying
of the Adam
Portal.
Second quarter
of the 13th century.
Diözesanmuseum,
Bamberg.

A LATE ASSIMILATION OF GOTHIC

The persistence of a late Romanesque sculpture of considerable renown delayed the wholehearted adoption of the Gothic style in the Germanic regions of the Empire. At first, penetration by the new plastic values of the French worksites came up against a strong local tradition which drew on Byzantine sources in the fields of wall painting and illumination. In only a few exceptional cases were façades receptive to the great sculptured programmes, although impressive decorative schemes were employed in the interior of churches, especially on choir screens. Wooden statuary, too, quickly adopted the innovations of the Gothic style.

It is with this in mind that the interior stucco decoration of St Michael's, Hildesheim, should be understood; the figures in the south side aisle are a little earlier (c. 1190) than the reliefs on the choir screen. The influence of tradition appears there very strongly in the use of stucco reliefs on stone arches. The latter form an architectural background reminiscent not only of similar older works (Gernrode), but also of the successful achievements of contemporary goldsmithery, which reached supreme heights at this moment in the region between the Rhine and the Meuse. Nevertheless, the relief, although pronounced, does not achieve the amplitude of contemporary sculptures in northern France.

In fact, the sculpture of Saxony developed its own way of assimilating Gothic. It followed a linear path, whose continuity is ensured by another choir screen at Halberstadt (Liebfrauenkirche), slightly later than the preceding one. Transposing the concept of a shrine or reliquary on to the monumental level, but still in stucco, the extremely natural figures are seated under arches, in draperies with an ample movement. The setting is close to that applied to tympana (St Godehard, Hildesheim). But this predilection for decoration of the interior led the master masons of Magdeburg Cathedral to reuse in the choir some statues and reliefs intended for an unfinished portal. The autonomy of the statue in the round was expressed in groups carved in wood, such as that around the great triumphal cross in Halberstadt Cathedral. When looking at such works, we fully understand the difficulty the artists of the Empire had in abandoning the habits they had acquired in making bas-reliefs. Echoes of this will recur, as we shall see, in the choir screen of Bamberg Cathedral.

If we were to linger on a regional history of sculpture, we should have to take into consideration the part played in Saxony by the Golden Door of Freiberg which is possibly the best regional synthesis of the elaboration of the style around 1225. The general arrangement of the portal with sculptured splays and arch mouldings derives from the late Romanesque portals in southern Germany and northern Italy, but the iconographic synthesis presented on it seems to be attempting a summation of everything the great Gothic façades introduced. Thus, the Epiphany occupies the tympanum, while the Coronation of the Virgin is represented above, in the centre of the first arch moulding. The Last Judgment figures on the other arch mouldings, which appear only at this late date in the Gothic of these parts. The Resurrection on the outer arch moulding has been compared, perhaps rather extravagantly, to contemporary French works. The originality of the style, fluid and baroque at the same time, in the elaboration of which the bronze-founders' art probably had something to do, is apparent in the great statues on the splays which do not stand out from their framework nor become incorporated in the column, but are presented as movable statues placed on a base and virtually lodged in niches.

Crucifixion group over the choir screen.
First quarter of the 13th century. Wood.
Halberstadt Cathedral.

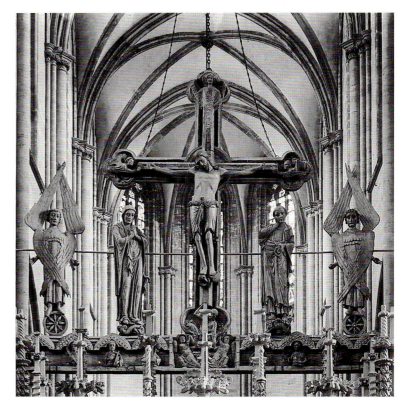

The Golden Door.
About 1225.
Freiberg Cathedral.

STRASBOURG CATHEDRAL

Benefiting by a privileged geographic situation on the periphery of the Empire and very receptive to innovations from northern France, Strasbourg Cathedral was an original and autonomous artistic centre. Indeed, the place that this building occupies in the latest contemporary history is not unconnected with the numerous studies it has inspired which seek to define its individuality between Germany and France. Reconstruction of the cathedral was begun in late Romanesque style with the eastern parts after the fire of 1176; and continued with the choir and the crossing around 1200. The north transept was finished between 1210 and 1225, about the time of the arrival on the work-site of one of the most brilliant Gothic masters, responsible for the sculptured masterpieces in the south arm of the transept: the Angel Pillar and the portals. These works have been dated towards the middle of the thirteenth century, but since a conference held at Strasbourg in 1968, there has been a tendency to push this date back to 1225-1235. That is when work began on the Rayonnant nave that differs so clearly from the choir and transept. The west

front belongs to a completely different moment in Gothic art, for the first stone was not laid until 1277 and its construction covered the whole of the fourteenth century.

The interior of the south transept contains the Angel Pillar and, outside, two symmetrical portals with splaying which, since the Revolution, no longer retain their original appearance, when they were adorned with twelve apostle statues. The lefthand portal comprises a tympanum with the Dormition of the Virgin and a lintel (restored in the nineteenth century) with her burial. The tympanum of the right-hand portal, which is original, is carved with the Coronation of the Virgin; the lintel expresses the fanciful nineteenth-century vision of the original theme of the Assumption. Between these two portals, the statue of King Solomon seated is modern, like its whole setting. The originals of the statues of the Church and the Synagogue from either side of the portals are preserved in the Musée de l'Œuvre Notre-Dame. In the interior of the transept, the famous Angel Pillar illustrates all the freshness of thirteenth-century sculpture. Three levels of four figures, which form part of the colonnettes of the pillar which correspond to the ribs, are backed against the central core and define an iconography of the Last Judgment. Below, the four evangelists are placed on bases representing their symbols; at the intermediate level, four angels are sounding trumpets; above, three angels bear the instruments of the Passion and Christ as Merciful Judge shows his wounds, seated on a throne whose base represents the Resurrection of the Dead.

The iconographic programme of the pillar is very unified. In contrast, the coherence of that of the portals has often been called in question. The existence of several successive stages has been suggested. On this supposition, the statues of the twelve apostles would form part of an original christological programme, while the Marian tympana and the lintels would belong to a modification to which the statues of the Church (New Law) and the Synagogue (Old Law awaiting Salvation) were added. For other scholars, the programme of the ensemble is homogeneous and incorporates those of the rose window and the pillar in the framework of an interpretation that is both Marian and eschatological, and might even include the slightly earlier north portal of the transept, which represents the Adoration of the Magi. In reality, the programme as a whole could have taken shape in successive stages, especially if we take into consideration the architectural alterations (south tympana not adapted to the arch moulding) and additions (bases and dies of the statues of Church and Synagogue).

If the iconographic conception takes local traditions very much into account, the stylistic interpretation incorporates many artistic concepts that come from outside. Indeed, before 1220, no creation from the Upper Rhine could be regarded as a signpost leading to the style of the sculptures considered here, as is demonstrated by the badly damaged statues of the north portal of the transept of Strasbourg or those slightly more recent and in better condition on the portal of the church of Eguisheim. In the sculpture of the pillar and the tympana art historians have seen echoes of Chartres (north porch, rood screen) and

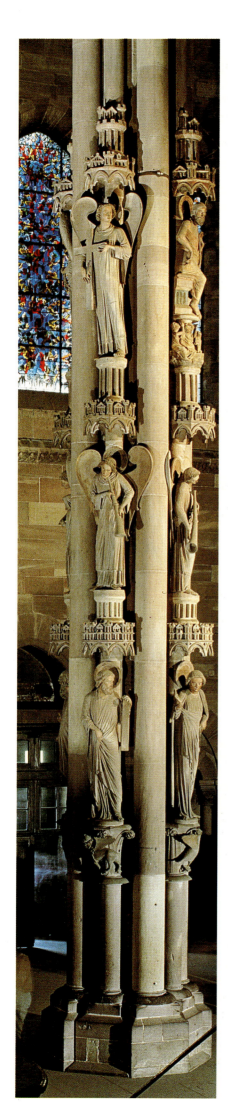

Angel Pillar.
Interior of the south transept.
About 1225–1235.
Strasbourg Cathedral.

The Dormition of the Virgin.
Tympanum, left portal of the south transept.
About 1225–1235.
Strasbourg Cathedral.

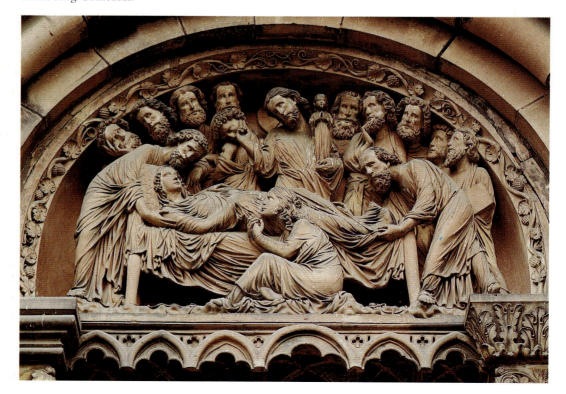

136

The Tempter. Statue from the west front.
The construction of Strasbourg Cathedral culminated in the west front, in the last decades of the 13th century.
Musée de l'Œuvre Notre-Dame, Strasbourg.

Burgundy (Dijon, Beaune, Besançon). These they have explained by the existence of a common denominator which was elaborated around 1200 at Sens Cathedral. But relations with the latter ensemble also exist without any intermediate stage, as is proved for example by comparisons between the head of St Stephen on the Sens trumeau and the heads of certain angels on the Strasbourg pillar, statues which, moreover, clearly reflect the art of Chartres. Born of these constant exchanges, the art of Strasbourg, characterized equally by the statues of the Angel Pillar and by the treatment of the drapery folds of the figures, the composition of the tympana and the statue of the Synagogue, has a most original quality which is also reflected in the positioning of the statuary in relation to the architecture. The inner evolution of the artists working on this ensemble of the south transept places the statues of Church and Synagogue among the most recent works. The basic artistic ideas were to be partly renewed by contributions from Reims when work on the rood screen began towards the mid-century.

Tympanum of the Last Judgment. Portal of the Princes. About 1220-1225. Bamberg Cathedral.

BAMBERG CATHEDRAL

Probably the most important ensemble of thirteenth-century sculptures in the northern countries, Bamberg Cathedral is at the heart of discussions about Gothic art, chronological polemics and studies of the exchanges with French cathedral sculpture. The present-day basilica, in which one can assess the full architectural influence of the Romanesque past, is no earlier than 1185. The beginning of the works cannot be very far from that date, because the worksite had already made rapid progress by 1225. The most reliable date is that of the building's consecration in 1237. It will be understood from the outset that the essential problem is to know whether the whole of the important sculptured programme of the cathedral was already completed at that date.

The building, with a nave and two aisles, a transept and a choir with two facing sections, has several sculptured portals on its exterior. On either side of the east apse open the portals known as the Adam Portal and the Portal of Mercy. The former presents some beautiful Gothic statues surmounted by baldachins added to the splays of an already finished portal which is wholly Romanesque. They comprise King Henry II, Queen Kunigunde and St Stephen on the left, and St Peter, Adam and Eve on the right. On the other side of the apse, to the north, is the Portal of Mercy, also with a Romanesque air, its tympanum being carved with a Virgin and Child accompanied by Saints Peter and George, and Henry II and Kunigunde once again. The style of this tympanum belongs to currents parallel to those of the Saxon stucco works already mentioned, although the relief is more assertive, as befitting sculptures executed in stone. It is the earlier style, from the first cathedral workshop, the one which was responsible for the original structure of the Adam Portal before the addition of the splay figures; consequently the latter illustrate the second stage in the sculpture of Bamberg. The first workshop adopted the local tradition wholesale, whereas the second partakes to the full in the international exchanges.

On the north side aisle the Princes' Portal forms a strongly projecting structure forming an *avant-corps*. On either side of the portal, on the outside wall, were the seductive statues of the Church and the Synagogue (today inside), whose feminine forms are subtly evident beneath their clothing. An original composition of prophets sur-

mounted by apostles figures on the splays. The Last Judgment stands out on the tympanum. The sculpture of this tympanum, especially the heads of the figures, is derived directly from that of Reims Cathedral.

Several groups of equally famous sculptures are preserved in the interior of the building. In the first place, the reliefs of the old choir screen which exhibits pairs of apostles (south) and prophets (north) in conversation. Their original arrangement and the style which belong to the first sculpture workshop denote artistic progress, possibly stemming from contact with goldsmiths, culminating in the most recent reliefs of the prophets and the Annunciation, in spite of the general features of the group common to all, such as the arrangement of the figures and the curvilinear movement of the drapery folds. One of the most famous figures is the Jonah with bared breast, the power of whose drapery is accentuated by the relief. Among the masterpieces inside the cathedral are the various statues, and especially the Visitation group executed by the second workshop. Recently it has been suggested that this Visitation couple should be separated, the theory being that the Virgin probably came from an Annunciation or might be Elizabeth, while the said Elizabeth could be a Sibyl or the Prophetess Hannah from the Presentation in the Temple. The universally famous Horseman on one of the piers of the nave facing the Princes' Portal was probably originally integrated with a broader icono-

The Prophets Jonah and Hosea. Choir screen. About 1230. Bamberg Cathedral.

graphic programme possibly in relation with the other statues (Epiphany?), unless it should be considered as an isolated statue at the very moment when royal and princely iconography was monopolizing the Gothic building. Its style is directly inspired by the head of "Philip Augustus" in Reims Cathedral.

The second workshop of Bamberg Cathedral is partially defined purely in relation to the sculpture of Reims Cathedral. However what is at stake is important for the chronology of the two cathedrals. Architectural analysis has shown that the tympanum of the Princes' Portal, partly influenced by Reims, is not later than 1225. No additional archaeological evidence can be relied on for the other sculptures of the cathedral, which are mostly statues independent of the masonry and the execution of which extends until 1237 at least. As far as this tympanum is concerned, most of the models of heads that one might call of Reims origin are found in the zone of the high windows of Reims. Moreover, many Reims sculptures comparable to those of Bamberg are located in the east parts of the cathedral, with the exception of some statues on the west front possibly coming from an initial project, which certainly poses chronological problems. Comparison of these two monuments involves a thorough rethinking of the relation which exists between the progress of the architectural works, the date of the execution of the sculpture and that of their actual putting in place.

Statue of the Virgin
from an Annunciation or Visitation group
with the angel of the Annunciation.
About 1230-1235.
Bamberg Cathedral.

◁◁ The Synagogue, from the Princes' Portal.
About 1225.
Bamberg Cathedral.

◁ The Synagogue, from the south
transept of the cathedral.
About 1225-1235.
Musée de l'Œuvre Notre-Dame, Strasbourg.

Calvary and rood screen of the west choir, portal.
Early second half of the 13th century.
Naumburg Cathedral.

two best known statues represent Count Eckehard and Uta. The style of this statuary (which recalls the rood screen of Mainz Cathedral) draws on the repertory developed by Parisian sculpture of the 1240s, translated here with special individualized accents, thanks to which the impressive masses are treated with delicacy. The date of this group, frequently disputed, cannot be earlier than the middle of the century, judging by the episcopal letter which mentions the founders in 1249. If Naumburg and Reims illustrate an identical stage of development in relation to Parisian sculpture, the Naumburg statues cannot be as late as 1270-1275, as has sometimes been suggested. Moreover, the output of this workshop continued, still in the west choir, with the reliefs which crown the screen and represent Passion scenes, distributed in groups of figures separated by colonnettes. The dense crowding of the figures, the depth of the relief and the baroque air of the groups derive from contemporary works in Germanic circles, especially the art of altarpieces.

It would also be desirable to mention many other groups, such as that of the west choir of Mainz Cathedral. Unconnected with the latter, the work of the Erminold Master, who takes his name from the tomb of the first abbot of the Benedictine abbey of Prüfening near Regensburg and with whom other ensembles are associated, includes the carved arch mouldings of the west portal of Basel Minster, the Annunciation group arranged on the transept pillars of Regensburg Cathedral, and the seated St Peter from the choir of the same cathedral today in the Regensburg museum. Among the sculpture of the last quarter of the century, we should mention the porch and main portal of the cathedral of Freiburg im Breisgau and especially the west front of Strasbourg Cathedral. We should also describe the influence that German groups (Bamberg) or Saxon sculpture (Naumburg, Meissen) had in countries like Hungary, where it was felt during the thirteenth century (Ják), replacing the tendency which

OTHER FORMS OF CREATION

When art historians have engaged in controversy in an attempt to understand how receptive German worksites were to French creations, they have sometimes forgotten the features peculiar to German sculpture, primarily the growing independence of the statue in relation to the architecture, which very soon led it to win autonomy in space for itself. Owing to the persistence of Romanesque architecture, the early Gothic statues were posed against a backdrop, so to speak, on the exterior, and even more in the interior, of buildings which as yet did not present all the advantages of the new architecture. This line of thought shows that French influence was primarily propagated in the small figures on the arch mouldings, for example, rather than in the big statues.

It is in that spirit that we must tackle the exceptional Saxon ensemble of Naumburg. The west choir of the cathedral contains twelve statues with heavy accents, backed against supports, not representing apostles or saints as one might expect, but the twelve founders of the building. Their clothing and attitudes relate to their rank in each case and the style betrays the hand of several artists; the

▷ Eckehard and Uta.
Statues in the west choir.
After 1249.
Naumburg Cathedral.

◁ Annunciation statues
illustrating the evolution
of the Swabian
style in the 14th century.
Heilige-Kreuzkirche,
Schwäbisch Gmünd.

French Gothic forms had hitherto imported into Central Europe (Esztergom).

The importance and significance of polychromy in stone statuary cannot be overemphasized. The polychromy found on the Regensburg sculptures tends to show that the range of colours during the thirteenth century in Germany was restricted. They were apparently applied on broad surfaces and matched the arrangement of the drapery and the modelling, with only a few special accents, on the lips and eyes, for example. If we generalize from the example of Regensburg, this polychromy would contrast strongly with that of earlier or later centuries which was closer to the use of colour on woodcarvings characterized by the highlights of superadded details which sometimes even ran counter to the sculpted form. That would call in question a number of nineteenth-century restorations which did not grasp this subtlety. Meanwhile, the study of polychromy needs to be undertaken at the regional level. Among the most important works of recent years figure the researches on the architectural polychromy of the church of St Elizabeth at Marburg (1235-1283) and its relations with the furnishings (stained glass windows, rood screen, funerary monuments). The original colours, executed during the last architectural stage (1265 and 1283) were distributed as follows: the walls, vaults, pillars, shafts and capitals were painted pink, with white joints, except on the capitals. The profiles of transverse ribs and arcades were painted alternately in white and yellow ochre, a colour also used for the ribs, and the tracery of bays was sometimes emphasized in white. The polychromy on the outside of the building was enhanced by a deep red to accentuate the profile of the cornices. Without attempting to be exhaustive, we may recall that the interior of Amiens Cathedral was painted grey on walls and pillars, and yellow ochre on the vaults, while the joints of the masonry were painted white. A harmony of yellow ochre and white also adorned the interior of Chartres Cathedral in the thirteenth century.

THE ORIGINALITY OF SOUTHERN GOTHIC

THE PÓRTICO DE LA GLORIA IN SANTIAGO DE COMPOSTELA

At the end of the first quarter of the twelfth century, work on the cathedral of Santiago de Compostela was still unfinished. It was not until the third quarter of the century that a famous master, Mateo, architect and possibly sculptor, undertook to close the nave of the building with an immense porch mounted on a lower structure. The work is as famous as its master, who was already active in Compostela in 1168 when King Ferdinand II of León granted him an annual pension so that he could devote himself wholly to the cathedral. The trumeau and tympanum of

the Pórtico de la Gloria were installed in 1188. An inscription celebrates the completion of the works, for this part of the central portal at least: "The year of the Incarnation of the Lord 1188, or 1226 of the [Hispanic] Era, the first of April, the lintels of the main doors of the church of Santiago were put in place by Master Mateo, who held the mastership from the foundations of these portals." The master resided in Compostela and is known from other documents. There is no doubt that he was already celebrated when he was awarded the royal pension, which helps us to date his work more accurately.

The three portals protected by a porch on the façade of the cathedral of Compostela open directly into the naves, just as they do at Vézelay. The stylistic and chronological continuity between the lower crypt and the façade proper, up to the level of the galleries, appears logical. As soon as the believer enters the porch, he is surrounded by the

Master Mateo. The Pórtico de la Gloria. Central portal. Late 12th century. Cathedral of Santiago de Compostela.

sculptural ensemble carved out of marble and granite. Of the three portals, only the central one has a tympanum and a trumeau on which stands the statue of the Apostle James. From the crypt to the galleries the unity of thought is built around the architectural representation of the Heavenly Jerusalem, whose historical deployment occupies the three inner portals of the porch. The righthand portal is devoted to the Last Judgment. The Resurrection of the Dead is represented on the twisted column of one of the pillars; on the archivolts appear Christ and the Archangel Michael separating the Chosen from the Damned. The tympanum of the central portal portrays Christ showing his wounds surrounded by the four Evangelists associated with the four beasts and angels who are censing or bearing the instruments of the Passion. In the background is a throng of the Chosen, while the Elders of the Apocalypse are represented on the archivolt. Recently the interpretation of the lefthand portal as illustrating the Descent of Christ into limbo has been convincingly upheld. The whole fits into a global reflection on the Revelation of St John and the Vision of Matthew in order to represent the Second Coming with its various historical and eschatological elements. The statues depict the prophets and apostles. The best interpretation of this ensemble is the one a medieval man has transmitted to us, the Armenian Bishop Martyrus, a pilgrim who journeyed to Compostela in the fifteenth century: "Above the door . . . one sees Christ seated on a throne, with the representation of everything that has happened since Adam and everything that will happen until the end of the world."

The iconographic and stylistic sources of the Pórtico de la Gloria, work on which continued until about 1200, are the subject of permanent study. Master Mateo occupies an original position between Romanesque and Gothic art. The iconography and conception of the porch are both a reflection of the monumental tradition from which the central portal of Saint-Denis also derives and an illustration of the Burgundian schemes at Vézelay and Avallon. Yet neither of these affinities explains the style of Master Mateo to whom we are also indebted for the stalls and the screen of the old cathedral choir, among other works. The presence of Byzantine features in the iconography and the style has been adduced. But the unity of the whole, the realism of the faces, the independent air of the statues, the freedom of execution and many other general and particular characteristics which we also find in San Vicente at Avila, have led art historians to think that Master Mateo had a Spanish training, leaning rather heavily on a comparison with the sculptures of the Cámara Santa of Oviedo, Carrión de los Condes and Silos. Nevertheless, there is an excessive tendency to conceal beneath the unity of conception and the name of a single master the variety of hands which can easily be distinguished by careful observation. It appears that Master Mateo's workshop had fully assimilated the various Hispanic trends of the second half of the twelfth century, especially the lessons of Silos, and that it was not unaware of what other great artists were doing in different parts of Europe. In spite of the enormous prestige of this place of pilgrimage, artistic echoes of the Pórtico de la Gloria do not seem to have crossed Spanish frontiers (Galicia, León, Zamora). At the beginning of the thirteenth century, the admiration felt for the quality of Mateo's work, which still appeared very traditional at the time, did not stand up when confronted with the new Gothic modernity.

Royal couple possibly from the west front. Second half of the 13th century. Burgos Cathedral.

BURGOS AND LEÓN: NORTH-SOUTH CURRENTS

Although Master Mateo's art still makes itself felt at Orense, his rejection is already obvious on the portal of Tuy Cathedral, also in Galicia, and then at Ciudad Rodrigo. The new vitality born of contacts with foreign parts was deliberately encouraged on the two most ambitious worksites of thirteenth-century Spain: the cathedrals of Burgos and León. The artistic exchanges facilitated by the influx of pilgrims became a permanent feature with the growing political relations of León and Castile with France and Germany. An original symbiosis of the strong peninsular tradition and northern French innovations came into being during the different stages of the construction and decoration of Burgos Cathedral. Begun in 1221 after King Ferdinand III granted an endowment to Bishop Maurice the Englishman, progress on the works of the cathedral had got as far as the level of the north transept in 1230, and its Coronería façade was already finished by about 1257. The worksite continued to be active for several decades in spite of the consecration in 1260. The west front, which was devoted to the Virgin, no longer exists. Among the sculptures which might have come from it figures the celebrated royal couple successively identified as Ferdinand III and his wife, and Alfonso X and Queen Violante. Recently their identification with Solomon and the Queen of Sheba in a typological programme

143

Annunciation. Portal of the cloister. Late 13th century. Burgos Cathedral.

great originality, a genuine stylistic revolution in the early stages of Spanish Gothic. The transept galleries of Burgos, for example, for which the progress of the works indicates a date in the 1260s, are not so close to those of Reims, while the relations of dependency are extremely close to certain aspects of the statuary at Amiens, and Amiens is probably the source of the idea of the superposition of two galleries: statues and windows with tracery. The originality of Burgos, to take only this example of detail, lies precisely in the interpretation one puts on Parisian and Amiens models, seeing that the lower parts of the façade are inspired by Soissons.

The influence of Burgos was very important (Sasamón, Burgo de Osma, even Bayonne) and it was primarily exerted on the largest group of sculpture still extant today, that of León Cathedral. The construction of the lower parts of León extends over the entire second half of the thirteenth century. Between 1260 and the end of the century, the three portals of the west front display, in the middle, the Last Judgment in a style inspired by the Coronería portal, with the White Virgin (María Blanca) on the trumeau, the Coronation of the Virgin on the right, and themes from the childhood of Christ in relation with the life of the Virgin, on the left. Impressed by the architectural contacts with Reims, art historians have often exaggerated the French influences alleged to have affected the sculpture of León, something which, apart from general considerations, does not stand up to serious criticism. The surprising disparity between styles and qualities, as well as the whole debate about the original position of certain statues, might be explained by the enormous financial difficulties the worksite experienced. The General Council of

Central portal of the west front with the White Virgin. Second half of the 13th century. León Cathedral.

has been suggested. The great sculptured groups are situated in the transept and in the interior of the building. On the tympanum of the south transept (El Sarmental) we find Christ in Majesty flanked by the evangelists with their symbols in between, on the lintel the apostles, on the splays the Elders of the Apocalypse among other images, and on the trumeau a bishop, probably one of the first in the town, rather than Maurice, the initiator of the works. To the north (Coronería or Apostles' Portal), the splays, which continue on to the façade, house apostle statues, while the tympanum, lintels and splays are devoted to the Last Judgment. There are galleries of statues of kings on the summit of the lateral façades and the west front. Lastly, on the portal of the cloister, which can be dated towards the very end of the century, we should mention the two pairs of statues on the splays: the Annunciation and David and Isaiah. Among the groups of statues attached to the pillars of the cloister, that of the Epiphany deserves special attention. If this brief description gives a feeling of the progress of the works, emphasis should be laid on the stylistic affinities of the sculptures of Burgos with those of Paris, Amiens and Reims (or between the tympana of the Coronería and the central portal of the south transept of Chartres as regards the iconography). It is a complicated problem which requires careful re-examination in the light of new research into French sculpture. It would bring out not the direct dependency which has been postulated but a very

144

1274 insisted once again on the need for money for the worksite and encouraged the faithful to give alms. A document of 1277 enables us to understand the wage problems of artists and stonemasons who were granted tax exemptions by King Alfonso X.

Equally representative of the sculpture of León during the thirteenth century are the many tombs extant in the cathedral and other churches in the region. They belong exclusively to ecclesiastics and the nobility, and consist of two types: the isolated sarcophagus of classical tradition and the sarcophagus set in a recess. The presence of scenes of a religious, funerary or profane nature enables us to establish comparisons with monumental sculpture, and the style illustrates the part their local schooling played in the sculptors' work, on the one hand, and the attraction of ultra-Pyrenean models, on the other. Thus the sculptor we might call the Master of the Last Judgment of the cathedral executed no less than eight tombs in local limestone (including that of Martín Fernández in the cloister). It should be said that, apart from our stylistic observations, we know nothing about the schooling and careers of such masters, their origins or their travels northwards.

The art of the cathedrals of Burgos and León is also reflected at Toro and in the Portal of the Apostles at Avila Cathedral. Lastly, the Puerta del Reloj (Clock Door) of Toledo Cathedral prompts us once again to dwell on the discrepancy between the architectural adoption of northern models (Bourges) and their diffuse reflection in the case of sculpture (not overlooking Italian innovations), in spite of the narrative structure of the Toledo tympanum on four registers. The most Parisian of the cathedral sculptures is the marble statue known as the White Virgin.

Puerta del Reloj (Clock Door).
Late 13th century. Toledo Cathedral.

Portal of the Apostles from the west front
(reordered in the 15th century). Last quarter of the 13th century.
Avila Cathedral.

THE MEDITERRANEAN FAÇADE AND CISTERCIAN ART

"We forbid the execution of sculptures or paintings in our churches and all dependencies of the monastery, for when attention is paid to them, the sense of right meditation and the discipline of religious gravity is often lost." In 1150 this chapter of the Cistercian Order issued clear directives about the sculptured decoration of monasteries. Discarding figurative decoration, on the whole, the new Cistercian foundations adorned if not their churches at least the cloisters and chapter houses with exceptional and sober decorative refinement. Without embracing the extreme austerity of Le Thoronet, Cistercian foundations in the new Catalonia sought to incorporate a form of sculptured decoration into the community life. During the thirteenth century in the monasteries of Poblet and Santes Creus, founded in the previous century, extremely delicate interlaces of wickerwork, foliage motifs and various plant themes adorned the capitals of cloisters and halls, keystones and rose windows. This aniconic tendency was not always the order of the day, as attested by the keystone devoted to St Nicholas in the larger church of Poblet, and it was less and less observed as the century advanced (chapter house of Poblet and cloister of Santes Creus). The portal of the north transept of the convent of Vallbona de les Monges was given a tympanum adorned with a Virgin and Child flanked by censing angels between 1250 and 1275.

During the thirteenth century Catalonia experienced a time of eventful historical change. The defeat of Muret near Toulouse and the death of Peter the Catholic (1213), the capture of Majorca (1229) and Valencia (1238), and then Sicily (1282) impelled the country towards the Mediterranean. So artistic production sees various trends co-exist or succeed each other in the course of the century. The worksites of the cathedrals of Tarragona and Lleida (Lérida), where this mixture of tendencies and Italian influences was given material form, have already been mentioned in the section dealing with the last phases of Romanesque art. Also involved is the whole problem of the persistence of this late Romanesque and the remarkable Cistercian continuity which ensured that the monasteries never broke the links established from their foundation with the northern groups of the Order.

Among the various aspects of this period and alongside the architectural renewal sought by the mendicant orders, we find the emergence of an early southern Gothic sculpture composed jointly of Mediterranean influences, the assimilation of late Romanesque and eclectic trends of the early 1200s, and a greater or lesser degree of receptivity to northern innovations. The work of Master Bartomeu illustrates this new pluralism. Known between 1277 and 1295, this artist from Gerona worked around 1277 on the façade of Tarragona Cathedral (lefthand portal) and carved the tomb of Peter the Great at Santes Creus between 1291 and 1295. His activity probably spills over into the fourteenth century. The tympanum of the Virgin and some capitals in the cloister of Gerona Cathedral, and the Calvary preserved in the museum are also attributed to him; they antedate 1277. On the façade of Tarragona Cathedral the Virgin and Child on the trumeau, probably carved towards the end of the century on a marble Roman column, is especially noteworthy. Master Bartomeu and his workshop prepared the advent of the great Catalan Gothic sculpture of the early fourteenth century and eclipsed the activity of other regional workshops which also, in spite of their isolation, tried to escape from the strong attachment to Romanesque art (central group of the Agramunt portal commissioned by the Confraternity of Weavers in 1283).

A similar approach would lead us to cite various examples in Mediterranean Languedoc and emphasize the part played by Carcassonne (choir statues of Saint-Nazaire)

View of the cloister. 13th century. Monastery of Poblet.

Virgin and Child. Trumeau, central portal of the west front. Late 13th century. Tarragona Cathedral.

during the second half of the thirteenth century. Study of the capitals of the Premonstratensian abbey of Fontcaude (Hérault) reveals in a cloister of modest dimensions the ambition of a community to break free from the predilection for capitals adorned almost exclusively with leafwork of other thirteenth and fourteenth-century Languedoc cloisters (Fontfroide, Villelongue, Saint-Papoul, Saint-Hilaire) by the introduction of historiated decoration (life of Christ). The many surviving fragments enable us to recognize in the style of different sculptors a clear reflection of Ile-de-France sculpture of the years 1240-1260. Can we associate the presence of these stylistic trends in the south of France (heavy drapery with full folds which break over the feet, faces with hair thrown back) with an opening of these regions to northern innovations as a result of their conquest by St Louis in 1258?

THE ITALY OF
FREDERICK II

Imperial bust, possibly an idealized portrait
of Frederick II. Second quarter of the 13th century. Stone.
Museo Civico, Barletta.

Presumed portrait of Charles I of Anjou (1227-1285).
Museo Capitolino, Rome.

The Italy of the thirteenth century (Duecento) can be defined by a few great names: Nicola Pisano, Arnolfo di Cambio, Giovanni Pisano, Cavallini, Duccio, Giotto, Dante. The century begins with Antelami, in other words with the intellectual and artistic advance which virtually leads from Romanesque art to Humanism. We chose to discuss Antelami in the chapter on Romanesque art because his art vitalizes the last phases of that style around the Mediterranean. Nevertheless, he was already conscious of the first Gothic decades of northern France and was well able to exploit their artistic concepts in a northern Italy that remained obstinately Romanesque. This absorption of the early Gothic currents was constantly renewed in Italy by contacts with the East and the incessant influx of Byzantine forms. To this was added the very important artistic role of the Cistercians (Fossanova) and the political will of Frederick II Hohenstaufen to revive the antique, classical roots of the imperial power. Under Frederick II (1194-1250), Emperor of the West from 1220, artistic Italy cannot be considered as cut off from imperial Germany; especially when we remember the role played by the emperor in the embellishment of certain monuments, such as Bamberg Cathedral.

Beyond a constant return to classical antiquity already manifested in the personalized portraits of Frederick II (or alleged as such) which is one of the characteristics of the sculptured output of thirteenth-century Gothic in southern Italy, the sculpture of the Duecento shows considerable independence in spite of its frequent contacts with the worksites of the Ile-de-France cathedrals. We observe the rejection of the French portal with column statues and arch mouldings. The statue's essential function is not so intimately subordinated to the architecture, and the actual significance of sculpture varies with the predilection shown for liturgical furnishings: ambos, fonts, etc.

Among the great works which can be associated with Frederick II in the field of southern arts, the prime example is the triumphal gateway at Capua (finished in 1239) which publicly proclaims a political iconography; but the im-

perial bust of Barletta, so directly related to the capitals with human heads from Troia, is also noteworthy. Our knowledge of the art of the period of Frederick II in central and southern Italy has been considerably renewed, bringing to light numerous regional centres, and rich networks of local and international relations which contributed to the elaboration of the new modernity, at once Gothic and classical. Thus, the sculpture of Castel del Monte derives from French Gothic, while that of Lagopesole (1242-1250 for the ground floor) looks rather to the Germanic world. In Campania, the furnishings of Salerno Cathedral (ambos and candlestick c. 1180), of La Cava dei Tirreni, Ravello (c. 1200), Caserta Vecchia (c. 1213) and Sessa Aurunca illustrate the evolution of a long tradition of marble-working fostered by a constant renewal of classical figurative elements. At Rome, the art of the Cosmati craftsmen, which also comprises sculptured elements, looks towards these southern creations. It was in this Gothic reinterpretation of the language of Antiquity, Late Antiquity in particular, that the first of the great personalities of Italian Gothic classicism, Nicola Pisano, who was also fully aware of the art of the imperial entourage in the Germanic milieu, was to be trained.

Frederician stronghold of Castel del Monte (Apulia).

Nicola Pisano.
Annunciation, Nativity, Annunciation to the Shepherds
and Bath of Jesus.
Pulpit, detail.
About 1255-1259. Marble.
Baptistery, Pisa.

Nicola Pisano.
Pulpit.
1265-1268. Marble.
Siena Cathedral.

NICOLA PISANO

The first of the great thirteenth-century Italian sculptors
was probably a native of southern Frederician Italy where
he would have familiarized himself during his youth in the
second quarter of the century with the artistic experiments
in those regions, if we are to believe the two documents
which mention him as "Nicola of Apulia." His biogra-
phers sometimes assign to him a period of training in Campania, sometimes an essentially Tuscan apprenticeship
with at least one journey to northern France shortly after
the middle of the century. These deductions as a whole
clearly account for the features of Nicola Pisano's style
during his known period of activity.

That activity comprises three great creations around
which other associated works are arranged. The pulpit of
the Pisa Baptistery is dated to 1260 (1259) and signed *Hoc
opus insigne sculpsit Nicola Pisanus*. Comparison of this
pulpit with that of Bartolommeo da Foggia at Ravello
bears out the theory that the sculptor had southern and
Campanian artistic origins. The hexagonal Pisa pulpit is
supported by six outer columns, three of them resting on
lions, and a principal column in the centre which rests on
a base carved with figures and animals. Plant-life capitals
bear the row of trefoil arches which is embellished with
corner statuettes (Cardinal Virtues, the Faith, John the
Baptist); the spandrels are also sculptured (prophets and
evangelists). The upper balustrade comprises five panels
adorned with narrative reliefs representing the Annunciation together with the Nativity and the Annunciation to
the Shepherds, the Epiphany, the Presentation in the Temple, the Crucifixion and the Last Judgment. The iconographic programme (christological cycle and allegories)
and the forms used (trefoil arches, foliated capitals) turn
the pulpit into a transcription of major monumental sculpture.

One of the novelties is the decorative reinforcement of
the angles with clusters of colonnettes and statues, while
the introduction of independent realistic panels recalls the
sarcophagi of Late Antiquity. Nicola's classicism, which
seems to have been enlisted for the glorification of the past
of the town of Pisa, is distinguished from the antiquizing
Romanesque style by his exceptional ability to reinterpret
the plasticity of antique sculpture.

The contract for the pulpit of Siena Cathedral drawn up
between Nicola Pisano and the church warden of the
cathedral, Melano, is dated 29 September 1265 and states
that the work should be executed by the artist and two
assistants, Arnolfo di Cambio and Lapo, soon to be joined
by Nicola's son Giovanni. A fourth assistant is mentioned
in 1267, a year before the pulpit was completed. On an
octagonal plan, the Siena pulpit presents panels separated
at the angles by figure groups representing episodes close
in their sequence to those of Pisa. The scale is smaller here
and the influence of Antiquity is less apparent. The Gothic
forms are firmer in the grasp of the sculptor (folds gathered
on the ground, facial structure) who seems to have a thorough knowledge of contemporary ivories, which, as we
know, travelled far and wide in the Middle Ages. The
documented presence of several artists means that an attempt can be made to single out the work done by each of

them. Obviously, art historians have had to use all their skill in this connection. Nicola's hand can be clearly distinguished in several corner statues and the Crucifixion panel. At Siena we begin to notice the work of the master's son, Giovanni (angels on the left of the Massacre of the Innocents) and of Arnolfo who was to become a famous artist in his turn (crouching figures to the right of the Crucifixion).

The great fountain of Perugia, planned as early as 1254, was finished by Nicola and his son Giovanni in 1278 after a year's work. Since then it has undergone two major reconstructions, first after the earthquake of 1349, and again after the Second World War. It is a monument that is essential for our knowledge of public sculpture and for our appreciation of the output of sculptors' workshops which took on both religious and civil commissions. The fountain, forming a twenty-five-sided polygon adorned with reliefs, has an elevated central basin embellished with statues at the angles. The reliefs represent the Labours of the Months, the Liberal Arts, fables, the story of Romulus and Remus, heraldic animals and Old Testament scenes. The twenty-four statues represent abstract personifications, towns and places, Old Testament figures, saints and contemporaries who had played a part in the erection of the fountain. The whole is a public illustration of harmony between Church and State. It was one of the last of Nicola Pisano's creations. Among the reliefs obviously carved by him figure the months of June and July, whereas the Liberal Arts reveal the style of his son. Among the other works executed by or attributed to Nicola Pisano are two reliefs at Lucca Cathedral which refer directly to the Pisa pulpit, the design of the tomb of St Dominic at Bologna, the altar of St James in Pistoia Cathedral (1273), and perhaps the direction of the works and the sculptures in the arches of the second level on the exterior of the Pisa Baptistery (c. 1270).

Nicola and Giovanni Pisano.
Main fountain.
1277–1278.
Perugia.

Nicola Pisano. Crucifixion. Pulpit, detail. 1265–1268. Marble. Siena Cathedral.

Giovanni Pisano. Crucifixion. Pulpit, detail. About 1297–1301. Marble. Sant'Andrea, Pistoia.

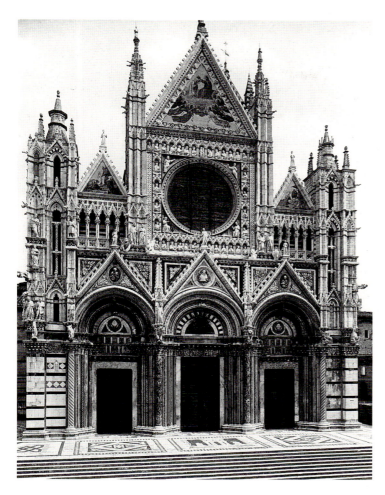

Giovanni Pisano. Façade of the cathedral. After 1284. Siena.

attributed to Pisano, especially the animals situated at the level of the portal lunettes and the statues placed immediately above them; today most of the latter are preserved in the Museo dell'Opera del Duomo. They fit into an iconographic programme which stresses the lineage of the Virgin and comprises prophets and figures from the Old Testament, as well as Plato, Aristotle, Balaam and the Sibyl, accompanied by inscriptions announcing the birth of Christ. A Virgin and Child, which appears in a fifteenth-century fresco, originally dominated the central portal. Even if the distant model for this façade can be sought in northern France, Pisano achieved in it a personal symbiosis between sculpture and architecture, rejected the archivolts of northern Gothic and splay statues, and adopted a very free positioning of the statuary in which each statue set on a base was completely independent. The statue emphasizes the ascending movement of the architectural ensemble by its imposing dimensions, the breadth of the base and the prominence assigned to the head.

At the turn of the century, Giovanni worked on the pulpit of Sant'Andrea at Pistoia; its completion in 1301 is recorded in an inscription. According to Vasari, he worked on it for four years. Of hexagonal plan, it is akin to the Siena pulpit, but its style is much more Gothic with more elongated figures, movements with violent undertones and dramatic expressions. To a familiarity with Roman sarcophagi is added, especially in the facial expression, an echo of the figure carving of the Germanic Gothic of Bamberg and Naumburg, as attested by a comparison of the deacons' heads on the pulpit with the Bamberg Horseman, for example. These accents, the most prestigious in thirteenth-century Gothic, are toned down in the pulpit of Pisa Cathedral (1302-1311) in favour of the new formulas peculiar to fourteenth-century Italy.

GIOVANNI PISANO

Son of Nicola Pisano and born at Pisa, the artist appears for the first time in 1265 helping his father to execute the Siena pulpit and then at Perugia in 1278. His last known major commission, the monument to Margaret of Luxemburg at Genoa, was undertaken in 1312. During his career, a comparatively large number of standing Virgins and Child have been attributed to him. The best documented are those of the Pisa Baptistery (c. 1295), the altar of the Scrovegni Chapel at Padua (c. 1305-1306) and the Duomo of Prato (c. 1312). Ivory statuettes, including the Virgin and Child in Pisa Cathedral, and wooden statues are also attributed to him. His activity extends over the first two decades of the fourteenth century.

Architect or master mason as well as sculptor, Giovanni attended to the decoration and installation of sculptured architectural ensembles, as his father had done in the Pisa Baptistery. Mentioned at Massa Maritima, his name is primarily linked with the erection of the façade of Siena Cathedral, a most important monument which the town wished to be especially sumptuous. Giovanni was employed there as early as 1284 and the last mention of his presence on the worksite dates to 1296. For the first time a great Italian Gothic façade was adorned with sculptures which even covered the upper parts. Needless to say, art historians have seen in it the echo of knowledge acquired from northern monuments (Amiens, Reims). In its present state, only the lower part of the façade can be

Giovanni Pisano. Pulpit. 1302-1311. Marble. Pisa Cathedral.

Giovanni Pisano.
Miriam, sister of Moses (?).
Statue from the façade of Siena Cathedral.
Between 1284 and 1296. Marble.
Museo dell'Opera della Metropolitana, Siena.

Giovanni Pisano.
Simeon.
Statue from the façade of Siena Cathedral.
Between 1284 and 1296. Marble.
Museo dell'Opera della Metropolitana, Siena.

Giovanni Pisano. Annunciation, Nativity, Annunciation to the Shepherds and Bath of Jesus. Pulpit, detail. About 1293–1301. Marble. Sant'Andrea, Pistoia.

ARNOLFO DI CAMBIO

Like Giovanni Pisano, Arnolfo di Cambio was trained as an assistant to Nicola Pisano, with whom he was first associated (1265) in the execution of the Siena pulpit (he was about twenty years old at the time), and then (1277-1278) in the making of the Perugia fountain. He may even have collaborated as early as 1260 on the pulpit in the Pisa Baptistery, and he certainly worked on the tomb of St Dominic at Bologna, probably at the time of the execution of the Siena pulpit. This tomb was composed of a rectangular sarcophagus borne by caryatids; the sides were ornamented with narrative scenes, and the four corners and the centre of the front and back with statues. The problem of what share Arnolfo had in this work compared with that claimed for Nicola Pisano or another of his pupils, Guglielmo, is still the subject of discussion. Two capitals in Siena Cathedral have also been attributed to Arnolfo.

His presence at Rome in the service of Charles of Anjou from 1277 is recorded. From this period date several tombs which confirm the large part played by Arnolfo in defining the type of recessed wall tomb which dominated production from the end of the thirteenth century. Moreover, the role of this sculptor was also decisive in the evolution of the funerary effigy with eyes closed. The tomb of Cardinal Annibaldi (died 1276) in St John Lateran, Rome, is a modern montage which includes two highly innovating fragments by Arnolfo, a frieze of clerics and the *gisant*; both, judging by the style, are posterior to the date of the cardinal's death. The evolution of Arnolfo's funerary art can be followed by studying the tombs of Pope Adrian V (died 1265) in San Francesco at Viterbo, the attribution of

which is disputed, and Cardinal de Braye in San Domenico at Orvieto, and the later monument of Pope Boniface VIII. The most famous is the tomb of Cardinal de Braye (died 1282), which originally possessed an architectural frame. Among the sculptured elements, we find two angels holding back curtains enabling the spectator to see the recumbent effigy of the cardinal, the Virgin and Child, two saints, one of them Dominic, and two censing angels now in the Orvieto museum. The influence of Roman marble masons is apparent in the decorative setting of the tomb, which is characterized by the presence of small sculptures, also by Arnolfo's hand, distributed over the monument. Even if this type of monumental tomb belongs to a French tradition of recessed tombs already used at Viterbo for the monument to Pope Clement IV (died 1268) by Pietro Oderisio, the theatrical introduction of the angels unveiling the *gisant* (unless they are closing the curtains on the defunct) is completely new. In 1980 the base of the baldachin was brought to light in Santa Cecilia, Rome. Signed by Arnolfo and dated 1293, it offers a welcome and useful landmark in his career. Coming after the Roman baldachin in San Paolo, it helps us to understand the Florentine work of this great architect-sculptor.

In later life Arnolfo di Cambio returned to Florence (1296) and embarked on the ambitious project for the façade of the Duomo, until 1302 at least, if not until 1310, depending on the date assigned to his death. It is known from paintings, a drawing and descriptions, which show that Arnolfo's façade then rose only to the height of the tympanum of the central portal. The sculptures on it included episodes from the childhood of Christ and the life

Arnolfo di Cambio.
Dormition of the Virgin
from the façade of the Duomo, Florence.
1296-1302 (1310?). Marble.
Skulpturen Sammlung, Staatliche Museen,
East Berlin.

of Mary, a Virgin and Child, and statues of prophets and saints, including Pope Boniface VIII. The museums of Florence (Museo dell'Opera) and Berlin preserve two sculptures of the Virgin reclining that come respectively from the Nativity and the Dormition, and the seated Virgin holding the Child famous for its inlaid glass eyes. Unlike the arrangement of the façade of Giovanni Pisano at Siena, that of Florence introduces statues in niches, thus covering the walls of the lower parts. Static and frontal, this arrangement is more in harmony with antique monuments, but the style is Gothic, as is the idea of displaying the Nativity and the Dormition of the Virgin on the tympana of the lateral portals. During the first half of the fourteenth century, Arnolfo di Cambio's style and manner did not enjoy the posthumous influence exerted by the art of Giovanni Pisano, which is well exemplified by Tino di Camaino.

Andrea Pisano.
Personification of Sculpture (Phidias).
From the Campanile of the Duomo, Florence.
About 1337-1340. Marble.
Museo dell'Opera del Duomo, Florence.

Arnolfo di Cambio.
Funerary monument of Cardinal de Braye (died 1282),
modern arrangement. Marble. San Domenico, Orvieto.

THE EVOLUTION OF THE SCULPTOR'S CRAFT

During the thirteenth century, the sculptor's position improved in comparison with other guilds of craftsmen, but a certain ambiguity remained about his status in relation to stonemasons. Etienne Boileau's *Livre des métiers* (Book of Crafts) is often wrongly invoked—wrongly, because it establishes only the status of image-makers and woodcarvers. In Italy the work of Nicola Pisano, who is called *Magister lapidum*, was considered as sculpture, according to inscriptions. The stained glass windows at Chartres offered to the cathedral by the brotherhoods of craftsmen show, among the artisans at work, both the stonemasons responsible for rough-hewing the blocks and carving the decorated architectural elements, and the sculptors who chiselled recumbent effigies and column statues in the workshop; here already is a certain degree of specialization. If we add to this the sources describing the work of Giovanni Pisano on the Siena façade and that of Arnolfo di Cambio at Florence, we see the whole complexity of defining a craft and how, in each case of monumental sculpture, the work of stonemason and sculptor on the one hand and sculptor and architect on the other could involve mutual encroachment.

Apprenticeship was served directly in the workshop or on the worksite alongside the masters of the craft. The material was of vital importance for the work of the sculptor, who did not perceive limestone and marble, for example, in the same way. Thus, the search for the right material was the subject of special attention before work began. As the archaeological study of statuary has shown, there was increasing specialization in the different parts of a sculpture. During the thirteenth century, the division of tasks

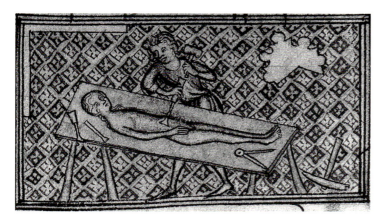

Direct cutting of a stone statue executed in a workshop.
14th century. Miniature from *The Romaunt of the Rose*.
British Museum, London.

became obvious. When architectural work became more and more standardized through the carving and pre-fabrication of various elements, monumental sculpture could only follow suit. This has been easy to demonstrate in connection with the prefabrication of sculptured splays before they were put in place and the preparation of complete programmes of statues before they were positioned. In the case of the restoration of the portal of Etampes, the observation of certain irregularities and the extraordinary simplicity of the assemblage and mounting of works made of yellow stone has even led to the suggestion that there may have been complete prefabrication in the workshop, possibly even away from the worksite, close to the quarry. Moreover, observation of the great worksites of American cathedrals, like that of Washington, now in the course of completion, clearly shows us the whole process of sculpturing elements on the worksite before their installation. In this general planning, drawings played an important part, both for the architectural design of the sculptured façade (Strasbourg, Orvieto), and as a preliminary sketch for the sculpture or as information useful to apprentices learning the craft. Drawings traced on the building under construction sometimes indicated the emplacement reserved for sculptures (Reims). During the second quarter of the thirteenth century, the celebrated sketchbook of Villard de Honnecourt, a native of Picardy, which is a

Sculptors in their workshop.
First half of the 13th century.
Stained glass window.
Chartres Cathedral.

Giovanni Pisano.
Virgin and Child.
Artist's signature on the base.
About 1305-1306. Marble.
Arena Chapel, Padua.

Villard de Honnecourt. King dispensing justice.
Design for a sculpture. Second quarter of the 13th century.
Bibliothèque Nationale, Paris.

▷ Drawing on parchment of the bell-tower on the west front
of Strasbourg Cathedral. Second half of the 14th century.
Musée de l'Œuvre Notre-Dame, Strasbourg.

Detail of the arch mouldings
(recently restored).
Original polychromy.
South portal.
Middle of the 12th century.
Notre-Dame, Etampes.

Stone cutters and sculptors
at work on the building site of a cathedral.
15th century. Miniature by Jean Fouquet.
Bibliothèque Nationale, Paris.

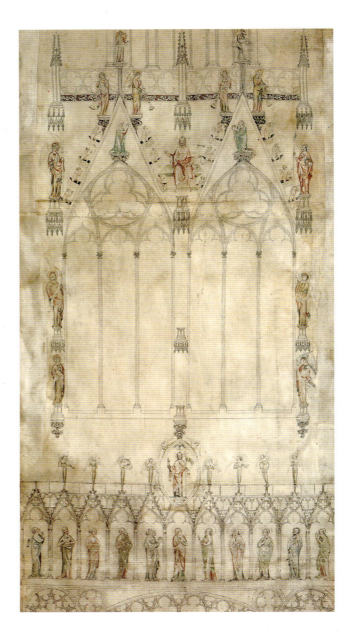

didactic work, in fact a technological treatise, often reproducing projects which Villard had learnt of in architectural agencies and the lodges of some great monuments, clearly shows the importance which that artist assigned to sculpture and the rendering of drapery, using the latter to define the style he observed around him which was common to sculptors, goldsmiths, illuminators and master glaziers. This observation of sculpture, characteristic of the great artists of the period (Giotto, Jean Pucelle), is at the very heart of the development of the craft.

A clear distinction must be made between carved church furniture and architectural sculpture, although they may sometimes have been executed by the same men or in similar conditions. The difference lies primarily in the organization involved in the making of the immense mass of sculptures that the commission for a façade represents. To explain the rapidity with which these great ensembles were created, it has recently been suggested that the technique of a preparatory model was already practised in the thirteenth century. Only the technical observation of a very large group of sculptures could support this attractive idea, which implies the existence of small-scale models and large maquettes dating back to this early period of Gothic art. At all events, we know that the sculpture workshop, especially the one charged with carrying out monumental projects, comprised, beside the master, many assistants responsible for various tasks, from the choosing

Two details of the polychromy
recovered on sculptures of the
porch and the south portal,
the so-called Painted Portal.
Christ on the tympanum
and figure on the arch moulding.
About 1220-1230.
Lausanne Cathedral.

and squaring of blocks to the carving and completion of different parts. Furthermore we have to assign the role of polychromy to its rightful place, for no sculpture was complete when the sculptor finished his work (except in Italy, owing to the use of coloured marble). There can be absolutely no doubt on this point: Etampes, Lausanne, Notre-Dame in Paris, Regensburg and many other discoveries and restorations have shown that colour was an essential component of the Gothic sculptor's craft.

In addition to our understanding of the sculptor's work, which is based on technical observations, documentary references and illustrations of all kinds, a few words about signatures are apposite. We have already seen that Romanesque sculptors and master masons signed their creations and that the myth of the Romanesque sculptor's anonymity should be rejected. Continuing this tradition in the thirteenth century, Roman marble-cutters, goldsmiths and many sculptors, particularly in Italy, continued to sign their works or are known to us from documents. The name of the architects of some cathedrals was engraved on labyrinths. But, paradoxically, the sculptured façade of Gothic France remains anonymous. Without neglecting the hypothesis of painted signatures, this anonymity of different elements of the façade confirms the growing standardization of the product and the rationalization of the work as essential features of the progress of the sculptor's craft in the thirteenth century.

157

COURT ART (1280-1400)

by Xavier Barral i Altet

INTRODUCTION

Georges Duby

Spurred on by the discovery of Aristotle's treatises which were successively translated from Arabic at the same time as the commentaries in which Islamic thought had encased them, the progress of intellectual research speeded up during the thirteenth century. The concentration of scholars at certain better equipped centers encouraged confrontations and controversies in a liberty gradually won within those associations for mutual defence which the emergent universities were. Theologians allied experience to logic in order to decipher the ambiguous and discordant messages that the Eternal had scattered throughout the text of the Scriptures and his creation. Faced with the complexity of living organisms, they were obliged to stick to methodical observation and the classification of phenomena. The eyes of scholars (and artists, too) were sharpened in these exercises. But reason was still their principal tool, as the increasingly dry severity of cathedral architecture testifies. The instrument of reason was apparently effective enough for Thomas Aquinas to believe he was capable of reconciling Christian dogma with Aristotle's teachings. This rash attempt was frightening, and at the end of the century the masters had to decide on a separation between them.

A frontier was drawn in the field of knowledge strictly demarcating the two domains of faith and reason. It was useless to seek to understand God. That could only be achieved by surrendering to the impulses of the heart in the hope of ultimate union with him in nuptials beyond the power of words. On the other hand, man was entitled to utilize unrestrainedly his faculties of understanding to win from nature all the gratifications of which it is the source and to order social relations within the terrestrial city with a view to the common good. Such a distinction was decisive, indeed we might ask whether the singularity and the destiny of Western Europe among the other civilizations in the world did not largely result from this choice. It corresponded to the aspirations of the ruling classes, because in the towns, whose populations were constantly growing, where business continued to prosper in spite of the recession now gaining ground in the country regions, the rich, who were becoming steadily richer, expected to be shown how to guarantee their salvation without depriving themselves of the good things of life. But most of all it was in profound agreement with the teaching of St Francis of Assisi which the Franciscan friars spread abroad from the cities, inviting all the faithful to reunite with the person of Christ, their brother, through love and compassion, and at the same time to praise the Almighty in all things good, beautiful and wonderful that he had created. This trend in Christianity had direct repercussions on sculpture. A summons to communicate by the effusions of the soul with the elements of suffering humanity assumed by God, entailed showing him in the most moving aspects, in the tenderness of infancy, in the afflictions of his torment, in placing near him the woman who had carried him in her womb and collapsed at the foot of the cross. On the other hand, affirming that God revealed himself in the beauties of nature authorized artists to bear witness to his grandeur in the eyes of the faithful who were increasingly sensitive to the quality of the objects with which they embellished their existence, to the delicacy of nuances and the elegance of forms, by using refined artistic treatment to enhance the charms with which the Creator endowed the visible universe.

The reconstruction of the State accentuated this tendency. Extorting ever more money from the now docile Church and the bourgeoisie greedy for privileges, concerned to show their power not only by the exhibition of military force, but also by luxury used to persuade their subjects, whose critical faculties were growing keener, and thus to develop a sort of secular preaching which, like sacred preaching, called for the help of the mise en scène, the masters of temporal power played a growing part in artistic creation. In the capital cities, beginning in the thirteenth century, the initial impulse came from the court.

A new culture was being forged in the courts. The prince's palace was thronged with ecclesiastics and was thus connected with university circles, but it was the men of war, the knights, who set the tone. The head of the house, himself a knight, shared their tastes. Like them, he loved to adorn himself. He enjoyed himself with them. The knightly culture, full of vitality, managed to work its way into the solid lasting forms in which only ecclesiastical culture had so far been expressed. It impregnated them with its own values. These were essentially those of sport and the pursuit of pleasure. Especially the pleasure afforded by women.

To be sure, all the princes were pious and the most munificent of them had been anointed when they were crowned. The money they devoted to artistic enterprises still served mainly to embellish the places where they went to pray. But knowing what would please the donor and his friends, sculptors gave more suppleness and charm to the statues of the Mother of God and the Foolish Virgins, and when they had to handle the theme of the Resurrection or the Earthly Paradise, they did not miss the opportunity of showing young bodies in all their seductive nudity. Under the pressure of courtly attitudes, sculpture gradually became courtly. This tinge of courtliness becomes noticeable as from the end of the thirteenth century. It then spread throughout the whole of Europe, flourishing in the entourage of the most generous sovereigns, the king of France, the king of England, the emperor in his Bohemian residences, the pope established at Avignon.

Whereas the tendency towards mannerism was barely beginning in religious art, the displacement of the currents of prosperity already entailed a shift of the poles of aesthetic innovation. Until then, French territory had been the most fertile. The wealth which supported the budding and then the flowering of monumental sculpture in those regions came from the land, from the profits of the rural seigneurie, which were more abundant than they were anywhere else. When the first agrarian expansion ran out of steam, France lost its advantages. The advance posts of a growth which henceforth stimulated the rise of foreign trade and banking were established at the extremes of that great country, some on the shores of the North Sea (and soon of the Baltic), others on the shores of the Mediterranean. The distance, already very appreciable in the Capetian kingdom, between a southern area, the cradle of Romanesque, and a northern area, the cradle of Gothic, was accentuated.

From then on, in spite of constant changes, the evolution of artistic forms, like every way of life and conception of the world, continued along divergent paths in north and south.

Scenes from the life of the Virgin.
French diptych.
Second quarter of the 14th century.
Ivory.
Museo del Bargello, Florence.

For a long time Italy led the way. Her sailors ventured ever further afield in the conquest of the Levantine economy. Her businessmen took on the fruitful management of enormous transfers of money set in motion by the improvements in the fiscal system adopted by the Roman Church, which had itself become a state and the most rapacious of all. Lastly, no one could deny that the seat of imperial dignity was on Italian soil, where the most obvious vestiges of past grandeur were on show, preserved in the stone of sarcophagi and the monuments still in use. They no longer inspired fear. Connoisseurs admired their force and beauty. Here the masters of the State, a state precociously freed from clerical ascendancy, commissioned artists to use them as models. Thus, one final renaissance, the great one, more vigorous than all those which had preceded it, started in Italy very early, beginning in the second quarter of the thirteenth century.

The first prince to invite sculptors to celebrate in the heroic Roman mode a power fortified by what the jurists exhumed from the constitutions of the Byzantine Empire, was the most eminent of all, the Emperor Frederick II. King of Germany, he was also King of Italy. He was descended from the Norman pirates who had conquered Naples and Sicily. It was there in the southern domains where he was born that he commissioned his own effigy surrounded by likenesses of his principal councillors, ordering that his face should look like Augustus's. After him, all the monarchs who picked up the fragments of his power in various parts of Italy followed his example. Charles of Anjou, for example, whose statue borrowed its ponderous majesty from the effigies of the last Roman emperors. In northern Italy, it was as horsemen, following the example of Marcus Aurelius, whose equestrian statue could be seen in the Lateran, that the "tyrants" wished to be represented in the plenitude of their sovereignty in the heart of the town whose seigniory they had taken over. And later the holders of that other power, intellectual power, in the aspect that linked it most firmly to politics, the masters of the University of Bologna, commentators on Roman law from which they drew the principles of regalian authority, also expected to be perpetuated in effigy in the city on bas-reliefs imitated from the antique.

In the towns of Umbria and Emilia, and those of Tuscany, the most powerful, enriched like Pisa by adventures on the seas, or like Siena by handling money and the trade in rare and costly fabrics, power belonged to the local government. It too proclaimed itself the heir of Rome and its magistrates were at pains to restore the emblematic decoration with which the city was once adorned in the public areas where the citizens assembled for debates and civic festivities. The arrangement of these esplanades took its bearing on the communal palace, but also on the cathedral and its baptistery or the basilica of the patron saint, and it was on these religious edifices that sculpture was concentrated. For the temporal power, however keen it was to defend its autonomy, felt that its first obligation was to give glory to God, and the sacred impregnated all its liturgies. To decorate the faces of pulpit or chancel, to represent Christ, the apostles, the Virgin Mother, the prophets or the symbols of the seasons, artists here did their utmost to rejoin the indigenous traditions in which the independence and pride of the town were anchored. To this end they burrowed far back in time. Sometimes, pushing back beyond classicism, their work rediscovered the accent of pre-Roman forms. As a result, we have the serene gravity which, in certain images of the Madonna on her maternity bed, seems like a distant echo of the funerary art of Etruria.

As for the first revivals of a secular sculpture, they appeared in public squares, in the decoration of fountains. A major element in antique town planning, the fountain in these arid climes had formerly symbolized man's power to control natural forces and demonstrated the benefits of political order simply by the spouting of water that had been harnessed. So that the communal fountain would repeat the same message, its sides were covered with images whose teaching was not entirely similar to that dispensed by the ornaments of the cathedral. Undoubtedly, by referring to the Scriptures, it, too, exhibited the concordances between the rhythms of nature and the constitution of human societies. Nevertheless, nurtured by the Latin classics, the moral it propagated was intended to be different. It was that of the good government of the *res publica*.

SCULPTURE AND THE COURTLY SPIRIT

Life of St Denis
the Areopagite.
Patron,
master mason,
construction scenes.
14th century.
Bibliothèque Nationale,
Paris.

DONORS AND PATRONS
IN A CENTURY OF CRISES

Fourteenth-century sculpture has been misunderstood, underestimated, and for a long time neglected. Indeed, the century itself, considered as a time of troubles, has not enjoyed the favour of historians, who have regarded it as a calamitous era of wars and economic decline. Painting alone has, in a small measure, escaped that incomprehension. The study of sculpture has suffered from its chronolo-

Giotto.
The donor Enrico Scrovegni presenting the model of the chapel.
Early 14th century.
Arena Chapel, Padua.

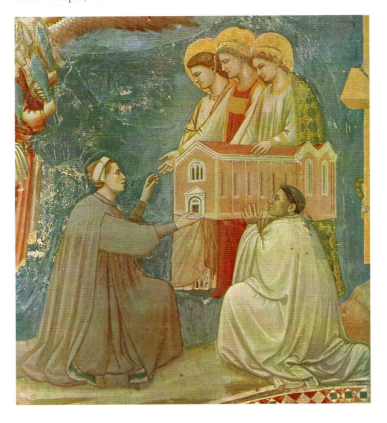

gical position between two great centuries: that of the cathedrals on one hand and that of Claus Sluter, flamboyant Gothic, Flemish painting, international style and the Italian Renaissance on the other.

The society of the fourteenth century was severely chastised by fate. The uncertainties of the Hundred Years' War paralyzed the activities of ordinary life, but provided a living for people whose business was war and nurtured the warlike ideal, of which *Le Jouvencel* (The Stripling) by Jean de Bueil says: "War is a joyful thing; there you see and hear many fine things and learn much that is good . . . Your heart softens with pity and loyalty at seeing your friend who so valiantly exposes his body in order to do and fulfil our Creator's bidding. And then you prepare yourself to go and live or die with him, and out of love not to abandon him. In that lies such delight that no man who has not attempted it can tell how good a thing it is." To this courtly ideal of the profession of war there came to be added commercial transactions tied to military acts. In 1379, while the war between Venice and Genoa (1378-1381) was in full swing, a Genoese merchant vessel was captured by the Venetians, who "embarked the best part of the booty: goods of all sorts, such as spices, woollen cloth, gold, silver and other things of great value." But the populations suffered heavily from the constant insecurity. "In those days, the only cultivating you could do in these parts [Ile-de-France] was around the towns, squares or castles, close enough so that from the top of the tower or bartizan the look-out's eye could spot the brigands swooping down on you" (1422). To this must be added the Black Death, which spread rapidly in the West, precipitating a demographic crisis and a generalized panic, reported in the *Decameron* in relation to the epidemic in Florence (1348), and of which we have so many accounts, such as that of the inhabitants of Messina in Sicily, who saw the Genoese galleys drop anchor in 1347: "The Genoese carried with them, in their bones, a disease such that all who spoke to one of them were stricken with this mortal sickness; this death, instant death which it was impossible to escape."

This negative vision of the century in the West is made complete by monetary difficulties and the economic crisis, with the bankruptcies of Florentine guilds, tax increases and insurrections that weakened the central authority. But the crises of the fourteenth century ended in the determination by the rich and powerful to make their role in society publicly known through great artistic commissions, often founded, in the case of kings and popes, on a new tax squeeze. Indeed, the Church, itself in crisis and experiencing the Schism, spread its influence artistically in Avignonese splendour. The economic and social changes arising from the transformation of the feudal nobility and the urban patriciate went hand in hand with an intellectual evolution brought about through the growth and multiplication of universities. Focal points of artistic activity were concentrated in the towns, in response to the demand of the guilds and wealthy commoners, or close to the court in the service of the king or the prince. The anxieties and contradictions of the century were directly expressed in artistic research aimed at defining a style that completely changed the relations between the sacred and the profane, between the public and private life.

The style of fourteenth-century sculpture, which saw the progress of mannerism and the abuse of seductive forms, came in response to the demand of a clientele of patrons, and spread thanks to the profusion of small commissions springing from individual piety. The greatest artists were called in to carry out funerary programmes or public statuary groups with a political purpose. The commission for a tomb often implied the building of a chapel to house it. Sculptural activity moved now from the exterior to the interior of the religious edifice, while in another respect it reached the street in the case of royal, princely or urban commissions. The effigy of contemporary figures, of the patrons themselves, was introduced into the decor of the church, castle or town. Each one wanted to leave his memory in this world, surviving, thanks to artistic commissions, a century of troubles. Rivalry in refinement created on one hand emulation among artists, but on the other, especially, the desire of the powerful to secure the services of the most renowned. Ownership of works of art became the sign of real wealth, and the taste for collecting grew among the patrons. Novelty in art was created in the shadow of the great system of patronage: papal (Boniface VIII, Avignon), royal (Paris, Prague), episcopal (Grandisson of Exeter, Wykeham of Winchester) or princely (Dukes of Berry or Burgundy, the Black Prince).

Modesty and self-effacement were no more: funerary art adopted the realistic portrait, and commemorative sculpture was used by the living for personal glorification. The individual was at the centre of artistic, philosophical or literary preoccupations. Enrico Scrovegni had himself painted by Giotto at the beginning of the century presenting the model of the Arena Chapel in Padua. At Toulouse Jean Tissendier had the chapel of Rieux built between 1333 and 1344 in the chevet of the church of the Cordeliers to house his sepulchre. His statue, a true portrait, as proved by comparison with the head of his recumbent tomb effigy, shows him as donor presenting the maquette, an authentic small-scale model of the chapel. In the same way, Charles V symbolically exhibited a model of the Portail des Célestins in Paris, thereby affirming his role as builder and patron. His statues were then as numerous in Paris as were those of Charles IV in Prague. This emphasis on the public-spiritedness of the donor can also be seen in monumental inscriptions. The pulpit carved by Giovanni Pisano for Pisa Cathedral between 1302 and 1311 bears two long inscriptions praising the work. The one relating to the patron, which was later placed in the cathedral, records the fact that "Burgundio di Tado caused the new pulpit to be made which stands in the Duomo." In Paris, at the back of the choir of Notre-Dame, an inscription anterior to 1344 reads: "Master Pierre de Fayel, canon of Paris, has given 200 pounds to help to make these stories and for the new windows of the choir herein." It is accompanied by a kneeling statue of the canon (it was made in his lifetime, and the artist Jean Ravy was also there), wearing a dalmatic and maniple; above him is the shield with his armorial bearings.

While the Pisa inscription still refers to the formulas in vogue in the previous century, the one in Paris lays emphasis on the new public image of the donors (stained glass window of Beatrix van Valkenburg from Oxford, preserved in Glasgow), who liked to be given a prominent position even when they only contributed in part to the financing of the work.

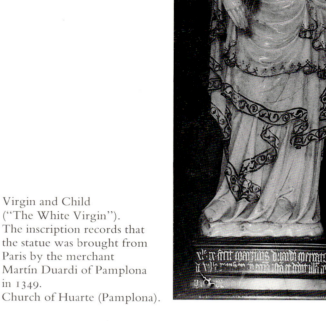

Virgin and Child
("The White Virgin").
The inscription records that the statue was brought from Paris by the merchant Martín Duardi of Pamplona in 1349.
Church of Huarte (Pamplona).

Jean Tissendier presenting the model of the Chapel of Rieux.
1333-1344.
Stone.
Musée des Augustins, Toulouse.

Woman's face from a tomb effigy.
First third of the 14th century.
Marble.
Musée des Beaux-Arts, Arras.

THE RETURN TO MARBLE AND ALABASTER

Marble was a deluxe material; it was costly, its price varying according to the conditions of quarrying, of transportation and the use to which it was put. In Italy it was used during the fourteenth century, as it had been throughout the Middle Ages, for there it was found in abundance. Quarries like those of Carrara were continuously worked, but many antique marbles were re-utilized and carved over again: ancient columns, for example, served for the carving of statues, and inscriptions turned back to front provided a plaque for a low-relief. In other regions where the preference for this material persisted, the use of marble posed a different problem because of its rarity and the slowdown in quarrying. Substitutes with a polish close to that of marble might then be employed (recumbent stone statue at Tournai and those of Saint-Denis).

In France, for example, where marble was in some regions used during the Romanesque period, it became rare during the thirteenth century and was then limited exclusively to the quarrying areas of Mediterranean Languedoc, Roussillon and the Alps. Indeed, it is to be observed that the major works of thirteenth-century sculpture in the north of France are not in marble. During the fourteenth century marble made its appearance for the first time in northern France, and its use was linked to the production of a luxury statuary in a royal or aristocratic milieu and the development of funerary monuments in those same circles. From other sources it is known that during the Middle Ages marble statues reaching these regions from Italy arrived at the ports of Normandy or South Brittany, travelling thence up the Seine or the Loire. Transport by the Rhone and the Durance is also recorded. Whereas the majority of the great Italian sculptors of the fourteenth century continued to be marble masons, and

the Avignonese sculptors too had the possibility of working in that material, in northern France most of the time only the head and hands of recumbent statues were of marble (mask of a man from Troyes in the Louvre). Some recumbent sculptures (mask of a woman, museum of Arras; recumbent figure, museum of Lyons) were carved from very thin slabs. Marble was also used for statues of the Virgin and Child.

Alabaster was the material par excellence for courtly sculpture. The softness of the stone stimulated the sculptor and charmed the client; but ever since the Middle Ages marble and alabaster have often been confused, as in the Virgin and Child whose provenance is Gosnay (museum of Arras), sculpted in marble by Jean-Pépin de Huy, which appears in the accounts of Mahaut d'Artois in 1329 as an "image of Our Lady in alabaster." Different marbles, moreover, were sometimes combined: thus, this same statue is said to have possessed a canopy and pedestal in black marble. The sculpted panels of altarpieces were often mounted on a base of black marble, which was a refined way of putting the accent on the polychromy (Arrest of Christ, Antwerp). An analogous formula is used in the fragments in the Louvre coming from the Sainte-Chapelle in Paris, but this time with white marble on a background of black marble.

In contrast to statues in stone or wood, those in alabaster are only slightly heightened by colours: most often the significance of the material is brought out by the aid of gilded parts. The Virgin in New York, from Pont-aux-

Angel of the Annunciation from Javernant.
Mid-14th century. Alabaster heightened with gold.
The Cleveland Museum of Art.

Entombment, from an altarpiece
formerly in the Sainte-Chapelle, Paris.
Second quarter of the 14th century.
White marble.
Musée du Louvre, Paris.

enough, he turned to the quarries of Chellaston (Derby-shire).

The search for alabaster constantly occupied the Catalan kings. Pedro III the Ceremonious (1319-1387), on deciding to build the family tomb at Poblet, engaged in 1340 Aloi de Montbrai and Pere de Guines; these two sculptors were joined in 1349 by Jaume Cascalls. The alabaster from the quarries nearest the monastery of Poblet was deemed deficient in quality. After investigations had been carried out it was decided to use the alabaster of Beuda (Besalú) in the region of Gerona. The distance was considerable. Routes were mapped and repaired for the transport of the material in wagons drawn by oxen towards the sea at Roses, whence it was shipped to Tarragona. Given the fragility of alabaster, the sculptors, after having supervised the extraction, took personal responsibility for the transport. While the tombs were being built the king regularly visited the workshops to give his opinion on the progress of the work, and occasionally to modify the project. Some fifty years later the sculptor Pere Joan, put in charge of the altarpiece for the cathedral of Saragossa, and having already used Besalú alabaster for the altarpiece of the cathedral of Tarragona, did not hesitate to undertake, after agreement with the parish council, two prospecting trips to those quarries, located over 460 kilometres distant, which implied the employment of the sculptor for over a year before the sculpturing of the altarpiece was even begun. We may thereby gauge the importance of the material in the artistic commission and the extreme care lavished on this choice by both sculptor and patron.

Dames, is a prime example of this. The alabaster patina is enriched by a painted or gilded decoration of lines and points, of flowerets and arabesques that emphasize the borders and punctuate the clothing. The inscription presented by the Angel of the Annunciation from Javernant (Cleveland) illustrates this aspect of the craft. Pieces of silverwork added on provided the finishing touch to alabaster statues, in particular a crown sometimes trimmed with precious stones and enamels.

During the fourteenth century the production of alabaster reliefs became a speciality of English workshops, which were soon known on the Continent. Beginning with the 1370s, rectangular panels, figures in high relief and statues were produced on a large scale and flooded the market during the fifteenth century. Alabaster was of local origin and was often carved in urban workshops, particularly at York, Burton-on-Trent and later at Nottingham. In the 1380s exports reached a watershed. In 1382 three statues are mentioned as leaving Southampton, and in 1390 a merchant from Dartmouth made shipments to Spain.

This trade, which at the end of the fourteenth century was not limited to specialized merchants, subsequently intensified, to judge from the lawsuit brought in 1491 by a Nottingham sculptor over payment for fifty-eight heads of St John the Baptist.

Alabaster was sometimes the object of highly specialized commissions, like that from Philippa of Hainaut, the wife of Edward III of England, who in 1362 had six wagon-loads of alabaster from the Tutbury deposits (Staffordshire) transported to London. In 1374 John of Gaunt prospected those same quarries for his own tomb effigy and that of his wife; but, finding the blocks there not large

The Arrest of Christ, from an altarpiece.
Second quarter of the 14th century.
Alabaster.
Museum Mayer van den Bergh, Antwerp.

Crucifix from the
Corpus Christi Chapel
in Wrocław.
First half of
the 14th century.
Muzeum Narodowe,
Warsaw.

THE REALITY OF THE BODY

In this century of hardships and recurring crises, artistic production did not slacken. It tried to surmount every pessimistic vision by stylistic beauty. An Italian chronicler, Matteo Villani, gives a beautiful description of this new flavour to life, a sort of reaction in the face of the Black Death and other calamities: "One might have thought that the men whom God in his grace had spared, having seen their nearest and dearest destroyed, and having been informed that suchlike things had happened in all the countries of the world, would have become better, humble, virtuous and Catholic... But now that plague has ended, exactly the opposite has occurred; for men, left in small numbers and grown rich in worldly goods thanks to legacies and inheritances, forgetting past events as though they had never happened, have led a more scandalous and disordered life than before... seeking after feasts... the delights of dainty food as well as games... looking for strange and unusual styles of dress... and common folk, men and women, owing to the excessive abundance of things, no longer wanted to practise their habitual trades... It was assumed that there would be plenty: instead, there was scarcity... It was thought that there must be profusion and abundance of clothing and of all other things the human body requires over and above life itself, and in fact... most things are now worth twice and more their usual price before the plague."

This happy-go-lucky attitude to material things, which masked harsh reality, was accompanied throughout the century by reflection on the soul, the body, and time. Sculpture expressed these anxieties by greater analysis of the reality of the body. Indeed, the fourteenth century is outstanding for studies of the nude, for research into realism in the portrait, and for anatomical investigations that led to the representation of the withered corpse (transi) and kept pace with the progression in university teaching of anatomy and surgery and with the profound advances in knowledge of the body. From 1306 to 1312 the first two treatises on surgery (Anatomy and Wounds) were written by Henri de Mondeville, surgeon to Philip the Fair. During the fourteenth century corporeal reality never ceased to be measured by the yardstick of medicine.

In the pulpit of the cathedral of Pisa Giovanni Pisano placed a series of standing statues (1302-1310) which flanked the supports. Among them the handling of the female nude of Prudence shows an assimilation of Gothic forms located at the opposite pole from the antique heroism incarnated by Force, previously sculptured, before 1260, by Nicola Pisano in the pulpit of the baptistery of Pisa. The concern to represent the female body realistically also appears when it is clothed, as evidenced in the statue of Force by Giovanni Pisano which adjoins that of Prudence at Pisa. The same interest respectfully extends to the representation of the Virgin, in whose body courtly seduction appears as a result of the hip-thrust of the figure and the moulding of the clothes which bring out the charms of the bosom (Virgin and Child of Giovanni Pisano in Padua).

The traditional opposition between the rendering of the naked bodies of the Elect and the Damned in representations of the Last Judgment became permanently estab-

Withered corpse of Guillaume de Harcigny
from the church of the Cordeliers, Laon.
Late 14th century. Stone.
Musée Archéologique, Laon.

lished in the century at Orvieto, before 1330, in the reliefs of the cathedral façade. To the smoothness of the bodies of Adam and Eve in the scene of the Creation, Lorenzo Maitani added anatomical details on a considerable scale in the representation of the Damned (joints, veins, muscles, bone structure, pubis).

The search for realism in the emaciation of the body became general during the course of the century in portrayals of Christ's agony. The Crucified, especially in Germanic surroundings, appears like a cadaver hung from the cross, and each detail of his suffering is inscribed on the body with overwhelming realism.

This whole preoccupation, which was based on a reflection on the individual and kept pace with the spread of realistic portraits of royal donors and recumbent tomb effigies (*gisants*) of all kinds, reached its culmination in the appearance of the withered corpse in funerary sculpture before the end of the century. Until then, during the fourteenth century the tomb effigy presented an idealized image of the deceased, a faithful portrait of the living person, henceforth asleep. The new reflection on death here joined that which was already far advanced on the body, and became generalized in the fifteenth century: "The death makes you shiver, turn pale, / your nose curve, / your veins tighten, / your neck swell, the flesh soften, / your joints and nerves grow and expand" (François Villon). In these circumstances is it surprising that one of the very first withered corpses, that of Guillaume de Harcigny (Archaeological Museum, Laon), carved after his death for the church of the Cordeliers of Laon, was a doctor's? The representation of the naked and fleshless cadaver reappears soon afterward in the monumental tomb of Cardinal de La Grange in the church of Saint-Martial of Avignon: beneath five levels of scenes from the life of the Virgin, of kings and persons of high rank, the withered corpse (*transi*) accompanies the recumbent tomb effigy (*gisant*), as if better to mark the transition between these two visions of death.

Giovanni Pisano.
Force and Prudence. 1302-1310.
Marble pulpit statues in
Pisa Cathedral.

Lorenzo Maitani and his workshop.
The Creation of Eve, detail from Genesis.
Before 1330.
Marble façade relief,
Orvieto Cathedral.

167

THE DECOR OF PRIVATE LIFE

Façade on the Piazzetta.
Second half of the 14th century and
first quarter of the 15th century.
Ducal Palace, Venice.

Scene of rural life, detail of the façade.
First half of the 13th century.
St Mark's, Venice.

The façades of fine townhouses continued to be lavishly adorned in the Gothic period (Reims, Maison des Musiciens, mid-thirteenth century). In the allegory of Good and Bad Government painted on the walls of the Palazzo Pubblico, Ambrogio Lorenzetti illustrated the appearance of the public buildings and houses of Siena around 1337-1339. There we see the house and loggia with colonnettes and decorated capitals, as well as the sober and impassive urban palace. In Venice the well-to-do house was built on two or three floors, equipped with an inner courtyard and with a development of the façade made necessary by the small amount of available land. The principal floor of the façade is distinguished by the balcony. The Ducal Palace corresponds to the summit of the social hierarchy of the city, surpassing even most of the Italian public buildings and town halls. A secular and religious iconographic programme is displayed on the outside.

Buildings of religious community life similarly received sculptured decoration. Generally the cloister was ornamented only by capitals, but the galleries were overrun by arched recesses and sculptured tombs. The main efforts were concentrated on the chapter house and the other outbuildings of the cloister. However, some monastery rooms received, in painted ceiling or sculptured decor, an ornamentation comparable to that of secular dwellings. The individualized heads of the present house of the Bishop, formerly the conventual hall of Ely monastery in England, supply evidence of this.

The luxuriousness of the private life of the great is displayed in the construction of castles and palaces: the distinction between them, moreover, is not always easy to make. The castles of Louis of Orléans are a case in point. They are situated at the height of the architectural displays of luxury to which princes and wealthy people aspired. Pierrefonds, La Ferté-Milon and Coucy have been called castles of extravagance. The relief of the Coronation of the Virgin on the monumental entrance gate of La Ferté-Milon illustrates this new synthesis of the religious and the secular, and testifies to the presence of sculptors of renown in the service of the great, which will be discussed hereafter. Near the entrance of the castle of Pierrefonds was to be seen a sculptured Annunciation. An illumination of the *Très Riches Heures* of the Duke of Berry preserves the memory of the castle, most of which no longer exists, of Mehun-sur-Yèvre, the chapel with its sculptured façade rising over the entrance tower–the meeting place of the most famous sculptors–of which Froissart wrote in his *Chronicles* in 1389-1392: "Meun-sur-Yèvre, a castle of his [the Duke of Berry], and with good reason one of the most beautiful houses in the world at that time, for the Duke of Berry had had it built and fashioned and embellished excellently well, and it cost fully three hundred thousand francs." Without equalling the luxury of the castles of Prague or Paris, the great hall of the Palace of Poitiers offered, after 1389, the statues of the Duke of Berry and Charles VI together with their wives, crowning the supports of the openwork tracery above the great fireplace.

The aim of the programmes was in keeping with the new idea of chivalry that spread especially starting in the second half of the century: an ideal of honour and personal glory united in a dream of heroism and love. This aspect of sculptured production may be grasped from the many groups expressing in stone the new chivalrous cult of the Preux and the Preuses. This group of nine heroes–three pagans, three Jews and three Christians (Hector, Caesar,

Siege of the Castle of Love. Ivory casket lid (iron fittings modern). Paris, second quarter of the 14th century. British Museum, London.

Alexander; Joshua, David, Judas Maccabaeus; Arthur, Charlemagne, Godfrey de Bouillon)–chosen for their relation to the chivalrous romance appeared at the end of the first quarter of the fourteenth century (Jacques de Longuyon). To them were rapidly added the series of nine Preuses: classic heroines redefined. The representation quickly became highly popular: armorial bearings were devised for them; they were represented in tapestries and placed alongside Bertrand du Guesclin. Such statues figured notably in the great hall of the castle of Coucy, on the eastern entrance tower of La Ferté-Milon (reliefs), on the towers of the castle of Pierrefonds and on the towers of the donjon of Maubergeon at Poitiers.

The decor of private life may also be conjured up by the treasures of the goldsmith's craft possessed by persons of importance, or by individual pieces of wrought gold, the symbols of social rise for the less wealthy. Ivory curios, like manuscripts or painted panels, were essential elements in the decor of the private chapel or of daily life. The lids of mirror cases consisted of a carved ivory surface on which courtly or romantic scenes or those of everyday life were often depicted. The Louvre preserves a fine series of them that brings to light the everyday world of ladies: chess games, loving couples in a garden, the court of the God of Love. Coffers exalting love, youth and the ideals of chivalry were also numerous and were given as wedding presents. The one in the British Museum is carved with courtly scenes, allegories and episodes from the romances of the Round Table. The one in the Louvre illustrates the story of the chatelaine of Vergi. The refinement of private life, which showed itself both in the manner of living and in the art of the table, reached one of its peaks in the taste of the wealthiest people for tapestries, emblazoned or used as soft furnishings; or for those more lux-

urious ones: historiated wall hangings. The passion for the latter swept the princes' courts from 1380 onwards, but as early as 1364 the Duke of Anjou possessed seventy-three tapestries, of which a large number were historiated and of large dimensions. The sculptor who developed in this environment daily imbibed a cultural atmosphere which he expressed in stone, marble or alabaster.

Game of chess. Ivory mirror case.
Paris, first quarter of the 14th century.
Musée du Louvre, Paris.

SCULPTURE AND POLITICS

THE PRINCELY AND ROYAL TOMB EFFIGIES

The tomb effigy or *gisant*, a representation of the deceased lying supine on his tomb, was the centrepiece of the fourteenth-century funerary monument. The source of this great medieval creation has not yet been brought to light; classical antiquity (funerary mosaics) or the early Middle Ages (Amay) have been considered as possibilities. The tomb effigy was used in Romanesque art (for example, the tomb of Isarn at Marseilles; monuments at Schaffhausen; the mosaic tomb of Guillaume de Flandres at Saint-Omer), but the fashion for it suddenly appeared in northern France towards the middle of the twelfth century (Childebert I and Clotaire II from Saint-Germain-des-Prés at Saint-Denis and the Musée Carnavalet), establishing its supremacy as the essential theme of funerary sculpture during the Middle Ages.

The pantheon of Fontevrault in Anjou illustrates the development of the form around the middle of the thirteenth century; in the necropolis of the Plantagenets are preserved the four royal *gisants* of Henry II Plantagenet (1154-1189), Richard the Lion-Hearted (died 1199) and Eleanor of Aquitaine (died 1204), all carved during the first quarter of the thirteenth century, and of Isabelle of Angoulême, whose tomb was carved in wood in 1256. A fifth effigy has just been discovered: a knight of the thirteenth century, with head, hands and legs badly damaged, lying on a sarcophagus with hands clasped, coat of arms and sword in its scabbard. The fine polychomy is well preserved. On the threshold of the fourteenth century, after 1274, the two tombs of the Infante Don Felipe and his wife Leonor Rodríguez de Castro at Villalcázar de Sirga (Palencia) in Spain show the increasing attention given to the tomb, the cult of the deceased person and the iconographic programme applied to it. At the summit of the hierarchy were the royal tombs.

Since remote times Saint-Denis has been the symbol of the French monarchy and the royal necropolis par excellence, which is not to say that kings have never fixed their choice on other abbeys, for example Royaumont: the queens were often buried elsewhere. During the thirteenth century the custom grew up of multiplying the sepulchres: the body, entrails and heart were buried separately. The burial of the entrails was due to the practice of disembowelment, widespread at a very early date in the Empire, in England from the time of Henry I (died 1135) and in France starting with Louis VIII (died 1226), whose viscera were deposited in Saint-André-de-Clermont. The heart very soon became the object of a cult. During the fourteenth century these various royal sepulchres served an elaborate monumental intention. The tomb effigy of the body of Charles V was the work of André Beauneveu

Tomb effigies of the Plantagenets. About 1200-1256. Painted stone and wood. Fontevrault.

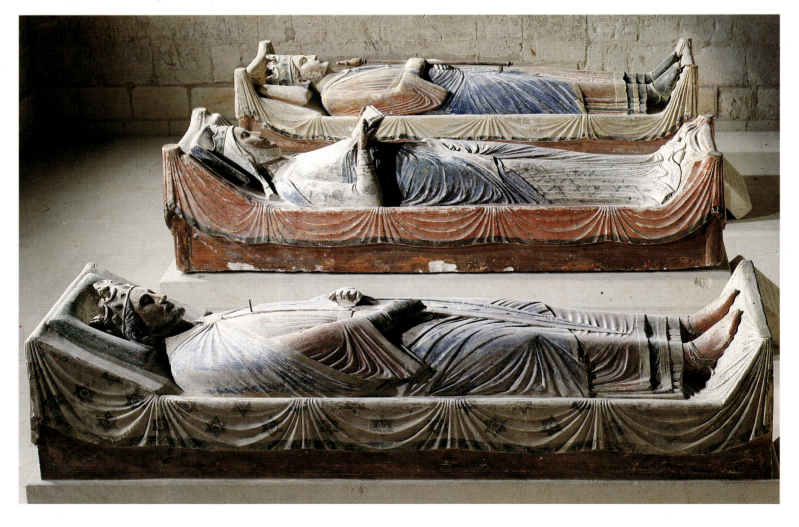

Tombs of the Infantes of Castile. After 1274.
Santa María la Blanca, Villalcázar de Sirga.

(1364-1366); the tomb of the heart intended for the cathedral of Rouen, known only from a drawing by Gaignières, was by Jean de Liège (1368) and also took the form of a recumbent figure holding the heart in its hand; the tomb of the entrails, executed after 1374, stood in the Cistercian abbey of Maubuisson (now in the Louvre), also represents the tomb effigy of the king. Here a *gisant* was used on each occasion, suggesting a genuine tomb for the whole body; it replaced the funeral urn.

The tomb effigy was soon integrated into a larger monument, the coffer-tomb descended from the sarcophagus, the baldachin-tomb, or the wall-niche tomb. These sepulchres became sumptuous monuments with a rich iconography, and were used for the great ones of the kingdom and the princes of the Church (tomb of Gerhard von Jülich and his wife at Altenberg). The custom rapidly extended to include the tombs of saints, whose former reliquary urn acquired the features of a monumental tomb. More and more venerated, the sepulchres were objects of pilgrimage and unfailing attraction, even inside the religious buildings themselves. At Avignon, Pierre de

Royal tombs of the Catalan dynasty (reconstructed).
14th century.
Transept crossing, Abbey Church, Poblet.

Tomb effigies of Robert the Pious (died 1031)
and Constance of Arles (died 1032).
Commemorative tomb commissioned by St Louis.
1263-1264 or shortly before (restorations).
Basilica of Saint-Denis.

Luxembourg, a saint especially venerated in the fourteenth century at the Saint-Michel cemetery, received "each day a hundredweight and more of candles, and there are already so many wax images that they number more than a thousand, of one kind or another. It is the greatest event and the greatest act of worship that has been seen for a hundred years. . . Only think that each night two hundred people sleep and keep worshipful vigil in this place. . . From outside, from the surrounding fortified villages, the lame, the crippled, the one-armed and the paralytic have come and are cured by the power of God and this saintly cardinal."

Each kingdom, each bishopric, each principality possessed its own licenced burial grounds, like Saint-Denis in France, Westminster in England or Poblet in Catalonia. The funerals were large-scale events and varied from place to place. Thus, for example, the funerals of the kings of France, at first inspired by the splendid ceremonies of the kings of England, were given a special sumptuousness beginning with Philip Augustus: it was both a political and a religious event, in which the emphasis on the principle of legitimacy by heredity was essential. Beginning with the thirteenth century the exhibition of the body of the dead king, dressed in the vestments of consecration and in full regalia, became general practice in Europe, on the model of Emperor Otto IV. The funeral mass, the strictly ordered funeral procession followed by the throng of the common people, were events that soon passed into the iconography of tombs.

THE OSTENTATION OF THE TOMB

Tomb effigy of Robert Curthose,
Duke of Normandy.
Oak.
Late 13th century.
Gloucester Cathedral.

The formula of tomb and effigy spread rapidly to include princes, knights at arms and influential rich persons, especially in urban circles. But during the fourteenth century it was not enough to possess the financial means to have an effigy carved; the effigy had to form part of a religious monument, and in cemeteries funeral monuments were rare. The tomb placed inside a church had to be provided with its own edifice, a chapel or at least a privileged space. Only the very great possessed such monuments, which considerably restricted the dissemination of funerary art, as well as the scope of its influence on other forms of sculpture. Rare are the testaments that, like the one of Jean Brancas (Avignon, 1455), mention, besides higher realms, the deceased's desire to have built "a tomb with a stone statue representing him with a tunic and his coat of arms, on the model of the tomb of Cardinal Anglic, in the charterhouse of Bonpas." The average tombs tended to be funeral slabs: flat-tombs used to pave the floors of churches.

In England the engraved stone or metallic slabs (brasses) were immensely popular (Higham Ferrers, Chartham, Northleach) and, contrary to the great sculptured tombs, came from specialized workshops. In England too, wood was often used for carving tomb effigies (tomb of Robert du Bois at Fersfield, Norfolk; tombs of Paulerspury), following a local tradition which we find echoed in the *gisant* of Isabelle of Angoulême at Fontevrault. The great funeral monuments were made in the workshops of sculptors who, like Jean de Liège, André Beauneveu or Jean de Marville, contributed to the general development of the form and style of sculpture. In London, where the production of funeral sculpture and engraved tombstones intensified during the second half of the fourteenth century, the dif-

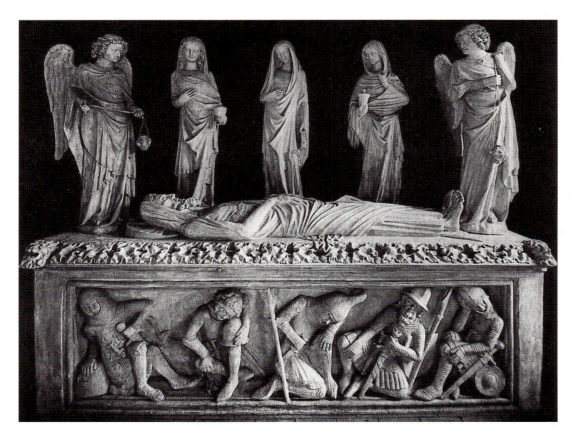

Holy Sepulchre.
About 1330.
Cathedral of Freiburg im Breisgau.

ference between the anonymous productions in series and the work of famous artists is quite distinct. Between the two, the case of the London marble-mason Henry Lakenham is exemplary. A contract in 1375 for carrying out the funeral monument of Sir Nicholas Loveyne testifies to the care paid by the patrons to finding the right place for the monument, to the shape of the tomb, to the choice of materials and to the deadlines for completion of the work. The tomb effigy in military dress, its feet resting on a lion, had to be stretched out on a coffer-tomb provided with inscriptions; it had to be completed in nineteen weeks and was to be paid for in instalments, the marble-mason being responsible for transport and assembly.

In the following chapters the subject will often come up of funeral sculpture and of extensive programmes placed around the deceased. The new custom of putting up a mausoleum during the lifetime of the important person had direct effects on the choice of iconographic programmes. The example of Jean de La Grange at Avignon is a significant one. The funeral monument takes up more and more space inside the church, from the thirteenth century onwards and not only in the case of royal or papal tombs (tomb of Inès de Castro, who died in 1355, Alcobaça, Portugal; tomb of the Bishop Kuno II von Falkenstein of Treves, at Koblenz). The tomb took part in the general iconography of the inside of the edifice and in the general stylistic evolution of the decor, for example at

Funeral monument of Bishop Domingo de Arroyuelo (died 1385). Burgos Cathedral.

The Percy Tomb.
Mid-14th century.
Beverley Minster.

Agostino di Giovanni and Agnolo di Ventura.
Funeral monument of Bishop Guido Tarlati.
About 1329-1332.
Arezzo Cathedral.

Tomb effigy of
Edward the Black Prince.
About 1377-1380.
Copper-gilt.
Canterbury Cathedral.

Salisbury in the tomb of Giles Bridport. The colossal tomb of the Percy family at Beverley (Yorkshire) represents, around the middle of the fourteenth century, one of the high points of funeral art by the dimensions of the whole, the monumentality of the programme with upright statues on the gables, and the central role played by its art in the stylistic development of the time (effigy of a lady at Alnwick; Clavering effigy at Staindrop; tomb of Welwick), in particular in the St Michael chapel in the church of St Mary at Beverley and in the highly diversified sculpture of Lincolnshire and Yorkshire.

Tomb iconography developed considerably during the fourteenth century. Polychromy, moreover, played a vital role in it, as did the choice and assembling of materials (different types of stone, marble, alabaster, metal). Elements of wrought gold or coloured glass inlays (head of the tomb effigy of Robert de Jumièges) set off the whole. Surrounding the effigy, the growing taste for pomp led to the introduction into tomb iconography of contemporary personalities and sometimes evocations of the gestures of the deceased. A hagiographic narrative was offered in the case of reliquary tombs of saints. The wall niche allowed the development of a mural iconography, supplementing that of the tomb, which could be either sculptured or painted (tomb of Bishop Tarlati, Duomo of Arezzo). Starting with the thirteenth century, two representations of the deceased were found in combination: dead as an effigy lying on the tomb and alive on the wall at the back of the wall niche (Royaumont, Saint-Médard at Soissons, SaintJean-de-Malte at Aix-en-Provence). It was a deliberate choice referring to the iconography of the resurrection of the body; however, the back of the niche was more frequently used for religious subjects (tomb of Bishop Domingo de Arroyuelo, cathedral of Burgos), which could present specific regional characters such as the Apostles/Coronation of the Virgin combination at Avignon. The tendency to increase the sculptured wall surface which had already appeared at the end of the thirteenth century (tomb of Fernando Alonso, cathedral of Salamanca) grew during the fourteenth century.

The dead man was portrayed asleep with closed eyes, and his effigy was sometimes unveiled by angels who partly opened the curtains; the coffer strictly speaking, once reserved for illustrations of important persons beneath a series of arches, apostles or saints, was henceforth taken up with funeral processions, an evocation of the new familial interiorization, mourners or weepers who formed the deceased's entourage. In the fourteenth century the procession became the essential ritual sequence of funeral ceremonies, and symbolized the separation between the dead man and the living. This procession was defined by the

Pere de Bonull and Francesc de Montflorit.
Tomb effigy of Blanche d'Anjou (restored).
1314-1315.
Former Abbey Church, Santes Creus.

Head thought to come from
the tomb effigy of Robert de Jumièges.
First half of the 14th century.
Inlaid marble.
Dépôt lapidaire, Jumièges.

Italian poet Frezzi (1346-1416) in his fear of old age as "a great crowd of people apparently living, each of them closely joined to his own stinking corpse."

The funeral corteges were in everyday reality veritable processions that crossed the town or village, particularly in Mediterranean countries, punctuated by cries and lamentations, to the extent that, by the end of the thirteenth century, the statutes of Valréas (near Avignon), prohibited under penalty of a fine anyone following the deceased person's body in the streets, church or cemetery to make lamentations, because they terrified the common people and hindered the holy service. To those cries and lamentations of the cortege were added the chants and prayers of clerics by the light of torches carried by the mourners. The representations of these corteges of mourners constituted one of the characteristics of the fourteenth-century tomb; they were popular in alabaster, standing out against black marble. Jean de Liège provided such mourners on the tomb of Philippa of Hainaut at Westminster and Jaume Cascalls made them famous at Poblet: dressed in a long tunic and hooded, the mourners, whose use spread massively during the fifteenth century, lift slightly with their clasped hands the cloth of the mourning mantle whose skirts fall to the ground.

THE VANITY OF THE PORTRAIT

Funeral sculpture also displayed one of the essential features of fourteenth-century sculpture: the quest for verisimilitude in the approach to the portrait. The head of the tomb effigy of Jeanne de Toulouse (Musée de Cluny, Paris) shows how this tendency began during the last decades of the thirteenth century. The line of the nose, unfortunately broken; the handling of the eyes, the eyebrows, the two small curly locks adorning the temples, the headdress with the wimple passing under the chin, the *touaille* (communion napkin) and the veil are all so many elements throwing light on artistic research into the representation of the portrait.

The mausoleum of Isabelle of Aragon, wife of Philip the Bold, in the cathedral of Cosenza in Calabria, the tomb effigy of Philip the Bold at Saint-Denis, and the statue of Mainneville from the castle of Enguerran de Marigny (not St Louis but presumably Philip the Fair), are like so many milestones in the conquest of the portrait, just as are the tomb effigy and (probable) statue of Sancho IV at Toledo, in the cathedral. The ordering of a tomb during the lifetime of its owner facilitated the realistic execution of the portrait *ad vivum*, from the living model. As regarded the deceased, the practice of the funeral mask, which is not recorded before Charles VI of France in the fifteenth century, probably already existed in the fourteenth century, to judge from the straightforward realism of many tomb effigies.

Woman's head from a funeral monument.
Last third of the 14th century.
Marble.
Musée du Louvre, Paris.

The funeral effigy of Marie de Bourbon, sister of the wife of Charles V, from the church of Saint-Louis at Poissy and today in the Louvre, presents the nun standing, hands joined together and wearing the hood, wimple and black and white dress of the Dominican order. This statue, exceptional for its polychromy and the finish of its materials, shows the search for psychological realism in the portrait. The famous statues of Charles V and Jeanne de Bourbon in the Louvre equally illustrate physical and psychological truth in the face and in the rendering of the headdress and clothing. Faithfulness in reproducing the features and the individuality was thus attained at about mid-century (painted portrait of John the Good). The attention to the portrait went together with the vanity inherent in representation when it becomes public and of genealogical interest. Donor portraits occupied a prominent position in the churches. Those of Charles V were as present in fourteenth-century Paris as those of the Emperor Charles IV in Prague. The bishops represented on tombs were also sculptured in their cathedrals, as at Amiens, where the future Cardinal La Grange had himself portrayed on the "Beau Pilier" buttress, in a royal environment of statues, outside his cathedral. At Poitiers the Duke of Berry placed full-length portraits in the Great Hall of his palace. Henceforth handled with realism, the portrait became a political instrument, a signpost between the private and public worlds (tomb of Lord Despenser at Tewkesbury Abbey, around 1375).

Presumed statue of
King Sancho IV.
Between 1289 and 1308.
Toledo Cathedral.

Tomb effigy of Bishop
Friedrich von Hohenlohe (died 1351).
Stone.
Bamberg Cathedral.

Standing funeral effigy of Marie de Bourbon
from the church of Saint-Louis, Poissy.
Shortly after 1401. Black and white marble.
Musée du Louvre, Paris.

The fashion for portraiture in the 13th century:
Hermann and Reglindis.
Statues in the west choir.
After 1249.
Naumburg Cathedral.

Bonino da Campione.
Funeral monument of Cansignorio della Scala.
About 1374–1376.
Santa Maria Antica, Verona.

PUBLIC SCULPTURE

The ambivalence of themes made it possible henceforth to represent the *Tale of the Three Quick and the Three Dead* on the portal of the church of the Innocents in Paris and the Coronation of the Virgin above the entrance to the château of La Ferté-Milon; it contributed to the integration of religious sculpture into urban space and to civil sculptures on the doorstep of religious precincts. Charles V and his wife Jeanne were represented on either side of the entrance gate of the Célestins of Paris, while the entrance of the town hall of Barcelona was presided over by a large statue of the archangel Raphael, the commissioning of which

from the sculptor Pere Ça Anglada was the object of a meticulous spelling out of contractual details by the municipality.

In the fourteenth century sculpture penetrated into the public domain of the town. The main tower of Almudaina of Palma de Mallorca (Majorca) was surmounted by a weathervane angel, highly popular, commissioned by Jaume I from the Perpignan sculptor Campredon in 1310. The town halls, like the most prominent houses, had sculptured façades. At Siena, as at Nuremberg, this phenomenon began in the fourteenth century. It continued everywhere into the fifteenth (loggia of Palma de Mallorca).

In Perugia the great fountain by Nicola Pisano offered passersby a complex religious, historical, political and symbolic iconography, anticipating the Nuremberg fountain. In Venice the Doges paid particular care to the programme of the exterior façades of the Ducal Palace. In Bologna the monumental mausoleums of the doctors dominated the town. In Prague the emperor had the Charles Bridge ornamented with sculptures. Thus the fourteenth century preceded the Renaissance in the installation of public and urban sculptured programmes.

One of the main symbols of the public sculpture of the fourteenth century was the representation of the horseman of great size, the civic statue par excellence since antiquity. The subject, known in the early Middle Ages, as witnessed by the bronze statuette of Charlemagne, was present during the period of Romanesque architecture on many church façades in the west of France, and in Italy at Lucca.

St Martin sharing his cloak with a beggar
(original now taken down).
First half of the 13th century.
Façade of the Cathedral of San Martino, Lucca.

The horseman is again found in the thirteenth century at Magdeburg and Bamberg, with an iconography of no greater transparency than that of most Romanesque horsemen: the Magi or famous personages. In Strasbourg, on the cathedral façade, Clovis, Dagobert and Rudolph of Habsburg on horseback were incorporated into the programmes of the late thirteenth century. A horseman, now time-worn, dominates the Portal of the Virgin on the west front of the cathedral of Sens. The goldsmiths, moreover, never ceased to exploit this theme, as may be seen from the inventories of church treasuries (Chartres). At Notre-Dame of Paris, a crowned horseman in painted wood, armed and helmeted on a caparisoned horse, is certified and known through document drawings. He was mounted on a pedestal and placed alongside the first southeast column of the nave. The cathedral of Chartres possessed one in its turn. They have been attributed sometimes to Philip the Fair, sometimes to Philip VI of Valois: the statue is said to have been offered in thanksgiving after a battle in 1304 or 1328. The former hypothesis seems more likely.

In Italy this theme had an extraordinary success. During the Middle Ages, the ancient equestrian statue of Marcus Aurelius, taken by many for Constantine the Great, occupied a conspicuous position in Rome in front of the Lateran basilica and palace. It is known from numerous plans and views of Rome, among which the most interesting to us is probably the fresco by Taddeo di Bartolo in the communal palace of Siena (around 1410). The equestrian statue of Marcus Aurelius was moved to the Capitoline Hill only under Pope Paul III in 1538.

Equestrian monument of Mastino II della Scala.
Before 1351.
Santa Maria Antica, Verona.

Horseman.
Second quarter of the 13th century.
Interior of
Bamberg Cathedral.

Among the most fashionable arrangements was the one adopted by the Della Scala and Visconti families in Verona and Milan respectively. In Verona the famous funeral monuments situated around Old Saint Mary (Santa Maria Antica), inside the sacred enclosure, appear in the form of an armed horseman on a pedestal base, in the case of the oldest ones (Can Grande della Scala, died 1324; Mastino II della Scala, died before 1351), or of a horseman standing on the summit of an immense funeral monument like the one built by Bonino da Campione, a Milan sculptor (known from 1349 to 1397), for Cansignorio della Scala, during the latter's lifetime (he died in 1375).

Mounted on columns, this monument in Verona is composed of a canopy, or tabernacle with arches, that symbolically protects the sarcophagus and tomb effigy. At the head of the sarcophagus are two angels, while the long sides are sculptured with six scenes from the life of Christ, and the small side-surfaces with the Coronation of the Virgin and the presentation to the Virgin by St George of Cansignorio della Scala. Above, on the architecture proper, are the personifications of the seated Virtues and angels presenting the family coat of arms. The summit is dominated by the equestrian statue of this Della Scala lord. The whole is finished off by tabernacles placed at the angles, which contain the statues of the warrior saints (George, Martin, Quirinus, Alvise, Valentine and Sigismund).

This monument, which was preceded at Verona by the formula of a simple canopy above the sarcophagus (Castelbarco tomb at Sant'Anastasia) is perhaps one of the best symbols of the dreams and mad aspirations of courtly society and its warlike and chivalrous vision of the world.

At Milan, another famous monument, that of Bernabò Visconti, today preserved in the museum of the Sforzesco

Bonino da Campione.
Equestrian monument of
Bernabò Visconti,
originally in
San Giovanni in Conca,
Milan.
Shortly before 1363
(sarcophagus after 1385).
Museo del
Castello Sforzesco,
Milan.

Castle, is also the work of Bonino da Campione. It is formed of two distinct parts: the sarcophagus sculptured after the death of Bernabò in 1385, and the equestrian statue which was carved some twenty years earlier. The latter had been made initially for the church of San Giovanni in Conca of Milan, where it was placed *in superficie altaris maioris*. On the sarcophagus Bernabò is presented by St George to Christ on the cross in the presence of saints and surrounded by various episodes involving the Virgin, St John, sundry saints, the Coronation of the Virgin, the Evangelists and the Church Fathers. The horseman, perhaps the only part attributable to the master's hand, is a cruel portrait of unflinching realism and startling violence.

This type of monument is the ultimate lifesize or over-lifesize expression, carried to its public paroxysm, of the social dream of being remembered and admired by posterity. From the English tombs which portray the knight at arms and exalt him with dignity by the original and characteristic position of crossed legs (tomb effigy of John of Eltham at Westminster) to the manuscripts and smallest objects of everyday use, such as seals or ivory carvings, the image of the horseman is everywhere present in the art of the fourteenth century. The bronze ewer and basin in the British Museum found in the Tyne, or the terracotta statuette from Nuremberg (around 1380), today in the Bode Museum of East Berlin, are objects of rare quality; they bear witness to the presence of the knight at arms in the everyday imaginative furniture of a society which associated the chivalrous conception of life with a courtly ideal made up of heroic feeling and fantasy.

SCULPTURE AND NEW DEVOTIONS

THE INDIVIDUAL CULT STATUE

In wood, in stone, in marble or in alabaster, individual statues formed the most numerous and most characteristic production of the fourteenth century. The beautiful and hip-shifting Virgin and Child were the focal point for all the feelings and fantasies of the dream of courtly love. At the same time the Virgin of Tenderness, the Beautiful Madonna, was the central element of the religious cult that, from the end of the twelfth century onwards, never stopped growing throughout the western world. The number of Virgin and Child sculptures which have been preserved reach into the thousands, and the study of them is made very difficult by the regional variations in stylistic advances and the differences in quality between the works of the great masters and the manufacture in series of local workshops.

The typological range of the Virgins was highly diversified. Standing or seated, wearing a crown or a veil, queen, mother or princess, the Virgin who had to fulfil feminine aspirations was no longer presented solely to accompany the Child as the Mother of God, as an instrument of Salvation: henceforth she was above all herself, throne of Wisdom, Queen of Heaven, the model of mother and of woman.

At once mother and spouse-symbol, the statue of Maxéville (Meurthe-et-Moselle) portrays the Child slipping the wedding ring on his mother's finger, while the belt glimpsed under the mantle symbolizes virginity. Conversing with the Child in a bond of tenderness, or beguiling it (Virgin of Champdeuil, Seine-et-Marne), the Virgin is always attired elegantly and with refinement, and represents the highest expression of the style of the century. In a play of curved lines, hip-thrust of the body, movement of clothes, the form of folds, the Virgin no longer hesitates to be a woman, and modestly, beneath the clothes, the forms of the body reveal themselves. She plays her role as mother publicly, and uncovers her breast to suckle the child. She can be seated right on the ground (Virgin of Humility, which appears in the Sienese painting of the second quarter of the fourteenth century). Mother of the Child, she is no less the mother of the crucified Christ; thus the theme of the Pietà appears, the Virgin receiving the dead Christ in her arms–that body of Christ on which the sculptors carried out their most elaborate anatomical investigations–, a type that was to blossom fully during the fifteenth century.

Objects of worship, the statues of the Virgin and Child were also a product of patronage: donors offered them to the churches and often had themselves represented kneeling in humility at the Virgin's feet; private persons dreamed of owning them. They travelled; for they were often commissioned from remote and reputed workshops. The Virgin and Child, alone or flanked by angels, was the statue above all others for the private chapel. On all levels of the social hierarchy the statues of the Virgin and Child were used for trade and gifts.

A few examples will serve to make these various uses clear. In 1341 the executors of the will of Guy Baudet, counsellor of King Philip VI and afterwards bishop of Langres, commissioned from Evrard of Orléans a statuary group representing the bishop kneeling at the feet of the Virgin, in accordance with Baudet's express wish. The seated Virgin and Child in the cathedral of Sens, famous for the reliefs that decorate the base of the throne, was

Virgin and Child probably from the abbey of Saint-Corneille, Compiègne. Second half of the 13th century. Limestone. Musée Vivenel, Compiègne.

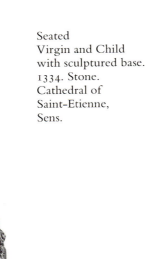

Seated
Virgin and Child
with sculptured base.
1334. Stone.
Cathedral of
Saint-Etienne,
Sens.

offered in 1334 by the canon Manuel de Jaulnes to adorn the altar of a chapel. An engraved inscription on the black marble base of the Virgin of Muneville (Manche) specifies that it was donated by the priest in charge along with a velvet chasuble in 1343. The examples could be multiplied endlessly, as could the references to restorations, repaintings or embellishments. In 1329 the accounts of Mahaut d'Artois recorded a payment made to the goldsmith Etienne de Salins for a gilded silver crown, set off by gems and enamels, for the Virgin and Child.

The great artists also made sculptures of the Virgin and Child. One need only recall the statue signed by Giovanni Pisano at Padua, or the attribution to Jean de Cambrai of the Virgin of Marcoussis: here, as in Prague or Paris, there is on one hand the problem of the non-specialization of the workshops, and on the other that of the relations with monumental sculpture and, finally, between different materials. The comparisons recently made between the heads of the tomb of Cardinal Petroni (cathedral of Siena), of Tino di Camaino and of the wooden Virgin and Child of Anghiari establish solid links between the different techniques. Commissions from faraway places given to prestigious workshops are evidenced by the marble Virgin known as the White Virgin in the church of Huarte (Pam-

Virgin and Child from Ile-de-France.
Second quarter of the 14th century.
Painted wood.
Staatliche Museen, Berlin.

Virgin and Child from Lorraine.
About 1330-1340. Stone.
Musée de Cluny, Paris.

Virgin and Child.
About 1330-1340. Marble.
Antwerp Cathedral.

Seated Virgin and Child.
About 1270.
Painted wood.
Schnütgen-Museum, Cologne.

Pietà from the Rhineland.
About 1300. Painted wood.
Rheinisches Landesmuseum, Bonn.

plona) with an inscription explaining that it had been brought from Paris by the Pamplona merchant Martín Duardi in the year 1349 and given to the church in honour of the Virgin Mary. Locally, statues could be offered in worship or as thanksgivings (Lesches, Seine-et-Marne).

The stylistic evolution of Virgin and Child statues shows a continuous progression during the fourteenth century towards the style of the Beautiful Madonnas, by an accentuation of the hip-thrust and the undulations of the mantle, and by a steady elaboration of a mannerist style. The regional groups make a subject of monographic studies for each country. The road leading to international Gothic and late Gothic is marked by an acceleration of the changes during the sixties of the fourteenth century, first in the handling of the faces, then, in the following decades, in the modification of the structural plan of the whole of the figure: but those are general characteristics of the sculpture of the century, particularly in the northern countries.

To the salience of the hip is added a swirling of the drapery and the twisting of the body. The movement accelerates in a kind of plastic turbulence; the clothes expand and become enveloping; the shoulders shrink and, notably in the Beautiful Madonnas of Bohemia, art takes off in complicated formulas, a challenge to the artist's skill. As a halfway house in his development we might select the statue of St Catherine of Alexandria in the church of Notre-Dame at Courtrai, which is attributed without conclusive proof to André Beauneveu and in which, to the current model of the Virgin and Child carrying the sceptre, the sculptor adds the wheel and sword of the saint.

This kind of transposition is common in the statues of saints.

Whether the saints were local or universal, hagiography also provided work for sculptors as a function of regional or private religious cults. The great wooden crucifixes formed another significant group of devotional statues. Set apart on a painted wall or placed on a triumphal beam at the entrance to the choir, the Christ on the Cross could also be inserted into a group between the Virgin and St John. It was a tradition common to groups of the Descent from the Cross that went back to the Romanesque period and culminated in the dramatic Christ of Sorrows of the fifteenth century. Just as the back surface of the wall-niche favoured the iconography of the Virgin over that of the Crucifixion (tomb of the cantor Aparicio, cathedral of Salamanca), so the production of Crucifixes never attained the scale of that of Virgins. Except in Germanic social circles, it was not until the very end of the century that the calvary of the charterhouse of Champmol by Claus Sluter (1395-1405; before 1399 for the crucifix), with its new form of emotive realism, opened the way to a new appreciation of the Crucified. The so-called Matthias Corvinus calvary in wrought gold from the treasury of the cathedral of Esztergom, in Hungary, underscores this same turning point in a different way.

Christ and St John
from Sigmaringen.
About 1330. Painted oak.
Staatliche Museen, Berlin.

THE CHAPEL AS SCULPTURE

The chapels founded by kings, princes, ecclesiastics, wealthy burghers or trade guilds had considerable importance for fourteenth-century sculpture. Lay donors and founders had themselves represented, and often buried, in them. The builders of funerary chapels were numerous in the different churches and even in those of the Minorites; the custom extended rapidly to important personalities, then to priests and canons, and finally to merchants. The case of papal Avignon is exemplary. There the great Italian families, Pazzi, Peruzzi, Gardini and others, tried to revive Florentine luxury, and installed themselves, for example, in the churches of the Minorites and the Carmelites (Bardi), in Notre-Dame-des-Doms, etc.

This custom indeed was not restricted to cardinals, for whom the choice of tomb was often accompanied by the construction of a chapel, but reached the more modest townspeople, the money-changers, the haberdashers, butchers or rich craftsmen. They had chapels built that grafted themselves onto churches in great numbers, splitting up and multiplying the oratories, the places of prayer or devotion. They had themselves depicted with their families, and commissioned altarpieces and sculptures. The

Portal of the chape
of the Episcopal Pa
Before 1343.
Tortosa.

Folding altarpiece.
About 1300.
Abbey Church, Cismar.

Pierpaolo and Jacobello dalle Masegne.
Marble altarpiece.
1388-1392.
Church of San Francesco, Bologna.

small portable triptych in painted wood of the Museum of Fine Arts of Angers constitutes a fine example of an object made to adorn a private chapel in which the person for whom the work is intended had himself painted on one of the panels in a kneeling position. To this piety also correspond the ivory triptychs or polyptychs, which, like the one in the Hôtel Pincé at Angers or the one in the Louvre, present a Virgin and Child at the centre, and angels and scenes of the life of the Virgin and Child on the movable side panels.

The proliferation of chapels contributed to the development of the altarpiece, which provided commissions for the workshops of sculptors in stone, wood, alabaster and ivory. Often organized and assembled from prefabricated parts, the fourteenth-century altarpieces are sometimes difficult to reconstruct, owing to the dispersion of the panels. The altarpiece of the high altar of the abbey of Maubuisson, for example, was executed around 1340 at the expense of Queen Jeanne d'Evreux, probably by Evrard d'Orléans, on the occasion of the founding of a chaplain's benefice dedicated to St Paul and St Catherine. In general, the altarpiece celebrated the theme of the Eucharist, and could form part of an overall programme together with the altar frontal. Often, moreover, because of the high cost of the labour, the different parts were executed at large

intervals of time (San Jacopo altar in the Duomo of Pistoia).

Among the major works of the century stands out the altar of San Francesco of Bologna, carried out by Jacobello and, especially, Pierpaolo dalle Masegne between 1388 and 1392. The fourteenth century here began the journey towards the sculptured altarpiece on a grand scale of the fifteenth century (cathedral of Vic by Pere Oller; cathedral of Tarragona by Pere Joan).

The palatine or episcopal chapel received special attention as a private oratory: for example, the shrine at Vincennes or Mehun-sur-Yèvre goldplated on the outside, or at Avignon on the inside; and in spite of the presence of decorative sculptures, it gave preference to wall decoration (Karlstein) or stained glass windows. The monumental sculpture is concentrated at the entrance, on either side of the door or on the tympanum, as in the chapel of the episcopal palace of Tortosa before 1343, where the Virgin and Child statue is seen flanked by two angels on the tympanum and the statues of two bishops in the splays. The multiplication of these different places of worship, filling the role of funerary chapel or private oratory and accommodating a more intimate and personal statuary, stressed the individual approach that nourished artistic creation and crystallized thought in images.

Altar and altarpiece of San Jacopo.
1287 to the 15th century.
Cathedral of Pistoia.

SCULPTURING GOLD

The inventories of the fourteenth-century church treasuries leave us flabbergasted, for it is hard to imagine translated into metal the vast quantities of objects amassed by the princes of the fourteenth century. The Emperor Charles IV assembled an unparalleled collection in Prague. The treasuries of cathedrals and churches possessed altar-pieces, crosses, reliquary shrines, chalices and monstrances, not to mention other objects such as censers, candelabra, etc.; there were many books, too, and they were sumptuously bound.

The evolution in the goldsmith's craft and in enamelling during the fourteenth century benefited from the development of the technique of making translucent basse-taille enamels, which, during the first half of the century, completely revolutionized aesthetics by the transparency of the fine layer of translucent enamel that allowed the chasing of silver or gold to be seen. The technique of stamping, of hallmarking, finds its highest expression in the celebrated cup of St Agnes in the British Museum. Goldsmiths were extremely numerous in Paris as in Tuscany. Many stone or marble sculptors were also, and primarily, goldsmiths, notably in Italy (Andrea and Nino Pisano) or in Catalonia (Pere Moragues).

This immense production of goldsmiths' work reached its height about 1400, and by then it constituted a kind of anthology of all the stylistic innovations made in the course of the previous century. If, from this abundance of fine work, we try to define a few major features, we must single out the sceptre of Charles V of France (Louvre). The statue of Charlemagne crowning the sceptre, and in particular the rendering of the face (after 1365), shows how closely the style of such work corresponded to the realistic tendencies of contemporary monumental sculpture.

The reliquary busts, very numerous in the fourteenth century, contributed directly to the history of the portrait by an in-the-round treatment of the figure (reliquaries of Charlemagne, John the Baptist and Cornelius in the Aachen treasury).

The most impressive piece of work produced by the goldsmiths' ateliers was the altarpiece, which attained great size and formed the luxurious and ostentatious version of the painted or carved altarpiece. During the second and third quarters of the century, the altarpiece of Gerona Cathedral, surmounted by an astonishing baldachin and composed of prefabricated parts assembled over a wooden core, shows in each of its details, particularly in the execution of figures and architectural structures, the monumental ambitions of the goldsmiths. They were in the forefront of stylistic research and probably originated most of the artistic innovations of courtly art. The goldsmiths' craft of the fourteenth century is equally distinguished by the range of a secular production in which the profane outstripped the sacred, and which represented the highest expression of court life.

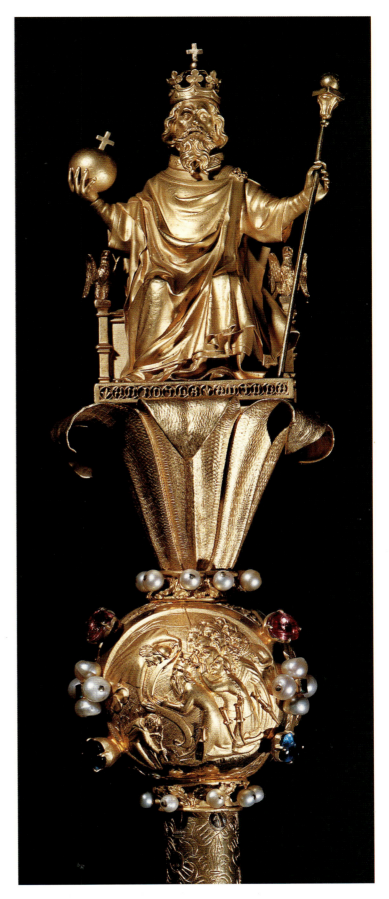

Sceptre of Charles V of France
with seated statuette of Charlemagne,
from the treasury of Saint-Denis.
1365-1380.
Enamelled, engraved and chased gold
with silver and stones.
Musée du Louvre, Paris.

Altarpiece. About 1325–1380. Silver-gilt and chased. Cathedral of Gerona.

Altarpiece from the Florentine Baptistery. 1366 to the 15th century. Silver. Museo dell'Opera del Duomo, Florence.

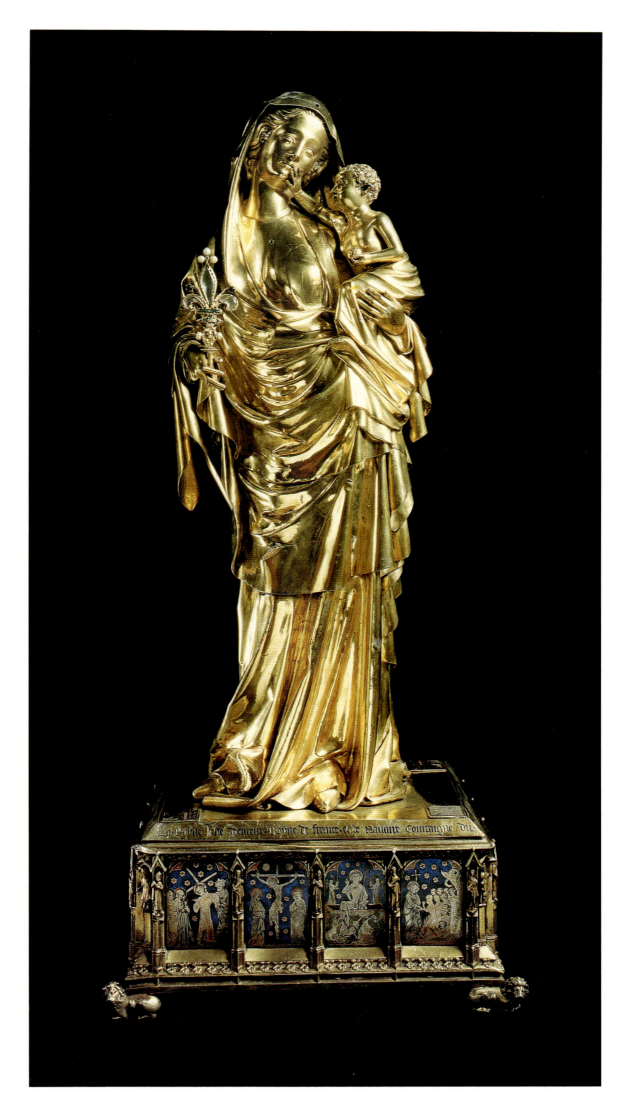

Virgin and Child
given by Jeanne d'Evreux
to the abbey of Saint-Denis
in 1339.
Silver-gilt, enamels,
gold, stones.
Musée du Louvre, Paris.

AN ORIGINAL IMAGERY: THE STALLS

Bench-end of the stalls with St George and the dragon.
About 1377. Wood.
Cathedral of Evreux.

The enclosing of the choirs of cathedrals and large religious edifices was accompanied by the installation of wooden stalls, generally arranged in two rows: the lower, more simple, at ground level, and the upper, reserved for canons and guests of honour, provided with sculptured backs. Choir stalls were one of the most freely and lavishly sculptured parts of the building. The seat was a moveable structure of rectangular shape, which, when closed, revealed the lower part; the misericord or smaller-sized seat, which took the form of a console, was then visible. At that location was a decoration in relief accompanied by other subjects on the arms and backs. The iconography was at once religious and secular; but the latter, with obvious moral implications, paradoxically dominated by revealing aspects of city life and the life of the couple, associated with personifications of the months and of occupations, with scenes of music and dance and a very broad plant or animal ornamental repertory. The marginal illustration of manuscripts played a large role in the conception of this iconography. The sculptured misericords spread throughout the

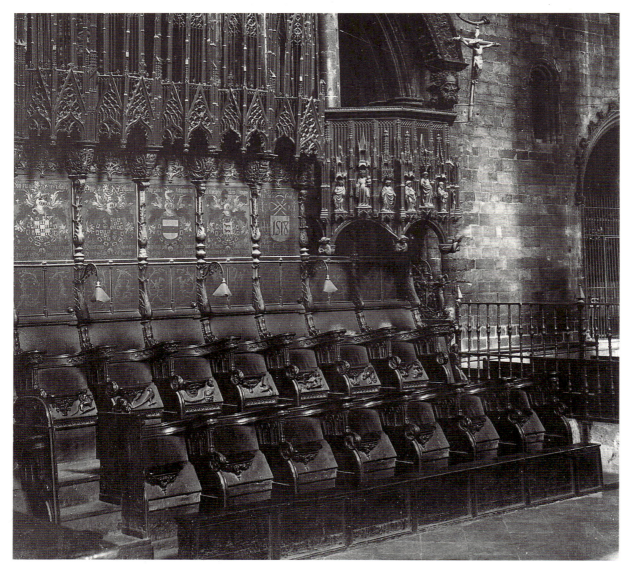

Pere Ça Anglada
and workshop
for the earlier parts.
Choir stalls and pulpit.
Around 1400 (lower part).
Barcelona Cathedral.

fourteenth century to enjoy a very great success during the two centuries that followed. In England fine sets of choir stalls are preserved at Winchester, Wells, Ely, Lincoln, Gloucester, Worcester, Exeter and Chester. In Germany the stalls of Cologne Cathedral denote by the style of the figures tendencies parallel to those of monumental sculpture. The relief carving of the stall in the church of St Bartholomew in Frankfurt is closer to metal-work (relief of Charlemagne). In France the stalls of the cathedral of Saint-Pierre of Poitiers, at the start of our period, have to be mentioned. In Catalonia, in adition to the stalls of Gerona, of which little remains, there is the well-preserved series of Barcelona Cathedral, a work entirely documented at the end of the fourteenth century but completed afterwards. This group, carried out in the workshop of the sculptor Pere Ça Anglada, which is known for an abundant production of monumental stone carvings, participated fully in the changes in Catalan sculpture which took place at the end of the fourteenth century. The restorations of recent years have given back all its lustre to the choir of Barcelona Cathedral, which possesses, in a perfect state of preservation, its original pulpit and episcopal throne (plausibly attributed to Pere de Sant Joan), both of them elegantly decorated with statuettes and pinnacles.

Noah's drunkenness.
Detail of the choir stalls.
Early 14th century. Wood.
Cologne Cathedral.

Detail of Noah's head.

PARIS AND THE NEW NORTHERN MODERNITY

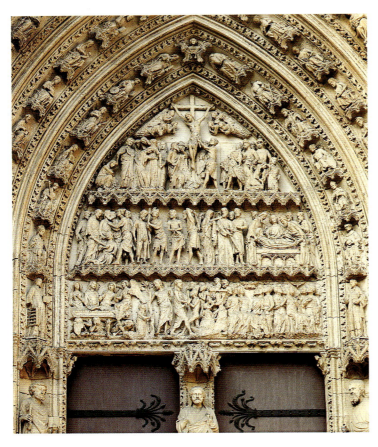

Portail de la Calende, south arm of the transept. About 1280-1306. Rouen Cathedral.

THE FLOWERING OF THE EARLY 1300s

At the end of the thirteenth century monumental sculpture underwent a new expansion on the building sites of many French churches and cathedrals then in the course of completion: Mantes, Meaux, Reims, Saint-Urbain at Troyes, Auxerre, Saint-Père-sous-Vézelay. In order to characterize those years with regard to the great portals, it is worth turning to Normandy, and above all to Rouen, where, most probably between 1280 and 1306, the façades of the cathedral transept were decorated. Comparing the two portals of Rouen Cathedral, we get a glimpse of what still harks back to the art of the thirteenth century in the Portail de la Calende to the south and of the constituents

of stylistic development in the Portail des Libraires to the north. The first presents in the tympanum the story of the Passion related on different levels, the apostles on the engaged piers surmounting the scenes of the Old and New Testaments as well as the life of local saints on the base; the whole capped by the Coronation of the Virgin and hagiographic subjects in the gables. The second shows the Last Judgment on the tympanum and statues of saints in the splays, with a cycle from Genesis and an encyclopedic programme; from here on, relief takes precedence over the statue, the decoration extends to the gables and the figure scenes inscribed in quatrefoils invade the base of the building.

In Paris, Philip the Fair (1285-1314) contributed to the revival of sculpture by his vigorous championing of the Capetian monarchy, his desire to increase the standing of the recently canonized Louis IX, and by his longing to draw inspiration from the model of Royaumont to which St Louis was so attached. Thus, the Saint-Louis priory of Poissy (from 1297 onwards) possessed a large sculptured programme, a kind of illustration of royal endeavours. In the transept, the statues of the royal family rose on the south wall; they are known through the drawings of the Gaignières collection, which reproduce the statues of six of the eleven children of Louis IX arranged in decreasing size on the consoles: Louis (died 1260), Philip the Bold (died

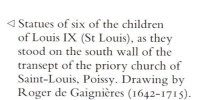

◁ Statues of six of the children of Louis IX (St Louis), as they stood on the south wall of the transept of the priory church of Saint-Louis, Poissy. Drawing by Roger de Gaignières (1642-1715).

▷ Isabelle de France. About 1304. Stone. Collegiate church of Notre-Dame, Poissy.

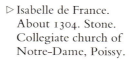

1285), Jean-Tristan (died 1270), Ysabelle (died 1271), Pierre d'Alençon (died 1283) and Robert de Clermont, then still alive, who is portrayed in a slightly different manner. The statues of St Louis and Marguerite of Provence were placed on the eastern pillars of the transept crossing, and other statues probably completed this genealogy reduced to two generations. We recall that the ceremonial hall of the Palais de la Cité in Paris presented the most customary formula illustrating monarchical continuity over a long duration. The acquisition by the Musée de Cluny, Paris, in 1987 of the statue of an angel from Poissy has made it possible to suggest the existence around the choir of Poissy of a series of angels bearing the instruments of the Passion, on the model (known by a triptych) of the choir of the cathedral of Arras; thus the angels of Poissy glorified the altar in which lay the relics of the sainted king. The statues and fragments from Poissy well illustrate a fluid style expressed in the handling of the folds of the clothing and in the roundness of the faces. This style, which asserted itself in the entourage of Philip the Fair and which has been defined as a synthesis of historical components and a stylistic classicism, determined the production of other important centres at the time (Ecouis). The Marian reliefs on the base of the north chapels in the choir of Notre-Dame, Paris, are particularly noteworthy in this respect (though still inadequately studied), inasmuch as they can be dated with certainty to the years between 1296 and 1318.

The influence of Paris, both of the style marking the period of St Louis (who reigned as Louis IX, 1226-1270) and of developments immediately following, can also be grasped from the success of the device of placing apostle

The Virgin Mary and Christ. Shortly after 1300. Painted stone. Choir statues, Cologne Cathedral.

Central portal of the west front. About 1280-1300. Strasbourg Cathedral.

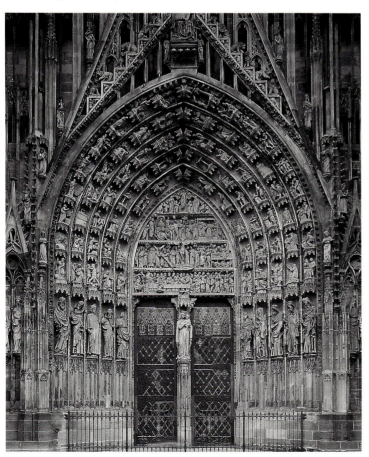

statues on the pillars, introduced at the Sainte-Chapelle and revealed at its consecration in 1248. At Cologne, for example, the cathedral begun that same year adopted this Parisian innovation before the consecration of the choir in 1322 and perhaps even around the early 1300s. In Paris the apostles from the church of Saint-Jacques-de-l'Hôpital, in the Musée de Cluny, bear witness to the fortunes of the formula well into the fourteenth century (1319-1327) and have often been considered as models for the Cologne statues. Today it is thought instead that the latter came before them, and go back to the development of Parisian sculpture in the second half of the thirteenth century.

Before returning to the many aspects of the Parisian centre and the role of its sculptors during the first decades of the century, it is appropriate to mention other, more distant cities that contributed equally to define the art of the 1300s, an art that for some years has received increasing attention. Among them, the building site of the western façade of the cathedral of Strasbourg, by the scope of its iconographic programme and the stylistic changes it proposed, seems to stand somewhat apart, even if considered as a driving force (Freiburg im Breisgau). The St Catherine chapel in Strasbourg Cathedral took over from it during the second quarter of the century with a large group of sculptures of highly diversified style (1331-1349), which was successful and followed up elsewhere (Colmar, Rottweil). In this chapel is to be found a type of funerary monument (Musée de l'Œuvre, Strasbourg) called Saint-Sépulcre (Holy Sepulchre), which enjoyed a certain popularity.

Jean Ravy. Canon Pierre de Fayel.
From the choir screen of Notre-Dame, Paris.
Before 1344. Stone. Musée du Louvre, Paris.

THE TRIUMPH OF NARRATIVE: THE CHOIR SCREEN OF NOTRE-DAME

The relations between text and image were at the heart of the new fourteenth-century sculpture. To the narrative sense and realistic stylistic tendencies was added a relationship to man, coupled with a cultural aspiration that sprang in many cases from an encyclopedic vision of the world and a rediscovery of basic Aristotelian ideas.

The dialogue opened by Giotto between man and the inanimate world, the sense of the narrative in episodes and its didactic purpose, became dominant during the second half of the thirteenth century but were already largely exploited by Giovanni Pisano. In northern France, where narration continued to invade the tympanum, imposing a division into registers, one above the other, the dialogue between sculpture and narrative found fertile ground in the choir screens. We have already seen the growing importance of the rood screen during the thirteenth century and its role in the iconography of the edifice, which has sometimes been underestimated owing to the dispersion of the principal ensembles (Bourges, Chartres, Saint-Denis). But at a time of profusion of movable sculpture and of the embellishment of the interior of the Gothic edifice, patrons and sculptors were ready to take the fullest advantage of the choir screen, which, cutting off the choir proper from the ambulatory, as in the cathedral of Albi, formed together with altar and relics a continuous narrative illustrating biblical history for the faithful.

The choir screen of Notre-Dame of Paris is the best preserved group, but is still insufficiently known. The screen originally closed off the whole of the church choir as far as the transept, where the rood screen stood. Only the north and south walls of the first three west bays are preserved. The programme is dedicated to the life of Christ, which can be followed step by step, from his birth at the north end, through the scenes on the south and up to the Passion (rood screen). The reconstruction of the decoration of the round parts of the choir screen remains a matter for conjecture. As to chronology, unanimity is also far from being reached; the north panels are the oldest, and their execution, later, of course, than that of the rood screen, comes before the end of the thirteenth century. At the south end, where the new stylistic tendencies blossomed, a keener sense of the picturesque is found, and a more modern way of handling clothes and faces. However, the making of each of the two parts is perhaps not as remote in time as once thought, and can easily be placed in the same stylistic climate of the Paris of Philip the Fair. The interest of the Notre-Dame screen lies equally in the effort it shows to translate select stylistic tendencies into a narrative language within everyone's reach.

The decoration of the round part of the choir of Notre-Dame of Paris disappeared, like the rood screen, at the end of the seventeenth century. According to old descriptions it is supposed that the lower part was ornamented with low reliefs of the story of Joseph. Above there were at least two reliefs representing the canon-donor, Pierre de Fayel, and the sculptor Jean Ravy, who, according to an inscription, had begun those "new stories" that were completed in 1351 by his nephew, Jean le Bouteiller. The fragment representing Canon Fayel, today in the Louvre, must have been carved before his death in 1344. A large gap thus divides the style of the north and south walls from that of the round part of the choir. Indeed, the style of representation of the Canon testifies to a decisive step forward in the personifying of the human figure, and a specifically stylis-

During the 13th century the carved rood screen was a prominent feature of the church: Sleeping soldiers, fragment of the rood screen. Shortly before the middle of the 13th century. Bourges Cathedral.

Giotto. Sequence of episodes from the life of Christ. Early 14th century. Arena Chapel, Padua.

tic development that can be followed through other Parisian works in the treatment of drapery folds. The exhibition of fourteenth-century French sculpture from the reserve collection of the Louvre, held at the Palais de Tokyo in Paris in 1985-1986, has made possible the identification of one of the reliefs of the eastern part of the choir screen.

It represents Joseph being caned in the presence of Potiphar, an episode traditionally paralleled by the flagellation of Christ and which throws a new light not only on the stylistic advance of Parisian sculpture but also on the dogmatic significance of the message conveyed by the choir screen of Notre-Dame.

Epiphany: The Adoration of the Kings. North wall of the choir screen. Shortly before the end of the 13th century. Notre-Dame, Paris.

195

Tomb effigy for the entrails of Charles V from the abbey church of Maubuisson. After 1374. Marble. Musée du Louvre, Paris.

THE ARTISTIC POLICY OF CHARLES V

After the entry of Charles V into Paris and the signing of the peace treaty with England, the king (1364-1380) displayed an intense artistic activity which earned him a lasting reputation as a patron of the arts. We have the eloquent testimony of Christine de Pisan in her *Livre des faits et bonnes mœurs du sage roy Charles V*, written in 1404. The military achievements included the building of the town wall (1358) with Vincennes (1361) and the Bastille (1370). In the civic domain he transformed the Louvre of Philip Augustus, fitted out the Palace, enlarged the Hôtel Saint-Pol and the manor of Beauté. Among his many interventions in religious buildings are the founding of the convents of the Célestins and of Saint-Antoine. But singular bad luck dogged the works of Charles V, most of which have disappeared. Only the Château de Vincennes bears witness today to the wide range of these royal enterprises. It amounts to more than a castle; rather, a real city whose rectangular wall encloses the castle proper and interior manor house. At the centre of the perimeter stands the Sainte-Chapelle with a single storey (not to be confused with the palatine chapel of the château of St Louis), the rectangular residence tower, while extensive grounds were set aside for the construction of private houses. It was thus a town for the king and the feudal lords. The castle of Vincennes retains a considerable quantity of decorative sculptures enabling us to define the artistic tendencies beginning with the 1360s. In the castle keep, between 1364 and 1369, the niches set above the Châtelet gate recall the presence of large statues of the royal family that surround the representation of a saint. Human figures or evangelist symbols are sculptured on the consoles or bases that catch the fall of the vaulting ribs; the sculptor has aimed there at resolving the problem of adapting figures to their setting. These sculptures are characterized by their monumentality, the treatment of folds which varies according to the artist but which shows a taste for curved lines and demonstrates great dynamism. In the Tour du Village, which dominates the north curtain wall, are preserved some sculptures close to the previous ones; consoles ornamented with figures of more controlled execution, but especially the fireplace of the first floor decked with foliage capitals, a plant decor and three angels. Four consoles on the first floor are sculptured with prophets or philosophers, whose new realism is close to bronze work. The third group dates from 1379, in the Sainte-Chapelle, of which the lower part dates from Charles V. The consoles that bore the statues stand out sharply from the wall and are adorned with figures which sometimes project outwards with a marked separation from the architecture. The clothes are sculptured in wide curved lines with great freedom, features to be found in the consoles of royal oratories and the arches of the portal. Of the latter nothing is known of the central pillar and tympanum, but the lateral engaged piers probably bore sculptures of Charles V and Jeanne de Bourbon, with perhaps the Virgin and Child on the central pillar. The scenes from the life of the Virgin seen on the arch mouldings, as well as the angels, could perhaps already be from the end of the century. The prophets probably stand at the end of the development and are characterized by the profusion of fabrics and the solemn look of the faces.

The style of Parisian sculpture under Charles V corresponds to the artistic progression of the city during the second half of the fourteenth century and the role it then played as a great capital of the arts. The realism of the face of Canon Fayel on the Notre-Dame choir screen stands at the beginning of a development which in the 1360s produced such works as the sceptre of Charles V in the Louvre, where the statue of Charlemagne reveals the essential features of the research into facial expression, in which great artists like Beauneveu (face of the tomb effigy of Charles V at Saint-Denis) participated. In a second phase during the 1380s, the construction of the whole sculptured figure was revolutionized by the presence of a twist to the body that introduced the third dimension. The essential landmarks in these investigations are found united in the craft of the goldsmiths of the early 1400s.

The destruction and dispersion of most of the groups sculptured under Charles V conditioned the interest taken in decorative sculpture. It would be unfair not to mention that the standing statues of the royal family figured at the Bastille and that the portal of the church of the Célestins in Paris presented the statues of kings, and an Annunciation in the tympanum. The famous statues of Charles V and Jeanne de Bourbon preserved in the Louvre were supposed to have come from the Quinze-Vingts hospice or to be those which, according to a print published by Millin in 1790, had adorned the engaged piers of the portal of the Célestins on either side of the statue of Saint Pierre Célestin, which stood on the central pillar; but if we accept the suggestion made in a recent study, they came from the façade of the eastern entrance of the Louvre. Their attributes are modern, and have been refashioned after old prints; originally the king must have held the sceptre and hand-of-justice staff, and the queen also a sceptre and perhaps a bouquet.

With that new and latest attribution the paternity of the two famous statues once again becomes controversial. For some years they were considered to be the work of the sculptor Jean de Thoiry, according to a payment made in 1378. The association with the great artists of the day of works preserved or simply known from illustrations or documents, opens multiple perspectives. Around Charles V gravitated many artists, some of them, like André Beauneveu or Jean de Liège, of great renown. Among the Louvre sculptors, there were, along with the two just mentioned, Jean de Saint-Romain, Guy de Dammartin, Jean de Launay and Jean de Chartres. In this domain we are directly dependent on monographic studies, essentially documentary, with added stylistic considerations. The reconstruction of the career of a sculptor may be attempted in some cases. It was done for Jean de Thoiry, a sculptor known during the second half of the fourteenth century and the early fifteenth. A native of northern France, having worked on the cathedral of Arras in 1365, he made his way to Paris drawn by news of the undertakings of

Charles V; he was mentioned there in 1378 when Charles V gave him the sum of thirty francs for a statue of Saint Pierre Célestin (portal of the Célestins). His reputation brought him commissions, including the tomb of Archbishop Lestrange of Rouen in 1375, and that, since destroyed, of the Duke and Duchess of Orléans in 1409. The contract for the latter, of 26 February of the same year, tells us how the sculptor worked. It contains a parchment on which the "portraiture" was sketched. The sarcophagus was to be lined with black marble slabs from Dinant and include a gallery carved in Pisa alabaster. The details of the decoration are mentioned, as well as the iconography with apostles or prophets chosen instead of mourners. The appearance of the tomb effigies is specified, and the wrought gold decorations that must embellish them, the figures that must surround them and the polychromy to set off the alabaster. For the execution of this tomb Jean de Thoiry committed himself not to exceed the span of a year's work and to assume responsibility for the installation. After him, his son Pierre de Thoiry became one of the great sculptors of the first third of the fifteenth century, confirming the family transmission of knowledge in the sculptor's craft.

Portal of the church of the Célestins, Paris, from a print published by A. L. Millin in 1790.

King Charles V of France and Queen Jeanne de Bourbon (the attributes are modern).
Statues thought to come from the portal of the Célestins in Paris, but possibly from the façade of the palace of the Louvre.
About 1365-1378. Stone.
Musée du Louvre, Paris.

Jean de Liège.
Tomb effigies for the entrails of Queen Jeanne d'Evreux and
King Charles IV the Fair, from the abbey church of Maubuisson.
About 1370-1372.
Musée du Louvre, Paris.

JEAN DE LIÈGE AND ENGLAND

The history of the fourteenth-century artists is the subject of constant investigations and of often revised attributions. Among the great names is obviously Jean Pucelle, an illuminator known to be active from around 1320 until his death in 1334, and the celebrated sculptor Claus Sluter, of Dutch origin, who worked between 1380 and 1406. Among the most famous sculptors of the French fourteenth century must be mentioned Jean-Pépin de Huy, known between 1311 and 1329, and often mentioned in the accounts of Mahaut d'Artois; Jean de Soignolles, known between 1349 and 1358, who first worked at Avignon before coming to Paris; then, towards the end of the century, Pierre Morel, known between 1370 and 1402, whose production was basically southern but who worked at Lyons between 1386 and 1390; and Jean de Cambrai, to whom we shall return. In Paris two names stand out as the sculptors of the century: Jean de Liège and André Beauneveu.

Jean de Liège was a past master in his native region in funerary art, and appeared in Paris in 1361, collaborating on the execution of a statue of Jeanne de Bretagne for the chapel of the Dominicans of Orléans. His prestige evident-

ly grew rapidly, since in 1364 he worked for the king on the "Grande Vis" (great staircase) of the Louvre under the direction of Guy de Dammartin, where he was made especially responsible for the statues of the king and queen. Afterwards he built the tomb of the heart of Charles V for the choir of Rouen Cathedral, known from a drawing by Gaignières. It was a commission from the king himself, a veritable political act with regard to the Norman duchy, and of which the advance paid to Jean de Liège in 1368 marked the beginning of a continuous activity in the service of the king and his entourage until his death in 1381. In 1369 Jean de Marville was mentioned as working with him. Shortly afterwards, around 1370-1372, Jean de Liège carved the tomb effigies for the entrails of Charles IV and Jeanne d'Evreux at the latter's request for the abbey of Maubuisson, near Pontoise. Charles IV, at his death in 1328, had been buried according to his wishes in three different places: his body at Saint-Denis, his heart with the preaching friars of Paris, and his entrails at Maubuisson. This practice, which his third wife Jeanne d'Evreux decided on immediately before her death (1371), increased the commissions for tomb-makers. The custom then began to spread. The monument at Maubuisson included a slab of black marble with a gilded inscription and canopies with gables and small columns that surrounded the tomb effigies enhanced with gold. These two tomb effigies preserved in the Louvre are of small size and bear the sceptre and the bag holding the entrails. The style of Jean de

Virgin and Child
attributed to Jean de Liège,
possibly from the church of
Saint-Antoine-des-Champs,
Paris.
About 1364. Marble.
Calouste Gulbenkian
Foundation, Lisbon.

Liège is shown there in the handling of the faces, the treatment of the hands (the queen's right hand is modern) and in the finely differentiated rhythm of the fabrics.

The inventory of property made after his death (1381) provides evidence of the great number of commissions given to Jean de Liège, since among the works still preserved then in his workshop or for which his heirs received payment figured two statues of the king and queen, a John the Baptist probably intended for the funeral chapel of Charles V at Saint-Denis, the tomb of Philippe d'Aulnoy, house steward of Charles V and his wife, as well as, among others, those of Blanche and Marie de France intended for Saint-Denis. The bust of Marie de France, daughter of Charles IV and Jeanne d'Evreux, was broken off from the tomb effigy during the Revolution; it is now in the Metropolitan Museum in New York. This head was the artist's masterpiece, characterized by the smile, the look, and the flecks of shadow contrived at the corners of the eyes. The place occupied by Jean de Liège among Parisian sculptors has earned him numerous attributions, such as the head of Bonne de France in Antwerp or the Virgin and Child in marble at the Calouste Gulbenkian Foundation in Lisbon. The latter, which may come from Saint-Antoine-des-Champs in Paris, is thought to have been done around 1364; the head of the Child is especially close to that of Bonne de France. The attribution of this work to Jean de Liège rests on the comparison of the drapery folds, particularly at arm-level, with those of the documented tomb effigy of Charles IV. Other attributions remain more uncertain, because of similarities of style with some facets of the art of André Beauneveu (Presentation in the Temple, Musée de Cluny, Paris).

After his spell at the Louvre, Jean de Liège appears in the English accounts, and, in around 1367, carried out for Westminster Abbey the tomb of Philippa of Hainaut, wife of Edward III. The artist's brief visit to England probably did not leave an impression on his art, for it was already fully formed. Nevertheless, let us recall the salient features

Jean de Liège.
Bust of the tomb effigy of Marie de France, from Saint-Denis.
About 1380. Marble.
The Metropolitan Museum of Art, New York.

of artistic realities during the long reign of Edward III (1327-1377), just at the moment when the Hundred Years War established contacts and, paradoxically, increased artistic exchanges between England and France.

We have already mentioned the exuberant development of the screen-façade, placing statues one above the other in niches on several storeys in the cathedrals of Lincoln and Exeter (around 1360-1365)–to which we must add the stone altarpiece of Christchurch–, and the attention of patrons to the choir decorations of the two

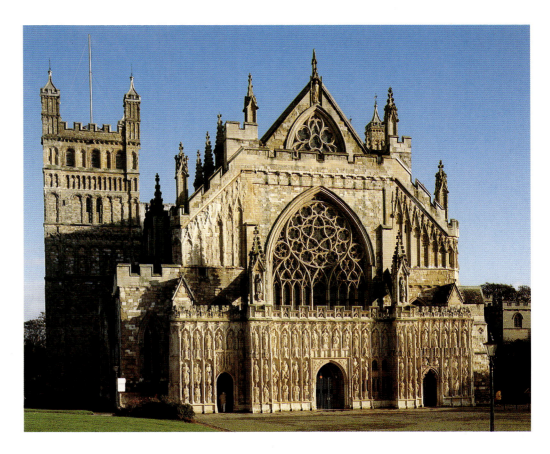

Screen-façade.
About 1360-1365.
West front of
Exeter Cathedral.

Statues on the west front of Lincoln Cathedral. About 1360-1365.

cathedrals (angels). A large part of the sculptural activity was carried on for the benefit of chapter houses which, like that of York, are the outcome of the decorative and stylistic tendencies of the previous century. During the fourteenth century decorative overabundance and refinement prevailed in the architectural sculpture of keystones. We have already referred to the importance of alabaster in the development of English sculpture. In the field of funerary sculpture, England retained quite a large number of monuments which are technically characterized by the increasing abandonment of Purbeck stone, by the use of the type of engraved copper flat-tomb which can sometimes be inserted into a stone slab, and by the gradual introduction of the theme of mourners into coffer-tombs. From the period of Edward III date the royal tombs of Edward II (died 1327) at Gloucester, of his son John of Eltham (died 1334) in Westminster Abbey, and of the sons

of Edward III at York and Westminster, all from London workshops. The tomb built by Jean de Liège was foreign to the English tradition, and even if it was admired, it remained isolated without much of a future in a production resolutely aimed, beyond a progression of realism in the treatment of faces, towards manufacture in series. As the end of the century approached, the workshops became specialized in the massive elaboration of alabaster panels for altarpieces and of highly stereotyped tombs, also in alabaster. The turning point in the quality of English sculpture has been linked to the ravages of the Black Death, which struck at the whole of English society in 1348-1349. However, this change in the mode of production had some success, and altarpiece panels were exported abundantly to the Continent. Such is the artistic reality of English sculpture during the visit of John of Liège, as he was called in England.

Tomb effigy of Edward, Lord Despenser.
About 1370-1375.
Tewkesbury Abbey.

Jean de Liège. Tomb effigy of Philippa of Hainaut.
About 1367.
Westminster Abbey, London.

André Beauneveu.
Tomb effigy of
Charles V of France.
1364-1366. Marble.
Basilica of Saint-Denis.

1366, only the tomb effigy is preserved at Saint-Denis; it is Beauneveu's only sculpture that is both preserved and documented. The king, in coronation dress, is attired in two tunics and a cloak. The sceptre, the hand-of-justice staff and the crown were in metal. His feet rest on two lions. The art of Beauneveu reveals itself in a mastery of the marble that makes itself understood beyond the apparent simplicity of the drapery folds and the handling of the face. The latter was sculptured from the living model, a novelty in the case of a royal personage. The king, who was then only twenty-seven but who appears older here, is stamped by naturalism, and stays clear of courtly mannerism. Monumentality and realistic sense of detail (the veins of the hand) are brought together here (the left hand is redone).

Like Jean de Liège, André Beauneveu is said to have visited England and is mentioned in 1372 at Tournai and two years later at Valenciennes and at Courtrai, where he worked until 1384 in the service of the Count of Flanders, Louis de Mâle, on the construction of a funerary chapel. His presence at Courtrai earns him today the almost unanimous attribution of the St Catherine of Alexandria in alabaster, probably intended for the funerary group. Conceived on the model of a Virgin and Child in which the Child has been replaced by the wheel, it displays a more elaborate style by Beauneveu. During all of this phase of his life the artist seems to have been established in the North, since he is to be found at Malines in 1374-1375, then in 1383-1384 at Cambrai and at Ypres.

ANDRÉ BEAUNEVEU

Alongside Jean de Liège the name of André Beauneveu dominates the century in the north of France. However, other undertakings with their source in the royal entourage contributed to the dissemination of the style elaborated in Parisian circles. Thus, for example, a great personage of the realm, the future Cardinal Jean de La Grange, who, involved in the Schism, had a tomb built for himself of exceptional size at Avignon, originated during his episcopate at Amiens (1373-1375) a programme of royal and secular glorification mounted on the summit of a cathedral. Around 1375 a series of statues–somewhat broken up and restored today–were installed on a buttress of the north tower of the cathedral of Amiens (Beau Pilier) which represent, in addition to the Virgin (redone) and John the Baptist, the king, his two underaged sons, the minister Bureau de la Rivière, the admiral Jean de Vienne and the Cardinal himself. La Grange turned to the Parisian workshops to commission works in a style distinguished by its relations with the famous statues of Charles V and Jeanne de Bourbon, but also with other Parisian productions of the time, such as those of André Beauneveu.

Around 1360 Beauneveu was probably working at Valenciennes, of which he was presumably a native. By 1364 he was an officially recognized sculptor, since he was already working in Paris in the service of Charles V, who regarded him as his "beloved Andrieu Biauneveu, our image-maker," and from whom he obtained commissions for the king's tomb effigy for Saint-Denis and those of his father, John the Good, and of his grandparents, Philip IV and Jeanne de Boulogne. Of the funerary monument of Charles V, for which there is a record of payments until

St Catherine
of Alexandria.
Statue attributed to
André Beauneveu.
Between 1374 and 1384.
Alabaster.
Church of Notre-Dame,
Courtrai.

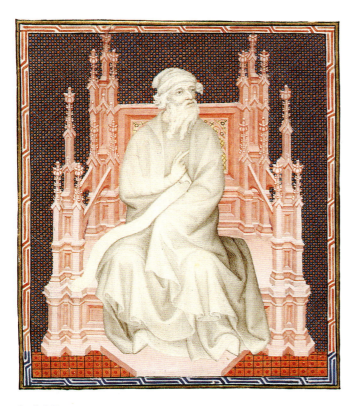

André Beauneveu.
Illustration in the Psalter of Jean de Berry.
About 1386.
MS. Fr. 13091, Bibliothèque Nationale, Paris.

If attributions are difficult to make during this period of Beauneveu's activity because he was working in the service of Charles V at the same time as Jean de Liège, the problem does not become any simpler afterwards, for, beginning in 1386 and until his death (before 1401), he was in the service of the Duke of Berry at Bourges and at the ducal castle of Mehun-sur-Yèvre, working there at the same time as Jean de Cambrai.

During this last period, André Beauneveu carried out the illuminations of the psalter of Jean de Berry (Bibliothèque Nationale, Paris, MS. Fr. 13091), as appears from the inventories which, from 1402 onwards, specify that the psalter should include at the beginning "several stories from the master hand of André Beauneveu." We do not know whether this initiative was the result of a whim of the patron's, the reputation which the sculptor already possessed in this field, or a desire on the part of Beauneveu for a change of technique at the end of his life. Be that as it may, the sculptured details of the painted thrones, the volume of the figures and the modelling of the drapery folds reveal the craft of the sculptor. Beauneveu's technical mastery is responsible for the attribution to him, which remains controversial, of sketches or cartoons for the stained glass windows of the Sainte-Chapelle of Bourges (today in Bourges Cathedral).

Beauneveu's activity as an illuminator raises once again the wider question of the relations between sculpture and painting during the second half of the fourteenth century; a discussion into which enters the handling of architectural structures and the figures of the Apocalypse tapestry of Angers.

▷ Statue of Jeanne de Boulogne
over the fireplace of the Grande Salle
in the Ducal Palace, Poitiers.
Late 14th century.

André Beauneveu.
Tomb effigy of Charles V
of France, detail.
1364-1366. Marble.
Basilica of Saint-Denis.

Decoration of the monumental entrance: over the gateway,
Coronation of the Virgin; on the towers, valiant knights.
Shortly after 1400.
Castle of La Ferté-Milon.

The prestige of royal commissions which implies the emergence of the new Parisian style led the princes and the great of the kingdom, following the royal models, onto the path of patronage of the arts. The example already mentioned of Cardinal La Grange is revealing in this respect. Within the very bosom of the royal family a rivalry sprang up to create peripheral centres in the image of Paris.

The Duke Louis of Orléans (1372-1407), second son of Charles V and brother of Charles VI, embellished the castles of La Ferté-Milon and Pierrefonds. While the works commissioned for this latter castle have disappeared, a solid reminder of this style so characteristic of the period is fortunately still preserved at La Ferté-Milon and at the castle of Coucy: the statues of valiant knights which the Duke had installed in the exterior niches of the wall towers. To the patronage of the Duke of Orléans is also due the Coronation of the Virgin carved at the end of the century for the entrance of the castle of La Ferté-Milon.

In this progression towards international Gothic and the art of the fifteenth century, the house of Anjou, founded by John II the Good, who elevated the county of Anjou into a duchy for the benefit of his second son Louis (1360), played a decisive role that in a large measure falls outside our period. Let us just recall that the famous tapestry of the Apocalypse of Angers was commissioned around 1373 by Duke Louis of Anjou, and that the latter possessed, as early as 1364, a collection of seventy-six tapestries.

At Bourges, on the other hand, Jean de France, Duke of Berry (1340-1416), third son of John II the Good, brother of Charles V and guardian of his nephew Charles VI, operated a system of patronage that seemed at first deeply loyal to Parisian circles. The Duke of Berry is known to be at the centre of the production of illuminated manuscripts, of which various books of hours have been preserved, and more particularly the psalter on which the sculptor André Beauneveu worked around 1386. The latter was in the Duke's service during the last decades of his life, before 1401. Froissart, who completed his *Chronicles* around 1400, explains that in the 1390s Beauneveu supervised the works of painting and sculpture at the ducal castle of Mehun-sur-Yèvre.

More study has been devoted to the intervention of the Duke of Berry in the field of illumination than in that of sculpture. His ventures into sculpture, however, are considerable. In 1385 the architect Guy de Dammartin built the Maubergeon tower of the ducal palace at Poitiers and decorated it with statues of important people, perhaps the Duke's counsellors; then Dammartin took a hand in the reconstruction of the great hall of the palace, and had the fireplace adorned with four large statues representing Charles VI and his wife Isabeau de Bavière, together with the Duke of Berry and his second wife Jeanne de Boulogne (c. 1389). The size of the statues, the place they occupy and the breadth of the style reflect the ambitions of the prince and the courtly refinement of his artistic pretensions. Almost at the same moment, between approximately 1391 and 1405, Jean de Berry undertook the building of the Sainte-Chapelle of Bourges, to house his tomb.

André Beauneveu and Jean de Cambrai are the two most famous sculptors of those attached to the Duke's court. They were preceded by others such as Jacques Collet, to whom are attributed the works of the first funerary chapel of Bourges Cathedral. Between André Beauneveu and Jean de Cambrai, who worked in parallel at Bourges for fourteen years under the same conditions, the attribution of sculptures is difficult (apostle's head from the chapel of Mehun, in the Louvre). Jean de Cambrai, a native of Rupy, near Saint-Quentin, is mentioned at Cambrai in 1374-1375 before travelling to Bourges, where in 1386-1387 he was "ymagier" (image-maker) for the Duke of Berry until his death in 1439. His name is attached to the building site of the Sainte-Chapelle of Bourges, where he was in charge of building the Duke's tomb (begun around 1404, the works were suspended at the death of the Duke in 1416). Jean de Cambrai himself presumably carved the tomb effigy, perhaps the canopy, from which is preserved the fragment of the sleep of the apostles, and five mourners. The simple style in which the body is concealed beneath the garment with long symmetrical folds, narrow and flattened, is characteristic of the work of Jean de Cambrai; and these features define the tendencies of the early

Angel holding up the armorial bearings of Jean, Duke of Berry,
from the castle of Concressault.
About 1400. Private Collection.

204

Angel's head from the palace of the Duke of Berry.
First quarter of the 15th century. Stone.
Musée de Berry, Bourges.

fifteenth century, confirmed by two angel's heads from the Duke's palace, today at Bourges and Issoudun respectively. Also attributed to Jean de Cambrai are the Virgin and Child in marble, given by the Duke of Berry to the Célestins of Marcoussis in 1408, the statues of Jean de Berry and Jeanne de Boulogne praying, and the groups of angels of Notre-Dame-la-Blanche, removed from the Sainte-Chapelle to Bourges Cathedral.

To sum up in a single work the style of the ducal court shortly before the turn of the century and its progression towards the international style, we can select the medallion recently brought back into prominence, portraying an angel holding up the armorial bearings of the Duke of Berry; it comes from the castle of Concressault (Cher). It can be attributed to the workshop of Drouet de Dammartin, mentioned as "ymagier" in 1400. The monumental implications of this small fragment, the very high quality of the execution of the drapery folds and the seduction and finesse of the face make it possible to connect it with other figures of angels like the ones already mentioned here or else with the music-making angels of Mehun or those bearing the coats of arms of the "Aligret" chapel of Bourges Cathedral, completed before 1412.

Another brother of Charles V, the fourth son of John II the Good, was Philip II the Bold. He drew inspiration from these different artistic successes in attempting to create another large cultural centre in Burgundy after 1363-1364. On the death of his father-in-law Louis de Mâle, Count of Flanders (1384), Philip came into the great Flemish inheritance. His son, John the Fearless, Duke of Burgundy from 1404 to 1419, continued, in spite of the struggles between Burgundians and Armagnacs, to support the artistic projects under way at Dijon. We find the

same appeal sent out there to artists of the royal court. Indeed, the sculpture programme of the Charterhouse of Champmol at Dijon, which Philip the Bold began to build in 1377 to house his tomb, was designed by the sculptor Jean de Marville, whom we have already met working alongside Jean de Liège. At his death in 1389 Jean de Marville probably had not been able to get beyond the façade and the tomb. Claus Sluter, who visited the building site of Mehun-sur-Yèvre in 1393, took over and became the initiator of a new style, monumental and baroque, which carried realism to extremes of dramatization.

THE SOUTHERN CROSSROADS

AVIGNON AND THE PATRONAGE OF THE POPES

By crowning Robert the Lame King of Naples in Notre-Dame-des-Doms at Avignon in 1309, Pope Clement V, former archbishop of Bordeaux, publicly affirmed the choice of Avignon as his residence. The political difficulties Italy went through during almost all of the fourteenth century led the popes to move away from it on a permanent basis, making Avignon the new capital of all Christianity until 1376, then, after the Great Schism of the West from 1378 to 1403, of only a part of it. There were many reasons for choosing Avignon: an advantageous

Apostle from the tomb of Cardinal
Guillaume II d'Aigrefeuille in the
church of Saint-Martial, Avignon.
About 1401. Alabaster.
Palace of the Popes, Avignon.

the fourteenth and the early fifteenth century was directly linked to the desire of the popes, distinguished figures and high-ranking clerics to have sumptuous monumental tombs built for themselves in the churches of Avignon and the surrounding districts: first at the cathedral of Notre-Dame-des-Doms, at Villeneuve, or in the monasteries of the mendicant orders. Five of the nine Avignon popes were buried there, as well as many cardinals. Most of the Gothic tombs of Avignon having been destroyed or broken up since the seventeenth century, however, the restoration of previous fragments and their identification is, though difficult, especially fascinating.

The first papal tomb was that of John XXII, who died in 1334 and who inaugurated the Avignonese formula of the canopied tomb. It was removed in 1840 to Notre-Dame-des-Doms, to the chapel located south of the choir built during the pontiff's lifetime (1316) to hold his funerary monument. The model, of northern or English origin, presented the tomb effigy (modern) lying on a chest surmounted by a high baldachin; the whole adorned by numerous small statuettes of which two, evoking the funeral procession, are preserved in the Petit Palais Museum. The tomb, now destroyed, of Benedict XII who died in 1342, was located in a chapel on the other side of the choir; so was that of Innocent VI who died in 1362 (Villeneuve-lès-Avignon); both took up the same model, referring stylistically to northern formulas. Despite these stylistic contacts with Parisian art, these Avignonese works fitted into a more realistic and personalized trend.

Resurrection scene
from the tomb of St Elzéar de Sabran
in the church of the Cordeliers at Apt.
Between 1370 and 1373. Alabaster.
Musée du Louvre, Paris.

geographical location on the Rhone axis between Italy and the Iberian peninsula at the gates of the kingdom of France, and a favourable political situation leading to the purchase of the city in 1348 from Joanna, Countess of Provence. The installation of the popes was accompanied by great architectural undertakings, foremost among which was the construction of the Palace of the Popes by Benedict XII (1334-1342), followed by Clement VI (1342-1352), Innocent VI (1352-1362) and Urban V (1362-1370). The popes remodelled the basilica of Notre-Dame-des-Doms and rearranged the wall areas in the papal quarter, in which the Petit Palais was also situated. Avignon rapidly became a very populous city (30,000 inhabitants?) and a wealthy one, an international trading centre, the seat of a university and a permanent building site during the course of the fourteenth century.

Avignon was transformed into an international capital, and the patronage of the popes attracted artists of renown, architects and master masons of course, but also painters, whose successive contributions defined an Avignon school which afterwards extended its influence. The presence of Giotto is probable, but the Avignonese centre is especially famous during this period for the activity of Simone Martini (1336-1344)–whose frescos from the porch of Notre-Dame-des-Doms are preserved–, by the secular decorations of the palace and by the work of Matteo Giovanetti (Saint-Martial and Saint-Jean chapels of the palace).

Only the portal of the Great Chapel of the palace, of which the stained glass windows had already been executed in 1354, was provided with a sculptured decoration, testifying to an attentive observance of contemporary trends in monumental art (Lyons, Rouen).

The exceptional, innovative and select development which Avignonese sculpture enjoyed during the course of

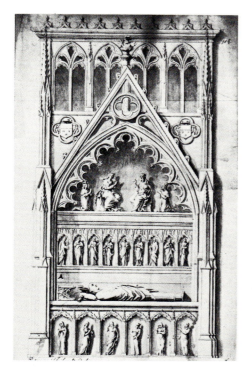

18th-century drawing of the tomb of Cardinal
Guillaume II d'Aigrefeuille, of about 1401,
in the church of Saint-Martial, Avignon.

Head of the tomb effigy of Cardinal Guillaume II d'Aigrefeuille.
About 1401. Alabaster.
Musée du Petit Palais, Avignon.

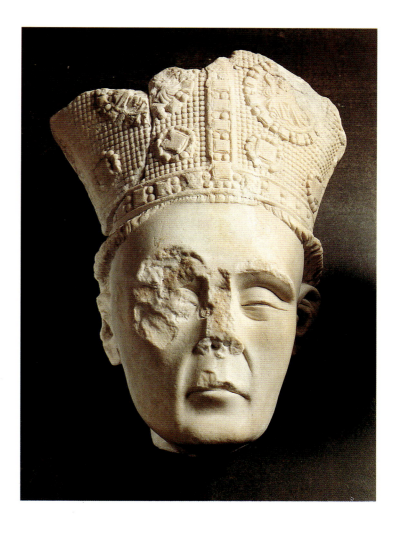

Among other tomb formulas was that of the coffer-tombs, to which belonged that of Clement VII (died 1394): the marble tomb effigy, which rested on a coffer ornamented with statuettes, is preserved. It was used as a model for the tomb of Cardinal Martin de Salva (died 1403), which was in the charterhouse of Bonpas, and of which seven statues are known. In this series among the most famous stands out the tomb of Cardinal Faydit d'Aigrefeuille (died 1391); its coffer, at Notre-Dame-des-Doms, was adorned with mourners standing beneath arches. Finally, the most frequently occurring funerary monuments are the recessed tombs placed flat against the wall (the recessed reconstruction of the tomb of Benedict XII at Notre-Dame-des-Doms is modern).

Some more exceptional tombs deserve separate mention. Urban V, who died in 1370, was buried in the crypt of Saint-Victor at Marseilles, but possessed a cenotaph in a recess at Saint-Martial of Avignon; only the tomb effigy survives today. The wall iconography displayed a Coronation of the Virgin with a Christ as Judge above it, accompanied by statuettes of saints and apostles. The association of the Coronation of the Virgin with apostles surrounding Christ, which was systematically used for many tombs, can be considered an Avignonese characteristic. The oldest example is the tomb of Cardinal Philippe de Cabassole (died 1372), formerly in the charterhouse of Bonpas, built by the workshop of Barthélemy Cavalier before 1377. The style of the alabaster statuettes preserved at the Petit Palais, at the Palace of the Popes or at Marseilles, reveals contacts with the Florentine milieu, and in a more general way with Italy. To this class also belongs the monument of Cardinal Guillaume II d'Aigrefeuille, formerly at Saint-Martial, Avignon, and of which are preserved, among several vestiges, an apostle figure,

the lower part of the body of the Virgin of the Coronation and the head of the tomb effigy. The tomb of Cardinal Jean de La Grange (in Saint-Martial), who died in 1402, must be accorded a place apart. Its religious and secular programme expresses the allegiance of the cardinal to the anti-Pope Clement VII and King Charles VI. The unusually developed wall niche is provided with five sculptured levels (life of the Virgin) above the withered-corpse figure, the tomb effigy and apostles. This naked decaying figure which represents the corpse with startling realism and exact anatomical study lies at the origin of a new iconographic type but here refers to the *Tale of the Three Quick and the Three Dead*. Among the other preserved fragments, and of which an increasingly doubtful attribution has been made to the sculptor of the Célestins, Pierre Morel, may be noted echoes of Parisian art of the late fourteenth century, and tendencies analogous to those developed by Claus Sluter beyond the period considered here.

The Avignonese school of sculpture, which developed during the second half of the fourteenth century out of northern influences and artistic exchanges with Italy, placed the accent on the latter beginning with Urban V, while emphasizing the realistic tendencies that contributed to the elaboration of a local style. The monument that best represents the artistic moment is the mausoleum tomb of St Elzéar de Sabran, which stood in the church of the Cordeliers at Apt. Of the reliefs carried out between 1370 and 1373, relating the life of the saint, six are preserved. The model of the canopied mausoleum which displayed them is Italian; the style of the sculptures, which departs from contemporary French production, brings out the blending of different external contributions and the hesitations over the choice of component elements of a local style.

Figure sculpture in the Bethlehem Chapel
of Narbonne Cathedral.
Last third of the 14th century.

and St Francis. The style of this group, to which must still be added the marble tomb effigy of Jean Tissendier, the modelling of which was brought out by the original polychromy, is not completely homogeneous, but well illustrates the tendencies of the day (which recur in the cathedral of Mirepoix). Added to the care for detail, the meticulousness in the search for expression, is the treatment of the clothing in folds now broad, now tightly rolled, which give the attitudes a mannered look. If northern sculpture of the second half of the thirteenth century seems to be at the origin of the art of heads and faces, the gentle expression of the features and the solid construction of the whole characterize this new virtuosity. In Bordeaux, at about the same time, the portal of the north transept of the cathedral derives from models provided by the south arm of the transept of Notre-Dame in Paris.

Towards the mid-fourteenth century the other important centre, Narbonne, already possessed a certain number of works which show the attention paid by the city and its region, as a result of changed political circumstances, to the Gothic art of northern France, and, more recently, to Avignonese creations. The tomb effigy of Guillaume Durand the Younger, Bishop of Mende, who died in 1330, which probably belonged to a cenotaph standing in the priory of Notre-Dame-de-Cassan at Roujan near Béziers, achieves this synthesis. To this background also belong the tomb effigy of Pope Clement V (Uzeste) and the vanished tomb of the Archbishop of Narbonne, Bernard de Farges (1311-1341).

THE ORIGINALITY OF LANGUEDOC

Gothic sculpture appeared belatedly in Languedoc, where edifices as important as the cathedral of Albi and the churches of the Jacobins and the Cordeliers at Toulouse are without it. We have seen in the previous chapter the introduction of the new style in a few sporadic cases during the thirteenth century and the part played by the choir statues of Saint-Nazaire at Carcassonne. Things changed in the course of the fourteenth century, not only because Languedoc experienced at that time the dissemination of an original type of Virgin and Child having a pronounced hip-swing (Azille-Minervois, Villardonnel, Notre-Dame-de-Paretlongue at Pennautier) but especially because the Languedocian Midi produced in the course of the century several popes who were natives of the region. Two centres stand out strongly: Toulouse and Narbonne.

At Toulouse Jean Tissendier, a native of Quercy and bishop of Rieux-Volvestre (1324), had built at the wish of Pope John XXII between 1333 and 1344 the Rieux chapel in the chevet of the Cordeliers church, which was to house his tomb. Since the nineteenth century the chapel no longer exists, but the sculptured model presented by the statue of the bishop preserved in the Musée des Augustins is of great architectural exactness. The sculpture programme of the chapel included an apostolic college of which eleven figures are preserved in the Musée des Augustins in Toulouse, an Annunciation and a Christ that are partially preserved at Bayonne (Bonnat Museum). In addition a statue of St Louis of Toulouse, a bishop of the city who died in 1297, accompanied St Anthony of Padua

Virgin and Child
(restored).
Mid-14th century.
Stone.
Parish church of
Azille-Minervois (Aude).

The Saint-Just cathedral at Narbonne, where the works of the choir with five radiating chapels begun by Jean Deschamps were undoubtedly completed by 1332, already contained by the middle of the fourteenth century a certain number of notable monuments, among which were the slabs from the tomb of Cardinal Pierre de La Jugie, Archbishop of Narbonne from 1347 to 1375, who during his lifetime had designed his own tomb, furnished with a great stone baldachin, highly ornamented, which rose above a cenotaph decorated with a double band of low reliefs. The bishops, clerics and canons of the sculptured cortege defined the stylistic features of the day, which combined the realism of faces, the hip-swing of the body attitudes and the fluidity of fabrics with the extreme

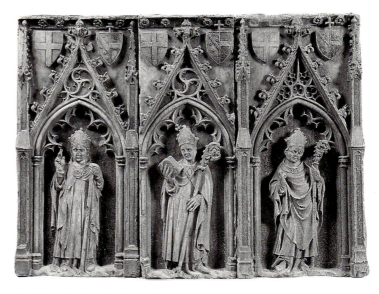

Reliefs with three bishops from
the tomb of Cardinal Pierre de La Jugie.
Third quarter of the 14th century. Marble.
Narbonne Cathedral.

Virgin and Child known as
Our Lady of Bethlehem.
About 1375-1380. Alabaster.
Narbonne Cathedral.

care lavished on the representation of wrought gold elements and a great attention to detail. Another fundamental monument was the alabaster tomb of King Philip III the Bold executed shortly before the middle of the century. It is known from descriptions of the seventeenth and eighteenth centuries, and a mourner is preserved from the funeral procession, which defines the essentials of a style close to that of the Rieux chapel.

For the sculpture of the last third of the fourteenth century at Narbonne almost all we possess is the beautiful statue of the Virgin and Child called Notre-Dame-de-Bethléem (Our Lady of Bethlehem), which was shown in 1981 at the great exhibition *Les fastes du gothique*. It stood in Narbonne Cathedral in a niche of the axial chapel above a fragment of low relief representing Hell. Since then one of the most astonishing discoveries of recent years has enabled us to reinsert this statue into a sculptured context that includes, above a base in which are presented two shields borne by angels, a first register of low reliefs representing Purgatory, Hell and the Old Testament patriarchs in limbo, surmounted by a second register with the Annunciation, probably the Nativity, the Epiphany, the Presentation in the Temple, the Entry into Jerusalem and the Crucifixion accompanied by statuettes of angels. Substantial traces of polychromy have been found. This decor, which was accompanied by wall paintings, reveals some aspects of a style distinguished by the arrangement of drapery folds and the care given to the execution of the faces, beards and hair. The Virgin and Child is by another hand, and probably the outcome of an independent commission. The reliefs of the Bethlehem chapel which follow Avignonese tendencies and look towards Italy were not isolated in the cathedral, to judge from the fragments recognized in the neighbouring chapel of St Peter and St Paul and the statuettes of the two saints preserved in the treasury. The group throws light on what it was desired to make of the new cathedral of Narbonne, which for financial reasons unfortunately did not extend beyond the choir. Between Avignon and Catalonia the reliefs of the chapel of Bethlehem at Narbonne constitute an essential landmark in our knowledge of southern sculpture in the fourteenth century.

TRADITION AND INNOVATION SOUTH OF THE PYRENEES

Portal of the chapter house, known as the Puerta Preciosa.
Before 1330.
Cathedral of Pamplona.

Tomb of Ermengol VII, Count of Urgell,
from the monastery of Santa Maria de Bellpuig de las Avellanas.
Early 14th century. Limestone.
The Metropolitan Museum of Art, New York,
The Cloisters Collection.

The penetration of French influences south of the Pyrenees, in Castile, León and Galicia during the thirteenth century, continued in the fourteenth in parallel with the emergence of local styles, which tended to define the characteristics of courtly Gothic in each region at the end of the thirteenth century but also in the fourteenth century in funerary sculpture and woodcarving.

In the cathedral of Burgos the tomb of Bishop Gonzalo de Hinojosa (died 1327) in a way illustrates two parallel developments: that of the massive autochthonous tomb effigy and that of the wall reliefs, which, like those of the altar frontal of St Paul, today in the Burgos museum, show an effort at composition and assimilation of courtly Gothic formulas leading to the creations of the later fourteenth century (tomb of Domingo de Arroyuelo, died 1385). At Burgos itself the portal of the church of San Esteban takes over the monumental heritage of the thirteenth century in the stylistic opposition of different sections of the portal. At Toledo the portals of the western façade of the Pardon, the Last Judgment and Hell took over where the Puerta del Reloj left off during the first half of the fourteenth century. The tympanum of the central portal (Pardon), which represents St Ildefonso kneeling and receiving the chasuble from the hands of the Virgin, is perhaps the most synthetic example of the stylistic tendencies of Castilian Gothic, at once simple and mannerist.

More closely related to the creations north of the Pyrenees, the refectory portal of the cathedral cloister of Pamplona, probably executed before 1330, illustrates a narrative style of great simplicity in which the statues of the Church and the Synagogue which flank the doorway build a bridge back to the previous century. Of higher quality and later in date, the portal of the chapter house (Puerta Preciosa) offers an iconographic programme dedicated to the Virgin. The episodes of her life are represented by groups of figures and arranged in registers on the tympanum. The summit is occupied by the Coronation of the Virgin. In this mannered Gothic, heavily inspired by northern ivories, the Pamplona artists played a mediating role in the transmission and dissemination of forms.

Catalonia and more generally the eastern part of Spain occupied a very different place in the geography of fourteenth-century Gothic. Receptive successively to northern and southern France, then to Italy, this area represents one of the rare examples of dissociation between a growing political and economic crisis and an artistic activity that showed none of its symptoms.

During the first third of the fourteenth century Catalonia kept pace with Europe, and Gothic sculpture there was the reflection of highly varied influences. The funerary monuments of the Urgell family, originally in the monastery of Bellpuig de las Avellanas, are today partly dispersed. Ermengol X (died 1314) had four tombs built for himself and his ancestors. The tomb of Ermengol VII, today preserved in the Cloisters Museum in New York, is provided with a sarcophagus resting on three lions and is sculptured with the Divine Majesty and the Twelve Apostles set beneath an arcade. The tomb effigy of Count

Altarpiece of San Lorenzo.
Third quarter of the 14th century.
Church of San Lorenzo, Lleida (Lérida).

Ermengol is placed on the lid, the hands crossed over the sword, and the head resting on a cushion. On the rear wall of the recess a relief was displayed with the representation of the funeral. A group of mourners surrounded the tomb effigy. The series of Urgell tombs is very coherent, and fits into a stylistic current indigenous to the region of Lleida (Lérida) which extends towards the south as far as Tarragona, and to which also belongs the altarpiece of the Virgin of Anglesola, preserved today in Boston. The tomb of Folch de Cardona (died 1322) at the monastery of Poblet belongs to the same artistic family.

The first third of the fourteenth century saw the creation of the tombs of Blanche of Anjou and of Jaume II at the monastery of Santes Creus. Four sculptors, all Catalan, had a hand in the making of this double tomb, from 1312 on; they were inspired by northern pantheons. At the same moment began an increasing flow of foreign sculptors in response to the new demands of Catalan art: Jacques Faveran of Narbonne, who was at Gerona in 1322; Master Alouns of Carcassonne, who worked on the main altarpiece of Puigcerdà in 1326; Pierre de Guines of Artois, who was at Majorca in 1325 and at Tarragona in 1338 and whose growing reputation earned him the commission for

the tomb of Pedro the Ceremonious in 1340; Jean de Tournai, at Barcelona in 1327, who imported Flemish designs and who is credited with the tomb of St Narcissus in the church of San Feliu (St Felix) in Gerona; and Reinard des Fonoll, an English master-craftsman, who was put in charge of the cloister works of Santes Creus between 1331 and 1341.

THE CATALAN MASTERS

While French and Italian artistic tendencies met and mingled in Avignon, Catalonia played an equivalent role in Spain as a centre of artistic exchanges. The arrival of foreign artists during the early decades of the fourteenth century did not eclipse the development of Catalan ateliers which, like that of Sant Joan de les Abadesses (Bernart Saulet or Bernat de Oleto), were able to carry out, in this case in alabaster, essentially narrative altarpieces over a limited period of time (1340-1348). At Gerona a goldsmith named Bartomeu was mentioned in 1325 for his work on the silver altarpiece of the cathedral before the intervention of André and Pierre Bernés in 1357-1358.

Aloi de Montbrai.
Statue of a king,
possibly Charlemagne,
formerly attributed to
Jaume Cascalls.
About 1350.
Polychrome alabaster.
Cathedral Museum,
Girona (Gerona).

him some time before 1365 when Cascalls returned to Poblet. There Cascalls carved the main altarpiece. His style is akin to that of Andrea and Nino Pisano. The polychromy of the Poblet altarpiece is known to have been the work of the famous painter Bernat Martorell. Cascalls' stay at Lleida generated an intense activity and he trained a number of sculptors, who in their turn were responsible for various tombs and several altarpieces. The heritage of Cascalls was taken up not only at Lleida but above all at Poblet by his former slave and apprentice Jordi de Déu (St Lawrence altarpiece at Santa Coloma de Queralt).

The last quarter of the fourteenth century was marked by the work of Jordi de Déu which culminated in the façade of the town hall of Barcelona, and also by the activities of the masters Pere Moragues and Guillem Morell. The first known document on the sculptor and goldsmith of Barcelona, Pere Moragues, is a contract of 16 October 1358 signed by the sculptor and the painter Ramón Destorrents for the making of seven wooden images, which throws light on the collaboration between different crafts. The work most characteristic of the art of Pere Moragues is the tomb of the archbishop Lope Fernández de Luna in Saragossa Cathedral, for which the sculptor received a

Jaume Cascalls. Pentecost, detail of the alabaster altarpiece.
About 1345.
Church of Corneilla-de-Conflent (Pyrénées-Orientales).

Starting with the end of the first third of the fourteenth century, Catalan art turned resolutely towards Italy. In the field of painting the best masters were Ferrer and Arnau Bassa; in that of sculpture the tomb of St Eulalia in the cathedral of Barcelona was the most significant work, closely followed by the tomb of the archbishop Juan of Aragon in the cathedral of Tarragona. These two funerary monuments, alien to the region, harked back directly to the art of the Tuscan masters, probably relayed to Catalonia by way of Naples.

Without any direct link with these works, Catalan sculpture of the fourteenth century is characterized, from the 1340s onwards, by the influence of the major masters, who are particularly well known from documentary sources. In an initial phase dominated by the advance of realism and the development of narrative formulas may be placed the work of the master sculptors Aloi de Montbrai, Jaume Cascalls and Bartomeu Robió. First mentioned in 1337, Aloi de Montbrai worked at Poblet on the execution of royal commissions, at Gerona (1345-1356), then at Tarragona; to him is sometimes attributed the statue of a king, possibly Charlemagne, in the Gerona museum. Jaume Cascalls, a native of Berga, was active between 1345 and 1379, first at Perpignan, then at Corneilla-de-Conflent, where he carved the famous alabaster altarpiece in about 1345. A detail which might seem anecdotal but which reveals the training of these masters is worth mentioning: in 1346 Cascalls married the daughter of the painter Ferrer Bassa, with whom he figured among the favourite court artists. The masters Aloi and Cascalls worked on the tombs of Poblet from 1347 for about ten years; then, from 1361 onwards, Cascalls remained alone there. The history of this sculptor is fairly well known. Around 1360 he was named master mason of the cathedral of Lleida (Lérida), where he was placed in charge of the execution of the great altarpiece and part of the cloister. Bartomeu Robió (recorded at Lleida between 1362 and 1375) took over from payment in 1379. Moragues is also credited with the statue of the Virgin of La Mercé in Barcelona. At Gerona, Guillem Morell carried out the tombs of Ramón Berenguer and the Countess Ermessenda around 1385, after having participated in the work on the Apostles' door of the cathedral. With these artists we approach the end of the century (portal of the church of Castelló d'Empúries, about 1400, attributed to the circle of Pere de Santjoan) and the end of the international style. The latter prevailed in Barcelona through the work of Pere Ça Anglada, one of the few sculptors on whom we possess a recent monograph. His creativity blossomed in the cathedral choir of Barcelona, and notably in the carving of the choir stalls (begun in 1394). The art of Ça Anglada reveals contacts with Parisian art and not, as has been supposed, with Claus Sluter. It enables us to revise what was known about the introduction of the international style in Catalonia, and to restore to sculpture a role slightly later than that played by manuscript illumination but probably earlier than that of painting. In the formation of a Barcelona school of sculpture around 1400 (Antoni Canet, Francesc Marata, Antoni Claperós, Llorenç Reixac, Pere Oller) the role of Ça Anglada–who, according to source documents, travelled across France and on to Bruges to obtain some Flemish oak and to study contemporary art before setting to work in the cathedral choir–appears decisive. Confirming the continuity of Mediterranean artistic exchanges, he was called to Sicily in 1407 to carve the Virgin and Child on the main altarpiece at Monreale.

Group of mourners from the Boil tomb.
Middle of the 14th century. Museo de Bellas Artes, Valencia.

Tomb of St Eulalia. About 1327–1339. Marble. Barcelona Cathedral.

THE QUICKENING OF ITALIAN ART

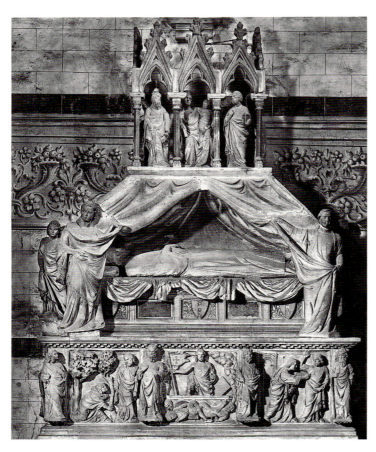

Tino di Camaino.
Funerary monument of Cardinal Riccardo Petroni (reconstructed).
About 1317-1318.
Siena Cathedral.

Tino di Camaino.
Statues from the funerary monument of the Emperor Henry VII
(modern reconstruction and reordering).
About 1315.
Campo Santo, Pisa.

THE RADIANCE OF TUSCANY: TINO DI CAMAINO

Italian Gothic sculpture of the fourteenth century follows on, without a break, continuing the achievements of the second half of the thirteenth century, thanks to the work of the great artists who, at the turn of the century, stood at the height of their powers. Two of them were Giovanni Pisano and Arnolfo di Cambio; both belong already in part to the new century. Schooled in the entourage of Giovanni Pisano is another, who represents the radiance of Tuscan art during the first third of the fourteenth century: Tino di Camaino.

The son of Camaino di Crescentino, himself a famous sculptor, Tino was born at Siena between 1280 and 1285. His early training owes much to Giovanni Pisano (pulpit of Sant'Andrea, Pistoia) and part of his apprenticeship was spent on the worksite of Siena Cathedral while Giovanni was working there. Tino himself returned there as master of works in 1319-1320, after having held the same position at Pisa Cathedral in 1315. Among the earliest works clearly bearing the mark of his hand were the baptismal fonts of Pisa Cathedral (1311), which were largely destroyed in the fire of 1595. More controversial are the scenes carved on the architrave of the main doorway of Siena Cathedral and the altar for the chapel of San Ranieri; this altar, on which work was going forward in 1306, is now in the Campo Santo, Pisa.

Tino di Camaino had by then acquired a high reputation as a master of funerary sculpture. One of the earliest commissions he received in this field (1315) was for the funerary monument of the Emperor Henry VII, who died in 1313. Now broken up and dispersed, this monument

Tino di Camaino.
Virgin and Child from the funerary monument
of Bishop Antonio Orso. 1321. Marble.
Museo dell'Opera del Duomo, Florence.

Tino di Camaino.
Hope. Caryatid from the funerary monument of Mary of Valois.
About 1333-1337. Marble.
Church of Santa Chiara, Naples.

included a sarcophagus with a tomb effigy *(gisant)* and several figures carved in the round, among them those of the emperor and four other men (possibly six, if one includes the head of a cleric recently discovered); but these figures in the round may have stood at some other point in the cathedral. The emperor's tomb was accompanied by an altar dedicated to St Bartholomew (the emperor had died on 24 August, that saint's feast day); its sculptures have recently been attributed to Tino.

During his time as master of works at Siena Cathedral, Tino executed, in part with his father, the tomb of Cardinal Riccardo Petroni, whose remains had been transferred to Siena in 1317. The present reconstruction dates from 1951, but it renders with precision and conviction the superb monumentality of this Gothic tomb. The high reliefs of the sarcophagus supported by caryatids represent the Resurrection and the apparitions of Christ, rhythmically enhanced by the standing figures. Above, the cardinal's tomb effigy is accompanied by four angels. The whole is crowned by a tabernacle, which houses the statuettes of the Virgin and Child and two saints.

From 1321, Tino worked in Florence for a period of two or three years, during which he executed three funerary monuments: those of Della Torre in Santa Croce, of Antonio Orso, bishop of Florence, in the Duomo, and of Bruno Beccuti in Santa Maria Maggiore. Among other works of this fruitful period was a Baptism of Christ for the baptistery; fragments of it are preserved in the Museo dell'Opera. This stage of his career is perhaps best represented by the Orso monument, identified by an inscrip-

tion, which received the bishop's body in 1321. Dispersed in the latter half of the nineteenth century, the surviving fragments are now in different European museums. They have been the object of several attempts at reconstruction. The sculptor innovated by portraying the bishop seated, with his eyes closed; this figure had its counterpart in the seated Virgin and Child which accompanied it.

Attracted by the brilliant, art-loving Angevin court in Naples, which had already patronized such masters as Simone Martini and Giotto, Tino di Camaino left Tuscany for South Italy in 1323 or 1324 and remained there for the rest of his life. Working in the immediate circle of Robert of Anjou, king of Naples, he designed and carved the tombs of Catherine of Austria in San Lorenzo, Mary of Hungary in Santa Maria Donna Regina, Charles of Calabria, and the latter's second wife Mary of Valois in Santa Chiara. This last-named work, still unfinished at his death in 1337, illustrates the artist's fondness for tombs recessed in the wall, with a baldachin. The caryatids supporting the sarcophagus personify Charity and Hope. They are among the most delicately carved works of Tino's final period (though admittedly they have not always been attributed to him). They show him moving away from the researches he had carried out in parallel with the paintings of the Lorenzetti brothers during his Sienese period (Petroni tomb). Tino di Camaino's work had a lasting impact both in Naples, among the Tuscan sculptors working there (Giovanni and Pacio da Firenze), and in his native Tuscany (Agostino di Giovanni, Agnolo di Ventura, Giovanni di Agostino).

Façade of Orvieto Cathedral
begun by Lorenzo Maitani after 1310.

THE FAÇADE OF
ORVIETO CATHEDRAL

Gothic Italy was dominated, and indeed shaped, by a succession of great sculptors and architects. They were in charge of the worksites on which these monumental buildings arose, and their activity there is fairly well documented. In these circumstances, it may be of interest to focus our attention on one outstanding work.

The façade of Orvieto Cathedral is one of the essential monuments of Gothic sculpture in central Italy. It permits us to see very clearly the respective shares which, in architectural creation, fell to bronze or marble sculpture, whether in relief or in the round, and to painting. Founded by Pope Nicholas IV in 1290, the church was adorned, to begin with, by several sculptors and master masons, notably Ramo di Paganello (1293) and Fra Bevignate (1295), the latter being best known for his work on the fountain of Perugia. Then, in 1310, the worksite was taken over by the Sienese sculptor Lorenzo Maitani, who remained in charge for the next twenty years.

Maitani's presence is recorded in Siena in 1290, and by the time he arrived in Orvieto his reputation stood high. The cathedral façade there is his major work, but his role as master of works is attested at Perugia, Siena, Montefalco and Castiglione del Lago. Among the essential questions that scholars have tried to answer is this: what was Maitani's direct share in the erection of the Orvieto façade? That is, were certain sculptures already carved by the time he arrived? And again: can his activity as architect (façade designs) be distinguished from his activity as

sculptor? And what about the work of Giovanni Pisano (façade of Siena Cathedral): to what extent did it influence Maitani? It must be remembered too that after 1330 work on the Orvieto façade was continued by other Sienese masters, Nicola di Nuto, Giovanni di Agostino, and after 1347 Andrea Pisano, his son Nino Pisano, and still others who ensured the Sienese continuity there until the beginning of the next century (with a brief intervention by Orcagna in 1358).

This west front of Orvieto Cathedral is divided into three sections, each corresponding in width to the doorway below, whose buttresses are prolonged vertically by salient pinnacles framing the three gables. The rounded arch of the central doorway emphasizes the formal continuity of Italian medieval art. The sculptured decoration corresponding to Maitani's period of activity is located in the lower parts of the façade: the buttresses carved with surface reliefs; the central tympanum on which stand out six bronze angels who, drawing back a curtain, disclose the marble group of the Virgin and Child; and the four evangelist symbols, also in bronze, standing on the buttresses above the sculptured reliefs. The marble reliefs on the lower buttresses actually flank the two side doors; on one side they represent scenes from Genesis, the tree of Jesse, and episodes of the Redemption preceded by some prophets; on the other, the Last Judgment and Paradise. Stylistically the two inner reliefs and the two outer ones hold

The Last Judgment. Façade relief.
Between 1310 and 1330. Orvieto Cathedral.

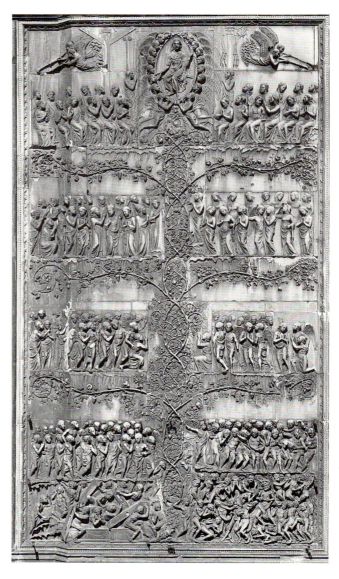

Virgin and Child with angels. Tympanum of the central doorway. Between 1310 and 1330. Marble and bronze (angels). Orvieto Cathedral.

together well enough, but all are thought to have been executed simultaneously and left unfinished. Attributed to Maitani, together with the evangelist symbols and part of the central tympanum, is the lower level of the Genesis and Last Judgment reliefs.

Iconographically, the lower level of the Orvieto façade was designed to convey a distinct spiritual message through the scope of the programme there deployed, the unusual choice of themes, and the theological implications of certain episodes, such as the prophetic scenes.

Stylistically and technically, this monument is unique, enabling us as it does to evaluate the relations then existing between marble work and bronze work: they are signally combined on the façade of Orvieto Cathedral. The marble buttress reliefs owe much moreover to the experience gained by bronze workers in casting the large sculptured doors. The Romanesque tradition has been invoked in the attempt to explain these reliefs. But even apart from the unmistakable knowledge of northern sculpture revealed in the nude figures of the Elect and the Damned, it would seem that here again the evolution of Italian painting, that of Siena in particular, went far to determine the decision to place the relief over a vast surface; a decision which could not fail to impress the great artists who, like Andrea Pisano, specialized in the art of combining marble work and bronze work.

Detail of the Damned in Hell. Last Judgment relief on the façade. Between 1310 and 1330. Orvieto Cathedral.

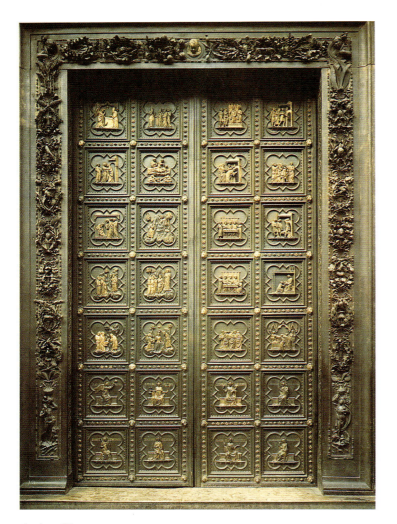

Andrea Pisano.
Bronze doors. 1330-1336.
Baptistery, Florence.

Andrea Pisano.
Scene from the life of John the Baptist.
Bronze doors, detail. 1330-1336.
Baptistery, Florence.

ANDREA PISANO

In the second quarter of the fourteenth century Florence gradually replaced Siena as the creative centre of Italian sculpture. The artist who best represents this Florentine flowering was born near Pisa, at Pontedera, about 1290-1295; his name was Andrea Ugolino, but he is better known as Andrea Pisano, from the region of his birth. The circumstances of his early life and career are unrecorded. All we know is that he was also a goldsmith, for he is described as a worker in bronze, gold and ivory. His fame is due almost entirely to two extensive pieces of work, one in bronze, the other in marble: the doors of the baptistery and the series of Campanile reliefs of the cathedral, both in Florence.

The making of the bronze doors of the Florentine baptistery is unusually well documented, from several different sources. An initial design is mentioned in 1322; it was for a wooden door enriched with gilt metal, to be made by Tino di Camaino. But nothing came of it. The idea was taken up again in 1329 and a representative of the drapers' guild was sent to Pisa to study and draw the bronze door of the cathedral, then to Venice in search of a master capable of doing the work. Wooden models were prepared in January 1330 and Andrea Pisano is mentioned as "master of the doors." In April of that year some wax models were ready (but probably not for the whole door). In 1331 two goldsmiths, Lippo Dini and Piero di Donato, were working with Andrea Pisano. In 1332 a Venetian, Lionardo d'Avanzo, began casting the door reliefs. The first leaf was finished by the end of that year (the one on the left according to a recent thesis), the second between July and December 1333. They were not put into place until 1336, once the lions' heads had been prepared and the hanging carefully adjusted. The baptistery doors, inscribed with the date 1330 and the name of Andrea Pisano, consist of a series of bronze reliefs cast separately and inserted in a frame, the whole being then heightened with gilding.

Taking as his model the doors with narrative reliefs made by Bonanno di Pisa, Andrea Pisano set out a sequence of fourteen rectangular panels in each leaf, with lions' heads at the intersections. The upper ten panels on each leaf are devoted to the life of John the Baptist, the four lower ones to the Virtues. The imagery here was manifestly influenced by the mosaic scenes inside the baptistery. Stylistically, northern goldsmith's work seems to have left its mark on Andrea, while the Santa Croce frescoes of Giotto inspired his conception of space. Andrea's style is characterized by elegant proportions, abundant draperies, and a lively sense of detail and narrative. This steady evolution or growth of a major artist, from goldsmithery to bronze work and then to monumental sculpture in marble, is interesting for an understanding of the influences which helped to shape the art of many sculptors of the Gothic age, among those who worked in stone or marble.

In the course of this work, Andrea Pisano probably executed a few sculptures in marble, such as the statuettes of Christ and Santa Reparata in the Museo dell'Opera, Florence. Possibly as early as 1336, he began working on the Campanile designed by Giotto to stand alongside the cathedral two years before. After Giotto's death in 1337, Andrea took charge of this project, being appointed master of works at Florence Cathedral in 1340; in 1347 he took over the same position at Orvieto.

Square in plan, this Campanile (i.e. bell tower) had only risen a few feet above the ground at the death of Giotto who, to decorate this lower part, had designed two levels of bas-reliefs, the lower ones hexagonal, the upper ones diamond-shaped. The iconographic programme, astonishingly wide in scope, amounted to something like an encyclopaedia: below, Genesis and the Arts and Crafts; on the upper level, the Planets, the Virtues, the Sacraments, and the Liberal Arts (some reliefs, replaced by copies, are now in the Museo dell'Opera). After the worksite was taken over by Andrea Pisano, the project was apparently modified by the addition of four niches on each side of the third level, intended to house statues; eight are preserved in the Museo dell'Opera, representing Solomon, David, the Sibyls and four prophets. Their attribution to Andrea Pisano has been much debated; today only the Solomon can arguably be assigned to him. Andrea's ability to carve large-size statuary has recently been confirmed by the attribution to him of a headless statue in the Museo dell'Opera; identified as St Stephen, it was executed in 1339-1340 for the church of Or San Michele in Florence.

The attribution of the Campanile reliefs to Giotto, Andrea Pisano or other sculptors of their workshops remains an open question, complicated by the fact that the original arrangement of them is conjectural. This is a problem which also concerns the position occupied first by Giotto, then by Andrea, within a major urban project of this type, and the role played by their respective workshops in the making and installing of the different pieces. By comparison with the reliefs of the baptistery door, the hand of Andrea Pisano would seem to be more present in the Genesis reliefs (fitted into the wall perhaps before Giotto's death) on the lower level (Creation of Adam, Creation of Eve, works) than in the reliefs on the upper level. These latter were once thought (already by Ghiberti) to be Andrea's; in reality they are only partly the product of his workshop. The progression of Andrea's style in relation to his earlier work on the baptistery door is especially noticeable in the relief representing the sculptor. Giotto's influence gained ground in Andrea's reliefs for the Campanile (so much that it has suggested, wrongly no doubt, the existence of detailed designs by Giotto himself). That influence vouches for the continuity of the craft, the collaboration between the two artists, and the admiration Andrea Pisano felt for Giotto when he took over the worksite.

Giotto and Andrea Pisano (?).
Tubalcain, artificer in brass and iron. Relief from the Campanile.
About 1334-1337. Marble.
Museo dell'Opera del Duomo, Florence.

Andrea Pisano.
The Creation of Eve. Relief from the Campanile.
About 1337-1340. Marble.
Museo dell'Opera del Duomo, Florence.

Angel.
Detail of a pillar of the Tabernacle of the Virgin.
1355-1359. Marble.
Church of Or San Michele, Florence.

ORCAGNA
AND NINO PISANO

From now on Florence played the leading part in the evolution of Gothic sculpture during the fourteenth century, in spite of economic difficulties and the plague epidemic known as the Black Death. The best work was done in the entourage of Andrea Pisano, chiefly by Andrea di Cione, nicknamed Orcagna, an all-round artist, painter, sculptor, master mason, architect, whose mature activity mostly dates from after the Black Death of 1348. He took charge of work on Or San Michele in 1355, on the cathedral of Orvieto in 1358, then on the cathedral of Florence in 1364-1366, and his building activity is as well known as his paintings. As a sculptor, however, he remains somewhat enigmatic. One major work at least can be assigned to him: the tabernacle ordered after the plague year to house the miraculous image of the Virgin, first in the Corn Market, then in Or San Michele, the church of the Florentine guilds. Vasari refers to this work, and Ghiberti had written of it: "Orcagna was a most noble master and unusually skilled in both arts. He made the marble tabernacle of Or San Michele, and a most excellent and singular thing it is, made with the utmost diligence. He was a very

Andrea di Cione, known as Orcagna.
Dormition and Assumption of the Virgin.
Back of the Tabernacle.
1355-1359. Marble.
Church of Or San Michele, Florence.

great architect and all the stories thereon are his handiwork. With his own hand he carved therein his own portrait marvellously lifelike. The price of the work amounted to 86,000 florins."

This tabernacle takes the form of a monumental altar; the ciborium above it stands on four colonnettes topped by statues of saints; the whole is crowned by pinnacles flanking a gable behind which rises a dome. The reliefs adorning the lower parts illustrate the life of the Virgin, the childhood of Christ, and the Virtues. On the front is a painting of the Virgin and Child by Daddi. On the back Orcagna carved the double scene of the Dormition and Assumption of the Virgin; there can be read the artist's signature and the date of completion, 1359. Characterized by polychrome inlays, the tabernacle is obviously the work of several hands besides Orcagna's. Readily distinguishable are the differences of style separating the reliefs of the life of the Virgin from the large composition on the back. The Campanile reliefs and indeed Andrea Pisano's work as a whole are reflected not only in the style but also in the narrative spirit of the stories. As compared with Andrea Pisano, however, Orcagna keeps closer to painted models (i.e. Giotto), a fact accounted for by his schooling as a painter. With Orcagna, Florentine sculpture stood in possession of a style which continued into the second half of the fourteenth century (Alberto Arnoldi) and evolved towards the Renaissance.

Of Andrea Pisano's two sons, Tommaso and Nino, only the latter made his name as a sculptor. Also a goldsmith and architect, Nino Pisano was master of works at Orvieto Cathedral in 1349. In 1357-1358 he made a silver antependium for Pisa Cathedral. His son Andrea continued the family tradition. Nino's style is not easy to trace, and the attribution to him of some works is controversial (Campanile sculptures in Florence, Madonna del Latte in the Museo di San Pietro in Pisa). For none of his work as a sculptor is there any documentary evidence. The only fixed points are three signed works: the Virgin of Santa Maria Novella in Florence, the Virgin of the Doge Cornaro tomb in SS. Giovanni e Paolo in Venice, and a bishop saint in the church of San Francesco at Oristano (Sardinia). With Nino Pisano, the Florentine style radiated outward. The Cornaro monument in Venice shows how well the statues made by Nino Pisano, and perhaps shipped from Pisa, fit into the typically Venetian conception of the tomb.

Nino is very much a man of his time. His art benefited by the artistic experience of his father, which he enriched with a thorough knowledge of Sienese painting and French movable sculpture. His Virgins and Child thus lend themselves to comparison with French works like the Virgin of Jeanne d'Evreux. For the evolution of his style, it is interesting to compare the signed Virgin and Child in Santa Maria Novella, Florence, one of his earliest works, with the marble statues of the Annunciation in Santa Caterina at Pisa attributed to Nino by Vasari (whose date for them, 1370, is probably just a few years too late): the angel shows the adoption of French Gothic forms, it also shows that new sense of naturalism and humanity which woodcarving was soon to take over and develop.

Nino Pisano.
The Angel of the Annunciation.
About 1365-1368. Marble.
Church of Santa Caterina, Pisa.

221

NORTHERN ITALY

In southern Italy, through the working of historical and political circumstances, the influence of French sculpture made itself felt as early as the thirteenth century; and there too, as we have seen, the prestige of Tuscan art prompted the Angevin rulers of Naples to call in and employ several Tuscan artists who, like Tino di Camaino, marked the beginning of an art current shaped and directed by the Neapolitan milieu. Likewise in northern Italy. The early Tuscan achievements brought their influence to bear during the second quarter of the fourteenth century, and they made a profound impress on the different local styles in the second half of the century.

Giovanni di Balduccio, who had worked on the cathedral of Pisa in 1317-1318, proceeded to dominate Milanese sculpture up to about 1360. Among his principal works are the shrine of St Peter Martyr in the church of Sant'Eustorgio, Milan, and the shrine of St Augustine in the church of San Pietro in Ciel d'Oro at Pavia, some twenty miles south of Milan.

The first of these two impressive monuments, signed and dated by an inscription to 1339, is modelled on the shrine of St Dominic in Bologna. Supported by eight caryatids, the sarcophagus is elaborately carved with scenes from the life of St Peter Martyr of Verona, who had

Giovanni di Balduccio.
Shrine of St Peter Martyr.
Finished in 1339. Marble.
Church of Sant'Eustorgio, Milan.

Possibly by Giovanni di Balduccio.
Shrine of St Augustine.
Lower part finished in 1362. Marble.
Church of San Pietro in Ciel d'Oro, Pavia.

died less than a century before, in 1252. These scenes are separated by statues of saints. The sarcophagus is crowned with eight statues of angels and surmounted by a pinnacled tabernacle housing statues of the Virgin and Child, St Dominic, and St Peter Martyr (who had been a Dominican).

The shrine of St Augustine in Pavia is attributed to Giovanni di Balduccio (admittedly with some reservations). It is a much later work, dated 1362. The form of the shrine refers back to the one in Milan. On the lower level, pairs of saints in high relief, set in an arcade, are separated from each other by salient figures of the Virtues. On the middle level, the arcading of the baldachin is borne by pillars, each with several statues of saints; in the centre is the tomb effigy of St Augustine accompanied by angels and saints. At the top are reliefs of the saint's life. Though not wholly the work of Giovanni di Balduccio, this shrine testifies to the diffusion of a style reshaped by contact with Lombard traditions; thus, for example, free-standing caryatids are replaced here by a sculptured partition.

While Balduccio's work illustrates the assimilation of Tuscan currents, northern Italy also gave birth to many artists trained locally. The most famous and characteristic are Giovanni and Bonino da Campione. Giovanni da Campione (active about 1340-1360) carved the corner figures of Virtues in the baptistery of Bergamo. Bonino is better known. He made the famous equestrian monument of Cansignorio della Scala at Santa Maria Antica in Verona (c. 1370-1375) and that of Bernabò Visconti (died 1385) originally in the Milanese church of San Giovanni in Conca, but now in the Castello Sforzesco, Milan. Just as the Angevin court patronized art in Naples, so did the Visconti, lords of Milan, in northern Italy between Milan and Verona, and the great tombs crowned with an equestrian monument are the most spectacular result.

In and around Venice sculpture took an independent line with respect to other parts of Italy, despite the influence already noted of Nino Pisano. The interaction there between Byzantine traditions and new Gothic forms can be seen in the marble plaque of the Virgin and Child (Madonna dello Schioppo) in St Mark's, Venice; it harks back to Byzantine sculpture of the Paleologan period. Among tombs, that of Doge Francesco Dandolo in the sacristy of the Frari church (1339) shows a marked departure from Byzantine traditions in favour of the new Gothic style. The latter is still more evident in the tomb of Raniero degli Arsendi by Andriolo de Sanctis (Padua, 1358): in the handling of the sarcophagus, the tomb effigy on the lid, the corner figures set out on the axis of the diagonals.

The major undertaking of Venetian art in the fourteenth century was the building and decorating of the Ducal Palace. An extensive series of capitals issued from the sculptors' workshops, carved with plant motifs and peopled by figures stemming from various sources. Schooled in Venice, these sculptors betray a familiarity with the local Byzantine tradition. The imagery is ambitious and encyclopaedic: cosmological and geographical themes, the Liberal Arts, the crafts, the Virtues and Vices, and Creation scenes. Here Venetian Gothic sculpture can be seen gradually breaking free, throwing off the weight

The Drunkenness of Noah.
Corner relief on the façade.
Third quarter of the 14th century.
Istrian stone.
Ducal Palace, Venice.

of the past, and attaining the peak of its stylistic autonomy —in, for example, the outside corner reliefs of the Ducal Palace, like the Drunkenness of Noah or the Fall of Adam and Eve. Traditionally dated to the mid-century, these reliefs belong more probably to the third quarter of the fourteenth century, if not to the 1360s. A few decades later, just before the turn of the century, Venetian sculpture evolved towards a new Gothic naturalism, with Jacobello and Pierpaolo dalle Masegne, first in Emilia (Legnano tomb from San Domenico, Bologna, now in the Museo Civico), then in Venice (iconostasis statues in St Mark's, 1391-1395).

TOWARDS INTERNATIONAL GOTHIC

The Emperor Charles IV and his wife.
Façade of the south transept.
About 1370-1380.
Marienkirche, Mühlhausen (Thuringia).

THE WORLD OF THE PARLERS

To the north, in central Europe, in what was then known as the Holy Roman Empire, a new mysticism arose in literature and art, entering strongly into the sculpture of the first half of the fourteenth century. That mysticism found expression chiefly in movable sculpture: altar-pieces, choir stalls, devotional images, goldsmith's work. And it did much to enrich the imagery of the sculptor's art. These innovations extended to monumental sculpture, affecting not only the figure of the Virgin but also that of Christ, more particularly the Christ of the Passion, often presented now in a group with St John, as the crucified, or lying dead on the lap of his Mother (Pietà).

Stylistically, the evolution towards a picturesque realism is distinctly present not only in the painting of altar-pieces but in sculpture as well. The influence of movable sculpture on monumental sculpture can be seen most clearly in the fact that the latter now becomes increasingly independent of architecture.

The steady progression towards an international style common to the different courts of Europe is most evident in the German-speaking lands of central Europe, and also in Bohemia where the Luxemburg dynasty maintained close relations with France. Charles IV succeeded his father John of Luxemburg as king of Bohemia, and in 1355 he was crowned in Rome as emperor of the Holy Roman Empire. Born in Prague in 1316, he was descended on his father's side from the Counts of Luxemburg, in western Europe, on the northern border of France; on his mother's side, from the Premyslide dynasty in eastern Europe. Taking his Christian name from his godfather King Charles IV of France, he was thus symbolically attached to the Carolingian heritage, which he affirmed by his lifelong cult of Charlemagne and by the gifts he lavished on the Palatine Chapel at Aachen, Charlemagne's ancient capital. At the same time he bore the baptismal name of Wenceslaus, signalizing his attachment to his distant ancestor, duke and patron saint of Bohemia.

This dual loyalty of Charles IV appeared in the preferential relations he maintained between Prague and Paris. In his youth he lived for seven years in France and learnt the language thoroughly. He married a French princess, Blanche de Valois. And the example of Paris was uppermost in his mind when he set out to make Prague the intellectual and artistic capital of central Europe. Which is indeed what it became by the middle of the fourteenth century. To Prague he summoned the French architect and sculptor Matthew of Arras to begin work on the cathedral of St Vitus, which after Matthew's death in 1352 was continued by Peter Parler. Thanks to this imperial patronage, the court of Prague became in the latter half of the fourteenth century one of the foremost art centres of Europe.

The extent of this prestige can be gauged by the lavish and stately reception given him by Charles V of France when the emperor revisited Paris in 1378. He was shown with pride all the best and most "modern" that French art could then boast of: the renovated palace of the Louvre, the château of Vincennes, the Hôtel Saint-Pol. The illuminated manuscript of the *Grandes Chroniques de France* enshrines the memory of that reception and the presents in gold and silver which went to enlarge the collection of the Emperor Charles IV, built up in the course of many journeys across Europe.

From 1356, when he was only twenty-one years old, the German architect and sculptor Peter Parler worked for Charles IV: he is the outstanding artist patronized by the emperor. A native of Cologne, he got his training at an early age under his father Heinrich Parler on the worksite of the Heilig-Kreuzkirche at Schwäbisch Gmünd in South Germany. Peter Parler is known to have had seven children. Among his brothers, Johann von Gmünd is recorded as a master mason at Freiburg im Breisgau about 1359, then in Basel; he was the father of Michael, architect of Strasbourg Cathedral (1383-1387/88), and of Heinrich, a master mason of some renown. With the Parlers, the family trade of architect and sculptor was handed down naturally from one member to another. One of Peter's brothers, Michael, was a stonecutter. So were many others of the family. Particularly well known is the second son of Peter Parler, master of works successively at three cathedrals,

Prague (before 1392), Vienna (around 1400), then Milan. Sifting out the handiwork of each member of the Parler family is understandably a difficult and absorbing task.

The tomb inscription of Peter Parler (1399) records the fact that he was responsible for the choir of Prague Cathedral, the All Saints church on the Hradschin in Prague, the church choir at Kolin on the Elbe, and the bridge over the Vltava (Moldau). Further, among the many works attributed to him, he is known to have made the tomb of Ottokar I Premysl in Prague Cathedral; for this he

Peter Parler.
Tomb effigy of Ottokar I,
king of Bohemia (1197-1230).
1377. Stone.
Cathedral of St Vitus, Prague.

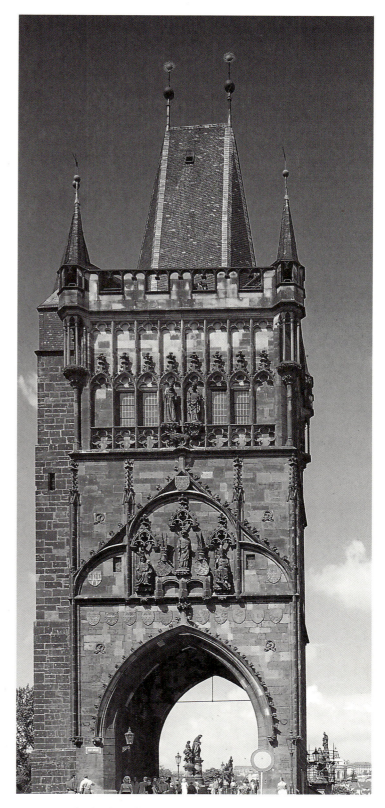

Tower on the bridge of Charles IV.
Façade facing the Old Town.
Last quarter of the 14th century.
Prague.

received a payment of 900 *gros* on 30 August 1377. While overseeing the work of architecture and sculpture on the cathedral, he received a weekly wage of 56 *gros*, to which were added various bounties.

Peter Parler is a signal example of the new social and economic standing achieved by a court artist who contributed directly to the definition of a style (the triforium busts in Prague Cathedral). To that style, in the field of painting, also contributed Master Theoderic from 1359 on (busts of Karlstein).

225

PRAGUE

Wishing to make Prague one of the first cities of Europe and a cultural centre with the added attraction of a university (the Charles University, which he founded in 1348), Charles IV sponsored a programme of construction, both public (hospitals, markets, town walls) and religious (monasteries, parish churches), and gave his personal attention to two projects in particular: the cathedral of St Vitus and the castle of Karlstein. From Avignon, which he had visited in 1344, and acting on the advice of Pope Clement VI, he summoned Matthew of Arras, who super-

vised the work on the cathedral choir until his death in 1352. With Matthew, he chose the building style of southern France; Narbonnese influence is plain in the plan of the choir. Then came Peter Parler, who took over the work-site in 1356 (and the share of these two men in the work is still a matter of debate). The choir of the cathedral was not vaulted until 1385.

With Peter Parler came a new conception of architecture, set forth in the vertical upthrust, the spatial unity ensured by the vaulting, a patterning of the walls in terms of broken lines, and a particular sense of light created by the openwork triforium. All these features stem from the schooling received by Peter Parler at Schwäbisch Gmünd,

Peter Parler and his workshop.
St Wenceslaus between two angels.
Probably 1373. Carved stone (St Wenceslaus)
and mural painting (angels).
Chapel of St Wenceslaus, Cathedral of St Vitus, Prague.

The architect Matthew of Arras.
About 1385. Stone.
Triforium of the
Cathedral of St Vitus, Prague.

and they reappear in Parler's work on the choir of the St Bartholomew church at Kolin on the Elbe and again at Kutna Hora. At Karlstein Castle in Bohemia, rebuilt from 1348 and completed during the 1350s, Charles IV chose a self-enclosed, rectilinear plan with suites of rooms.

Like his nephew Heinrich, Peter Parler directed a series of sculpture projects which contributed to situate this art at its true and merited level in terms of the imperial undertakings. Stylistic realism appears already in the set of tombs of the kings of Bohemia, which began with that of Ottokar I (1377) and continued with those in the choir chapels of Prague Cathedral. The best example of the combined use of sculpture and painting in the service of a style occurs, just before the last quarter of the fourteenth century, in the St Wenceslaus chapel of the cathedral: it represents the patron saint of Bohemia, carved in stone, standing between two painted angels. Here the new stylistic trends, prompted by the innovations of Parisian art, are rendered with an unusual forcefulness, a vivid and lifelike polychromy, a spirited realism and a monumental sense which lends a spatial dimension to the sculpture. This work stands in contrast both with the art of the Parlers' homeland, Swabia, and with the earlier works in Prague (tympanum of Our Lady of the Snows). Yet these trends are already to be seen before 1377 in the south doorway of Prague Cathedral.

Among the major works of Peter Parler and his workshop or entourage are the bust portraits of the Bohemian royal family and of archbishops, master architects and other personalities in the triforium of Prague Cathedral.

St Catherine holding a book.
Closing phase of the style of the Beautiful Madonnas.
Shortly after 1400. Painted wood.
Castle of Karlstein (Bohemia).

The Virgin Mary, known as Mary in Hope.
An example of the "Fine Style."
Late 14th century.
Statue lost during the Second World War.
Formerly Muzeum Okregowe, Torun (Poland).

Martin and George of Cluj.
St George slaying the Dragon,
formerly decorating a fountain
in the courtyard of the castle.
1373. Bronze.
National Gallery, Prague.

Statue of Anna von Schweidnitz.
About 1385. Stone.
Triforium of the
Cathedral of St Vitus, Prague.

Among the monumental building projects in Prague,
one was the cathedral of St Vitus. Another was the statuary
on the tower of the Charles Bridge, the *Karlovo most*, probably by Peter Parler; on the side facing the Old Town are
statues of Charles IV, Wenceslaus IV, and St Vitus,
St Adalbert and St Sigismund. Many other items are ascribed to Peter Parler or his workshop, like the Virgin of
the town hall in Prague or the decoration of the Tyn
church. The workshop of the Parlers and its forcible style
dominated Bohemian art in this period, despite the
presence in Prague of other artists of renown. Among
these are Martin and George of Cluj, who made the bronze
statue of St George slaying the dragon, cast in 1373 (now
in the National Gallery, Prague)—though a case has recently been made for attributing this St George to Peter Parler
himself. The background of these two artists, from Cluj
(Koloszvar) in Transylvania, speaks for the interchanges
with Hungary and the more southerly regions of Europe,
including Italy. On the threshold of the international
style, the art of Prague radiated outward towards Austria
(cathedral of St Stephen, Vienna) and to western Europe
as well, as shown by the movement of artists towards
Cologne.

COLOGNE

Flowing alongside the Paris–Prague axis, the artistic exchanges between Prague and Cologne have been investigated and clarified in recent years. In Cologne, capital of the Rhineland, the most representative work is the St Peter portal of the south tower on the west front of the cathedral, the creation of Prague sculptors and members of the Parler family in Cologne. Their activity has been made better known to the public by the Parler exhibition of 1978–1979, and by the famous polychrome bracket console representing the bust of a woman (Schnütgen-Museum). But for specialists the debate centres on the sculptures of this Petersportal (some of them now in the Diocesan Museum).

Comprising splay statues, sculptured archivolts and a carved tympanum, the St Peter portal is not a homogeneous work. The apostle statues standing in the splays are apparently the oldest parts, certainly the most archaic: they stem on the one hand from the local tradition of sculpture and on the other from the style of French sculpture in the early second quarter of the fourteenth century (hospice and church of Saint-Jacques-de-l'Hôpital, Paris).

Bracket console bearing the mark of the Parlers.
Bust of a woman.
About 1380–1390. Stone.
Schnütgen-Museum, Cologne.

Apostles.
Splays of the St Peter portal
of the cathedral.
About 1370. Stone.
Cologne Cathedral and Diözesanmuseum, Cologne.

However, the facial features of Peter, Paul and Andrew (Diocesan Museum, Cologne), together with the handling of garments, tie in with other Rhenish work of the 1370s. In contrast with this archaism is the novel character of the seated prophets over the doorway. They vouch for the arrival of another workshop of slightly later date (1380–1390) which had resolutely adopted new formulas.

The arch mouldings and tympanum, despite differences of style and quality, derive from the art of Prague. The head of St Catherine on the St Peter portal invites comparison with the bust of Anna von Schweidnitz in the triforium of Prague Cathedral, or with the bracket console bearing the Parler mark in the Schnütgen-Museum, Cologne. As for certain heads on the Cologne arch mouldings, it is their kinship with the tomb effigy of Ottokar I in Prague which has suggested the presence of Peter Parler and his workshop among the sculptors of the Petersportal. In the spatial detachment of the figures in the arch mouldings and in their movement, one discerns elements which, stemming from Prague and leaving little further trace in Cologne, introduce the stylistic formulas of the late Middle Ages. This new style was largely diffused from central Europe, during the 1390s, by movable sculpture and by the so-called Beautiful Madonnas.

Claus Sluter.
Bust of the crucified Christ from the Calvary of the Chartreuse de Champmol.
1396–1399.
Stone with traces of colour.
Musée Archéologique, Dijon.

230

GLOW AND AFTERGLOW OF GOTHIC (1400-1530)

Sophie Guillot de Suduiraut

INTRODUCTION Georges Duby

When did the Middle Ages end? What criterion should we adopt to mark the termination of this period of history, to draw a boundary which will be indecisive in any case? If it is a question of art, the reference is obviously to the forms we call Gothic. But did Gothic ever exist in Sicily? Clearly it is a question of geography, rather than chronology. From this point of view, Italy had undoubtedly left the Middle Ages behind by the end of the fourteenth century. Having entered the Renaissance, its influence radiated. As early as 1400 the humanists of the court of France were fascinated by the ideas emanating from Italy and yet, much later, the men who designed the church of Saint-Eustache in Paris remained faithful to the Gothic spirit. In the last analysis, it must be admitted that sculpture remained medieval all over Europe, with the exception of Italy, throughout the fifteenth century.

In our eyes, it had by then ceased to hold first place among the arts, giving way to painting. It is by no means certain that the men of those times had the same feeling. To them, fine work required the collaboration of various bodies of craftsmen. Sculptor and painter were expected to work together; indeed the sculptor was often a painter as well. Such cooperation seemed particularly necessary when the making of an altarpiece was undertaken, a field now much enlarged by public commissions. Placed above the altar, the altarpiece offered a permanent display inside the church complementing the other sacred representations that diligent brotherhoods erected outdoors on the parvis, on all sides, with immense success during the great feast-days of Christianity with the aim of teaching the people and maintaining their piety. So that the altarpiece, too, should fulfil the same function appropriately, the executants of the commission were invited to bring all the artifices of the theatre into play, adding to the persuasive force of the relief that of colour and perspective, and if necessary that of trompe-l'œil. Here sculpture was called on to enhance the effect.

If henceforth it was a source of enjoyment for many, sculpture remained a sacred art in its dominant expressions. Its new features were impressed on it by the new religious attitudes. In the fifteenth century Christianity completed the process of popularizing itself: it had finally become a popular religion. But to achieve their ends, the Mendicant Friars who persisted in conducting the enterprise by preaching had to make their speeches fit in with the ways of thought and feeling of the majority, in particular agreeing to allot the secular an increasingly unrestricted place among the images which backed up their discourses. The faithful were absolutely determined to see with their own eyes in detail, and in terms of the crudest realism, not only the unfolding of a tale, the successive episodes of the infancy of Christ, his passion and resurrection, but also hell, paradise, the actual mystery of the Trinity and the other mysteries, just as they had achieved their object of being shown the host during the mass at the moment of the elevation. The points that had had to be conceded to the masses to attract and keep them in the fold spread irresistibly in the upper strata of secular society. Thus religious art as a whole sacrificed more and more to the pleasing, the surprising and the emotionally moving.

This change was combined with another vital change. The work of art became mobile. Its format was reduced. It tended to become an object possessed by individuals and thenceforth private commissions won the day. Here social changes came into play. The movement which for generations had gradually freed the individual from collective constraints made both wealth and pleasure increasingly personal. Now people took their pleasures in private and salvation was also won in private. During its development, pastoral action had established a sort of turning inward of piety. Devotion, in its most modern aspect, moved away from public places. The ardour of his desire led the Christian to withdraw, far from the bustle and din of the world, into seclusion to advance in his imitation of Jesus Christ. Sculpture responded to this trend. It withdrew into the domestic space. Perhaps not as an individual possession, but at least belonging to the household, the family line, from then on it mainly served to decorate chapels and tombs.

Everyone who had the means engaged the services of a salaried clerk, built a private altar and fitted up a place in which to pray, follow the service and recite the hours in company with his household. If possible he placed some relics in it, but at all events he there installed some of the images he relied on to touch the heart and bring him nearer the divine. In its earliest origins, the chapel had been royal, available for the orisons of the divine monarch, Charlemagne at Aachen, St Louis in his Parisian palace, the Emperor Charles IV at Karlstein. For a long time, all the heads of houses who had seized regalian powers, followed the kings' example. The rich imitated them in their turn. By the fifteenth century the chapel, too, had become fashionable. It established itself in even the least important châteaux and in patrician dwellings. It invaded the side aisles of urban churches where the great families of the city obtained the concession of a site reserved for their own devotions. Founding a chapel was a sign of social success. So the chapel was a place of ostentation, strewn with heraldic signs clearly designating its owners, whose power and wealth were measured by the profusion and brilliance of a decoration in which, as on the furnishings of the choir and the great altarpieces, sculpture was associated with painting and goldsmiths' work, on a smaller scale, but with the same concern to move and convince.

One of the chapel's main functions was funerary. It housed the tombs of the family ancestors and thus preserved their memory. In accordance with their last wishes, masses were said there for the repose of their souls. Fifteenth-century preachers gave vivid pictures of the punishments in store for sinners in the next world. They also taught that the sojourn of the dead in purgatory could be cut short by the prayers of the living. Consequently who would not be preoccupied with staying alive in the memory of those who survived them? Every man who possessed some property and, thinking about his last end, arranged for its transmission, accordingly took pains, not only to institute religious services which would be repeated until the end of the world on the anniversary of his passing, but to prepare his own tomb, engage sculptors or leave money with which to pay them to his heirs (his wife in particular, since care of the dead was a woman's business), ordering the artists to fashion on this memorial the obvious signs which would remind every visitor of the duty to help him whose mortal remains rested under the slab with his intercessory prayers.

Very soon, the wealthiest men had made such arrangements. From the end of the twelfth century sculpture's task was to perpetuate the pomp of funeral ceremonies. On such days the deceased was exhibited in a final parade in all the brilliance of his life on earth. Made up, adorned with the attributes of power, his body stretched out on the catafalque remained exposed to the view of those who mourned him. It was in this magnificent aspect that great men wanted to be represented so that their presence among men would be prolonged. Carved in wood or stone, the *gisant* found his place on top of the tomb. So that the dead could be recognized by other means than their coats of arms, artists were soon asked to reproduce the features as preserved by the death mask. Faces became portraits. Lastly, as the desire to survive demanded even more, contracts between sculptors and the representatives of great lords stipulated that the band of mourners should figure on the mausoleum and that the image of intercessors, the Virgin, patron saints and sometimes the allegory of the saving virtues should be placed near the effigy of the deceased. Some of these contracts involved representing the body several times, not only as he looked at the moment when the soul left his body, but also as the forces of corruption consumed him in the tomb, as he appeared during his lifetime in devotional postures and lastly as he would be at the time of his resurrection when the angels welcomed him to paradise. In the end this relentless attachment to conquering death gave the tombs of cardinals and princes the complexity and monumentality of the most imposing altarpieces.

Thus the ultimate masterpieces of medieval sculpture were not to be found in the palaces which the sovereigns adorned with trivial decorations for the pleasure of the court, but at Champmol and Brou, in the necropolises which they installed so that they could make periodic retreats to them, convincing themselves before the tombs of their predecessors of the vanity of worldly things and meditating on their own death in the company of the austerest monks, before they themselves came to rest in this sanctuary of sleep and peace.

Virgin enthroned with
Christchild writing.
France, about 1400.
Polychrome limestone.
The Cleveland Museum of Art.

INTERNATIONAL GOTHIC STYLE

At the dawn of the fifteenth century, the international Gothic style opened the last chapter in the history of medieval sculpture–a chapter too often underrated by criticism and overshadowed by the great creators of northern painting and of the Italian Renaissance. It might be said in defence of this final flowering that Claus Sluter and Nicholas of Leyden are as great as Jan van Eyck, that Michel Colombe is the equal of Jean Fouquet or Hans Leinberger of Altdorfer, and lastly that Vasari, who despises the barbarous manner of the "Goths," nevertheless extols the beauty of the St Roch by Veit Stoss. But above all these works undertook to arouse the attention of the indifferent. Thus, to take two examples of the purest emanations of the international Gothic style, the contemplation of a "Beautiful Madonna" from Bohemia delights us quite as much as that of an illumination by the Limbourg brothers.

This vast movement, which flourished around 1400 for several decades, is called international, in the phrase of Louis Courajod, in order to express its dissemination on a European scale, from northern Italy and Spain to Germany and the Netherlands, and from England and France to Bohemia and Hungary. The exceptional unity of artistic language forged at that time was the fruit of constant exchanges between different European courts, particularly those of Prague, Paris, Avignon, Milan, London and Dijon. Works, ideas and styles travelled just as much as did people, artists and patrons, so that the place of origin of some works is still doubtful.

The crowning achievement of fourteenth-century court art, international Gothic enjoyed the favour of princes and their entourage, fulfilling the aspirations of that ostentatious clientele which sought refuge in its own chivalrous dreams by providing it with an unreal vision of the world, an extreme elegance of forms and a remarkable fluidity of lines. Yet, undulating silhouettes, draperies with melodious rhythms, soft and dreamy expressions or delicate gestures are nonetheless accompanied by descriptive details: touches of the familiar and picturesque. Religious art was thereby humanized as secular subjects were developed alongside it. Preciousness of language and artificiality of linear rhythms, moreover, posed no obstacle to the increasing taste for a faithful rendering of facial lineaments or studies of movement and plastic density reflected in the amplification of volumes set out in a three-dimensional space. Those tendencies, already present at the end of the fourteenth century, had a great future in store for them. Through them, international Gothic also paved the way for the subsequent renewal of style in the fifteenth century.

◁◁ Virgin and Child from the north portal.
Ile-de-France, about 1400.
Stone.
Church of Le Mesnil-Aubry.

◁ Virgin and Child.
Netherlands (?), early 15th century.
Alabaster.
Rijksmuseum, Amsterdam.

THE BEAUTIFUL MADONNAS

The heir of medieval court art, a new conception of Marian statuary (i.e. dedicated to the Virgin Mary) was born around 1400 in the creation of images of a beauty at once idealized and real; possessing ethereal grace, yet wholly human. These innumerable sculptures bear witness to the fervour with which the Virgin was worshipped and echo the hymns which, like the *Tota pulchra*, celebrated at length Mary's physical beauty: the perceptible sign of her beauty of spirit.

The *Schöne Madonnen*, the Beautiful Madonnas of Germany and Bohemia, termed *pulchrum opus* (beautiful work) from the beginning of the fifteenth century, have a grave gentleness and a sweet charm that makes them particularly moving. One of the most perfect examples, the Virgin and Child from Cesky Krumlov in Bohemia, displays an extreme delicacy in the treatment of the small, fine face, long, bowed neck, and hands with tapering fingers that sink into the flesh of the naked Infant. This naturalistic detail, which tellingly conveys the humanity of the Son of God, contrasts with the unreality of the sinuous and slender silhouette of the Virgin with its salience of the hip, broadened by an ample cloak whose superabundant and voluminous folds fall in two cascades of lateral scrolls in repeated curves flowing down to the ground. Thus freed from strict frontality, the sculpture becomes part of the space around it, promoting a new plasticity following the line of research into form during the second half of the fourteenth century.

The type of the Beautiful Madonna, which presented many variants and spread irresistibly throughout the Germanic countries, was devised in eastern Europe, probably in Prague, where it had its roots in the art of the Parlers and in Bohemian painting of the late fourteenth century. The term *weicher Stil* (literally, soft or gentle style) well conveys the sweetness of the expression and the velvety aspect of the drapery, the chief characteristics of this "fine style" or "softened style" which forms the Bohemian and Germanic version of international Gothic.

Concurrently there appeared in France, but in varying interpretations, the same concern for grace and elegance; a similar taste for the melodious play of unctuous folds and the amplification of volumes, also derived from the previous stylistic evolution. The precious gesture of Mary delicately holding back a corner of her mantle and the fineness of her childlike features are especially typical of French works like the Virgin Enthroned and Christchild Writing in the Cleveland Museum. Some come from Paris or its region, like the Virgin and Child from the abbey of Saint-Victor in Paris (Musée de Cluny) or the one from the church of Le Mesnil-Aubry (Val d'Oise); but others, of unknown origin, are difficult to localize because of the relative unity of style that prevailed around 1400. The Virgin and Child in Amsterdam, formerly attributed to the Ile-de-France or Burgundy, more probably originated in the Netherlands, as indicated by the somewhat heavy

"Beautiful Madonna" from Cesky Krumlov, Bohemia, about 1400.
Polychrome limestone.
Kunsthistorisches Museum, Vienna.

facial features. It is also distinguished by the mundane look of its willowy silhouette outlined by the long fluid folds of the robe, gathered by a wide belt worn very high following a model then fashionable and frequently represented in contemporary illuminations. The refinements of court life, its gestures and sartorial fashions, permeated religious just as much as secular art as the fifteenth century began.

THE EVOLUTION OF ICONOGRAPHY

Virgin and Child on the crescent moon,
with the Three Magi (left) and St Romanus (right).
Tabernacle altarpiece from Raron/Rarogne (Valais).
Early 15th century.
Polychrome wood.
Swiss National Museum, Zurich.

The dead Christ supported by an angel.
Upper Rhine, about 1420–1430.
Polychrome limewood.
Staatliche Museen, Berlin.

The enrichment of Marian iconography was stimulated by the growth and spread of this new worship of the Mother of God. Most of the iconographic subjects, old or new, henceforth became fixed, and reflected the evolution of spirituality under the influence of mysticism. Born of thirteenth-century Franciscan thought, rekindled by spiritual speculations or narratives of the ecstasies of such great fourteenth-century mystics as Meister Eckhart, Johann Tauler, Heinrich Suso and St Bridget of Sweden, a dual sensibility at once gentle and tragic pervaded the works produced up to the end of the Middle Ages. And in response to the more personal piety of believers came the proliferation of isolated holy images, independent of any narrative context, either in church decoration or for domestic use. The devotional image (*imago pietatis, Andachtsbild*) whether sculpture, painting, precious object or single illuminated page, became the aid to personal contemplative meditation.

Some representations of the Virgin Mary presented hardly any iconographic novelties, finding their natural place in the evolution of style, such as the ivory triptych of the "Glorious Virgin" in Berlin, which, in a refined manner close to the works of the Middle Rhine, takes over a motif often used by fourteenth-century Parisian ivory carvers. The traditional theme of Christ crowning the Virgin is also frequently illustrated in carved altarpieces, and appears in monumental decoration: the Coronation of the Virgin in the church of Saint-Jacques in Liège innov-

ates by the plasticity of form of the two figures that move in space, clothed in soft and voluminous drapery; the Coronation in the château of La Ferté-Milon, built by Louis of Orléans, recalls the ostentation of a princely ceremony.

Other iconographic types, devised in the fourteenth century under the influence of mysticism, acquired an increased popularity around 1400 which remained unfailing until the end of the Middle Ages. But the tone can be seen to change. Touching groups of the Virgin of Pity, the theme known as Pietà, were created in the style of the Beautiful Madonnas of Germany and Bohemia. In these, the Mother does not exteriorize her grief as strongly as she did at the start of the fourteenth century; instead she manifests it in a restrained way, the lyrical expression of lamentation blending harmoniously with the refined handling of the form and the polychromy (Virgin of Pity from Seeon).

It was thus in the last quarter of the fourteenth century that the image of the Virgin and Child appeared on the crescent moon, a theme afterwards extremely popular, especially in the Germanic world and the Netherlands. Mary, likened to the "woman" of the Apocalypse described by St John as "clothed with the sun, and the moon under her feet, and upon her head a crown of twelve stars" (XII, 1), provides the symbolic image of the belief in the Immaculate Conception: the Virgin, conceived of as being immaculate, is exempt from the burden of Original Sin. A changing star, the moon under her feet is the sign of her power over the evil courses to which earthly life is prone. The approval of the doctrine of the Immaculate Conception by Pope Sixtus IV in 1476 and the circulation of the legend of the Sibyl of Tibur showing the Emperor Augustus the Virgin in a sun-like glory, helped to spread those representations.

The new form of the Annunciation, inspired in particular by the *Meditationes Vitae Christi* of the Pseudo-Bonaventure, a thirteenth-century Franciscan monk, was also propagated and embellished with homely details so as to set the scene in the contemporary world. A small household altarpiece in the Diocesan Museum in Cologne shows the angel kneeling to greet the Virgin, who is at prayer in her room adorned with furniture—prayer stool, bench, wall hangings—all carefully painted and carved. The secular life of everyday invaded the religious sphere in keeping with the new desire of the faithful, springing out of mystical thought, to come near the Virgin Mary, to penetrate into the intimacy of her life and that of her son. The childlike prettiness of the two faces, characteristic of the creations of the Middle Rhine in the early fifteenth century, further adds to the charm of this tender evocation of the Annunciation.

If mystical writings magnified the surge of tenderness for the Virgin and her Child, they also stirred the pity of believers for the sufferings of Christ or martyred saints, depicted with extreme precision and a piling on of pathetic, even horrible details. Tauler describes the bloody tracks left by Christ walking onward after the Flagellation, and Bridget insists on the gory aspect of the corpse of the Crucified.

◁ St Lucy.
Portugal, first half of the 15th century.
Polychrome limestone.
Ernesto de Vilhena Collection,
Museu Nacional de Arte Antiga,
Lisbon.

Ivory triptych of the "Glorious Virgin."
Middle Rhine (?), last quarter of the 14th century.
Staatliche Museen, Berlin.

Pere Joan.
Predella with the martyrdom of St Thecla,
detail of the altarpiece.
1426–1436.
Polychrome alabaster.
Main altar of Tarragona Cathedral.

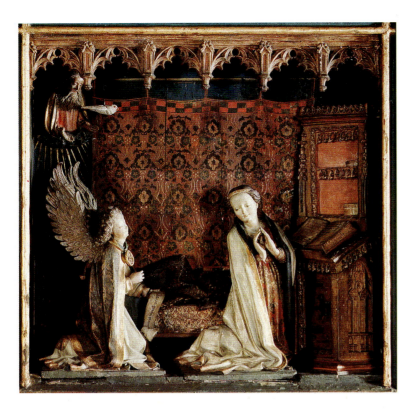

The Annunciation, detail
of a household altarpiece.
Middle Rhine, about 1440.
Polychrome wood and terracotta.
Diözesanmuseum, Cologne.

Inspired by the vision of St Gregory, the image of the dead Christ emerging from the tomb supported by one or several angels often figures at the end of the fourteenth century on small-sized objects of worship, marked by a pathetic, softened feeling specific to international Gothic, such as the delicately carved limewood relief from the Upper Rhine, in the Berlin museum. In the fifteenth century the diffusion of this theme, whose popularity was linked with the obtaining of indulgences, was facilitated, like that of other representations, by the production of woodcuts which made such motifs widely known.

The ubiquitousness of Christ and the Virgin in iconography cannot conceal the homage paid to male and female saints, whose worship did not cease to spread with the close of the Middle Ages. To the traditionally venerated saints like Catherine, John the Baptist and Michael, a throng of succouring and popular saints were added whose iconography was enriched by the tales of the *Golden Legend*. Their effigies peopled the churches and private oratories; the episodes of their martyrdom or their glory are displayed on countless altarpieces.

Around 1400 the special tonality of the international style bathed in a serene sweetness those scenes in which young women saints, smiling amid lions or beneath the executioner's stroke, offered to the faithful a lesson of hope and resignation.

Virgin of Pity from the monastery of Seeon.
Prague, about 1400.
Polychrome limestone.
Bayerisches Nationalmuseum, Munich.

MATERIALS AND TECHNIQUES

Around 1400, in several centres of the Netherlands and the Empire, materials like clay or cast stone, less costly and easier to work with than traditional stone, marble or wood, came into current use. The practice of casting made it possible to produce statues and statuettes in series and at lower price, often with widespread distribution.

The different regional variations of the "fine style" in the Germanic countries are illustrated by numerous works in moulded cast stone (*Steinguss*): Beautiful Madonnas, Virgins of Pity, male and female saints. Examples of sculptures are preserved, if not from the same mould, at least from moulds cast from the same model, as shown by the Virgins from Hallgarten and Eberbach, whose refined lyricism is characteristic of a whole group of works of the Middle Rhine region.

In the course of archaeological digs in the Low Countries at Utrecht and Liège, casts have been unearthed of statuettes and reliefs that were used in the fifteenth century to manufacture small terracotta objects, often exported. The earlier sets of such works have their place in the mainstream of international Gothic.

Virgin and Child from
the abbey of Eberbach.
Middle Rhine, about 1420.
Polychrome cast stone.
Musée du Louvre, Paris.

Virgin and Child.
Middle Rhine, about 1420.
Polychrome terracotta.
Parish church,
Hallgarten.

Young beardless apostle (St John?).
Nuremberg, about 1400.
Terracotta.
Germanisches Nationalmuseum, Nuremberg.

Modelled so as to produce statuettes of special charm, clay was a favourite medium at Nuremberg in Franconia, also in Swabia and along the Middle Rhine. It made possible a subtle relief and great delicacy in the handling of details, in harmony with the flowing drapery and sweetness of expression. An extreme care was taken in modelling the back of free-standing sculptures, such as the series of apostles at Nuremberg.

Clay could also be used, like plaster, to fashion maquettes or models of sculptures frequently mentioned in documents from the end of the fourteenth century onwards. At the Charterhouse of Champmol, just outside Dijon, founded by the Duke of Burgundy in 1383, the Dutch sculptor Claus Sluter had a model made in plaster for the "Well of Moses," perhaps lifesize: during the winter of 1398-1399 a teamster of Dijon spent sixteen days "hauling fine sand to make a plaster cast. . . and putting the markings on it for the construction and stonework of the fountain."

Once the work was carved or modelled, the materials employed were generally not left in the natural state. Stone, wood, clay or cast stone received a carefully applied polychromy using complex techniques which gave the sculpture a perfect finish. Alabaster and marble, sometimes wood as well, were partially heightened with colours and gold, which set off the parts left uncovered. But the fragility of this added colouring and the defacement or weathering it has suffered over the course of centuries (when it has not disappeared entirely) usually prevent us today from appreciating the play of gilding and colour, the beauty of painted decoration and the fineness of flesh-tints in their original brilliance.

Master of the Rimini Altarpiece.
Crucifixion from Santa Maria delle Grazie
near Rimini. About 1430. Alabaster.
Liebighaus, Frankfurt.

Master of the Rimini Altarpiece.
The Entombment. About 1440. Alabaster.
Hermitage Museum, Leningrad.

THE MASTER OF THE RIMINI ALTARPIECE

The international Gothic style also brought with it a growing taste for small-sized sculptures, mainly in terracotta and alabaster. Isolated devotional images or elements of altarpiece decoration, these statuettes and reliefs, easily transportable because of their reduced format, are sometimes difficult to attribute precisely to any particular region in the absence of signatures or documents.

Such is the case with the alabaster sculptures carved by the mysterious Master of the Rimini Altarpiece, the creator of the Crucifixion altarpiece formerly in the church of Santa Maria delle Grazie near Rimini.

A large group of alabaster carvings from the first half of the fifteenth century, very consistent in style, are ascribed to this master and his workshop or to the sculptors who followed in his wake. They are to be found widely dispersed over Italy, France, Silesia, the Rhine valley, the Netherlands and elsewhere. The extent of this diffusion can be explained by the mobility of the artists and the importance of commercial exchanges, as confirmed, for these sculptures, on two occasions. In 1431 the abbot of the monastery of Sand at Wrocław (Breslau) purchased from a Parisian trader a Crucifixion in alabaster (preserved fragment: the Holy Women in the Silesian Museum, Wrocław); and in 1432 the abbot of the Saint-Vaast monastery at Arras acquired from a German merchant some alabaster statuettes portraying the twelve apostles and the Coronation of the Virgin, which were painted in 1434 by Jacques Daret at the same time as he painted the wing panels of the altarpiece for which the statuettes were intended. The dearth of details about the makers of these sculptures, the geographical distances separating the places where they were commissioned and the different nationalities of the merchants show how difficult it is to locate the production of these alabaster statues with precision.

Proposed by Georg Swarzenski, the identification of the Master of the Rimini Altarpiece with Master Gusmin of Cologne, a goldsmith active in Italy and extolled by Lorenzo Ghiberti in his *Commentarii*, is rejected today. Nevertheless, the hypothesis of itinerant workshops, possibly originating in the Rhineland, has since been often adopted. On the other hand, a certain stylistic kinship with the Flemish painters of the first half of the fifteenth century has also led to consideration of the southern Netherlands as a possible source for the art of the Rimini Master.

Alabaster, a choice material, was handled with a subtle blend of dryness and extreme delicacy. The typical method of chiselling thin and angular forms, the minute rendering of anatomical details, garments, hairstyles and deeply undercut beards, sets off the precious appearance of the material enlivened by a few polychrome highlights. The draperies with tight folds, fluid but breaking over the ground, adopt the formulas of international Gothic. Attitudes and expressions help to create a strong dramatic tension, yet one that is softened by refinements of style, especially in the finest creations like the figures of the Rimini altarpiece or the Entombment in Leningrad. Indeed, despite similarities of form and the repetition of set themes (Virgin of Pity, Apostolic College, Annunciation), within that abundant output of small alabaster carvings, there exist notable differences of quality.

Pere Ça Anglada.
Misericord of a choir stall, with two musicians.
1394-1399.
Oak.
Barcelona Cathedral.

DIVERSITY OF FUNCTIONS

One of the trends in monumental sculpture around 1400, continuing a development begun during the fourteenth century, lay in an emphasis on small fine forms, anecdotal details and a profusion of decorative elements. Carved by Madern Gertener around 1420, the Adoration of the Magi on the small tympanum of the Liebfrauenkirche in Frankfurt is like an enlarged illumination in which the figures are clustered in a picturesque landscape. At the cathedral of Milan, the portal of the south sacristy was carved around 1393 by Hans Fernach and his workshop. It presents a highly dense composition, setting out the three scenes in tiers within an elongated tympanum inserted in an elaborate frame. The style of these reliefs, and of numerous statues executed around 1400 for the adornment of the cathedral, is typical of international Gothic, particularly esteemed in the court circles of northern Italy.

On the worksite of Milan Cathedral, artists of all nationalities mingled freely. The presence of German sculptors like Hans Fernach (who is also said to be a native of Como) helped to introduce the new styles of expression, which were also adopted by Italian artists like Jacobello and Pierpaolo dalle Masegne or Jacopino da Tradate.

In all buildings, civic or religious, the innumerable brackets and consoles were choice locations for sculptors, who there displayed a freedom of invention and a zest for secular subjects at times carried to the point of caricature. Images full of life and picturesque details are also carved on the misericords of choir stalls. Those of the cathedral of Barcelona, executed from 1394 to 1399 by Pere Ça Anglada, one of the first representatives of international Gothic in Catalonia, present a varied repertory of subjects borrowed from fable, satire or mythology.

Carved church furniture thus continued to be enriched, enlivened, diversified. The altarpieces exhibited new designs that flowered in the course of the fifteenth century, and the number of statues independent of a supporting wall thereafter never ceased to grow.

Nevertheless, indoors and out, pride of place was still reserved for monumental statuary, which revealed by turns the general tendencies of late Gothic art towards amplification of volumes, dynamic effects and refinements of form. The programmes were worked out under the princely patronage; they made much of the new ideas instituted at the beginning of the fifteenth century in France and taken up in Prague in the days of the Parlers.

Thus, in parallel with traditional religious statuary (prophets of Bourges by André Beauneveu and Jean de Cambrai) and with effigies of contemporary donors introduced into church decoration (the Duke and Duchess of Burgundy at Champmol by Claus Sluter), sculptured groups celebrating the power of a ruler and the glory of a dynasty increased in number.

Among the many surviving examples may be mentioned the statues of English kings on the choir screen of Canterbury Cathedral, the remains of statues from the royal palace of Buda or else the effigies of the Duke

Hans Fernach.
Door of the south sacristy.
On the tympanum, Virgin of Mercy (top), Virgin and Child enthroned between John the Baptist and St Andrew (middle) and Virgin of Pity with the dead Christ (below).
On the arch mouldings, scenes from the life of the Virgin.
About 1393.
Milan Cathedral.

Andreas Herneysen.
Design for the repainting of the
Schöner Brunnen ("Beautiful Fountain")
in Nuremberg. 1587.
Watercolour on paper.
Germanisches Nationalmuseum,
Nuremberg.

Isabeau of Bavaria, statue adorning the fireplace
in the palace of the Duke of Berry at Poitiers.
About 1390.
Plaster cast of the stone original.
Musée des Monuments Français, Paris.

Julius Caesar and Joshua,
sandstone statues from the Schöner Brunnen
in the Hauptmarkt.
Nuremberg, 1385-1396.
Germanisches Nationalmuseum, Nuremberg.

Jean de Berry and his wife and of King Charles VI and Queen Isabeau, standing over the fireplace of the great hall of the palace of Poitiers, a fireplace designed and built for the duke by Guy de Dammartin around 1390. Unlike the retrospective images offered by other royal series, these effigies were representations *ad vivum* testifying to the quest for physical lifelikeness and psychological convincingness, characteristic of late fourteenth-century art. The expressive face of Isabeau of Bavaria and the undulation of her elegant silhouette render with great skill the queen's disturbing power of seduction.

In the Empire, similar commemorative cycles decorate and embellish cathedrals or princely homes, as well as municipal edifices like town halls and fountains. Commissioned by the town of Nuremberg, the Schöner Brunnen ("Beautiful Fountain") was erected in the market place from 1385 to 1396 under the direction of Heinrich Beheim the Elder, a member of the Parler family. It was taken down and replaced in the nineteenth century, and important fragments of it are preserved in the museums of Nuremberg and Berlin. Following a complex iconographic programme, this monument to the civic glory of Nuremberg housed an ascending series of different symbolic figures. On the lowest level of the central interior edifice the seven Electors, representatives of the imperial power and guarantors of civic order, are associated with the Nine Valiant Knights, ideal images of chivalry and princely virtues widely disseminated in fourteenth-century art and literature. Above, the eight Prophets look more like defenders of justice in their role as councillors of the kings of Israel than like heralds of Christ's coming. This political manifesto was put back into a religious context by the presence on the basin rim of statuettes of the Evangelists and the Church Fathers, together with Philosophy and the seven Liberal Arts.

But above all, by means of this utilitarian edifice standing in the sight of everyone, the city proclaimed its faith in imperial justice. This intention comes as no surprise, since imperial cities such as Nuremberg were among the Emperor's most faithful vassals.

FUNERARY ART

Despite the scale of destruction, the innumerable tombs that have been spared give a good idea of the host of funerary monuments of all kinds which populated the churches and cloisters of the Middle Ages. If the pride of princes and churchmen shows itself all too clearly in imposing, lavishly decorated monuments, the necessarily modest tastes of less wealthy clients were content with simpler tombs or votive reliefs. But the desire to stay present in the memory of the living is common to them all.

The type of tomb with a sculptured recumbent figure (*gisant*) and weeping mourners beneath a series of arches, was now firmly established and spread universally (tomb of Bishop Ramón Escales by Antoni Canet, 1409-1412, Barcelona Cathedral). It lasted down to the end of the Middle Ages with some variations touching, in particular, the arrangement of the funeral procession or the handling of the deceased person's effigy.

On the tomb of Philip the Bold, Duke of Burgundy, commissioned from Jean de Marville in 1384 and continued by Claus Sluter and Claus de Werwe, the mourners are no longer conceived as applied reliefs placed side by side in the niches but as independent statuettes circulating beneath a veritable gallery of arcading. The revival of portraiture, which stems from the fourteenth century, bursts out in some of the recumbent figures: the ugly face

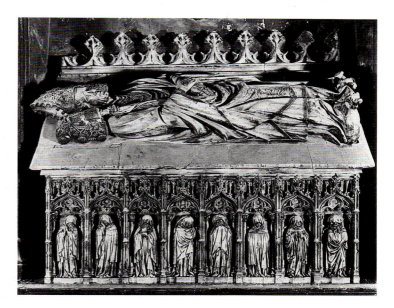

Antoni Canet.
Tomb of Bishop Ramón Escales.
1409-1412.
Alabaster.
Barcelona Cathedral.

Claus Sluter and Claus de Werwe.
Mourners from the tomb of Philip the Bold.
About 1404-1405.
Alabaster.
Musée des Beaux-Arts, Dijon.

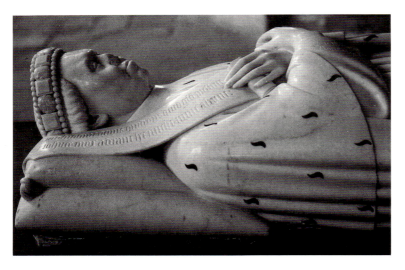

Jean de Cambrai.
Tomb effigy of Duke Jean de Berry, detail.
Between 1405 and 1416.
Marble.
Crypt of Bourges Cathedral.

Tomb of Archbishop Johann II von Nassau (died 1419).
Sandstone.
Mainz Cathedral.

of Jean de Berry is uncompromisingly rendered on the tomb statue at Bourges carved by Jean de Cambrai between 1405 and 1416, the date of the duke's death.

From the idealized image to the faithful portrait of the deceased, the evolution of funerary sculpture also led to the representation of the emaciated or withered corpse (*transi*), which reproduces the grim visions of the plague and recalls the vanity of the things of this world. In France, the oldest withered corpse statues, contemporary with the first dissections of the human body authorized in 1396, are those of the physician Guillaume de Harcigny (died 1393) who attended Charles VI (Archaeological Museum, Laon) and of Cardinal Jean de La Grange (died 1402) at Avignon. The latter, remarkable for its anatomical accuracy, is accompanied by an inscription which gave to the macabre portrayal its full significance: "If all see, great and small, to what state they shall be reduced... then wherefore pride? For thou art dust and like me thou shalt again become a fetid corpse, ashes and food for worms."

The tomb La Grange had built for himself in the choir of Saint-Martial of Avignon was remarkable for its size, its wealth of decoration and the range of its iconographic programme; this is clear from a seventeenth-century drawing and the surviving elements in the Petit Palais Museum at Avignon. Above the withered corpse, the tomb effigy and the College of Apostles, five successive storeys rose some fifty feet from the ground and showed La Grange, Louis of Orléans, Charles VI, Charles V and Pope Clement VII each kneeling and commended by a patron saint before a scene from the life of the Virgin. The theme of the Coronation of the Virgin, image of Paradise, and that of the Apostolic College, which evoked the desire to unite the Avignon Curia with the Apostles and thereby affirm its legitimacy, recall the traditional formula of the cardinal's tomb at the time of the Schism.

The first example of this type, carved under the direction of Barthélemy Cavalier from 1372 to 1377, was the funerary monument of Cardinal Philippe Cabassole; its design and layout may have inspired the great Neapolitan tombs of the late fourteenth century.

But La Grange enriched the usual design with a taste for pomp and a purpose of political commemoration already obvious in the statues of the "Beau Pilier" at Amiens Cathedral, which he had commissioned about 1375. Adviser to King Charles V of France and instigator of the schismatic election of Pope Clement VII in 1378, Cardinal de La Grange chose to have portrayed on his tomb as the representatives of his spiritual family the Pope and the Royal House of France. The sculptures, of varied styles and uneven quality, bear witness to the diversity of influences mixing in the Avignon crucible and engendering international Gothic art. One of the main currents had its sources in France in the royal or princely circles of the end of the century.

On German soil, episcopal pomp found a new mode of expression: the wall-tomb, which, in a profusely ornamented frame, presented the sculptured image of the deceased in a standing position, supported by the wall or a pillar and no longer recumbent on a tombstone (Johann II von Nassau, died 1419, Mainz Cathedral).

Other funerary sculptures answered the ever growing needs of a vast clientele with relatively modest financial resources. Mass-produced and widely traded, they had a creative value that was sometimes limited, but revealed the religious practices of the period just as reliably as the more

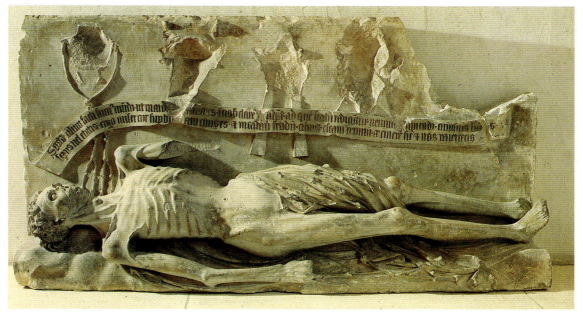

Tomb of Cardinal Jean de La Grange
(died 1402) formerly in the
church of Saint-Martial, Avignon.
Anonymous drawing of the 17th century.
Barberini Collection,
Vatican Library, Rome.

△△ Louis of Orléans commended by an apostle and Annunciation
from the tomb of Cardinal Jean de La Grange (died 1402)
formerly in the church of Saint-Martial, Avignon.
Alabaster.
Musée du Petit Palais, Avignon.

△ Withered corpse of Cardinal Jean de La Grange (died 1402)
formerly in Saint-Martial, Avignon.
Stone.
Musée du Petit Palais, Avignon.

prestigious monuments. The sign of hard times marked by wars, epidemics and famines, the longing for individualization in the face of the anonymity of omnipresent death asserted itself in all ranks of fourteenth-century society. Accompanied by long and explicit epitaphs, the engraved images of the dead person stretched out on the funeral slab, or the reliefs that showed him under the protection of his patron saint, imploring divine indulgence, express this concern to conjure up the deceased's personal fate.

These two kinds of monument, common from the fourteenth century onwards, spread to a remarkable degree around 1400 and throughout the fifteenth century.

The funeral slabs, thin sheets of copper or brass (copper and zinc alloy) cast and afterwards engraved, have come down to us in substantial quantities. The workshops produced them from models that were faithfully repeated over a period of several decades, albeit with some minor modifications, notably involving armorial bearings and the texts of inscriptions chosen to fit each commission. Thus the funerary image did not necessarily appear as the authentic portrait of the deceased but might evoke his social position (figure of a knight in armour), family ties (married couple holding hands) or physical death (tomb effigy lying wrapped in a shroud).

Sepulchral brass of
Joris de Munter (died 1439)
and his wife (died 1423).
Cathedral of Saint-Sauveur, Bruges.

Sepulchral brass of
Lord and Lady Camoys.
About 1419.
Church of Trotton (Sussex).

In the southern Netherlands, this standardized production was shipped abroad, in particular from the port of Bruges, which was undoubtedly the chief manufacturing centre in Flanders. The slabs, large rectangles made of several assembled sheets, were laid flat on a flagstone of the same size. One formula fashionable in the fourteenth and fifteenth centuries replaced the architectural decoration surrounding the figures by a richly wrought background simulating a fabric ornamented with oriental motifs. The inscription was punctuated all around by quatrefoils bearing coats of arms and the symbols of the evangelists (brass of Joris de Munter, died 1439, and his wife, died 1423, cathedral of Bruges).

The English sepulchral brasses are somewhat different. The brass plates, cast and left blank, were imported from Flanders; then, in London workshops, they were cut to size, engraved and set into Purbeck marble slabs. Highly popular in England, these funerary monuments reveal a dominant fifteenth-century stylistic uniformity and stereotyped formulas echoing those of alabaster tombs with sculptures carved in the round (Lord and Lady Camoys, about 1419, Trotton, Sussex).

From quarries near Tournai, in Hainaut, a carboniferous limestone of dark colour was extracted that took a high polish. It was admirably suited for sculptured tombs with recumbent effigies and, above all, for the abundant series of funerary reliefs applied to church walls. The latter are preserved in great numbers at Tournai and neighbouring regions such as northern France (exported by the Hainaut workshops or imitated by local sculptors?), and the same compositional designs were consistently adopted for all of them. One of the customary formulas depicts, above the engraved epitaph, the donors and their patron saints placed symmetrically on either side of the enthroned Virgin, to whom they address their prayers (funerary relief of Jean du Bos, died 1438, and his wife Catherine Bernard, Tournai Cathedral).

Funerary relief of Jean du Bos (died 1438) and his wife
Catherine Bernard, commended to the Virgin by
John the Baptist and St Catherine of Alexandria.
Limestone.
Chapel of Saint-Eleuthère, Tournai Cathedral.

CLAUS SLUTER

The genius of Claus Sluter dominates the art of his time from the outset. Luckily, his career in Dijon is fairly well known, thanks to the accounts of the court of Burgundy, which supply precious information about his works, as compared with the almost general anonymity of sculptures around 1400, subject to the changing game of attributions. A native of Haarlem in the County of Holland, recorded as being in Brussels about 1380, Claus Sluter came to Dijon in 1385 to work in the service of Philip the Bold, Duke of Burgundy, in the workshop of Jean de Marville whom he succeeded as the duke's image-carver in 1389, until his death in January 1406.

At the Charterhouse of Champmol near Dijon, founded by the luxury-loving patron to receive his sepulchre, Sluter broke up the static design for the church portal provided by his predecessor. The vivacity of the Virgin placed in the centre, the movement of the two patron saints who present the kneeling duke and duchess to her, are accompanied by ample draperies deeply creased with folds, and the handling of the faces brings out the thickness of the features.

The celebrated "Well of Moses" is in reality the base of a monumental Calvary ornamented with prophets and angels in tears, bathing in the waters of a fountain. Built by Sluter in the centre of the cloister of the charterhouse from 1396 to 1405, and famous since its creation, it drew inspiration from the symbolic theme of the Fountain of Life. The imposing figure of Moses sets the tone of this potent art

Claus Sluter and his workshop.
The "Well of Moses,"
base of the Calvary in
the cloister, adorned with
prophets and angels
(left Moses, right David).
1396-1405.
Polychrome stone.
Chartreuse de Champmol,
Dijon.

247

which translates into stone the superhuman grandeur of the visionaries of the Old Testament, harbingers of the Passion of Christ. But the accent is also placed on the vigorously characterized faces with intense expressions, by turns meditative, inspired or wrathful. The illusion of life had to be strengthened to begin with by a few accessories, like the bronze spectacles of the prophet Jeremiah or the copper strings of David's harp, and by a rich polychromy entrusted to Jean Malouel, court painter of the duke, and to Hermann of Cologne.

And yet the notion of realism frequently applied to the sculptures of Sluter seems excessive and too limited. His extraordinary talent passes easily from one register to another, from the vehemence of the prophets to the living dynamism of the Virgin or the sensitive pathos of the magnificent bust of the crucified Christ, the principal relic of the Champmol Calvary. And how are we to imagine the pastoral scene commissioned by Philip the Bold for his château of Germolles, portraying the duke and duchess as shepherd and shepherdess seated beneath an elm surrounded by sheep? The exact degree of participation of Sluter's many collaborators, too, still needs to be assessed, in particular that of his nephew Claus de Werwe,

who joined the Dijon workshop in 1396 and took charge of it in 1406 after his uncle's death.

Comparative criticism has shown how novel Sluter's art was. That novelty is already evident in the cortege of mourners on the ducal tomb, with which he probably began the work. Indeed, one looks in vain in the sculpture of Brussels or Holland for any true equivalents or forerunners of his style. And his contacts with contemporary sculptors–in 1393 he visited the worksite of Mehun-sur-Yèvre supervised by André Beauneveu in the service of the Duke of Berry–have no particular echoes, at least in his surviving works. However, if the master's creations opened new perspectives rich in possibilities, they are also totally in keeping with the embryonic fourteenth-century tendencies that burst into bloom around 1400. The different versions of international Gothic are marked, on several accounts, by that common taste for dynamic figures, ample volumes deployed in space, thick and flowing draperies, and individualized faces.

But Claus Sluter bends these plastic themes to the daring inventions of his personal touch. He creates a style whose powerful ascendancy made itself lastingly felt in fifteenth-century Burgundy, and even far beyond.

Claus Sluter.

◁◁ Philip the Bold kneeling, commended by John the Baptist. Splaying of the church portal. Set in place in 1391–1392. Stone.

◁ Virgin and Child. Central pillar of the church portal. Set in place in 1391. Stone.

Chartreuse de Champmol, Dijon.

248

Michael and Gregor Erhart. Altarpiece on the main altar.
Central panel: Virgin and Child with St Benedict, John the Baptist, St John the Evangelist, St Scholastica.
Wing panels: Nativity and Adoration of the Magi. Predella: Christ and the apostles.
Crowning: Christ of Pity, Virgin and St John, Fathers of the Church and saints. Ulm, 1493-1494. Polychrome limewood.
Abbey church of Blaubeuren (Baden-Württemberg).

ALTARPIECES

Of all the creations of late Gothic art, the carved altarpiece is beyond all doubt the most fascinating. It is in the decoration of the altar, holiest of holy places, on which all eyes are turned, that the artists' imagination and virtuosity scored their triumph. The wall standing behind the altar, rising vertically above the slab of the altar, took on unprecedented breadth and complexity. The art of the altarpiece, born well before the fifteenth century, experienced a remarkable flowering during this period.

In the Germanic countries and the Netherlands, the altarpieces in carved and painted wood, fitted with folding wing panels, developed from fourteenth-century examples: the vast reliquary altarpieces, which associated the holy receptacles on several levels with an ornamentation of statuettes placed side by side beneath arcades; or the small altarpieces shaped like tabernacles, which housed the holy image in the centre. When closed, the painted (sometimes carved) wing panels enabled the sculptures and relics to be protected; when open, to be presented on the altar for adoration by the faithful.

At the end of the fourteenth century, potentially far-reaching changes affected the shrine or casket (*Schrein* in German, *screen* in Flemish), the central part of the altarpiece. This shrine, being deeper, could receive narrative compositions in high relief beneath the architectural elements, and its median bay was elevated, breaking with the rectangular form and creating a vertical axis at the centre. That was the case with the Crucifixion altarpiece commissioned by Philip the Bold in 1390 from Jacques de

Baerze, a sculptor of Termonde, for the Charterhouse of Champmol. The way was open for formulas typical of the Netherlands around 1500, where scenes with multiple figures placed on rising ground were composed by small reliefs carved separately, then fitted together and arranged in tiers in the different compartments of the shrine. The form of those compartments and their architectural setting, composed of flamboyant fenestration, vaults, colonnettes, gables and pinnacles, evoke the interiors of Gothic churches. The Dortmund altarpiece of about 1420 already offers an accomplished example of this type of shrine, called *Kapellenschrein*. But the attempt to suggest depth of space is restricted by the material confines of each compartment. In compensation, it brings with it a kind of miniaturization of forms and proliferation of details placed at the service of expressive and narrative values. The anecdotal episodes, picturesque costumes, and concrete elements rendered in minute detail help to situate the narratives drawn from the Bible or the lives of the saints in the sculptors' contemporary world.

The monumental figure carvings standing in the shrines of the German altarpieces produce a different effect. In both cases, however, the altarpiece is conceived as a whole (*Gesamtkunstwerk*). Shrine and wing panels must be considered together, according to the opening and closing of the altarpiece as required by the necessities of the liturgical calendar. There is a deliberate progression of forms and imagery in the passage from the simpler paintings on the wing panels (often grisaille on the outside and more coloured representations or else low reliefs within) to the sculptures of the central shrine, where the most sacred and elaborate images stood. When closed, the altarpiece wears,

Altarpiece on the high altar.
Main panel: Crucifixion
with the twelve apostles.
Southern Netherlands, about 1420.
Polychrome wood.
Reinoldikirche, Dortmund.

Altarpiece from Saluzzo (Piedmont)
with scenes from the life of the Virgin and the Childhood of Christ.
Brussels, about 1500. Polychrome wood. Musée de la Ville, Brussels.

Mallet, hallmark of the Brussels sculptors
stamped on the head of a figure.

Altarpiece from Saluzzo (Piedmont).
Detail: Presentation in the Temple.
Brussels, about 1500.
Polychrome wood.
Musée de la Ville, Brussels.

as it were, its everyday face, adapted to days of toil or mourning; when open on feast days, it shows itself in all its splendour.

The production of carved and painted altarpieces in the southern Netherlands, already considerable in the course of the fifteenth century, became extremely abundant at the close of that century and the start of the next. Strictly organized, and in some cases almost standardized, this line of work was extensively commercialized, as shown by exports to France, the Iberian peninsula, the Balearic and Canary islands, and the Germanic and Scandinavian countries. Two centres, Antwerp and Brussels, were predominant, while the workshops of Malines specialized in the manufacture of statuettes. Several craftsmen collaborated in the construction of an altarpiece: joiners and cabinetmakers who devised the shrine, sculptors, painters and gilders who were responsible for the polychromy. The statutes of the craft guilds to which they belonged laid down precise conditions of work and production. Each town's hallmark was affixed to its works as a guarantee of their origin and quality. The varieties of wood most frequently used were oak, walnut and some fruit trees.

In Brussels the mark of the cabinetmaker was stamped on the outer panels of the oak shrine and depicted his tools: a plane between the branches of an open compass. It was often accompanied by the wooden mallet, the mark of the Brussels sculptors, which was carved on the wood, generally out of sight: on the head or back, or beneath the base, of the figures. On the other hand, the rectangular mark bearing the word BRVESEL, which was impressed in the still fresh preparatory coat before the application of the gold, and guaranteed the quality of the polychromy, was placed in evidence on the front of the shrine (Saluzzo altarpiece) or on the pedestals of free-standing statuettes. Some workshops might also use their own hallmarks, and sometimes the sculptors, like the famous Jan Borreman, even signed their works (altarpiece of St George, 1493, Royal Museums of Art and History, Brussels).

△ Altarpiece from the church of Pailhe
with scenes from the life of the Virgin
and the Childhood of Christ;
in the centre, the Tree of Jesse; above, the Crucifixion.
Antwerp, about 1510. Polychrome oak.
Musées Royaux d'Art et d'Histoire, Brussels.

▽ Detail: central panel with the Tree of Jesse.

Two hands and a castle,
the Antwerp hallmark stamped
on the altarpieces made there.

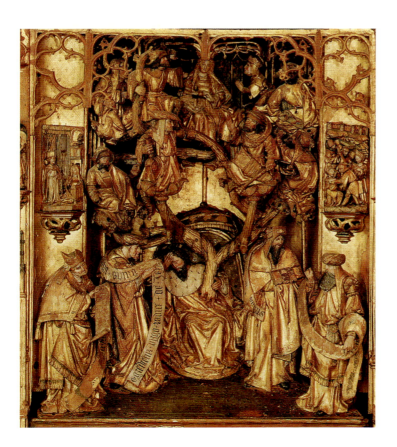

The care taken in the execution of the Brussels altarpieces, the quality of the carving and the refinement of the polychromy are admirable. Each decorative element, each architectural detail, is delicately chiselled and the slim, elongated figures display an elegance and restraint in facial and bodily expression characteristic of the sculpture of Brabant. The gold or silver and the colours, laid over the priming coats applied to the wood and then embellished with various decorations using complex techniques, put the finishing touch to the sculptor's work.

An outstandingly well-preserved example of that intrinsic complementarity between sculptured form and colouring, the Saluzzo altarpiece was made in Brussels around 1500 for the Italian family of Pensa di Mondovì in Piedmont (it was later transferred from Mondovì to nearby Saluzzo, then sold to the City of Brussels in 1894). The figures in the Presentation to the Temple are arranged in tiers on a tiled floor viewed in perspective, as in the paintings of the primitives. The scene is set in the choir of a small church and, to heighten the illusion, the altar behind the figures has a painted triptych resembling a miniature altarpiece which represents the Sacrifice of Abraham, a prefiguring of the sacrifice of Christ. The subtle play of chromatic values and the contrasts between bright and mat surfaces were ingeniously enlisted to heighten the volumes and render the tactile sensations of fabrics and materials: thus, transparent green lacquer was applied on gold for the enamelled tiles, and mat white was used for the striped stuff of the turban worn by the maidservant standing behind St Anne. The complicated technique of "appliqué brocade" consisted in laying premoulded motifs over the colours or directly on the priming coat. These motifs in slight relief, picked out with gold and colours, made it possible to simulate orphreys (borders of the golden cloaks of the Virgin and St Anne) or rich silks brocaded with threads in precious metal (curtains to protect the small painted triptych).

The Antwerp hallmarks were branded in the wood: a severed hand, recalling a local legend, was placed clearly in evidence on the sculptured parts, and vouched for the quality of the wood and workmanship; the castle of the town, often with two hands above it, was stamped on the shrine and certified the high finish of the altarpiece.

In the early sixteenth century, production in Antwerp was stepped up remarkably and surpassed that of Brussels. Rapidly executed, almost mass-produced, both for the regional market and for export, the Antwerp altarpieces were turned out with great skill but generally with less care than the Brussels pieces. The sculptors faithfully reproduced the same types from one scene and from one altarpiece to the other, to the point where some figures seemed interchangeable. More care was given to picturesque effects and expression, and often the iconography repeated unvaryingly the same themes, such as the Tree of Jesse which bears the ancestors of Christ, or scenes from the life of Christ and his Passion (altarpieces of Pailhe and Oplinter in the Brussels museum). The structure of the altarpiece became more complicated, and in particular it relinquished the delicate openwork band running along the base of Brussels works. In addition to painted or hallmarked decorations, the polychromy frequently included the technique of scratchwork: after the gilding was entirely covered with a coat of opaque colour, the paint was partly removed with a stiletto, tracing designs that allowed the polished gold beneath to show through.

Malines coat of arms
with three stakes, hallmark
of the Malines sculptors.

Household altarpiece:
Carved central panel: Virgin and
Child between St Catherine and
St Barbara.
Painted wing panels: St Agnes
and Mary Magdalene.
Malines, about 1500.
Polychrome wood.
Museum Mayer van den Bergh,
Antwerp.

At Malines (Mechelen), too, the sculptors kept consistently to the established models, carving–with skill it is true, but without invention–statuettes of the Virgin and Child, and male and female saints who all look alike with their charming, childish, doll-like faces. The Malines workshops also produced altarpieces with narrative compositions, but the chief activity was the carving of these "dolls" of stereotyped prettiness. Hundreds of examples are still preserved, easily recognizable even if they do not carry the marks of guarantee: the three stakes of the Malines coat of arms, the sculptors' hallmark applied to the back of statuettes, and, on the front, the letter *M*, engraved on the gold leaf, or the rectangular imprint *MECHLEN*, with an escutcheon between the *H* and the *L*. A Malines sculpture might also be given a Brussels polychromy, certified in that case by the hallmark on its base. Of modest size, the Malines statuettes were above all for private use, displayed separately or in the shrine of small household altarpieces with painted wing panels like those in the Mayer van den Bergh Museum at Antwerp and the church of Saint-Galmier in the Forez (central France). Later, in the "closed gardens" composed by the Beguines, such statuettes were mingled with other sculptures and holy relics in a shimmering decor of artificial flowers.

In contrast to these compartmented altarpieces of the Netherlands, the specifically German type of altarpiece, appearing from the second third of the fifteenth century onwards, offers a light and spacious composition. From a distance the monumental effect is impressive, and the tall sculptured figures, often lifesize, which rise in the shrine stand out strongly. From the outset the eye takes in the various articulations of the whole and progresses according to the rhythms which animate it, in no way hampered

Attributed to Niklaus Weckmann.
Altarpiece from the church of Thalheim.
Detail of the central panel: Virgin and Child with two angels.
Ulm, about 1510-1515.
Polychrome limewood.
Württembergisches Landesmuseum, Stuttgart.

Swansea altarpiece
or altarpiece of the Joys
of the Virgin.
Detail: Adoration of the
Magi, Trinity, Resurrection.
England, second half
of the 15th century.
Polychrome alabaster.
Victoria and Albert Museum,
London.

by the rich flamboyant decoration subordinated to the overall structure. At Blaubeuren, the central axis is strongly emphasized. Around the Virgin and Child are the matching silhouettes of the four saints placed on lower pedestals, then the large low reliefs carved on the folding wings and complemented by the painted landscapes on the upper section.

The Gothic altarpiece of the Germanic countries commonly soars upward from the carved or painted predella, which raises it above the altar table, to the church vaults brushed by the tips of the pinnacles of its aerial crown surmounting the shrine. Architecture within architecture, it fits harmoniously into the interior space of the church or chapel. And the sculptures are doubly inserted into this space in which the air circulates around the altar. Let the illumination from the high Gothic windows only be favourable, and the light envelops the altarpiece and accentuates the transparency of its crowning. The impression of lightness and clarity is further heightened when the back of the shrine is patterned with openwork and the sculptured figures are lit from behind, as in the Heiligblutaltar at Rothenburg, carved by Tilman Riemenschneider and consecrated in 1478.

As in the Netherlands, joiners, sculptors and painters in Germany took part in the making of these large altarpieces, which could also be sold abroad, to far-off places. The sculptures are generally in limewood in South Germany and often in pine in the Alpine regions. The colouring techniques differ little from those already mentioned for the Netherlands, but some processes, types of decorations or colour schemes are peculiar to the German workshops and denote an extremely refined taste and admirable skill: hence the smoothness, as if enamelled, of the flesh tints, and the little locks delicately painted on foreheads and cheeks at the edges of the sculptured hair; the large motifs, made of "appliqué brocade," scattered over a solid-colour background so as to imitate silk fabrics; the ornamental elements painted or traced by the scratchwork technique on the edging of garments and the designs engraved in the priming coat before the application of gold leaf on the gilded backgrounds (Thalheim altarpiece). The natural colour of the limewood may also be enhanced, tinted slightly with a gum impregnated with tannin and locally heightened with colour (eyes, lips, sometimes beards and hair). Tilman Riemenschneider, Veit Stoss and Daniel Mauch have used this technique of semipolychromy so well calculated to set off the chiselling. All too often, unfortunately, the original polychromy has flaked off, or been rubbed off, and many altarpieces have been broken up or destroyed. Those that remain *in situ* and the many fragments preserved in museums attest to the imposing number–several thousand–of German altarpieces produced in the later Middle Ages: on the eve of the Reformation, Ulm Cathedral alone had fifty of them.

The use of materials other than wood, rare in the Germanic world and the Netherlands, was frequent elsewhere, even if the altarpieces still intact are far less numerous. The English altarpieces with juxtaposed alabaster reliefs set in a wooden case closed by shutters (Swansea altarpiece) remain exceptional today compared with the multitude of isolated panels spread throughout England and the Continent. Few examples still exist of the altarpieces composed of terracotta reliefs and statuettes produced in the northern Netherlands, in particular at Utrecht, and sold abroad (altarpieces of Santa María la Real, Segovia).

In France, the exports from Brussels, Antwerp and England, whose importance can be seen from the surviving examples and a few written records, exerted some influence locally. In the early sixteenth century the sculptors of Champagne and northern France thus drew inspiration from the formulas characteristic of the southern Netherlands, which they transcribed in stone and interpreted in their own style (altarpiece of Rumilly-les-Vaudes). During the second and third quarters of the sixteenth century, in the Beauvais region, the belated production of altarpieces in carved and painted wood also derived from northern models. Sometimes it is difficult to distinguish imported from local works, which, moreover, may have been executed by foreign-trained sculptors. In polychrome stone, the most common medium used in France in the late Middle Ages, other altarpieces display different types, some inherited from fourteenth-century creations, like the fifteenth-century series from Burgundy and Berry adorned with Christ or the Virgin surrounded by apostles (Nolay altarpiece, Louvre, Paris).

Spain worked out a particularly original type of altarpiece from traditional designs. The back is divided into panels ornamented with low reliefs or paintings set out around a statue of the Virgin and Child. This scheme was in use during the fourteenth century. The Catalan examples in alabaster already had monumental dimensions at the start of the fifteenth century. Grown to giant proportions by the end of the Middle Ages, the Spanish altarpiece in carved wood rises up like a wall in the church choir. An immense rectangle, higher than it is wide, it fills the space entirely and is joined to the side walls without the effects of transparency and mobility peculiar to German altarpieces. The division into horizontal and vertical registers forms a strict grid, whose regularity is scarcely broken by a wider axis at the centre in the *Retablo Mayor* of Seville Cathedral. Within the compartments, the narrative high reliefs, disposing several figures in tiers in the Netherlandish manner, seem squeezed between the flamboyant canopies and the pilasters overloaded with statuettes.

Indeed, these Spanish altarpieces in various respects show the influence of altarpieces imported from the Netherlands, and of the northern sculptors or painters who came in large numbers during the fifteenth century to work in the Iberian peninsula. Thus Pieter Dancart, expressly described as *alemán*, was engaged for the altarpiece of Seville by the cathedral chapter, and probably supplied an initial design (*traza*) around 1481-1482. The origin of the teams which followed him and carried out the work on the altarpiece, whose central part was completed in 1526, is not known precisely; however, the style of the sculptures shows obvious links not only with the southern Netherlands but also with the regions of the lower Rhine. The woods used are extremely varied: walnut (often for the carved figures), poplar, chestnut, pine, oak, cedar, cypress, etc., of local provenance or from further away, as with the *madera de Flandes* for which Dancart received payment in 1481 and 1482.

In Spain as elsewhere, an altarpiece was a collective work involving the *entalladores* who did the joinery and decorative elements; the sculptors, also called *entalladores* or *imaginarios*; and the painters, *doradores*, *estofadores* and *encarnadores*, responsible for gilding and colouring the fabrics and flesh tints. Gold is lavished in profusion on these huge historiated altarpieces, thick and gleaming, which are displayed in Spanish churches. In Seville the polychromy of the central area belongs to the final stage of execution in 1524-1525 and develops a redundant taste for decorations painted on gold or traced by the scratchwork technique. The motifs, stars, arabesques, dots, and plant, floral and geometric elements, cover the surface of most of the clothes and many accessories. Their diversity, breaking with the relative simplicity of late fifteenth-century polychromy almost free of scratchwork, and the richness of their shimmering effects characteristic of the Spanish Renaissance, heralds the brilliant luxuriance of the Baroque sculptures of the Iberian peninsula.

Altarpiece
with Bearing of the Cross, Crucifixion
and Resurrection.
Champagne, set up in 1533.
Polychrome stone.
Church of Rumilly-lès-Vaudes, near Troyes.

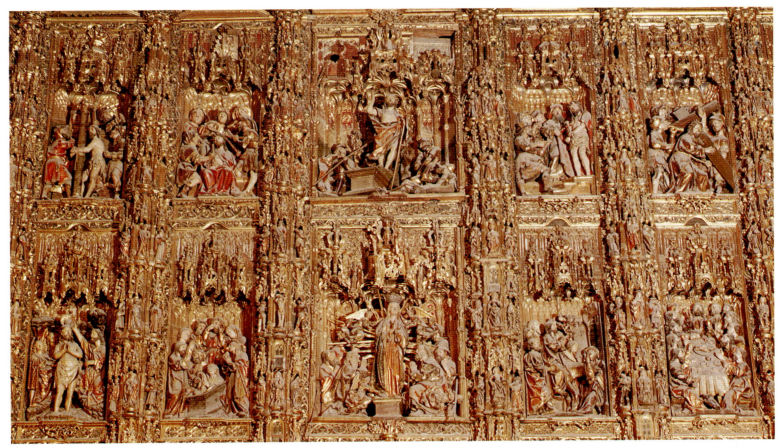

THE SCULPTORS

What do we know of these men, of these "artist-craftsmen" (the distinction is blurred in the Middle Ages)? What do we know of their working conditions, their social status, their personal lives? Truth to tell, in spite of increasing research into written records and the works themselves, we are still badly informed. If documents for some regions are fairly abundant, they are often rare or not explicit enough for others, and the vast majority of extant sculptures remains anonymous. Yet, in spite of everything, light can be thrown on several aspects of the craft and on the role of the Gothic sculptor.

In the fifteenth century independent urban workshops replaced the great religious building sites. The statutes of the guilds to which the sculptors belonged, particularly well known in the case of German towns, regulated the profession with the aim of controlling production and hindering foreign competition. At Ulm in 1496 the master builder had to be a burgess of the town: if he gave work to a sculptor from another city he had to pay a special tax. The number of journeymen attached to the same workshop was not restricted, but the number of apprentices was limited to two and the minimum length of apprenticeship was four years. Elsewhere are specified the length of service as a journeyman and the modalities for executing a piece of work qualifying for mastership. Most of the time the master was assisted in his workshop by one or two journeymen and one or two apprentices. In France, Michel Colombe was aided in building the Nantes tomb by two journeymen, including his nephew Guillaume Regnault, and by two Italians responsible for the decorative elements. But the popular workshops could be very much larger in numbers, like that of Riemenschneider at

Workshops of Pieter Dancart, Master Marco, Pedro Millán, Jorge and Alexo Fernández.
Altarpiece on the main altar.
Detail: middle registers with Assumption of the Virgin and scenes from the life of Christ.
Seville, 1481-1526. Polychrome wood.
Seville Cathedral.

Veit Stoss.
Altarpiece from the Carmelite church at Nuremberg.
Central panel with Nativity.
1520-1523. Limewood.
Bamberg Cathedral.

Würzburg, which between 1501 and 1517 had twelve apprentices and several journeymen.

Frequently the handing down of the craft took place in a family context favourable to a precocious apprentice, and the workshop was passed on to a close relative: thus Regnault kept on his uncle's workshop at Tours. Sometimes veritable dynasties were formed, like that of the Viguiers in Rouergue and in Albigeois. Family ties were also formed between representatives of different professions—joiners, sculptors, painters, goldsmiths, glass painters—who often lived close to each other in the same neighbourhood and joined forces to carry out a commission. The Swabian sculptor Daniel Mauch married the daughter of the painter Jörg Stocker in 1503 or thereabouts; in 1502-1504 Gregor Erhart undertook an altarpiece for the monastery of Kaisheim together with his brother-in-law, the joiner Adolf Daucher, whose son Hans was trained by Erhart himself; from 1508 to 1525 the sculptor Jorge Fernández and his brother Alexo, a painter, collaborated on the altarpiece for Seville Cathedral.

From all too rare documents filters personal information about the sculptors. Thus we learn of the quarrelsome temperament of Jean de La Huerta, convicted in 1448 of having insulted and drawn his dagger against Philippe Mâchefoing, counsellor of the Duke of Burgundy; or of the fatigue, towards the end of his life, of Michel Colombe, described as "quite old and heavy... gouty and sickly from past labours," who refuses to carve unaided the tombs of Brou for Margaret of Austria. Nevertheless, nothing explains the individual choices reflected in the works, which, if they were specified, might help us better to understand how certain stylistic mutations occurred.

Veit Stoss.
Design for the altarpiece from
the Carmelite church at Nuremberg.
Pen and ink drawing.
University Museum, Cracow.

As for the sculptors' material and social situation, it remained extremely variable in the late Middle Ages. Some owned a house and a few chattels, but their prosperity was modest as compared with the wealth of other professional classes. The salaries and amounts of payment often seem small when measured against the cost of living, even if those sums were accompanied, as was the custom, by compensation in kind and by settlement of additional expenses, arising, for example, from the transport of the work and the furnishing of materials. The use of gold, silver and expensive pigments such as azurite blue, partly explains why painters might receive relatively higher sums than those granted to sculptors. Furthermore, not enough is known about the relation between wealth and social standing. Master sculptors could profit from a high position in the city or enjoy the consideration of the great: Tilman Riemenschneider was burgomaster of Würzburg in 1520-1521 and Olivier Le Lœrgan, who made the Le Faouët rood screen, was ennobled in 1469 by the Duke of Brittany.

Written sources tell us more about the fame of some masters who were sought after, showered with praise, or became for a time sculptors by appointment to a ruler without actually being attached to him (holding, in France, the enviable title of valet de chambre), as in the European courts around 1400 and during the Renaissance. The sculptor of the waning Middle Ages generally appears more as a "bourgeois craftsman" than as a "court artist," the precise difference between the two terms "artist" and "craftsman" moreover being difficult for the period to grasp. Described as "image-carver" or "image-maker" (Bildhauer, Bildschnitzer, Beeldhouwer, imaginario, etc.), he was also called "workman" (Werkman) without any deprecatory intention, since the word might be accompanied by flattering adjectives. Michel Colombe was described as a "great workman" and La Huerta as a "very good workman at his trade of image-making and famous for it." The term, however, places the accent on the work the sculptor does with his hands, and allows us to suppose a distinction, though not necessarily qualitative, between the practice of the painter and that of the sculptor, who faced more restrictive material problems and had to expend physical energy on his work. In any case, both painters and sculptors, who sometimes practised the two trades concurrently, were conscious of the value of their works, as testified by some inscriptions.

The rarity of signatures, a general phenomenon at the end of the Middle Ages, does not necessarily suggest that the men effaced themselves behind their creations and were indifferent to their fame. Many of the most highly reputed omitted to sign, whereas sculptors now considered less talented or less inventive, such as Jan van Steefeswert, active in the middle Meuse in the early sixteenth century, put their name to their productions several times. In a collaboration the name of the painter, joiner or architect might appear on the work or in the contract, while the sculptor remained unknown. Germany provides many examples of altarpieces that bear the painter's signature only: that of Nördlingen, for instance, signed and dated by Friedrich Herlin, while its celebrated sculptures are anonymous and have led to controversial attributions; the altarpieces of the Nördlingen painter Sebastian Dayg in the former abbey church of Heilsbronn; or those of the Strigel painters of Memmingen. The signer was usually the master, who concluded a contract with the person who

Unfinished statuette.
Burgundy or Dauphiné, 15th century.
Stone.
Musée de Peinture et de Sculpture, Grenoble.

furnished the funds; he provided a design for the altarpiece (*Visierung, Riss*), sub-contracted for the different parts to be executed and collected payments. This role of intermediary was also often held by the joiner or cabinetmaker (*Schreiner, Kistler*), for example Jörg Syrlin the Elder who in 1474 designed the altarpiece for the high altar of Ulm Cathedral, or his son Syrlin the Younger, long mistakenly regarded as a sculptor, who supervised the execution of many works. Similarly in Spain the *entallador* might make a sketch (*traza*) but the sculptor himself was, as elsewhere, frequently responsible for the overall plan. Of the designs that have come down to us, very few match surviving works, like the design by Veit Stoss for the altarpiece still in Bamberg Cathedral. In the absence of preserved evidence, several documents also mention the use of full-scale models or maquettes made by the sculptors, such as in France the famous examples of stone or terracotta models requested of Michel Colombe. In 1474 he was paid by the treasurer of Louis XI "for having carved in stone a small model in the shape of a tomb at the command of the king and with his portrait and likeness" (doubtless from the sketch painted by Jean Fouquet, who was paid at the same time); in 1511 Colombe agreed to provide terracotta models (based on drawings by the painter Jean Perréal) "in small size" for the Brou tombs.

The execution of a design or sculptured model often accompanied the written contract, which came into general use in the late Middle Ages. The contract, which bound the executant and his client, laid down certain specifications for the work: materials, completion dates and modes of payment. Sometimes it listed in detail the demands of the client, who for example prescribed the iconographic programme, cited a model for imitation or stipulated the use of specific colours. In 1504 Bishop Diego de Deza imposed the altarpiece of the college of Santa Cruz at Valladolid as a model for the high altar of Palencia Cathedral and provided designs for the decorative parts; in 1505 he laid down the iconography of the figures, listed in an annotated plan added to the contract, and he chose the sculptor Felipe Bigarny, ruling out Alejo de Vahia, who had been previously engaged by two members of the cathedral chapter. At Bordeaux the shoemakers' guild, having struck a bargain with Jean Baudoyn in 1497 for two wooden statues, respectively of St Crispin and St Crispinian, signed a contract with the painter Philippe Perlant which specified very precisely the parts to be gilded and the appearance of the furs on the robes, the one being "of the colour of martens and the other of cats."

But the artists did not always respect the written instructions. They could take some liberties with the initial project or else, if they had several irons in the fire at once, delay carrying out the works or leave them to their collaborators. It is understandable that the contract for the pulpit concluded in 1500 between the St George worksite at Haguenau and Veit Wagner stipulated that "Master Veit must work on the piece himself" ("*sol der genant meister Vitt selbs an solichem werg arbeiten*") and that the work must not be entrusted to "journeymen, servants or other underlings" ("*knechten, gesinde und andern ussrihten*").

The carrying out of commissions led the sculptor to travel, sometimes quite far from his native town, either because he was sought after for his talent, like Nicholas of Leyden who was summoned by the emperor, or because he needed to find a more open market. The case of Jacques Morel is well known: his career took him from Lyons, where he was born, to Toulouse, Rodez, Montpellier, Avignon, Souvigny and Angers. On the other hand, Michael Pacher made the altarpiece for the St Wolfgang church in the Salzkammergut in his workshop at Bruneck, in South Tyrol; and Michel Colombe carved at Tours the tomb sculptures of the Dukes of Brittany, which were then shipped down the Loire to Nantes. But many were the artists who emigrated in search of a clientele and who, taking advantage of political and economic ties existing between countries, married and settled in an adoptive town, like the painters and sculptors from Germany and the Netherlands who moved to Spain in the fifteenth century.

Representations of the sculptor at work, and above all the works themselves, provide considerable information on the purely technical aspects of the craft, often revealed by thorough scientific examination. Many sculptors, like Riemenschneider, carved wood, stone, marble and alabaster all at the same time. The choice of materials was, moreover, the object of attentive care. In 1459 Pierre Viguier went several times to the Magot quarry to oversee the extraction of blocks destined for the doorway of the cathedral of Rodez. A few unfinished pieces, like the Grenoble statuettes, enable us to see how the sculptured form emerges from the rough-hewn block and takes shape, down to the detailed chiselling of the surface. Special procedures and marks left by the tools appear as evidence of the habits of workshops and traditions of particular countries, as do the cutting and assembly of ele-

St Barbara.
Burgundy, late 15th century.
Polychrome stone.
Church of Millery, near Lyons.

St Barbara.
Burgundy, late 15th century.
Polychrome stone.
Musée Rolin, Autun.

St Barbara.
Burgundy, late 15th century.
Polychrome stone.
Palm branch and left hand modern.
Church of Moutier-Saint-Jean, near Dijon.

ments composing a figure in carved wood, or the grooves worn in the base of statues by the raised ledge behind the altar in the region of Semur-en-Auxois at the end of the fifteenth century (Virgin of Pity of Montmorot, St Barbara of Pontaubert).

Similarly, the polychromy, the final stage in the completion of a sculpture, testifies to specific usages which often reveal the origin of works, as the study of altarpieces has already shown. As a general rule polychrome application was entrusted to specialized craftsmen, but sometimes also to reputed painters or to sculptors themselves, despite the possibility of lawsuits between guilds. Several sculptors, like Michael Pacher or Veit Stoss, who attended to the colouring of the St Lawrence Annunciation at Nuremberg, practised both trades. The work of the painter might be done long after that of the sculptor and the altarpiece might be completed by wing panels years later, as in the case of the altarpiece for the religious brotherhood of Our Lady at 's Hertogenbosch (Bois-le-Duc) carved in 1475-1477 by Adriaen van Wesel and furnished with wing panels painted in 1488-1489 by Hieronymus Bosch. And unfortunately, it must be repeated, the original polychromy on stone, wood or other materials may, in the course of centuries, have been partially or wholly done over (and even scoured off). In spite of the recent progress achieved in scientific analysis and the restoration of art works, we all too often have only an inkling of the refinement and splendour of medieval polychrome sculptures. The knowledge of technical procedures is indispensable to

Alejo de Vahia. Two statues of the Virgin and Child.
Castile, about 1500. Polychrome wood.
Parish church of Monzón de Campos and
church of Santiago at Medina de Rioseco.

259

Master E.S.
Virgin and Child with
Lily of the Valley.
About 1450. Print.
Graphische Sammlung
Albertina, Vienna.

The Dangolsheim Virgin and Child.
Strasbourg, about 1460.
Polychrome walnut.
Staatliche Museen, Berlin.

their study and must be added to that of formal and iconographic types.

Indeed, to understand late Gothic sculpture, we must take into account the old medieval system of reproducing images, already widespread in the fourteenth century, which subsequently developed in scope, favoured by the structure of the workshops and the growing demand of the clientele. Collective work with specialization of tasks under the direction of a master was the rule in the workshops. The master distributed and supervised the work of his helpers, putting his personal mark on the production of the atelier, which presented a homogeneous style and could faithfully reproduce a popular model. The many Virgins Suckling the Child by Alejo de Vahia, active in Castile around 1500, and the Virgins and saints from the atelier of the Master of Elsloo in the middle Meuse at the beginning of the sixteenth century, resemble each other like sisters. But the influence of a pre-eminent master might go beyond the confines of the workshop and exert a lasting effect on former journeymen who had become masters in their turn, or it might leave its mark on simple followers who adopted the prevailing fashion. This phenomenon is common in all German sculpture. Similar types are thus found reproduced without their precise attribution always being possible in the absence of signatures or documents. Criticism then hesitates to choose: the Virgin and Child from the Örtel collection (Kunstmuseum, Düsseldorf) is sometimes attributed to Daniel Mauch, sometimes to a sculptor of his immediate entourage, conventionally called the Master of the Örtel Madonna. On the other hand, in Burgundy, several St Barbaras from Auxois, although very much alike, display nuances of style and expression suggesting they are by different hands. So it frequently happens that the medieval sculptor, caring not a jot for originality, takes up once more at leisure the same designs, the same stylistic and iconographic conventions, drawing his inspiration from pioneer works admired for their innovative qualities, famed for their beauty or especially venerated. Thus, in the fifteenth century, the paintings of Rogier van der Weyden had a considerable formal impact on the altarpiece sculptures of Brussels.

The transmission of models occurred by various routes. In addition to the direct experience of reference works or of the imitations they inspired, there was the role played by graphic sources, essential in the Germanic countries. Prints, mainly those of Master E. S. and Dürer, provided a vast repertory of motifs and compositions which the sculptors translated into three dimensions. The typical overcrossing of the mantle folds in the Virgin with Lily of the Valley by Master E. S. reappears in the celebrated Virgin and Child of Dangolsheim. In the presence of stylistic variants based on the same type, like that of the Issenheim Virgin and Child, the existence may be suspected of a print that helped to disseminate the model, and it may be supposed that the engraving preceded the sculpture.

Thus the multiplication of examples, deriving, to be sure, from the same basic design but never slavishly copied without changes in interpretation, was current in this concluding phase of the Middle Ages, when the notion of an original work was still vague. Mention has already been made of the success of mass-produced pieces in the Netherlands and in England: the Antwerp altarpieces, the Malines "dolls," the sepulchral brasses, the alabaster reliefs. This intensive production, stimulated by the needs of a huge clientele whose tastes and devotional practices it reveals, was fostered by the economic prosperity of the towns and the organization of the marketplace. Art works travelled the same routes as merchandise. The sculptures were shipped together with woollen cloth, raw materials, or various products from the ports of the Netherlands, bound for the Scandinavian countries, Normandy, Brittany or the Cantabrian coast, and were transhipped up the Seine or other rivers. The Swabian altarpieces took the trade routes leading south over the Alps, and English alabasters followed the maritime routes to the Continent. Trading on a European scale and local commerce in regional fairs were the province of merchants: purveyors, like the "haberdashers" of Rennes, of art works, goods and commodities of all kinds, and often carrying on banking activities on the side.

Virgin and Child from the
Antonite monastery of Issenheim (Alsace).
Upper Rhine, late 15th century.
Limewood.
Musée du Louvre, Paris.

Hans Geiler.
Virgin and Child.
Fribourg, about 1525-1530.
Polychrome limewood.
Musée d'Art et d'Histoire,
Fribourg (Switzerland).

Christ of Palm Sunday from Sundgau (Alsace).
16th century.
Polychrome wood.
Musée d'Unterlinden, Colmar.

WORSHIP AND LITURGY

Both joy and grief find an outlet in the religious imagery of the late Middle Ages, suffused as it is with mystical thought, the moments of tenderness of the childhood of Christ and the dolorous episodes of the Passion. Nativities are as common as Crucifixions. However, several themes from the Passion cycle, particularly moving and rich in meaning, were held in special favour, being directly related to popular worship and the liturgy.

Independently of any reference to the Gospel text, Christ was imagined after the ascent to Calvary, seated at Golgotha, hands and feet bound during the preparations for the agony. Crowned with thorns, he is stripped to the waist, the mantle of derision having slipped to the ground, and he bears the marks of the Flagellation. Head bowed, mouth partly open and eyes half-closed, he seems to meditate on man's estate, and wears an expression of restrained suffering fit to arouse commiseration. The many portrayals of the Suffering Christ or Christ in bonds, often placed in cemeteries or funerary chapels, are evidence of the fervour of the faithful for this subject, from which they drew a lesson of resignation in the face of pain and death. In the Hospital of Beaune a Suffering Christ was placed on a console at one end of the "Great Ward of the Poor": it was offered to the patients' view, like the Last Judgment of Rogier van der Weyden, an image of faith in the Resurrection that in the past had been placed opposite, on the altar. In the late fifteenth and during the sixteenth century, statues of the Suffering Christ in wood or stone were produced in abundance in Brabant, Hainaut and several French regions such as Burgundy and Champagne. In Germany the representations laid more emphasis on the human distress of Christ put to the torture (*Schmerzensmann, Christus im Elend*), withdrawn in his sorrow, his head resting on one hand in accordance with an iconographic formula probably derived from images of Job on his dunghill and illustrated in particular by Dürer in the *Little Passion* of 1511.

Not only the expression of feelings by the play of facial features and attitudes, but also the monumental scale and polychromy of the sculptures, often lifesize and freestanding, attempt to give the illusion of life. Indeed, to bring the divine closer to the world of humans is a constant feature of the art of the late Middle Ages. The ceremonies in which statues played a role in the quasi-theatrical representation of episodes from the Gospels testify still more pointedly to the desire of the faithful to confer a visual form on the great mysteries of the Faith. Much written or sculptured evidence of the rites practised during major festivals of the liturgical calendar is still preserved, mainly on Germanic soil. A few examples make it possible to grasp the importance of the ties between those practices and the carved images.

Christ on the Mount of Olives.
North Tyrol, about 1510.
Polychrome limewood.
Cemetery chapel, Mils bei Hall (Tyrol).

On Palm Sunday, to commemorate the Entry of Christ into Jerusalem, it was the custom in most German towns to carry in procession a wooden effigy of Christ on a donkey (*Palmesel*) and to throw clothing and palm branches on the ground as it passed. On the evening of Holy Thursday a religious ceremony often took place outside the church before a sculptured representation of the Gospel story of Christ praying on the Mount of Olives (*Ölberg*), showing Christ kneeling and the three sleeping apostles in the garden of Gethsemane. On Good Friday a statue of Christ lying dead (or else a wooden crucifix with movable arms folded back) might be placed, along with the consecrated Host, in a small, tomb-shaped structure (*Depositio*) on the breast of the crucified Christ. At Easter, to celebrate the Resurrection, the Host was carried back into the tabernacle and the effigy of Christ removed from the tomb and carried in procession (*Elevatio*). On Ascension Thursday a crucifix or a wooden sculpture of Christ giving blessing, standing on clouds, with a suspension ring fitted on its head enabling it to be hoisted in the air by a cord, disappeared through an opening provided in the vaulting of the church. An image of the Virgin was thus lifted up in some

Martin Gramp.
Christ of the Ascension
from the collegiate church
of Saint-Nicolas, Fribourg.
1503.
Polychrome limewood.
Musée d'Art et d'Histoire,
Fribourg (Switzerland).

Suffering Christ.
Brussels, about 1500.
Oak.
Musées Royaux d'Art et d'Histoire, Brussels.

towns during the feast of the Assumption. At Pentecost, the same opening in the roof vault could serve for lowering a wooden dove representing the Holy Ghost, surrounded by strips of incandescent paper simulating tongues of fire.

Among these customs, occasionally recorded in very early times, as far back as the tenth century in the West for the Palm Sunday procession, some became widespread in the late Middle Ages, developing into ritual acts around the official liturgy in which laymen actively participated and which thereby gave direct expression to the popular piety of the time. But the excesses that were liable to accompany many ceremonies, the abuses of the games, songs and dances, even inside the church, were sharply reproved by the ecclesiastical hierarchy, which tried to prohibit or curtail some manifestations by dissociating them from the liturgy. The mystery plays acted on the squares in front of the churches were born of that sacred theatre originally integrated into traditional liturgical rites.

Venerated or even miraculous images, the statues carried or set up during processions and ceremonies had a devotional purpose in addition to their material contribution to the performance. They were rich in the symbolic meaning given to the Gospel scene to which they referred. On the Mount of Olives the anguished prayer of Christ offering himself to redeem humanity in dramatic contrast to the sleeping apostles recalls the prayer of the believer and his faith in Redemption. This may explain the frequency of the subject, represented apart from other scenes of the Passion in large-sized cemeteries, on funerary reliefs applied to the walls of churches and cloisters, and on small alabaster sculptures for private use.

Comparable significance is given to sculptured groups representing the Anointing of Christ or his Entombment. The iconographic theme takes as its source the canonical

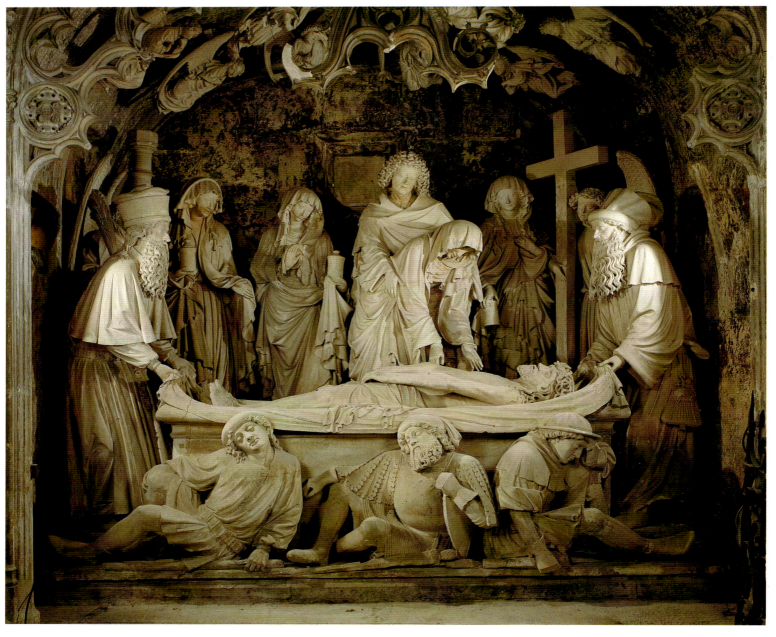

The Entombment.
Lorraine, first third of the 15th century.
Stone.
Church of Saint-Martin, Pont-à-Mousson, near Nancy.

Gospels enriched by the contribution of apocryphal texts. The Germanic formula of the Holy Sepulchre, which symbolically brings together the dead Christ, the Holy Women, the angels and sleeping guards, and the theatrical staging of the mystery of the Passion which enacted the episode of the burial shrouding, probably played a role in the genesis of sculptured representations of the Entombment on a monumental scale.

These appeared in the early fifteenth century, in particular in the southern Netherlands, Burgundy and the neighbouring regions (Entombment of Mainvault and of Fribourg in Switzerland). In the fifteenth and sixteenth centuries, and especially in France, the examples recorded are remarkably abundant. Around the corpse of Christ lying in his shroud, carried by Joseph of Arimathea and Nicodemus, stand the motionless group of Holy Women, the Virgin and St John, to whom may be added, as in Lorraine, the angels with the instruments of the Passion and, on the front of the sarcophagus, the dozing guards. If

the clothing, hairstyles and accessories recall contemporary fashions, and perhaps the picturesque costumes of the mystery plays as well, the regard for realism and descriptive detail does not impair the serious tone of the whole, without excessive display of a grief that remains interiorized.

The atmosphere of reverence is further heightened by the penumbra enveloping the large sculptured figures in many chapels of the Holy Sepulchre, low-lying and half-buried, as at Tonnerre, Chaource and Puiseaux, to evoke the Holy Sepulchre of Jerusalem. The donors often asked to be buried in the chapel near Christ's tomb, serene in the face of death and trusting in his promise of eternal felicity.

Other scenes drawn from the Passion cycle, such as the Bearing of the Cross or the Flagellation, are fixed in stone or wood by lifesize sculptures which seem to bring the Gospel narratives alive. These evocative images answered the desire of the faithful to ascribe to holy personages earthly emotions which they might thereby share.

Rodrigo Alemán.
Friar blessing a woman,
misericord of a choir stall.
After 1497.
Oak.
Cathedral of Plasencia.

"THE BITTER TASTE OF LIFE"

"The men of that time," writes Johan Huizinga, "always oscillate between the fear of hell and the most naïve joy, between cruelty and tenderness, between harsh asceticism and insane attachment to the delights of this world, between hatred and goodness, always running to extremes" (*The Waning of the Middle Ages*, 1924). A clear reflection of the contrasting character of medieval mentalities, late Gothic sculpture intimately mingles the sacred and profane. It expresses in turn a deep piety and an ungoverned fantasy: the taste for life and the obsessive fear of death.

Death is personified in the form of an emaciated corpse, a worm-eaten skeleton with its skin still sticking in places to the bones, as on the withered corpses (*transis*) figured on the tombs. This ghastly image which punctuates the dances of death was set up in the cemeteries to arouse scorn for the perishable flesh, to proclaim the ephemeral nature of earthly life and the equality of all before death. The glow of beauty and the youth of the body ineluctably yield to the ravages of old age; to sagging flesh, the prelude to death, as shown by Gregor Erhart's "Vanitas," a coloured woodcarving which presents back-to-back a pair of young people and an emaciated old woman. The moral idea is already defined here in a Renaissance manner.

However, physical death is but a passage leading on to eternal life if the menace of Hell is kept at bay. On funerary reliefs, therefore, the deceased are placed under the protection of patron saints and kneel before the divine image to beg its indulgence. On the Zlichov altarpiece carved by Master I. P. (National Gallery, Prague), the right hand of the knight is grasped by that of a frightful skeleton which makes ready to drag him off and brandishes an hour-glass. But Christ separates the two hands, not to save the knight from death, which is inevitable, but to lead him to eternal life. The presence of the Virgin and St Andrew interceding in favour of the deceased strengthens the meaning of this scene: the victory of death is temporary; faith is affirmed in divine mercy and in the resurrection of the body.

In counterpoint with macabre portrayals, images of life abound in religious art, expressing the tenderness of human feelings, the innocence of childhood, earthly joys and carnal beauty. As for profane subjects, they are scattered in profusion in the churches of Europe, where sacred subjects appear alongside burlesque or licentious scenes of low life. The late medieval examples best known today and preserved by the thousands are provided by the misericords of the choir stalls. From the picturesque incidents

Gregor Erhart.
"Vanitas."
Augsburg, about 1500.
Polychrome limewood.
Kunsthistorisches Museum, Vienna.

Erasmus Grasser.
Moorish dancer.
1480.
Polychrome limewood.
Städtisches Museum, Munich.

given up to earthly pleasures. But the intention was not always critical or instructive in images which invite to laughter and careless joy, like that of the loving couple consisting of an elegant and frivolous young woman and a seductive jester who clasps her tightly, carved on a towel rack by Arnt van Tricht. The profane sculptures adorning these objects of daily use, at once decorative and utilitarian, have seldom come down to us; they are often better known through paintings or prints. In Germany and the Netherlands, lamps made of reindeer antlers and carved allegorical or ornamental figures decked out town halls and might be the work of the greatest artists: in 1522 Veit Stoss carved a ceiling lamp with dragons for the town hall of Nuremberg, modelled on a drawing by Dürer.

Veit Stoss.
Ceiling lamp with antlers and dragons.
1522.
Polychrome limewood.
Germanisches Nationalmuseum, Nuremberg.

Arnt van Tricht.
Towel rack.
Kalkar, about 1540.
Polychrome oak.
Städtisches Museum Haus Koekkoek, Cleves (Kleve).

or aspects of everyday life to the comic, sometimes vulgar nature of fabliaux and proverbs; from the grotesque in satirical farces to the monstrous in tales and legends, an entire world of imagery echoes popular beliefs and local customs, a memorable witness to the richness of an oral culture which it is hard today to fully apprehend. Again and again the meaning of the scenes escapes us or seems rash to interpret (moralizing intention or conscious irreverence? naïve fantasy or deliberate impiety?).

Music and dance, the indispensable accompaniments to popular merrymaking and princely feasts, were present everywhere in church decoration as they were in private dwellings or civic buildings. Mural paintings, tapestries, prints, objects of personal use, all testify to the popularity of these images of pleasure and diversion.

In sculpture mention must be made of the outstanding series of Moorish dancers by Erasmus Grasser, carved in 1480 for the recreation room of the Munich town hall, and the reliefs ornamenting the balcony of the *Goldene Dachl* erected in 1500 at Innsbruck by Nikolaus Türing to commemorate the festivities held for the marriage of the Emperor Maximilian I to Bianca Sforza. The dancers vividly convey the excitement of the dance, the surrender of the body to rhythm and music which prompted the Church to try to curb such entertainments. The crossover steps, the arched or bowing postures, the contrasted gestures of arms and hands render the vivacity of the Morisco (morris dance), a fashionable dance from Spain punctuated by leaps, tapping of the feet and the sounds of bells tied to legs and wrists. The grimacing expressions of the face and the complicated costumes also recall the pranks and dumbshows of the clowns at princes' courts or of female impersonators of the jesters' feast. On that day, when all excesses were given free rein, the dance and its acrobatic pirouettes formed a part of the merrymaking.

The jester, with his ass-eared cap, coxcomb and bell, recurs often in pictorial representations to denounce the disorders of society or parody the waywardness of men

LATE GOTHIC

After the gradual waning of international Gothic, new formal languages developed during the course of the fifteenth century with the emergence of "national" styles. While Renaissance Italy followed its own path, in the Germanic regions and the Netherlands, in France, England and Spain, Gothic traditions were revitalized by powerful innovative currents continuing down to the Reformation and sometimes even extending further into the sixteenth century. The directions taken, contradictory or complementary, swung between tension and sweetness, exaggeration and simplicity, caricature and inwardness as the case might be, gradually paving the way for the adoption of the first Italianisms, as in France, or on the contrary promoting almost "pre-baroque" expressive values, as in the Germanic world.

Nicholas of Leyden.
Woman's head (the Sibyl of Tibur?) from the doorway of the Chancellery of Strasbourg.
1463-1464. Red sandstone.
Liebighaus, Frankfurt.

THE GERMANIC WORLD AND THE NETHERLANDS

NICHOLAS OF LEYDEN

Detectable before the mid-fifteenth century, the renewal of style was essentially achieved in the work of Nicholas of Leyden, which lies at the very source of late Gothic sculpture (*Spätgotik*) in the southern part of the Empire. In Swabia, Hans Multscher (recorded in Ulm from 1427; died before 1467) had already begun to stiffen the pose of his figure carvings, with their compact and solid silhouettes; to harden the pliant folds and soft curves of international Gothic, on which he nevertheless remained dependent. The break was finally made by Nicholas of Leyden. Probably of Dutch origin as his name

indicates, he was also called, more rarely, Nicolaus Gerhaert after his father. Nothing is known of his training and we have records for only eleven years of his life, from 1462 to 1473; years marked by a few undisputed works (only four are extant), by his arrival in Strasbourg in 1462 at the latest, and by his departure in 1467 for the court of the Emperor Frederic III in Vienna and Wiener Neustadt, where he died in 1473. That is little indeed, measured against this remarkable sculptor's personality.

The tomb of Archbishop Jakob von Sierck at Trier, signed and dated 1462, is already a work of his maturity. The plastic density of the recumbent figure is well served by the sweep of the draperies, hollowed or distended with sharp and broken folds conferring live movement upon this tomb effigy of an all too often static type, formerly

Nicholas of Leyden. Tomb of Archbishop Jakob von Sierck. 1462. Stone. Dom- und Diözesanmuseum, Trier.

Nicholas of Leyden.
Leaning bust of a man.
About 1467.
Red sandstone.
Musée de l'Œuvre Notre-Dame,
Strasbourg.

accompanied by a withered corpse effigy. The doorway of the Strasbourg Chancellery, erected in 1463-1464, was ornamented by Nicholas of Leyden with a Virgin and Child, the armorial bearings of the town, and two busts: an old man and a young woman probably representing the Emperor Augustus and the Sibyl of Tibur, who were known from earlier casts (only the two heads in red sandstone are preserved, in Strasbourg and Frankfurt). The stock theme of the half-length figure leaning on a window ledge, whether handled in painting as in the portraits by Van Eyck or inserted in an architectural setting as in the Jacques Cœur palace at Bourges, is here completely remodelled. Leaning over the windowsill, advancing a shoulder and inclining the head in a skilful play of contrasting lines, the two figures of the Chancellery have a mobile posture that lends an inner dynamism to the carved bust and suggests spatial recession. The Epitaph of a Canon in Strasbourg Cathedral, signed and dated 1464, and the admirable Leaning Bust of a Man in the Notre-Dame Museum of Works, attributed to Nicholas of Leyden and sometimes regarded as his self-portrait, give the same sensation of life, thanks to the naturalness of the gestures and the movement of the bodies. Added to the delicate rendering of facial expression–the attentive gaze of the

Emperor and the Sibyl, the lowered eyes of the leaning man sunk in thought–is a sharp and exact treatment of the features which inscribes in detail on the stone surface every line, every wrinkle, every fold of flesh. This focus on the human, going beyond the mere transcription of reality, places Nicholas of Leyden in the line of the great innovative painters of the southern Netherlands and in more distant descent from sculptors like Claus Sluter. The elongated body of Christ on the cross at Baden-Baden, another signed work dated 1467, takes over devices used by Van Eyck and Rogier van der Weyden, also disseminated by the prints of Master E. S. The Crucifix of the Nördlingen altarpiece (1462), because of its kinship with that of Baden-Baden, has been attributed to Nicholas of Leyden and would thus be his only extant woodcarving. His altarpiece for the cathedral of Constance (1465-1467) was destroyed at the Reformation and the other figure carvings of the Nördlingen altarpiece are ascribed to an anonymous Strasbourg master directly in touch with Nicholas, the maker of the Dangolsheim Virgin and Child. The slim and pliant silhouette of the Virgin is concealed behind the flaps of the cloak flung far out from the body, which stands back, creating empty spaces that seem to penetrate the sculptured form.

This new and complex plastic conception, worked out in Strasbourg and adopted along the Upper Rhine, was diffused through South Germany by the prints that propagated the Upper Rhenish repertory of forms: it constitutes one of the dominant features of late German Gothic sculpture. The widespread use of limewood, light and soft, allowed sculptors to carve freely and deeply in the material in order to chisel with virtuosity those intricate forms so characteristic of Germany, and to release broad flights of drapery rhythmically broken by folds with sharp edges and acute angles.

THE "LEANING BUST" THEME

Fully to appreciate the extent of Nicholas of Leyden's influence, we may take as a point of reference the theme of the "leaning bust." In Strasbourg itself and in the Upper Rhine, the popularity of this theme was considerable

Anton Pilgram.
Self-portrait from the decoration of the pulpit. 1515. Stone.
Cathedral of St Stephen, Vienna.

Façade decoration of the palace
of Jacques Cœur
at Bourges (partially restored).
Mid-15th century.

269

among the the great master's followers. But they seized above all on the anecdotal character of these "spectator" figures and lingered over the minute delineation of human features, sometimes almost trivially emphasized to the detriment of inner life. Expressive power prevailed in the work of Nicholas of Haguenau, recorded in Strasbourg from 1485 to 1526, who carried out varied and important works such as the altarpiece of the high altar of the cathedral, the *Fronaltar* (1501), and who is credited with the carvings of the famous Issenheim altarpiece (Unterlinden Museum, Colmar). His contemporary, Veit Wagner, active from 1492 at Haguenau and Strasbourg, also repeated the leaning bust theme, almost caricaturally, for the altarpiece, commissioned in 1500, for the Strasbourg church of Saint-Pierre-le-Vieux.

In the footsteps of Nicholas of Leyden, in Constance and in Vienna, sculptors like Heinrich Iselin (active at Constance from 1477 until his death in 1513) and Anton Pilgram (active at Heilbronn, Brno and Vienna from 1481 to 1515) interpreted in their turn the traditional model introduced into the decoration of stalls, pulpits and tabernacles. However, in Ulm Cathedral the leaning figures, attributed to different sculptors, which surmount the reveals of the stalls commissioned from the joiner Jörg Syrlin the Elder in 1469 and completed in 1474, adopt only the formal aspect of the subject and betray a spirit alien to the style that issued from the Strasbourg milieu.

Nicholas of Haguenau.
Leaning bust of a man.
About 1500.
Polychrome limewood.
Musée de l'Œuvre Notre-Dame, Strasbourg.

Attributed to Michael Erhart.
The Libyan Sibyl on a choir stall.
Ulm, 1469-1474.
Oak.
Ulm Cathedral.

Veit Wagner.
St Egidius and St Benedict from the altarpiece
of Saint-Pierre-le-Vieux in Strasbourg.
1500-1501. Limewood and cherry-wood.
Musée des Beaux-Arts, Mulhouse.

TYROL AND AUSTRIA

The echo of Strasbourg art reverberated in different ways in the Alpine regions in the late fifteenth century: distinctly in Austria and around Constance, Zurich and Fribourg in Switzerland; more discreetly in the Tyrol. The personality of Michael Pacher, who is first mentioned at Bruneck in South Tyrol in 1467 and died at Salzburg in 1498, was indeed original. From his workshop came several carved and painted altarpieces intended for Tyrolean churches like that of Gries (1471-1475) or for more distant places: such are the famous altarpiece of St Wolfgang (1471-1481) in the Salzkammergut and that of Salzburg (1484-1498), destroyed in 1709. Stylistic divergences between the painted panels and the sculptured sections led to the mistaken belief that Pacher was not both the painter and sculptor, as he is now generally regarded to have been. While the scenes viewed in perspective on the St Wolfgang wing panels reveal specific contacts with Italian painting, in particular the works of Jacopo Bellini and Andrea Mantegna, showing a conception of space already inspired by the Renaissance, the luxuriant Coronation of the Virgin which occupies the central panel is one of the great masterpieces of late Gothic. Its style derives mainly from the art of the Swabian sculptor Hans Multscher, represented, precisely in the South Tyrol, by the Sterzing altarpiece (1456-1458), without overlooking some Strasbourg innovations of the 1460s. The scene forms a complex whole of a profuse but skilfully ordered richness centred around God the Father and the kneeling Virgin. The monumental figures are enveloped in ample garments with breaks and tubular folds running through them which form broad, well-defined transversal lines between the smooth areas. The broad fleshy faces, typical of Pacher, resemble those of the painted figures which also display the same plastic density as the sculptures.

The influence of this so personal art was felt by the Tyrolean sculptors of the following generations, like Hans Klocker, mentioned at Brixen from 1478 to 1500, who ran a very active workshop in which many altarpieces were crafted. However, Klocker can be clearly distinguished from Pacher, in particular by his more incisive manner and the more angular forms of his sculptures.

Pacher was also known to the woodcarver who, between about 1491 and 1498, made the Kefermarkt altarpiece in Upper Austria: he is identified tentatively with Martin Kriechbaum, recorded as working in Passau from 1473 to 1508. His style bears in addition the imprint of Strasbourg formulas transmitted either by the intermediary of Austrian followers of Nicholas of Leyden or directly, since the master probably came to Passau in 1469. But the nervous mobility of the figures in the central panel of the Kefermarkt altarpiece, their tormented faces, the almost metallic crumpling of the draperies hollowed by violent shadows and deployed in space, and the sharp chiselling of the accessories and decorative elements, have no equivalents. Everything points to a highly singular talent which unfortunately is no longer represented today except by this altarpiece and the Deacon statuette in the Louvre.

Hans Klocker.
St George slaying the dragon.
About 1485.
Polychrome cembra pine.
Formerly Staatliche Museen,
Berlin (destroyed in
the Second World War).

Altarpiece on the high altar.
Passau (?), about 1491-1498. Limewood.
Parish church, Kefermarkt (Austria).

Altarpiece on the high altar.
Central panel: St Wolfgang between St Peter and St Christopher.
Passau (?), about 1491–1498.
Limewood.
Parish church, Kefermarkt (Austria).

Michael Pacher. Altarpiece on the high altar.
Central panel: Coronation of the Virgin between St Wolfgang and St Benedict.
1471–1478.
Polychrome pine.
Parish church, St Wolfgang (Austria).

FRANCONIA

Upper and Lower Franconia display contrasting faces in their two main art centres, Nuremberg and Würzburg, where two outstanding creators, Veit Stoss and Tilman Riemenschneider, occupied the first rank.

At Nuremberg, after the middle of the fifteenth century, the influence of Hans Multscher, which confirmed a traditional taste for calm and compact figures with mild expressions, was challenged by the influence of the Upper Rhine transmitted through the prints of Master E. S. and Martin Schongauer or by direct contact with actual works (Nördlingen is not far from Nuremberg). It was a mobile style, angular but marked by mildness and a fragile grace, that prevailed in Nuremberg in the years 1470-1480, and which is notably illustrated by the sculptured parts of the altarpieces painted by Michael Wolgemut (Nuremberg, 1434 or 1437-1519). Veit Stoss shattered this relatively tranquil art.

Master Pavel of Levoča.
Altarpiece on the high altar.
Detail of a wing panel: the martyrdom of St John.
1508-1517.
Polychrome wood.
Church of St James, Levoča (Slovakia).

VEIT STOSS

The training and early career of this sculptor born at Horn on the Neckar, who left Nuremberg in 1477 for Cracow where he stayed nearly twenty years, remain obscure. At all events the teachings of Strasbourg were assimilated and transgressed by the passionate, deeply original temperament of Veit Stoss.

His two chief undertakings at Cracow were the marble tomb of King Casimir IV and the great altarpiece in polychrome wood in the church of St Mary which he and his workshop carved from 1477 to 1489. In the central scene of the Death of the Virgin the dramatic emphasis and intensity of expressions, heightened by the gesticulation and mimicry of the figures, are admirable. The bodies disappear beneath tumultuous flights of draperies as if buffeted by a violent wind, but an extreme care is lavished on faces and hands, chiselled with the prodigious virtuosity that was the master's hallmark. The powerful and craggy features of the apostles, the full oval of the Virgin's delicate face, the exuberant curls of the voluminous beards and hair were the many characteristic features displayed as well in the works Veit Stoss carried out after returning to Nuremberg in 1496.

There he worked in sandstone to produce the three scenes of the St Sebaldus Passion commissioned by Paul Volckammer (1499), which vied with the anecdotal reliefs of the stone carver Adam Kraft, maker of the celebrated tabernacle in the Nuremberg church of St Lawrence (1493-1496). But Stoss carved mainly in limewood, which he coated either with an ultra-refined polychromy, as in the Annunciation (1517-1518) hanging in the choir of the St Lorenzkirche, or, preferring to bring out the material itself, with faint coloured highlights. Several figure carvings attesting to the growing preference for this process in the early sixteenth century rank among the master's finest creations, namely Tobias and the Archangel Raphael in the Nuremberg museum, St Andrew in the Nuremberg church of St Sebaldus or St Roch in Florence celebrated by Vasari in the *Lives*, which in each case exhibit new formal inventions. The broken and arbitrary lines of the draperies show with a still more heightened spiritedness in the copperplate engravings made by the sculptor.

Unlike the Nuremberg bronze-founders, Peter Vischer the Elder (1460-1529) and his sons, Stoss remained a stranger to the Italian novelties introduced by Albrecht Dürer (Nuremberg, 1471-1528). Stoss's last work, the altarpiece of the Carmelites (1520-1523), today in Bamberg, once again affirms his mastery and the force of his personal genius, which had a tremendous impact on many sculptors, whether pupils or followers, such as Master Pavel, active at Levoča in Slovakia.

Veit Stoss.
The Annunciation, detail of the Virgin with the dove of the Holy Ghost.
1517–1518.
Polychrome limewood.
St Lorenzkirche, Nuremberg.

Veit Stoss.
Altarpiece on the high altar.
Detail of the central panel: the death of the Virgin.
1477-1489.
Polychrome wood.
Church of St Mary, Cracow.

TILMAN RIEMENSCHNEIDER

The progress of the long, fertile and illustrious career of Tilman Riemenschneider is well known–a rarity in the Middle Ages–thanks to the abundance of documents and works that have been preserved. Born at Heiligenstadt in Thuringia towards 1460, journeyman in 1483 and master in 1485 at Würzburg, where he was in charge of a large workshop receiving extensive and numerous commissions, the sculptor held an established position in the city, of which he was mayor in 1520-1521.

The conditions of his apprenticeship and first professional engagements, however, are unknown. His first recorded commission, in 1490, for the parish church of Münnerstadt, was the Mary Magdalene altarpiece installed in 1492 and today dismembered. There followed the sandstone statues of Adam and Eve (1491-1493) for the gate of the chapel of the Virgin, the tomb of the prince-bishop Rudolph von Scherenberg (1496-1499) at Würzburg and that of the Emperor Henry II (1499-1513) at Bamberg, as well as many other sculptures in stone, marble, alabaster or wood and several large altarpieces, some still preserved *in situ*, such as those of the Holy Blood (*Heiligblutaltar*) at Rothenburg (1499-1505) and of the Virgin at Creglingen (around 1505).

The stylistic vocabulary of Riemenschneider is easy to characterize. His feminine figures, with some minor variants, all have a slender stature–narrow bust, frail limbs, fine hands–, hair set in peaceful waves, a sweet face with smooth modelling and a broad flat forehead, eyes slanted towards the temples and circled by a fold of skin, a long nose and small mouth with a slight swelling of the lower lip. The masculine faces, built on the same plan, with, of course, thicker and more rugged features, present some distinct types found in many combinations in Riemenschneider's various works, as witnessed by the apostles of Rothenburg and Creglingen. The play of draperies, animated by uneven folds broken into multiple facets, is complicated but without excessive agitation. The calm features, delicate gestures and tranquil attitudes show a melancholy sweetness even when emotion or pain are expressed.

An extreme care is taken over details and the treatment of the surface. The limewood is often left exposed and merely accented by a partial polychromy which brings out the subtlety of the polished volumes and emphasizes the finesse of the varied motifs barely chiselled on the surface of the wood. The process was used, in particular, for the altarpiece of Münnerstadt, afterwards painted by Veit Stoss between 1502 and 1504 (this colouring has now disappeared).

Tilman Riemenschneider.
Altarpiece of the Holy Blood.
Detail of the central panel: the Last Supper.
Würzburg, 1499-1505.
Limewood.
Church of Sankt Jakob. Rothenburg.

Tilman Riemenschneider.
Adam and Eve from the gate
of the Chapel of the Virgin, Würzburg.
1491–1493.
Sandstone.
Mainfränkisches Museum, Würzburg.

The sources of this sensitive and lyrical art may be assumed to lie in Swabian tradition and in the artist's familiarity with the sculpture of the Upper Rhine. But the original talent of Riemenschneider, working free of external influences, created a new style which enjoyed a brilliant and prolonged success. In his workshop the sculptor imposed his style on his fellow-journeymen and on his apprentices, all the more so in that he kept consistently, in their joint undertakings, to the same physical types described above. The former disciples of the master, established outside Würzburg, and the imitators inspired by his works, spread his stylistic formulas widely throughout Franconia, Thuringia and Saxony.

SWABIA

The artistic landscape of Swabia in the third quarter of the fifteenth century was profoundly marked by the art of the Ulm sculptor Hans Multscher, who died in 1467. On that tradition built the new generations active towards the end of the century, from which emerged the personality of Michael Erhart, whose name appears in Ulm from 1469 to 1522. With the exception of the Crucifix of

Gregor Erhart.
Mary Magdalene, known as "La Belle Allemande."
Augsburg, about 1500.
Polychrome limewood.
Musée du Louvre, Paris.

Schwäbisch Hall signed and dated 1494, practically all the sculptures which documents ascribe to him have disappeared, as for example the figures of the high altar of Ulm Cathedral, commissioned from the joiner Jörg Syrlin the Elder in 1473 and destroyed during the Reformation. For that reason the attribution to him of doubtful works continually sparks off fresh controversies.

Erhart is, however, credited by general consent with the Virgin of Mercy from Ravensburg (State Museums, Berlin) who shields two groups of the faithful from divine wrath beneath the skirts of her protective mantle. Her svelte and upright figure, scarcely bowed, exhibits firm outlines and a placid sweetness inherited from Multscher and alien to the open and dynamic volumes characteristic of Upper Rhenish sculptures. Erhart introduced a new grace evoked by the elegant but reserved bearing of the Virgin, the delicacy of her gesture and her fine face carried on a long thin neck and skilfully set within the round outline of the veil. As with Riemenschneider, his search for an idealized beauty is expressed in the creation of images of the Virgin Mary: harmonious, serene, almost disembodied. At Blaubeuren, the figure carvings of the altarpiece dated 1493 and 1494 and probably made in the workshop of Michael Erhart in collaboration with his son Gregor (born at Ulm, died at Augsburg in 1540), possess more ample forms and drapery and have more broadly modelled faces; but they present a nobility of tone and a quiet grace in the same spirit.

The Ulm workshops, numerous and very active around 1500, adopted and enriched this Erhartian language, reflected in the languid look of many figures with subtly balanced attitudes, full but elegant forms and gentle features. Partial inheritors of this style, the works of Niklaus Weckmann (mentioned at Ulm from 1481 to 1526) and his workshop revived the types of drapery animated by more complex folds with voluminous bulges between deep hollows (Thalheim altarpiece). The rapid propagation of formulas devised by Weckmann, repeated or interpreted by his pupils and followers throughout all Swabia and even beyond, maintained a relatively uniform, at times somewhat monotonous style for several decades. In the least successful works the forms verged on flabbiness and the expressions seemed drowsy, which rendered the fashionable types uninteresting.

The refined and subtly shaded art of Daniel Mauch (Ulm, 1477–Liège, 1540) led to a similar infatuation. Mauch, coming from an Ulm milieu, interpreted the traditional elements in a personal manner, inventing his own compositions and intensifying the lyricism of expressions. In the Holy Kinship altarpiece of Bieselbach, signed and dated 1510, which he chose to leave in monochrome, he also adopted Renaissance decorative motifs transmitted by Augsburg, which was rapidly penetrated by southern influences.

At Augsburg settled Mauch's contemporary, Gregor Erhart, whose name is mentioned in this city from 1494 onward, after his presumed participation in the altarpiece of Blaubeuren, and who held the foremost place there at the beginning of the sixteenth century. On the basis of comparison with the Kaisheim Virgin of Mercy, a work authenticated as his but unfortunately destroyed in 1845, several sculptures are now attributed to Gregor Erhart, in particular the celebrated Mary Magdalene in the Louvre, also called "La Belle Allemande," for which a woodcut by Dürer from around 1500 may have served as a model. The

harmonious and quite earthly nudity of the saint, at once emphasized and concealed by the long hair, and the elegance of her pose pivoting in a slight *contrapposto*, reveal a desire for carnal beauty already in the Renaissance spirit and very far from the still Gothic interpretation which Riemenschneider had given to the same theme some ten years before.

Michael Erhart.
Virgin of Mercy from Ravensburg.
Ulm, about 1480-1490.
Polychrome limewood.
Staatliche Museen, Berlin.

Adriaen van Wesel.
Music-making angels and Joseph, fragment of a Nativity from
the altarpiece of the brotherhood of Our Lady at 's Hertogenbosch
(Bois-le-Duc).
Utrecht, 1475-1477. Oak.
Rijksmuseum, Amsterdam.

NETHERLANDS, WESTERN AND NORTHERN GERMANY

In this rapid survey of German lands where the richest talents too often leave secondary but important masters in the shade, the West and North of Germany and their ties with the Netherlands may be referred to only in broad terms.

The episcopal city of Utrecht was the most active art centre of the northern Netherlands in the second half of the fifteenth century. Gradually moving away from the international Gothic style and receptive to the influences of the southern Netherlands, in particular Brabant sculpture and Flemish painting, the art of this city had its own specific language. Several sculptors are recorded in Utrecht, such as Jan Nude, mentioned from 1450 to 1494, and Adriaen van Wesel from 1447 to 1489-1490. The latter carved numerous altarpieces, notably the one, now dismembered, for the brotherhood of Our Lady at 's Hertogenbosch (1475-1477). As in the southern Netherlands, the scenes were composed of small polychrome wood reliefs, juxtaposed in the compartments of the shrine, and affirming a pronounced taste for anecdote, for concrete and picturesque elements. Adriaen van Wesel caught the familiar gestures and the expressive features of his figures with a charming vivacity, but also with a sweetness that places him still in the mainstream of international Gothic.

His contemporaries often handled their forms with a certain hardness. Thus many feminine figures, slim and straight, combine stiff drapery falling in cylindrical folds with delicate and gracious facial types, and show extreme accuracy in rendering the finely chiselled details in oak or

stone (St Ursula in the Beguine convent of Amsterdam, attributed hypothetically to Jan Nude; male and female saints of the Master of Koudewater).

This elegant and biting style had direct extensions in the regions of the Lower Rhine, close geographically and historically, since Cleves and Kalkar formerly belonged to the bishopric of Utrecht, itself part of the archbishopric of Cologne.

The most influential personality here was that of Master Arnt, who had a workshop at Kalkar (from 1460), then at Zwolle (from 1484 until his death in 1492), which carried out important commissions such as the choir stalls for the church of the Franciscans at Cleves (1474) and the altarpieces of St George (around 1480) and of the Passion (1490-1492), for the high altar of the St Nicholas church at Kalkar. The mark of Arnt's style, at once tense and gracious, linear and solid, and of his incisive treatment of the surface, was determinant for the sculptors of Kalkar and Cleves, Jan van Halderen and Dries Holthuys, and also influenced the chief master established in Cologne at the end of the fifteenth century, Tilmann van der Bruch (first mentioned in 1467). A new stylistic modulation was later added by much sought-after sculptors like Heinrich Douvermann (mentioned at Cleves and Kalkar from 1510 onwards), the Master of Elsloo (active in the Middle Meuse, early sixteenth century) or Arnt van Tricht (active c. 1522-1560 at Antwerp and Kalkar).

In the north, too, the influence of the art of the Netherlands made itself felt after the abandonment of the international Gothic style, giving a peculiar appearance to sculpture, distinct from that of southern Germany. Trade relations and the growing wealth of the Hanseatic city of Lübeck promoted, in addition to the penetration of Western models, the activity of painters' and sculptors' workshops and the export of their creations to Scandinavia

Master Arnt.
Dominican saint
(St Thomas Aquinas?).
Lower Rhine, about 1490.
Oak.
Kunstmuseum, Düsseldorf.

Bernt Notke. Calvary. 1477. Polychrome wood. Lübeck Cathedral.

and the countries bordering the Baltic Sea. Of Pomeranian origin and probably trained at Tournai in Hainaut, Bernt Notke made a name for himself in this important art centre. He is mentioned as a painter in 1467 after he had painted a Dance of Death on canvas, some hundred feet long, for the Marienkirche in Lübeck. But he is best known as a sculptor. Here his work includes the monumental Calvary (1477) commissioned by Bishop Albert Krummedik, erected in the middle of the nave of Lübeck Cathedral; the gigantic St George in the church of St Nicholas (Storkyrka) in Stockholm, completed in 1490; and several altarpieces like that of the church of the Holy Ghost at Tallinn in Estonia (1483). Beyond general formal

relationships with the Netherlands, Notke's plastic language shows peculiar accents of which the expressive force is tempered, as in the Lübeck Calvary, by the gentleness of facial features and restrained gestures, even in pain; by the refinement of the carved details, by the polychromy and sumptuousness of the ornamental elements.

Notke's many pupils and followers freely repeated the master's formulas. Alone, Henning van der Heide, mentioned at Lübeck from 1485 to his death in 1521, possesses a more personal tone. The renewal of style, however, was accomplished by another generation of sculptors: that of Claus Berg and Benedikt Dreyer, belonging to the final stage of late Gothic.

Antoine Le Moiturier.
Angel holding up the cross
from the Last Judgment
altarpiece
in the collegiate church of
Saint-Pierre in Avignon.
1463. Stone.
Musée du Petit Palais,
Avignon.

FRANCE
THE HERITAGE
OF CLAUS SLUTER

It is tempting to consider fifteenth-century Burgundian sculpture solely from the angle of its dependence on Sluter—so evident is the great master's mark—and to exaggerate the degree of his influence outside the boundaries of Burgundy. That, however, would be inaccurate, for the nuances introduced by the sculptor's successors at the head of the ducal workshop of Dijon diversified and transformed even the specifically Sluterian language. And in the other French provinces, the taste for individualized faces, for ample forms and draperies, did not necessarily signify a Burgundian influence but also followed the general trends of the period.

The temperament of Claus de Werwe, who completed the tomb of Philip the Bold after the death of his uncle Claus Sluter in 1406, opposed Sluterian vehemence by a calmer sensibility, full of a lyricism tempered with gentleness, as revealed in the Christ on the Cross at Saint-Bénigne in Dijon, which is attributed to him. Jean de La Huerta, of Aragonese origin, who after Claus de Werwe's death in 1439 was made responsible in 1443 for carving the tomb of John the Fearless and Margaret of Bavaria, brought more forcefulness and complexity into his creations; more search for effect into the drapery of his figures.

Some fifty years after Champmol, the Virgin and Child and the John the Baptist in the church of Rouvres, probably carved by Jean de La Huerta for the mayor of Dijon, Philippe Mâchefoing, still followed in the tradition of Sluter's works but without retaining their unusual vitality, despite the remarkable beauty of the flowing draperies, owing to a certain heaviness acquired by the figure types.

Numerous sculptures of the first half of the fifteenth century have been located in the two masters' sphere of influence by comparison with rare authenticated works like the angels and mourners of the ducal tombs. A charac-

teristic series of Virgins of meek aspect—small, thick-lidded eyes, slightly elongated and pointed nose, ball-shaped chin and round cheeks–, enveloped with clothes that are heavy but animated by simple and subsiding folds, seems akin to the art of Claus de Werwe (Virgin and Child of Meilly-sur-Rouvres). Other feminine figures in stone or alabaster exhibit square faces with more sharply defined features, often slightly sulky expressions and hair sprinkled with little hook-like curls, typical of the sculptures attributed to the chisel of Jean de La Huerta.

Reproduced in a workshop or imitated by various hands, the same models with minor variants were thus adopted for the facial types, the iconographic formulas and compositional schemes of the draperies (Virgin and Child statues at Auxonne, about 1447, at Pluvault, in the cathedral of Autun and at Sully). The short silhouette of some Virgins could be particularly broadened by the movement of the large mantle passing over the free arm, which moves far out from the body. This type of drapery, distantly derived from the art of Champmol, gave rise to different stylistic interpretations of high quality (Virgin and Child at Bézouotte, at Poligny, and in the rue de la Porte-aux-Lions in Dijon, today in the Louvre). But the less skilful Burgundian sculptors did not always prevent the solid plasticity of these figures from becoming ponderous, the fullness of the drapery from verging on heaviness, and their expressive values from lapsing into monotony.

Attributed to Jean de La Huerta.
Virgin and Child.
About 1448. Stone.
Church of Rouvres-en-Plaine,
near Dijon.

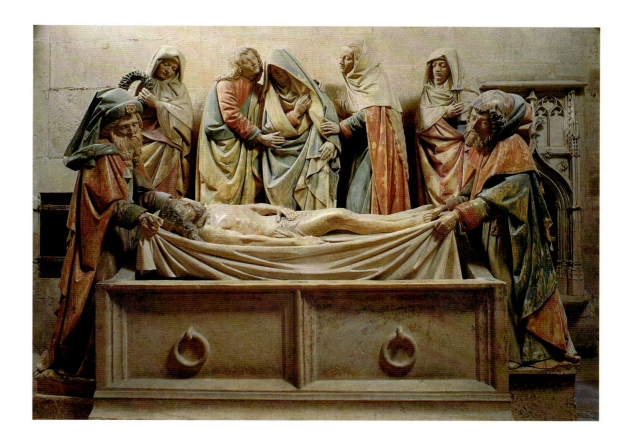

Workshop of
Antoine Le Moiturier (?).
Entombment from the local
Carmelite monastery.
Set in place in 1490.
Polychrome stone.
Church of Notre-Dame,
Semur-en-Auxois.

THE "EASING UP"

After the middle of the fifteenth century a new spirit gradually came over sculpture, a phenomenon which the art historian Louis Courajod has called *la détente*, the "easing up" of French art, in order to stress the contrast between the tension and emphasis of Claus Sluter and his Burgundian following and that tendency towards quieting down, towards the search for grace and equilibrium. In reality this new style, more complex than a simple reaction to an opposing current, was nourished by traditions from the beginning of the century, still hardy after several decades. And although this later art sometimes shows a hint of Netherlandish influence, it totally diverges from the experiments being carried out in the Germanic lands.

Jacques Morel, often considered to be the prime mover behind the "easing up," ensured the continuity of the muffled and peaceful manner of the early fifteenth century, accompanied by the habitual penchant for individualized features and heavy fabrics with soft and ample folds. Among the works created during the itinerant career which led Morel from Lyons, where he is mentioned in 1418, to Toulouse, Rodez, Avignon, Souvigny and Angers, where he died in 1453 in the service of King René of Anjou, there is preserved only the funerary monument of the Duke of Bourbon at Souvigny (Allier), commissioned in 1448 on the model of the tombs of Champmol.

The latter left Dijon in 1456, and it was Antoine Le Moiturier of Avignon, assumed to be the pupil of Jacques Morel, who in 1466 was given the job of completing the tomb of John the Fearless and who helped to reorient the Burgundian style in accordance with the general trend towards a "relaxed" art. The two angels surviving from the altarpiece, now destroyed, of Saint-Pierre-le-Vieux at Avignon, commissioned from Le Moiturier in 1463, enable us to define the plastic language of this sculptor who simplified forms, accentuating the angular lines and large empty areas of the breaking folds; precisely delineated the fringes and braid of the clothing on the surface of the stone; and enhanced the sweet and childlike expressions of the rounded faces. There was no superfluous complication in this style, quiet and sober but without roughness, in which the formal vocabulary, blending with the specifically Burgundian tradition, was abundantly and diversely utilized by the prolific workshops of the Auxois and the Autunois in the late fifteenth century.

Several sculptured groups are doubtfully attributed to Le Moiturier, including the Entombment of Semur-en-Auxois (1490). On the other hand, the famous tomb of Philippe Pot (Louvre, Paris) cannot be from the master's hand: the idea of enlarging the mourners almost to lifesize and making them carry the slab on which the tomb effigy lies is daring, and testifies to an original conception that gives the old formula a new lease of life; but in detail the execution is weak and the handling dry and perfunctory.

Jacques Morel.
Tomb of Duke Charles of Bourbon and his wife
Agnes of Burgundy. Commissioned in 1448. Marble.
Church of Saint-Pierre, Souvigny.

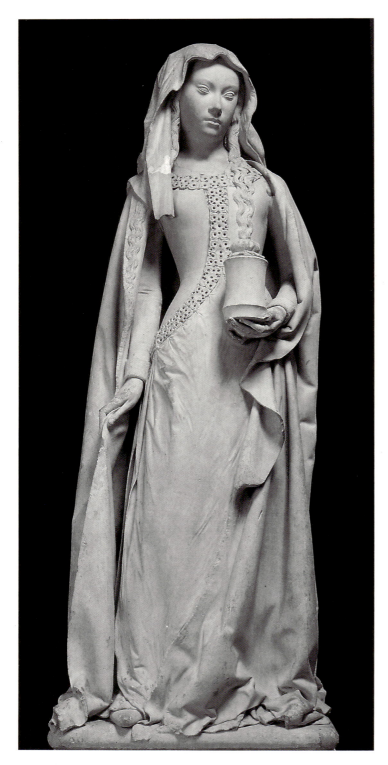

Mary Magdalene.
Bourbonnais, late 15th century. Stone.
Church of Saint-Pierre, Montluçon.

LOIRE VALLEY

In the regions washed by the Loire and its tributaries, the "easing up" of French art made itself felt with a particular brilliance, thanks to royal, princely or bourgeois patrons who quickened the art centres of Berry, the Bourbonnais and Touraine. There, too, the artistic climate of the early fifteenth century had paved the way for this later flowering.

At Bourges, after the death of Jean de Berry in 1416, halting the work on the ducal building sites, the workshops kept up some activity, which increased with the installation there of the royal court in 1422 and the great undertakings of Jacques Cœur at mid-century. Father of

the celebrated Michel Colombe, the sculptor Philippe Colombe, whose authenticated works have not survived, is recorded at Bourges from 1434 until his death in 1457. Jean de Cambrai, the Duke's image-maker, died only in 1439. We may connect with various aspects of his style, rooted moreover in the fourteenth century, several anonymous sculptures, preserved from this first part of the century, in which the density and solidity of forms and the calm rhythm of solid folds prevail, without excluding a tender and charming vivaciousness in the childlike faces.

In Touraine, too, a measured power, far removed from all dramatization, a naturalism exact without excessive attention to detail and a quiet gentleness reigned from the middle of the century in the statuary which revealed indisputable affinities with the art of the painter Jean Fouquet, established in Tours, where he died around 1480. Thus the energetic handling of the Virgin and St John on Calvary, originating perhaps in the abbey of Beaugerais, has often been related to the exceptional plastic and monumental sense shown in Fouquet's painted figures. Several oak sculptures, images of worship or decorative panels, bear witness to the activity of woodcarvers at Tours, also certified by documents. Works in stone, like the angels of the tomb of Jeanne de Montjean at Bueil (around 1460, Archaeological Society of Touraine) or the statues of the castle chapel of Châteaudun consecrated in 1464, present equivalent stylistic characteristics, later heightened and enriched in the Touraine workshop of Michel Colombe.

Colombe's creations, known from texts, at Bourges where his name appears in 1457 and at Moulins where in 1484 he worked for the luxury-loving Duke of Bourbon, have unfortunately been lost. They would doubtless have enabled us to evaluate the role of this sculptor, coming in fact from the Berry milieu, in the evolution of a specific-

▷ Virgin and
St John on Calvary,
from the
abbey of Beaugerais (?),
Touraine, late 15th century.
Walnut with traces
of polychromy.
The Metropolitan Museum
of Art, New York (Virgin)
and Musée du Louvre,
Paris (St John).

◁ Attributed
to Jean de Chartres.
St Anne and the Virgin as
a child from the chapel of
the Château de Chantelle.
Bourbonnais, 1500-1503.
Stone.
Musée du Louvre, Paris.

ally Bourbonnais style, illustrated by many sculptures from the time of the master's sojourn or of later date, such as the works of his disciples who remained at Moulins after his departure around 1490. There, notably, was elaborated a particular type of feminine face, regularly oval, sometimes slightly plump, with small features, a large convex forehead and almond-shaped eyes under blurred eyebrows, a type that recalls the meek-looking Madonnas painted around the same period by the Brussels painter Jean Hey, the Master of Moulins. To the serenity of expressions, the harmonious balance of forms and calm fall of the draperies, is added the exquisite delicacy of gestures that emphasize the fineness of the hands, and a painstaking handling of details of dress chiselled in the stone.

Majesty prevails in the monumental statues of St Peter, St Anne and St Susanna from the Château de Chantelle, carved in the very first years of the sixteenth century, probably by Jean de Chartres, Colombe's chief collaborator at Moulins. But the face of the Virgin as a child, standing beside St Anne, further refines the type that had become habitual, and the elegance of Susanna reveals a mind that is almost worldly. Bearing witness to the influence of these formulas, even beyond the boundaries of Bourbonnais, many series of saints show kinship in their slender silhouettes, delicate face and informal grace tinged with preciousness and coquetry. One of the most famous is the Mary Magdalene of Montluçon.

The new tonality that henceforth marked Bourbonnais sculpture is part of the general evolution of the Loire country under the dominance of the art of Michel Colombe, which it is at last possible to apprehend. The

Virgin and Child ("The Education of the Child").
From the chapel of Longvé.
Bourbonnais, late 15th century. Stone with traces of polychromy.
Musée du Louvre, Paris.

tomb of François II and Marguerite de Foix at Nantes, ordered in 1499 by Queen Anne of Brittany and made from 1502 to 1507 in the workshop at Tours, where Colombe's name is mentioned from 1496, enables us to define the master's style at the close of his life. If it draws extensively on the traditional Loire heritage, it also introduces innovative conceptions blending smoothly with the recent contributions of the Italian Renaissance. In the Nantes tomb, Colombe did not content himself with adopting the antique decorative repertory brought from beyond the mountains by the court sculptors of Charles VIII and of Louis XII, and already present in the ornamentation of châteaus or figure groups such as the Entombment of Solesmes, dated 1496. The corner statues of the Cardinal Virtues on the Nantes sarcophagus express the ideal of noble and serene beauty which inspires the sculptor; these statues portray his search for compact and balanced volumes, his care for the human form in the sensitive modelling of the body and the construction of faces with features more sharply drawn than previously. The old Gothic idealism revitalized during the fifteenth century did not oppose Italian art; it opened itself to new ways and encouraged the harmonious meeting of traditional and Renaissance style in this final phase of the Middle Ages on the banks of the Loire. The nephew and collaborator of Colombe, Guillaume Regnault, to whom is ascribed the famous Virgin and Child from Olivet (Louvre, Paris), kept alive at Tours the final style of his master, who died around 1514, when the mannerist tendencies of the Fontainebleau court were already making headway.

St Cecilia, back of the rood screen. About 1500. Polychrome stone. Cathedral of Sainte-Cécile, Albi.

The Virgin and a Holy Woman.
Detail of the Entombment from the Château de la Combéfa.
Albigeois, about 1490. Polychrome stone.
Chapel of the Hôpital Saint-Jean, Monestiès-sur-Cérou, near Albi.

SOUTHWESTERN FRANCE

The serene clarity of the Loire statuary is embellished, moreover, with particular accents which contrast or harmonize with the monumental simplification and the picturesque details, the inward expressions and gracious effects. Southwestern France, the north and Champagne display different facets of these tendencies in the regional variants of French sculpture at the close of the Middle Ages.

A touch of suavity brings out the childlike and languid charm of many anonymous sculptures, in polychrome stone, of the third quarter of the fifteenth century in the

Annunciation.
Rouergue, about 1460–1480.
Polychrome stone.
Church of Inières (Aveyron).

regions of Toulouse and Rodez. As usual, the works of the masters, Jacques Morel, active at Rodez in 1448, or Pierre Viguier, recorded at Villefranche-de-Rouergue and Rodez from 1451 to 1497, are now destroyed or very fragmentary, making it difficult to identify for certain the originator of this personal tone in Languedoc and Rouergue sculpture.

"Nostre Dame de Grasse" at Toulouse and the Annunciation at Inières bear charming witness to this style which blossomed and diversified at the end of the fifteenth century, spreading its influence towards Albi and Moissac as well. The generous gifts of Louis I of Amboise, bishop of Albi from 1473 to 1502, spurred important undertakings: the monumental Entombment carved for his Château de la Combéfa, and the teeming flamboyant decor of the rood screen and chancel screen of Albi Cathedral, where the figure carvings renewed the traditional local types, gain in weight and complexity and are brightened by picturesque strokes of inspiration.

A graver sentiment, related to the art of the Loire, emanates from the figure groups created at the beginning of the sixteenth century in Périgord and in Bordelais by the workshop of the Master of the Biron Entombment, which makes much of the Italianizing ornamental repertory.

Preaching of
St Firmin, first
bishop of Amiens,
on the tower of
the choir.
Picardy, about 1490.
Polychrome stone.
Amiens Cathedral.

CHAMPAGNE AND PICARDY

In a style familiar and fashionable by turns, the Champagne workshops produced, around 1500, long anonymous processions of devotional images in stone or polychrome wood, in marble or alabaster: Virgin and Child or male and female saints, at whose feet was often carved the donor's diminutive kneeling figure. The wholly Gothic plastic density of these statues, their poised gestures, their gentle, delicate and regular faces, are accompanied by many anecdotal details and coquetries of dress–embroidered braid, small hanging chains, studded belts, pleated and knotted ribbons–even more abundant than in other regions of France. Concurrently the dolorous themes of the Passion are treated in a serious and reserved tone, stripped of pomp or pathos, in a large and famous collection of works gathered around the St Martha of the church of the Madeleine at Troyes and the Entombment of Chaource (1515).

To explain the decorative excesses of Champagne sculpture, reference has often been made to the influence of the Netherlands, of which Nicolas Halins, established in Troyes from 1494 to 1544, could have been one of the transmitters, but not, as has wrongly been said, the only one. Indeed, the penetration of northern formulas through imported objects or the influx of foreign artists, forms part of a general movement, which in sculpture partially included Champagne as well as Picardy, Artois and Normandy, and broadened in scope through the circulation of engraved models. The art of altarpieces especially, which interpreted the examples of Brussels and Antwerp in stone or wood, owed much to this influence. The work of the Picardy cabinetmakers and image-makers who carved in oak the stalls of Amiens Cathedral from 1508 to 1522, and the frames of the first "Puys" (medieval religious societies) of Notre-Dame also show acquaintance with the narrative style, alive and racy, of the Netherlandish workshops. The large stone reliefs of the cathedral choir tower mark the stages of a different stylistic development, more typical of Picardy, which extends from the first scenes from the life of St Firmin (about 1490), arranging tiers of calm figures clad in stiff and simple draperies, to the last episodes in the story of John the Baptist (1531), highly ornate in taste, in which the suppler figures are swathed in animated fabrics enhanced by refined polychromy. The Gothic sculpture of Picardy, little affected by Italian novelties, had an exceptionally late flowering, whose luxuriant effects invaded the great façades of flamboyant Gothic buildings and continued to influence altarpieces well after the middle of the sixteenth century. In Normandy, too, the abundance of sculptured decoration was linked to the last creations of Gothic architecture, marked more rapidly, however, by the intrusion of Renaissance motifs.

Statue of the Virgin from Henry VII's Chapel.
1503-1512.
Stone.
Westminster Abbey, London.

ENGLAND

The widespread destruction wreaked during the English Reformation, especially of monumental statuary and decoration, together with the conservatism prevailing in funerary sculpture and the production of alabaster reliefs, augment the difficulties in the study of the stylistic development of English sculpture at the close of the Middle Ages.

Largely exported to the Continent by the workshops of Nottingham or other towns, the overabundant production of small carved and painted alabaster panels, whether independent devotional images or elements of altarpieces, indeed became repetitive after the middle of the fifteenth century. Since the documents corresponding to extant works are often missing and since the sculptors consistently re-employed the same iconographic and stylistic formulas, the English alabasters are difficult to date accurately. But it is easy to recognize them thanks to their simplified, highly typical treatment—lean forms, stereotyped faces, crisp draperies—and their refined polychromy, which delicately brings out the natural colour of the alabaster.

The large output of alabaster or stone tombs followed the general evolution of funerary art, adopting in particular the twin representation of tomb effigy and withered corpse, the deceased reposing on the tombslab in all the paraphernalia of his earthly glory above the macabre image of his cadaver (tomb of John Fitzalan at Arundel or, at Ewelme, Oxfordshire, tomb of the Duchess Alice of Suffolk, who died in 1477).

Inside the churches, the sculptured decoration consisted chiefly of rows of figures in stone sheltered by canopies on the chancel screens and in funeral chapels (chantries), built in large numbers in the late Middle Ages. The statues of English kings adorning the choir screen of Canterbury Cathedral (1411-1427) have a quiet density scarcely enlivened by a few sinuous falls of drapery, also appearing, at mid-century, in the figures of angels and saints ornamenting the funeral chapel of Richard Beauchamp in the church of St Mary at Warwick. This style has been related to the activity of John Massingham, mentioned at Canterbury in 1436, at Oxford, where he was responsible for the decoration of All Souls College from 1438 to 1442, and in London in 1449.

Several sculptures from the chapel of Henry V at Westminster Abbey (about 1441-1450) issue from a similar spirit but others, like the Angel and the Virgin of the Annunciation, clearly reveal the influence of painted or sculptured models from Brabant and Flanders by their physical types and conception of draperies with broken and hollowed folds.

But it was at the end of the fifteenth century and the beginning of the next, at the moment of the full flowering of artistic activity, that several sculptors are mentioned as coming from the Netherlands or Germany to work at the English court. Unfortunately, the teams collaborating on the rich decoration of the chapel of Henry VII at Westminster (1503-1512) remain anonymous. On all the walls unfolds a frieze of angels carrying armorial bearings placed above a row of statues. The energetic treatment and expressive force of these sculptures, which verge on dryness and stiffness in the least successful works, evoke in some aspects the art of the Lower Rhine at the end of the fifteenth century and recall the figures of the Divinity School at Oxford (1481).

This harshness, which also appears in stone tombs and in woodcarving–choir stalls, benches, beams, rood screens–is one of the characteristics of English production of the late Middle Ages, unreceptive to Italian novelties. The style of the Florentine master Pietro Torrigiani, summoned to build the tomb of King Henry VII (1512-1518), indeed presents a complete contrast with the pieces from the Gothic workshops of London or regional centres, whose activity was suddenly broken off by the English Reformation in the 1540s.

▷ Statue of a prophet from Henry VII's Chapel.
1503-1512.
Stone.
Westminster Abbey, London.

▽ Coronation of King Henry V.
Part of the south side of Henry V's Chantry.
About 1441-1450.
Stone.
Westminster Abbey, London.

Workshops of Copín de Holanda, Sebastián de Almonacid
and Felipe Bigarny.
Altarpiece on the high altar
with scenes from the life of Christ and the Virgin.
1498–1504.
Polychrome wood.
Toledo Cathedral.

290

SPAIN AND PORTUGAL

While the last traces of the international Gothic style faded away, the picture of Iberian sculpture at the close of the Middle Ages was coloured by new values dominated by northern influences.

The manner of the foreign sculptors from the north, however, changed on their contact with Spanish surroundings and their style was transposed by the indigenous masters into a specifically Spanish key. The boom in production was concentrated mainly in the Castilian regions, as well as Catalonia, Andalusia and Portugal, after the middle of the fifteenth century. Often the artists' names leave no doubt as to their northern origin.

In Toledo, Hannequín de Bruselas, *maestro mayor* of the cathedral, put up the door of the south transept, the Puerta de los Leones (1462-1465), whose sculptured decoration was the work of Juan Alemán and his collaborators, among whom was Egas Cueman, Hannequín's brother.

From the start northern influences prevailed in this portal. The stiff, impassive, monumental statues of the splays and the figures in relief of the Tree of Jesse on the inner tympanum are clearly defined by a linear rhythm emphasized by the prominent verticals or diagonals of the tubular folds between the smooth areas. This tense and graphic style, not without delicacy in the treatment of feminine and juvenile faces, hands and details of clothing, presents undeniable resemblances with the sculpture of the Lower Rhine, linked, as we know, with Netherlandish art.

These masters of Toledo, probably schooled in the north before settling in Spain, represent a stylistic phase parallel to that of their contemporaries from Brussels, Utrecht or Kalkar, such as Master Arnt, in the second half of the fifteenth century. Here as there, the forms and imagery show the dominance of the great Flemish painters, known very early in Spain, as witnessed by the works of Egas Cueman for the abbey of Guadalupe (Cáceres), which interpret some typical designs of Rogier van der Weyden. But from the prolific production of Toledo

Attributed to
Jorge Fernández.
The Massacre of
the Innocents.
Detail of the altarpiece
on the high altar.
1508-1518.
Polychrome wood.
Seville Cathedral.

Workshop of Juan Alemán. The Tree of Jesse.
Detail of the inside tympanum of the Puerta de los Leones.
1462-1465. Stone.
Toledo Cathedral.

modelling statues or reliefs distinguishes several series of Sevillian works. Those of Mercadante on the portals of the Nativity and the Baptism (1466-1467) of the cathedral embellish their somewhat stiff robustness with an emphasis on expression in the rounded and smiling feminine faces. His successor in practising this technique, Pedro Millán (mentioned from 1487 to 1507) softened still further the physiognomies of his polychrome terracotta figures, several of which bear his signature, such as the Christ of Sorrows from El Garrobo (Museo de Bellas Artes, Seville).

The enormous altarpiece in polychrome wood on the high altar of Seville Cathedral, begun from a design by Pieter Dancart around 1481-1482, and continued by various teams, notably from 1497 to 1506 by Master Marco, then by Pedro Millán mentioned in 1506-1507, and from 1508 to 1525 by Jorge Fernández and his brother the painter Alexo, had its central part completed only in January 1526. This shows how difficult it is to estimate the share of each in this collective work. Some figures, like those of the Birth of the Virgin, rather suggest the art of Pedro Millán by their regular oval faces and quiet draperies. Others, like the figures of the Raising of Lazarus, have more vivacity, more individualized features, and belong to a later stage, perhaps that of Master Marco and Jorge and Alexo Fernández, which seems to echo the style of the Kalkar workshops in the entourage of Master Arnt.

At Burgos flourished the singular genius of Gil de Siloé, the great name of late Gothic Spanish sculpture. Was he a

Pedro Millán.
Christ of Sorrows from El Garrobo.
Late 15th century. Polychrome terracotta.
Museo de Bellas Artes, Seville.

emerged a peculiar tonality attributable to the local milieu. The typically Iberian predilection for ornamental richness showed itself everywhere inside religious buildings: in the teeming flamboyant decor of the choir screen in Toledo Cathedral, the *capilla mayor* carved from 1483 on under the direction of Martín Sánchez Bonifacio and Juan Guas; in the vast altarpiece in polychrome wood on the high altar (1498-1504) which sets out the sculptured scenes in superimposed compartments in the Netherlandish manner and was the joint work of sculptors of such diverse origin as Copín de Holanda, Sebastián de Almonacid and Felipe Bigarny (i.e. from Burgundy); or yet again in the Toledo church of San Juan de los Reyes, originally destined to house the tombs of the Catholic Kings, where an astonishing heraldic decor punctuated by figure carvings, conceived by Juan Guas, covers the walls (1478-1495).

In funerary art the Toledo sculptors or their Castilian emulators also affirmed their specific manner, precise and vigorous, with an acuteness verging at times on dryness, as shown by many examples, such as the tombs by Sebastián de Almonacid of the constable Alvaro de Luna (died 1489) and his wife (cathedral of Toledo); or that, justly famous, of the knight at arms Martín Vásquez de Arce (died 1486) (cathedral of Sigüenza), which, unusually, presents the deceased leaning on his elbows and reading, thereby transforming the traditional type of recumbent figure in a humanist mode.

At Seville as well, the foreign masters who are mentioned after the middle of the fifteenth century (like Lorenzo Mercadante de Bretaña, Pieter Dancart, who is called *alemán*, Master Marco Flamenco) introduced rigid, energetically outlined forms, physical types and compositional schemes at once stemming from the Netherlands or Lower Rhine and displaying various autonomous accents according to personality. The original use of clay for

northern master who had emigrated to Spain? A Spaniard trained in the north? The question remains unresolved because of the absence of explicit documents and the perfect fusion his art reveals of northern characteristics and Iberian traditions. For the charterhouse of Miraflores, Gil de Siloé created three masterworks: from 1489 to 1493 the alabaster tombs of the parents and brother of Queen Isabella the Catholic–King John II, Isabella of Portugal and the Infante Alfonso–and from 1496 to 1499 the monumental altarpiece in polychrome wood. Other works, like the Tree of Jesse altarpiece in the St Anne chapel of Burgos Cathedral (donated by Luis de Acuña, bishop from 1456 to 1495), were made in his workshop as well as the tomb of the queen's page, Juan de Badilla (died 1491), for the monastery of Fresdeval (Museo Provincial, Burgos).

The scope of these works, carried out over approximately two decades, implies a large number of collaborators whose names are unknown, with the sole exception of Diego de la Cruz, referred to as both sculptor and painter. Despite perceptible nuances in treatment due to the

◁ Lorenzo Mercadante.
St Justa, detail.
Splay of the Puerta del Bautismo.
1466-1467. Terracotta.
Seville Cathedral.

▽ Gil de Siloé.
Tomb of the Infante Alfonso.
1489-1493. Alabaster.
Cartuja de Miraflores, near Burgos.

Façade of the Colegio de San Gregorio.
1488-1496.
Stone.
Valladolid.

decorative effects of unprecedented pomp: witness the intricate, although strictly organized compositions, and the proliferation of ornaments which invade everything, backgrounds, frames, accessories, draperies. To cover a surface entirely with repeated motifs indeed constitutes one of the basic principles of Hispano-Moorish art. In the funerary effigies, the simplicity of the volumes contrasts oddly with the extraordinary complexity of the pattern of decorative elements chiselled in the alabaster with an almost metallic dryness and a skill that grows tedious.

Everywhere the profuse and capricious detail is subordinated to the unitary conception of the whole. Thus the church façades take on the aspect of monumental altarpieces in stone forming vast rectangles which, within the limits of a sharply defined grid, are filled with sculptured figures and motifs. At Valladolid the luxuriant façade of the Colegio de San Gregorio (1488-1496) is attributed to the workshop of Gil de Siloé or to that of Simón de Colonia, the master mason of the celebrated chapel of the constable Pedro Fernández de Velasco (1492-1498) in the cathedral of Burgos, which also displays a superabundant sculptured decoration. It is particularly difficult to pick out individualities in the midst of the many anonymous executants of the decorative parts of these monuments. The art of the altarpieces offers more varied talents and a few names, like that of Alejo de Vahia (maker in 1505 of two sculptures for the altarpiece of Palencia), who represents the last Gothic phase of Castilian sculpture, while

"Capelas imperfeitas,"
view of the decoration.
Early 16th century.
Stone.
Monastery of Santa Maria da Victoria.
Batalha (Portugal).

participation of these different hands, stylistic unity reigns supreme and testifies to the hegemony of a principal master who conceived the works, provided the designs (in 1486 for the Miraflores sculptures) and supervised the execution. The physical types and the arrangement of the draperies, repeated many times in alabaster and wood with secondary variants, emphasize the connections with the northern Netherlands and the Lower Rhine. For example the upright and rangy silhouettes of the saints of the Miraflores altarpiece, their delicate, full-cheeked faces, their constrained gestures to hold up a robe or mantle falling in stiff folds in keeping with a conception of clothes more graphic than plastic—all spring from the same spirit as the sculptures of the Master of Koudewater, active around 1460-1480 in the region of 's Hertogenbosch (Bois-le-Duc). And other general relationships may be detected, notably with the works of Kalkar or Cleves associated with Master Arnt and his emulators in the late fifteenth century.

Gil de Siloé, of course, subordinates these foreign borrowings to his own vision, whose bold novelty springs from specifically Iberian values. The *mudéjar* tradition has often been called in to explain the choice of an octagonal form for the royal tomb and especially the emphasis on

Gil de Siloé.
Altarpiece on the high altar of the church,
with Crucifixion, scenes from the life of Christ, and male and female saints.
1496-1499. Polychrome wood.
Cartuja de Miraflores, near Burgos.

new generations were already turning to the art of the Renaissance.

Portugal, which was opened to Spanish influences during the reign of King Manuel (1495-1521), also favoured ornamental profusion, traditionally esteemed, thanks to the contributions of *mourisco* art, the Portuguese counterpart of Spanish *mudéjar* art. Exuberance and fantasy are the rule in the decoration of Manuelian monuments. The mixture of composite elements, flamboyant, Moorish, or exotic and introduced by Portuguese navigators, gives a strange accent to this final flowering of late Gothic in the Iberian peninsula.

Albrecht Altdorfer.
Madonna on the halfmoon
(the Schöne Maria of Regensburg).
1518. Ink on grey-green paper.
Staatliche Museen, Berlin.

BETWEEN GOTHIC AND BAROQUE

chromy (some bearing the sculptor's monogram), which reflect the strange atmosphere of Danubian works and a characteristic taste for the vegetable kingdom. In the moving scenes of martyrdom or the Passion, the natural elements, like the falling branches of the great spruces on the banks of the Danube, seem quickened by the same inner movement as the figures, their hair, their clothing and even some accessories. The lines play freely and mingle in an apparent but skilfully controlled confusion. Both in works of very small format and in monumental figures, the poses and drapery, far more than the faces, render the emotions with a power of expression and a capacity of invention that puts Leinberger in the front rank of the sculptors of his time and makes him the equal of the great Danubian painters. His influence pervades a large number of anonymous Bavarian sculptures of varying qualities, often hard to classify into distinct groups, like the

Hans Leinberger. Virgin and Child. Central figure in the altarpiece on the high altar. About 1511-1514.
Polychrome limewood.
Parish church, Moosburg (Bavaria).

If the taste of late Gothic artists for ornamental luxuriance became more pronounced in architectural decoration, as in Picardy or the Iberian peninsula, without any genuine renewal of plastic language, in the Germanic lands on the contrary sculpture moved into a strange and violent world reshaped now by the social and religious upheavals of the age. The afterglow of a style, this "baroque Gothic" is fascinating to an eye and mind willing to accept its excesses and vagaries. Within a broad movement essentially affecting the southern part of the Empire and involving a new generation of sculptors active from about 1510 on, the tendency described as "Danubian" asserted itself with force and originality.

Over and above controversies concerning the notion of a "Danube school" in painting (*Donaustil*), there is general agreement on a close community in spirit and forms between the works of the main representatives of the Danubian style and the sculptures produced concurrently in the same Austro-Bavarian region. The genesis of the new plastic style occurred within the late Gothic tradition, taking the old methods a step further while developing new rhetoric in perfect osmosis with the contemporary graphic and pictorial language, as shown by the sculptures of Hans Leinberger, mentioned at Landshut from 1510 to 1530. If, for example, the tumultuous draperies clothing his figures and soaring far out from the body in arbitrary folds spring from the previous Gothic conception, their treatment avoids angles and breaks in favour of floating undulations at the edges and large inflated folds, tracing long diagonals interrupted here and there by little stiff crinkles on the surface of the fabric: a treatment closely corresponding to the manner of Albrecht Altdorfer (Regensburg, c. 1480-1538), as seen in his pen and ink drawings on a dark ground where white highlights bring out the forms and billowing folds with festooned curves and parallel bands.

Leinberger, who, moreover, worked in 1518-1519 at the same time as the painter for the new Schöne Maria pilgrimage church in Regensburg, appears to have transformed Altdorfer's graphic inventions into volumes. At the very least he exploited plastically the new formal possibilities offered by the Danubian style, as also initiated by other artists such as Lucas Cranach the Elder (Cronach 1472 - Weimar 1553) and Jörg Breu (Augsburg, c. 1475-1537). The pictorial component is even more present in Leinberger's limewood or boxwood reliefs without polyone formed by the works of the Master of the Altötting Doors, a personality more independent than the mere imitators of the master.

Leinberger also exerted a certain influence on the Salzburg and Passau workshops, connected by their common links with the Danube school. The Master of Irrsdorf, Andreas Lackner, or the sculptors who worked with the painter Wolf Huber (c. 1485 – Passau 1553), notably on the Feldkirch altarpiece (1515-1521), borrowed extensively from engraved or painted models for the compositional designs and formal types of their carvings in relief or in the round.

The mysterious Master I.P., maker of several small panels in pearwood without polychromy carved with a subtle virtuosity, was active during the 1520s, perhaps at Passau or Salzburg, and more doubtfully in Prague, where sculptures attributed to his workshop are preserved (altarpieces of Zlichov and the Tyn church). The Mourning over the Dead Christ in Leningrad, signed with the monogram I.P., shows how the master absorbed and transformed Leinberger's vision, amplifying the pathos and sense of space, which he developed further in depth and suggested by foreshortened bodies, delicate shadings and increased emphasis on natural setting. In the Original Sin reliefs at Gotha and Vienna (the latter dated 1521), inspired by a Dürer engraving of 1504, the accent is placed on the fabulous landscape, the fantastic rocks and tall trees with rough and knotty trunks, made in the image of the Danubian painters. The free attitude of the two nude figures, Adam turning seen from behind, and Eve animated by a slight *contrapposto*, shows a concern for the representation of the body marked by the humanism of cultivated circles, for whom, moreover, these small cabinet pieces highly prized by collectors were intended. Master I.P. thereby links up with the new art of the Renaissance, although his tall slim figures with their rugged features remain alien to antique balance and regularity, and later seemed to evolve towards a mannerist formulation.

On the edge of the Danube region and outside it, countless works of traditional use, altarpieces and devotional images, were made in ateliers that followed the general trend of style in the 1510s and 1520s and seem more resistant to the Renaissance spirit even when they resort abundantly to an antique repertory of ornament, with garlands, pilasters and putti. Regional or individual nuances shift the common tendencies towards an overwrought accentuation of forms, lines and expression: the leering and gesturing figures in the altarpiece of Mauer near Melk (Lower Austria); the giddy swirling movement that galvanizes the Zwettl sculptures (Lower Austria); the monstrously overblown tulip of Hans Witten's pulpit in the cathedral of Freiberg (Saxony); the brutal dynamism of Claus Berg's apostles in the cathedral of Güstrow (Mecklenburg); or the tentacular sprouting of the Tree of Jesse in Douvermann's altarpiece at Kalkar (Rhineland).

In addition to the garments buffeted by a violent wind, as in Claus Berg, or blistered and quivering as in the sculptures of Leinberger and Master I.P., a type of drapery with parallel folds had a widespread success in quite different regions such as Carinthia, Tyrol and Swabia, where the output of the Memmingen workshops was characteristic of this *Parallelfaltenstil*. Thus the Master of Ottobeuren (possibly Hans Thoman, active at Memmingen from 1514 to 1525), named after the Annunciation and Nativity reliefs preserved in the great Benedictine abbey of

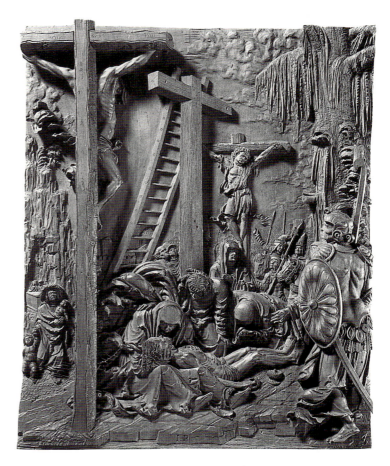

Master I.P.
Mourning over the dead Christ.
About 1525. Pearwood.
Hermitage Museum, Leningrad.

Hans Witten.
Tulip pulpit.
About 1510. Stone.
Cathedral of Freiberg (Saxony).

◁ Heinrich Douvermann.
Tree of Jesse. Predella of the altarpiece
of the Seven Sorrows of the Virgin, detail.
1518-1522. Oak.
Nikolaikirche, Kalkar.

▷ Erhard Schön.
"Klagrede der armen verfolgten Götzen..."
(Complaint of the poor persecuted idols).
About 1530.
Woodcut.
Germanisches Nationalmuseum, Nuremberg.

Master of Ottobeuren.
Nativity, detail. About 1520-1525. Limewood.
Klostermuseum, Ottobeuren (Baden-Württemberg).

Master H.L.
Coronation of the Virgin, detail of God the Father.
Altarpiece on the high altar, central panel. 1523-1526.
St Stephansmünster, Breisach (Baden-Württemberg).

Ottobeuren, patterns the limewood surface with a strange network of curved and regular lines which is carefully organized and sets up a play of light and shadow. At the same time the forms of his figures, whose quiet self-possession is very much in the Swabian tradition, acquire a genuine plasticity which seems to echo the new humanism; it recurs in most contemporary works, beginning with those of Leinberger and the Danubian sculptors. On the other hand, the reliefs place the figures in tiers on ascending levels in almost complete contempt of the representation of space.

Master H.L. carried the tension and instability of lines to their peak. His monogram appears on several prints dated from 1511 to 1522 as well as on the Breisach altarpiece, completed in 1526, without our being able to ascertain whether this engraver was also the sculptor or merely the designer of the carvings. And his training remains equally obscure, since the manner of this sculptor, who has affinities with Danubian art, is strikingly original. The swirling eddies of the clothing, hair, vegetation and clouds tend to submerge the figures in the Breisach Coronation of the Virgin and completely fill the area of the shrine. But extravagance here is restrained with supreme mastery. The intricacy of the forms does not weaken the expressive force, and the overall view of the work is never blurred by excessive ornament. The monumental effects peculiar to late Gothic German altarpieces full of large figure carvings are enhanced here by the power and plastic authority of the divine personages. A sublime work, this Breisach altarpiece, which, as against the serene assurance of the Renaissance, opens up a magic world and points the way to Baroque.

THE DESTRUCTION OF IMAGES

New times arrived. But alongside the flowering of humanism and the Renaissance, a grave moral and spiritual crisis shook the Church. Alas, the changes were accompanied by violence and destruction of extreme brutality, owing to the iconoclastic fury of the Protestants.

Indeed, the adherents of Church reform condemned holy images, basing themselves on Biblical prohibitions: "Thou shalt not make unto thee any graven image, or any likeness of any thing that is in heaven above, or that is in the earth beneath, or that is in the water under the earth: thou shalt not bow down thyself to them, nor serve them" (Exodus, xx, 4-5).

In its materiality the image is deceiving; the danger exists that the true believer may venerate the image itself more than what it represents. The image, by its power of seduction, may lead the senses astray instead of inciting to prayer. By its excessive cost, the image encourages the egoistic pride of rich donors and not their charitable duty towards the most deprived; God must be served through his poor rather than by vain expenditure on sculptures and paintings of excessive proliferation. Those were some of the arguments set forth, with variations, by all the leaders of the Reformation in their works, their sermons or their pamphlets. Luther was relatively moderate, insisting on the educative role of narrative subjects while denouncing temptations to idolatry and the squandering of money. Thus he blamed Carlstadt's iconoclastic zeal at Wittenberg in 1522 and condemned the violence of "criminals and pillaging hordes of peasants" at the time of the peasant revolts of 1524-1525 in South Germany. In Switzerland, first Zwingli, then Calvin, criticized sacred images more radically, urging their suppression or destruction.

As the ideas of the Reformation, mingled with material and social demands, made headway in Europe, the manifestations of iconoclasm multiplied in diverse forms: sporadic outbreaks or intense explosions like that in the Netherlands during the year 1566; spontaneous acts of handfuls of individuals driven by poverty and religious fanaticism, or movements orchestrated by civic authorities won over to the new doctrines. Thus at Strasbourg beginning in 1524, under the auspices of the town council, paintings, crucifixes, altarpieces and other images began to be removed from religious buildings and systematically destroyed or sometimes carefully dismantled. Inevitably, in many towns, sculptors in want of commissions were reduced to expatriating themselves or to begging for living allowances, and often ended up in poverty.

The printing press played a considerable role in the spread of the Reformers' doctrines, in particular those of Luther and Calvin. And preachers everywhere carried on the most active propaganda, for example thundering against the scandalous figures of female saints adorned more luxuriously than prostitutes, a veritable incitement to voluptuousness and not to pious thoughts.

At Steenvoorde in Flanders, on 10 August 1566, following a sermon by Sebastian Matte, some twenty members of the audience stormed the monastery and laid waste all the images. The destructive rage reached its height during the Beggars' Revolt; the inhabitants of Tournai sacked the churches of their town, looted the treasuries, profaned the relics and smashed the statues. In France the Huguenots also engaged in blasphemous demonstrations and wholly devastated many religious edifices, in the south and southwest especially. In England, under the auspices of the monarchy, the Anglican Reformation entailed, over and above the suppression of the monasteries and the sale of their goods, the systematic destruction of monumental figures decorating the church choirs and chapels.

Thousands of sculptures accordingly perished in the agonies of the *Bildersturm*, annihilated in the flames of pyres and beneath the blows of pickaxes or irreparably mutilated. Works fallen forever into oblivion or illustrious works of which surviving records preserve the memory, sharpening our regret at their loss, such as the altarpiece by Nicholas of Leyden on the high altar of the cathedral of Constance destroyed during the Zwinglian iconoclasm, or the altarpiece by Michael Erhart and Jörg Syrlin the Elder in the cathedral of Ulm, torn down by the Lutherans.

Other agonies, military or revolutionary, later contributed, it is true, to the disappearance of many medieval images. And this is not to forget changes in taste and the desire to renovate or purify church decoration, largely responsible for multiple destructions of Gothic altarpieces, stalls, rood screens and choir screens. If the reforming iconoclasm banned religious art, the Church of the Counter-Reformation, which defended it, wanted it to be above reproach and called for austerity and decency.

"The Middle Ages ended on the day the Church itself condemned them," wrote Emile Mâle, deploring the death of medieval iconographic traditions after the Council of Trent (1545-1563). But we also know that in spite of everything the Middle Ages remained strongly present, as Henri Focillon affirms: "They have not disappeared, they have not been wiped out. It would seem the West is nostalgic for them. The nostalgia became a conscious longing in England in the eighteenth century, with the neo-Gothic style dear to Horace Walpole. It gathered strength with the progress of Romanticism, and the nineteenth century finally gave it the tone and power of an historic force... This marks the beginning of a vast inquiry which, starting from a reaction of taste and ever sustained by more intense forces, ends in a wider knowledge of the past, in a more complete possession of mankind."

Altarpiece of the Holy Kinship. Early 16th century. Polychrome stone. Jan van Arkel Chapel, Utrecht Cathedral.

CONCLUSION
Georges Duby

The majority of sculptors dealt with in this book were anonymous. We shall never know the name of the artist who carved one of the most amazing figures of God made man in Burgundy stone on the tympanum of Vézelay. In any case, who was the actual author of that work? The sculptor who had been engaged because he was known for his excellence in executing commissions, assisted by the companions of his team and who, before receiving the sum of money that remunerated his work from the chamberlain, had shared the coarse bread baked for the servants of the abbey with cowherds and wheelwrights in the refectory? The monastic community which had worked out the project at chapter meetings? Or the monk whom his brothers had made responsible for choosing from the maquettes and ensuring that the work closely matched the image which the servants of God together had devised of the unknowable, while singing the Psalms and meditating on the text of the Scriptures?

We know next to nothing about what conditions were like in the Middle Ages for those workmen we now call artists. Except that, in a strictly hierarchized society, they belonged to the dominated masses, they ranked among the very poorly paid. The John of Pisa whose name appears around 1300 in the accounts scrupulously kept by the administrators of the cathedral and whom we are surprised to discover was not paid much more than the masons, was he not the great Giovanni Pisano, one of the brilliant forerunners of the Italian Renaissance? We have to imagine the sculptors, like the mercenaries engaged by the kings for their military prowess, as grouped in small companies led by a sort of captain. The latter negotiated with the patron, the prior of a monastery, the canon responsible for work on the cathedral, or, as from the thirteenth century, with the architect overseeing the work, with the prince's steward, with the merchant who used his profits to adorn his tomb. The leader of the team offered his services to these men. He promised to follow their directives faithfully, to respect the clauses of a contract specifying the material he had to use, laying down in minute detail the gestures and costumes of the personages he was asked to represent, and defining the composition of the work, that is to say its meaning. For we should not forget that the work was not inconsequent; it fulfilled a function, it carried a message and its significance was essential. So where did the artist's freedom begin?

Especially as his freedom was curtailed by other limitations. As soon as the reviving towns got organized, the sculptors who lived in them were enrolled in a guild, like the other craftsmen. This association subjected its members to strict constraints in order to avoid competition, dominate the work-force and monopolize the local market. There is no doubt, however, that a number of masters managed to retain a free hand. These men were not established in a particular city, they moved with their workshop, they went from site to site. To be sure, they were the most skilful craftsmen, those whose fame had spread abroad and who were summoned from afar. Long before archive documents supplied proof of this mobility and made it possible to retrace their itineraries, close study of forms enabled experts to attribute works that were scattered far and wide to a particular artist whose style they recognized. In fact, the promoters of major art made enquiries about artists and picked out the best, quarrelling over them, like the barons who vied with each other on the eve of a tournament to win over the champion who would bring victory to their colours at the next encounter. As the sponsors were anxious to retain the most talented artists, it is quite conceivable that they agreed to give the latter a margin of personal initiative favourable to the flowering of their gifts. It is obvious that at a very early date, from the eleventh century, sculptors enjoyed a consideration that made them less submissive to the injunctions of their patrons.

That was the case with those whose signatures we find carved on their work, although we may ask, with reference to the oldest works, whether this name did not belong to the deviser of the project rather than the executor. With the passage of time, the question no longer arose: the mark was indeed the sculptor's. A moment came when he dared to introduce his own portrait into the composition, admittedly in a recess, in the background, yet in the vicinity of the donor's portrait and the faces he gave to Christ, the saints and the angels. The advent of the artist succeeded the advent of sculpture with four hundred years' delay.

Nevertheless, Gothic Europe at the end of the fifteenth century was still far from raising sculpture to the rank of the liberal arts. It kept it on a lower level, among the mechanical arts, following the principle that the free man is he who thinks, that manual work enslaves, and firm above all in the conviction that the fleshly should remain under the strict domination of the spiritual. Sculpted work had always been considered as a means of communicating with the invisible. Its deeper meaning, in other words its value, was not conferred on it by the artist, but by the men of prayer and learning who, in the silence of chapels and libraries, had imagined what it should signify and established the terms of the commission in consequence. How could common sense have recognized the quality of the true creator in the sculptor and, seeing that he himself handled the hammer or the gouge, if only to finish with one stroke what assistants under his control had fashioned after the sketch, how could it help confusing him with the men simply following a trade, the craftsmen?

Statue of a Sibyl (?).
Detail of the tomb of the Duke of Savoy
Philibert le Beau (died 1504).
1516–1522.
Alabaster.
Church of Brou, Bourg-en-Bresse (Ain).

LIST OF ILLUSTRATIONS

The works illustrated are listed according to their place of origin.

The index and bibliography will appear in volume I of this series: ANTIQUITY OR THE INVENTION OF SCULPTURE.

316

SKIRA

PRODUCED BY THE TECHNICAL STAFF OF
ÉDITIONS D'ART ALBERT SKIRA S.A., GENEVA

COLOUR AND BLACK AND WHITE,
FILMSETTING AND PRINTING BY
IRL IMPRIMERIES RÉUNIES LAUSANNE S.A.

BINDING BY MAYER & SOUTTER S.A.
RENENS/LAUSANNE

Printed in Switzerland